MILITARY HISTORY FROM PRIMARY SOURCES

ON CAMPAIGN WITH THE BRITISH ARMY IN THE ZULU WAR OF 1879

Charles Norris-Newman

THE ILLUSTRATED EDITION

EDITED AND INTRODUCED BY
BOB CARRUTHERS

BOOKS LTD

This book is published in Great Britain in 2013 by
Coda Books Ltd, Office Suite 2, Shrieves Walk, Sheep Street, Stratford
upon Avon, Warwickshire CV37 6GJ.
www.codabooks.com

Copyright © 2013 Coda Books Ltd

ISBN 978-1-78158-326-5

A CIP catalogue record for this book is available from the British Library.
All rights reserved. No part of this publication may be reproduced or
transmitted in any form or by any means (electronic or mechanical,
including photocopy, recording, or any information storage and retrieval
system, without the prior permission in writing from the publisher.

This book was first published by W.H. Allen & Co., Ltd, London, in 1880

CONTENTS

FOREWORD 5
DEDICATION 6
PREFACE 7
INTRODUCTION 8
CHAPTER I 17
CHAPTER II 34
CHAPTER III 41
CHAPTER IV 50
CHAPTER V 58
CHAPTER VI 67
CHAPTER VIII 78
CHAPTER IX 98
CHAPTER X 106
CHAPTER XI 120
CHAPTER XII 125
CHAPTER XIII 134
CHAPTER XIV 141
CHAPTER XV 145
CHAPTER XVI 153
CHAPTER XVII 162
CHAPTER XVIII 167
CHAPTER XIX 181
CHAPTER XX 190
CHAPTER XXI 202
CHAPTER XXII 208

CHAPTER XXIII 214
CHAPTER XXIV 222
CHAPTER XXV 229
CHAPTER XXVI 235
CHAPTER XXVII 240
CHAPTER XXVIII 247
CHAPTER XXIX 257
CHAPTER XXX 265
CHAPTER XXXI 275
CHAPTER XXXII 280
CHAPTER XXXIII 300
CHAPTER XXXIV 304
CHAPTER XXXV 314
APPENDICES 328
  APPENDIX A. 328
  APPENDIX B. 329
  APPENDIX C. 335
  APPENDIX D. 341
  APPENDIX E. 342
  APPENDIX F. 343
  APPENDIX G. 344
  APPENDIX H. 347
  APPENDIX I. 367
  APPENDIX K. 382
  APPENDIX L. 390
  APPENDIX M. 396

FOREWORD

CHARLES NORRIS-Newman was an ex-British officer who served as special correspondent for The London Standard in the Zulu War. He attached himself to Lonsdale's Natal Native Contingent and was with Chelmsford's column when Isandlwana was attacked. His report on the battle was the first by a war correspondent. Norris-Newman also took part in the relief of Eshowe and took an active part in the campaign by riding ahead of the relieving forces to become the first man to enter the fort.

In Zululand with the British Army is an essential addition to any Zulu war library. It is the work of an excellent and thoroughly professional writer who was eyewitness to many of the events of the war. He saw the events unfold from disaster at Islandlwana to the final victory and was able to provide a vivid account of the war from the British perspective as it unfolded . Norris-Newman had the right credentials to be able to attach himself to the British Army and as a result he was fortunate enough to avoid the Islandlwana debacle. He accompanied Lord Chelmsford's expeditionary force into Zululand as a special correspondent and, were it not for his decision to attach himself to the staff would have been one of those killed at Islandlwana. In the event he was able to provide a description of the British Camp as it was when he surveyed it before the battle, and the scene of desolation which awaited him on his return. Norris-Newman remained with Chelmsford for the remainder of the war and was able to produce a comprehensive and visceral pen portrait of the Zulu War of 1879 which is essential reading. In Zululand with the British Throughout the War of 1879 was first published by W H Allen & Co in 1880 and was dedicated to Lord Chelmsford.

DEDICATION

LORD CHELMSFORD

**TO LIEUTENANT-GENERAL LORD CHELMSFORD, K.C.B., ETC. ETC.
Late Commanding the Forces in South Africa.**

This personal narrative of the events of a war—which, however unfortunate in its beginning, was yet brought to a final and effective close by the persistent working out of a preconceived plan of a campaign ending in the battle of Ulundi—is dedicated, with the highest feelings of respect and admiration, by the author.

PREFACE

They say that "self-praise is no recommendation," but I must, in fairness to my readers, explain that I was the first and only officially appointed special correspondent that was in the field with the troops daring the early days of preparations and our first entry into Zululand; which ended so disastrously, as every one knows, on that fatal 22nd January at the camp of the Head-quarters column at Isandwhlana. Having been sometime previously residing in Natal I knew something of the country, and of the native language and customs; and throughout the whole campaign I was constantly about with the different Divisions of our forces. Thus I was able to get a more general view of the whole conduct of the war than if I had attached myself to any one Division throughout. I have in this work tried to confine myself to a concise (but I hope interesting) description of facts, as they occurred, and as I saw them, without going into any detailed criticisms; and the descriptions of those events, some of them very important, at the occurrence of which I was not present, have been compiled from the official reports and the letters of my confreres. This work does not pretend to be a complete history—military, political, and general—of the war, its causes and effects; and, in fact, is hardly as voluminous as it was my original intention to make it; but a very severe illness which attacked me after leaving Sir Garnet Wolseley at Utrecht, and from which I am only now slowly recovering, must plead as my excuse for any shortcomings.

CHAS. L. NORRIS-NEWMAN.
Pietermaritzburg, Natal 1880.

INTRODUCTION

THE NARRATIVE of my personal experiences in the late Zulu Campaign would be incomplete without a short sketch of the political causes which led up to the outbreak of the war; and I shall, therefore, endeavour to lay before the reader, as briefly as possible, a statement of the relations between Zululand and our South African colonies, and more particularly between that country and the Transvaal and Natal, which both lie contiguous to it.

It has been very commonly and repeatedly, but very inaccurately, stated that Sir Bartle Frere "caused the war." The truth is that a difficulty, likely to culminate in war, had existed in connection with Zululand for fully a quarter of a century before Sir Bartle Frere set foot in South Africa; and the existence of this difficulty was well known to the Home Government. Sir Bartle Frere was sent out as High Commissioner to endeavour to put an end to the trouble, without war if possible; and events proved that the Zulus would not yield to any of his requests unless he showed himself willing, if necessary, to enforce them. He was thus placed in the position of deciding whether he would leave the danger, which threatened Natal and the Transvaal directly, and the whole of our South African Colonies indirectly, unchecked; or would insist, if need were, by force, upon such securities being given by Cetywayo, the Zulu King, as would make our colonies secure from invasion in the future.

From the earliest days the constitution of society (if society it can at all be called) in Zululand was that of one vast camp. The nation was founded early in the present century by the renowned Charka, who laid waste Natal, with its then peaceful native inhabitants—so much so that the early settlers, in the year 1810,

Dingaan orders the killing of Piet Retief's party of Voortrekkers. c.1847

found it almost depopulated, the only inhabitants at that time being miserable refugees from the Zulu despot. In 1828, after an iron reign, Charka was assassinated by his brother Dingaan, who threatened the early English settlers with war, on the ground of their harbouring the refugees from his brother. This difficulty was smoothed over; but the Dutch settlers, who later on found their way to Natal from the Cape over the Drakensberg, became involved in similar difficulties. "Dingaan," to quote the words of Mr. Trollope, who aptly and succinctly describes this portion of the history of the Zulus, " did not add much to the territories of his tribe, as Charka had done; but he made himself known, and probably respected, among his subjects by horrible butcheries of the Dutch pioneers. The name of Dingaan then became dreadful through the land. It was not only that he butchered the Dutch, but that he maintained his authority and the dread of his name by the indiscriminate slaughter of his own people. If the stories told be true, he was, of all South African savages, the most powerful and the most savage. He met the end common to tyrants, and was murdered, after having, however, been first defeated by his brother Panda, whose cause the Dutch settlers espoused, vanquishing Dingaan, and driving him out of his land."

Panda then ruled in his stead. He was an easy-going man, not inclined to war, and disposed to keep on good terms with his neighbours. So long as this state of affairs continued, it was comparatively easy to keep peace with Zululand; but Panda, on his death, was succeeded by Cetywayo, who turned out to be a man of a very different stamp to his father, and openly declared that he intended to emulate the warlike policy of his uncle Dingaan. How far Cetywayo was influenced in this by his personal disposition seems open to question. Those who are best acquainted with him do not seem to consider that he was, by instinct, a warrior, though he took deep interest in wars. In a great measure he was probably influenced by the undoubted fact that his people, or at any rate the younger portion of the nation, were beginning to chafe under the peaceful policy of Panda, and were anxious (to use the expression familiar among them) to "wash their spears," that is, to go to war with some neighbour. Cetywayo, like his predecessors, found himself able to maintain his despotic authority only by acts of cruelty and oppression, and by keeping up the military system founded by his uncle Charka. The "young men" of his army were not permitted to marry until they had fought some enemy and obtained the King's permission; and this powerful lever was used to keep the army together around him. Cetywayo, however, at first avowed friendship for his English neighbours in Natal; and in 1875 he consented to go through the form of coronation at the hands of Sir Theophilus Shepstone, who went into Zululand, accompanied by a company of volunteers, for this purpose. Whether this act of humility was sincere, or was, as is quite possible, intended only to put us off our guard, is not even yet quite clear; but it was not long before reports arrived, from missionaries and others, to the effect that the King was steadily increasing his army, and that guns and ammunition were being imported in large quantities into Zululand. So long, however, as the Dutch held the Transvaal, he confined his quarrels to them, and was content to maintain peace with Natal, in the hope, doubtless, of pitting the English against the Dutch, should a serious quarrel arise with them. In 1877 the Transvaal was annexed to the British Crown; and, this motive for maintaining friendship no longer existing, Cetywayo began to show his hostility more openly. On Sir Henry Bulwer, the Lieutenant-Governor of Natal, remonstrating with him for his cruelty to his subjects, contrary to his promise, when crowned, that he would not take their lives without trial, he sent back a defiant answer, "that he would kill his people if he liked, and that he did not ask the Governor of Natal not to kill his own."

The messengers sent by the King to attend the enquiry which was set on foot about this time, as to the boundary with the Transvaal, concerning which there was a dispute when we took the territory over (and to settle which a Commission was appointed), used haughty language, and were very independent; saying that "they had only been sent there to declare what the

King said." About the same time an armed raid was made across the Buffalo into Natal by the sons of Sirayo (a border chief in Zululand of bad repute), who seized two women on our territory, and dragged them across into Zululand, where they were barbarously put to death, merely on the ground that they had run away from their husbands. All these circumstances, combined with the undoubted fact that Cetywayo was evidently preparing his hordes for war, and that we were the only neighbour he was likely to attack, made it absolutely necessary for the Home Government to take the matter in hand. Accordingly His Excellency Sir Bartle Frere, Governor of the Cape Colony and High Commissioner of South Africa, was ordered to proceed to Natal, to confer with Sir Henry Bulwer, and decide upon measures for inducing Cetywayo to govern his people in a manner more in accordance with the dictates of humanity and less threatening to his neighbours. Towards the end of September, 1878, His Excellency arrived in Pieter Maritzburg, took up his abode at Government House with our Lieutenant-Governor, and proceeded to obtain the necessary information with a view to this end.

It has only recently come to light how critical matters at that time appeared to be, when they were investigated. In the last Blue Book it is shown that on the 12th October, 1878, Mr. John Dunn, a confidential adviser of the Natal Government in Zululand, reported that Cetywayo was already moving his forces. It is not improbable he was incited to this by observing that the forces in Natal had been increased shortly after the arrival of Lord Chelmsford (then General the Hon. F. A. Thesiger, C.B.), which had taken place early in August. Much has been made of this fact, as showing that we brought about the war, by assuming a needlessly aggressive attitude. But Sir Bartle Frere saw clearly that Cetywayo was likely to be difficult to deal with, if this was the attitude he assumed, from the moment it seemed likely that we should demand with firmness that he should adhere to the promises he had made when crowned by Sir T. Shepstone. As further showing the state of affairs then existing, I may quote the opinions of the best authorities in Natal at that time, viz.: Sir T. Shepstone, Sir Henry Bulwer, and Lord Chelmsford. Sir T. Shepstone expressed his firm belief that Zululand must be made amenable to civilised ideas and Government, the military organisation be done away with, and British officers received as Residents. These changes he deemed absolutely necessary, "before any commencement could be expected in the change which was required to make the Zulu people safe neighbours and an improving community." Sir Henry Bulwer expressed his opinion that these changes should be demanded; significantly saying, "there can be no question as to the right of interference to such extent as is necessary to secure the objects in view, namely: the better government of the Zulu people, and the security of British territory from constant danger." He farther added "in the measures proposed by the High Commissioner in his present Minute, His Excellency (Sir Bartle Frere) has not, in my opinion, gone beyond what is necessary to secure these objects." Lord Chelmsford said that there was "no doubt in his mind that the guarantees demanded were absolutely necessary for the future peace of South Africa."

After carefully feeling his way and ascertaining the true state of affairs, as well as the opinions of those best qualified to judge of them. Sir Bartle Frere sent his celebrated message or ultimatum to Cetywayo on the 11th December, 1878, after having given due notice to the King to send messengers to hear it read, receive it, and then convey it to him. It was delivered to these messengers by the Hon. C. Brownlee, representing the High Commissioner, and the Hon. John Shepstone, Secretary for Native Affairs, who were attended by several officers, Mr. Fynn, R.N., Mr. Fynney, our Border Agent, who acted as interpreter, and a small escort, at a spot just below Fort Pearson, near the mouth of the River Tugela. The demands therein made were that the brother and sons of Sirayo—who had been connected with the armed raid into Natal, and seizure of two women refugees—should be given up and a fine of cattle paid for the offence; and farther, that the numerous promises made at Cetywayo's coronation should be fulfilled, that he should cease to kill his subjects without trial; that his threatening army should be disbanded; and the right of a British Resident to live in Zululand be recognised. Twenty days were given him in which to give up Sirayo's relations and pay that fine; and an extension was made of another ten days, making thirty days altogether, for the final answer of the King and payment of the fine inflicted upon him for the previous non-fulfilment of his promises. The message also treated of the settlement of the long dispute as to the territory bordering on the Transvaal. In this Sir Bartle Frere followed the award made by the Commission which had sat previously at Rorke's Drift to decide the question, and much to the surprise of many he also gave back to the Zulus a strip of land which, it was stated upon very good authority, belonged to the Dutch, but which the Commissioners had held to be part of Zululand. It was, however, understood, with a view if possible of satisfying both sides and doing justice to all concerned, that Sir Bartle Frere would, if his ultimatum had been accepted, have endeavoured to arrived at an arrangement whereby, while recognising the sovereign rights of the Zulu King over this portion of the land, he would secure to the Dutch farmers who had settled upon it such individual rights as they were entitled to, or compensation for losing them.

    Such, briefly, was the state of affairs existing in South Africa which led up to the Zulu war, and the part which Sir Bartle Frere played in them. Now, more than ever, can we see that the war was inevitable; and had the matter only been quietly shelved for a little while, we should most likely have been the invaded instead of the invaders. The Colony of Natal had long been threatened with invasion by the Zulus, and the utmost care and tact on the part of our authorities had been required to prevent some outbreak long before. When Sir Bartle Frere came round to Natal he found it was absolutely necessary that definite steps should be taken to obviate this danger. Indeed there can be little doubt that he was expressly commissioned to do so by the Home Government. Whether it might have been possible for two or three years longer to continue living on the edge of such a political volcano may be an open question. Possibly matters might have held together for a short time; but it was certain that the danger, already formidable, would continue to increase every year, nay, almost every month; and that the difficulty of dealing with it, which might arise from immediate and decisive action, would be proportionately augmented by delay. Parleying with Cetywayo had long proved useless, and it was hopeless to expect to bring him to reason without some display of force. Sir Bartle knew that the demands which he was thus compelled to make would be unpalatable to Cetywayo, but he still hoped that the Zulu King would be disposed to yield, rather than face going to war with us, when he perceived that we were prepared if necessary to enforce our demands. It was reasonably considered that, in the event of a refusal, the troops which Lord Chelmsford had under his command would prove sufficient to awe Cetywayo into submission; and though preparation for ulterior measures was compulsory there seemed every reason to hope to the last that the Zulu King would concede the terms which we demanded. It may be noticed that even Bishop Colenso, who all along has been, and still is, a strong opponent of Sir Bartle Frere and his policy, admitted that the demands as a whole were justifiable and necessary; although he took exception to the proposed plan of recognising the territorial rights of the Dutch farmers on a part of the disputed boundary land, to which I have before alluded. But to the surprise of all, it was found that, even before the receipt of the message, Cetywayo had been actively preparing for war; and on the 25th November, a fortnight before the ultimatum was issued, Lord Chelmsford reported that Zulu piquets were within rifle-shot of our own men. There thus appeared to be every probability, nay, almost a certainty, that, long before Sir Bartle Frere could have referred the matter home and received his answer (the telegraph not being established at the time), the Zulus would have invaded Natal. Lord Chelmsford had declared—and the whole course of the war shows that he was justified in his opinion—"that Natal could only be protected by our acting on the offensive;" and the case was clearly one in which promptitude as well as firmness was required. Delay would have given Cetywayo the greatest possible temptation to attack the colony. He would have seen that we marched our troops forward, and that we hesitated to do more; and this hesitation would infallibly have been construed as the results of fear. How thoroughly prepared he was to carry out his threats was only too well shown by the furious onslaughts made against our forces on the sad and memorable day at Isandwhlana, and by the subsequent desperate attack of 4,000 Zulus upon our small fort at Rorke's Drift, in Natal.

The time allowed by the ultimatum for compliance with the demands having expired, and no answer being received from Cetywayo, Sir Bartle Frere made over the settlement of the whole question to Lord Chelmsford, who marched our troops in five Columns, at different places, across the frontier from the 6th to the 11th January, without opposition from the enemy, and thus commenced the first campaign in Zululand.

CHAPTER I

EVER SINCE the commencement of the Cape War against the Gaikas and Galekas, at the end of 1877, signs had not been wanting that disturbances were likely to break out, not only among the small surrounding tribes along our Natal border and that of the Transvaal; but also it was found that even Cetywayo himself was fomenting these smaller quarrels, so as to enable him to carry on his own projects with greater success. Secocoeni and Umbelini, two of the most noted, powerful, and independent predatory chiefs in the Transvaal and Zululand—or just beyond the north-west corner of Natal—were the first to show signs of what was impending; and, having for some time successfully waged a desultory warfare with the inhabitants of their surrounding neighbourhoods, while the Transvaal was under the Government of a Dutch Republic, they doubtless thought that the opportunity was come for doing so on a still larger scale when the British annexed the country and took over the Government. They, however, greatly miscalculated the power of their new foe. In order to check these lawless mountain chieftains, the regiment then at Pretoria (the 13th P.A.L.I.) was strengthened in August, 1878, by the 80th "Staffordshire Volunteers," and several mounted Volunteer corps were raised locally; while forts were built along the line of communications, thus enabling the troops to keep the forces of those chiefs in check, until we should be able to enter into a regular campaign against them. In Natal itself, owing to the dispute on the boundary question being again raised by Cetywayo, and other news from Zululand, the first and second battalions of the 24th "Warwickshire" regiment were added to the 3rd "Buffs," at that time the only regiment quartered

Sir Henry Bartle Edward Frere, 1st Baronet, GCB, GCSI, (1815 – 1884). He was made High Commissioner for Southern Africa in 1877.

in Natal. Shortly after this, matters had come to such a pass between our Government and the Zulu King, that it was clearly seen that some decisive steps would have at once to be taken, in order to put an end to the outrages and insolent behaviour of Cetywayo. Under these circumstances, His Excellency Lieu-tenant-General the Honourable F. A. Thesiger, C.B., came round from the Cape in August, and made the necessary preliminary arrangements, so as to protect our own territory and enable us to resort to force, if nothing else would suffice. The advent of the General was quickly followed by that of His Excellency Sir Bartle Frere, K.C.B., Governor of the Cape, and Her Majesty's High Commissioner in South Africa; as well as by the arrival of large reinforcements of troops from the old colony, including the 88th "Connaught Rangers;" Wood's Column, consisting of the 90th regiment, a battery of artillery and some mounted infantry; the Frontier Light Horse, which had originally been raised by Captain F. Carrington, 1-24th regiment, but were then 200 strong and specially commanded by Major Buller, C.B., 60th rifles, who had with him as second in command the late Captain Barton, Coldstream Guards; the "Kaffrarian Riflemen," under Commandant Schermbrucker; and drafts from every other branch of the service. These were again supplemented in January by the arrival from England of the second battalion 4th "King's Own" regiment, and the 99th "Duke of Edinburgh's." The navy also contributed its share, a large naval brigade being landed from H.M.S. Active, Flag Ship of the Cape Station, flying the pennant of Commodore Sullivan, C.B., and placed under the command of Captain Campbell, R.N. Three regiments of a Native Contingent were also formed, two having two battalions, and the third, three, of 1,000 men in each (of the formation of which I shall give full particulars farther on). Troops of mounted natives were raised to act as scouts, and every Mounted Volunteer corps in the colony—eight in number —was called out; while Town Guards were established at Durban and Pieter Maritzburg, and arrangements were made to put all the "laagers" throughout the colony in a defensive state. The Natal Mounted Police, a purely colonial force, was also much strengthened and called out for active service.

Our forces were stationed at various posts along the Border, and divided into five Columns. No. 1 Column was commanded by Colonel Pearson, and encamped at the Lower Tugela Drift (where Fort Pearson was built), with Durban for its base, and Stanger as an advanced depot. It numbered about 1,900 whites and 2,000 natives—a total of 3,900 men. No. 2 Column was that under the command of the late Lieutenant-Colonel Durnford, R.E., and was stationed at Kranzkop, Middle Drift, with Grey Town as its advanced depot, and Pieter Maritzburg as its base. It consisted entirely of natives, with the exception of their white officers, and bad about 150 whites and 8,800 natives —together 8,450 men enrolled. No. 3 Column, with which went the Head Quarters, was commanded by Brevet-Colonel Glynn, C.B., and was the strongest of the five. It was organised at Helpmakaar and Rorke's Drift, having Pieter Maritzburg as its base, with Ladysmith on the main road, and Grey Town on the Border road, as advanced depots. It numbered about 2,200 whites and 2,500 natives, or 4,700 in all. No. 4 Column was under the command of Colonel Wood, V.C., C.B., and was stationed at Conference Hill on the Blood River, with Utrecht for its base. The original strength of Colonel Wood's Column has not been precisely ascertained, as be was constantly adding more Irregulars and Dutch Volunteers; but at the beginning be had a nucleus of about 1,800 whites and 500 natives, that 18 2,800 men. No. 5 Column was hardly intended for offensive purposes against the Zulus, but was left behind at Luneberg and in that district, to check Secocoeni. It was commanded by Colonel Rowlands, V.C., C.B., and numbered about 1,500, of whom 1,000 were whites, and 500 natives. So that altogether, exclusive of the Dutch Volunteers, the Irregular corps then being raised at the Cape, and the Swazie levy, Lord Chelmsford had under his command a force of nearly 16,000 men, made up of 7,000 whites and 9,000 natives.

The following is the official List of our Army in the field at the commencement of operations:—

NATAL AND TRANSVAAL.

Lieutenant-General Commanding the Forces,—F. A. Lord Chelmsford, K.C.B.

Personal Staff.

Assistant military secretary, Brevet Lieutenant-Colonel Crealock, 95th foot; aides-de-camp, Brevet-Major Gosset, 54th foot, Captain Buller, R.B., and Lieutenant Milne, R.N.

Head-quarters Staff.

Colonel Pearson

Deputy adjutant and quartermaster-general, Brevet-Colonel Bellairs, C.B. (unattached); deputy assistant adjutants and quartermasters-general, Brevet-Major Spalding, 104th foot, Brevet-Major Grenfell, 60th foot; officer commanding Royal Artillery, Lieutenant-Colonel Law, R.A.; commanding Royal Engineers, Colonel Hassard, C.B., R.E.; commanding Natal Mounted Police and Volunteers, Major Dartnell, N.M.P.; district commissary-general, Commissary-General Strickland, C.B.; commissary-general (ordnance). Deputy Commissary-General Wright; district paymaster. Staff Paymaster Ball; principal medical officer, Deputy-Surgeon Woolfryes, C.B., M.D.

No. 1 Column.

Colonel commanding. Colonel Pearson, 3rd foot.

Staff—Orderly officer, Lieutenant Knight, 3rd foot; principal staff officer, Brevet-Colonel Walker, C.B., Scots Guards; general staff duties, Captain McGregor, 29th foot; transport duties, Captain Pelly Clarke, 103rd foot; senior commissariat officer. Assistant Commissary Heygate; sub-district paymaster, Paymaster George (hon. captain); senior medical officer, Surgeon-Major Tarrant.

Corps—Royal Artillery, two seven-pounders (mule), Lieutenant Lloyd; Royal Engineers, No. 2 company, Captain Wynne, R.E.; 2nd battalion, 3rd foot, Brevet Lieutenant-Colonel Parnell; 99th foot (six companies), Lieutenant-Colonel Welman; Naval Brigade, Commander Campbell, R.N.; No. 2 squadron Mounted Infantry, Major Barrow, 19th hussars; Natal Hussars, Captain Norton; Durban Mounted Rifles, Captain W. Shepstone; Alexandra Mounted Rifles, Captain Arbuthnot; Stanger Mounted Rifles, Captain Addison; Victoria Mounted Rifles, Captain Saner.

2nd Regiment Natal Native Contingent—Major Graves, 3rd foot; staff officer. Captain Hart, 81st foot; 1st battalion. Major Graves; 2nd battalion. Commandant Nettleton; No. 2 company, Natal Native Pioneer Corps, Captain Beddoes.

No. 2 Column.

Commanding, Lieutenant-Colonel Durnford, R.E.

Staff—For general staff duties. Captain Barton, 77th foot; for transport duties. Lieutenant Cochrane, 82nd foot; senior medical officer. Civil Surgeon Cartwright Reed.

Corps—Rocket battery (mules), Captain Russell, R.A.

1st Regiment Natal Native Contingent—1st battalion. Commandant Montgomery; 2nd battalion. Major Bengough, 77th foot; 3rd battalion, Captain Cherry, 82nd foot; Sikali's Horse; No. 8 company Natal Native Pioneers, Captain Allen.

No. 3 Column.

Commanding, Brevet-Colonel Glynn C.B., 24th foot.

Staff—Orderly officer. Lieutenant Coghill, 24th foot; principal staff officer, Major Clery; for general staff duties. Captain Gardner, 14th hussars; for transport duties. Captain Essex, 75th foot; senior commissariat officer. Assistant Commissary Dunne;

Colonel Anthony Durnford of the Royal Engineers was killed in action at Isandlwana on 22 January, 1879, while in command of No. 2 Column.

sub-district paymaster. Paymaster Elliott (hon. captain); senior medical officer, Surgeon-Major Shepherd.

Corps—N battery, 5th brigade, Royal Artillery, Brevet Lieutenant-Colonel Harness; Royal Engineers, No. 5 company. Captain Jones, R.E.; 1st battalion, 24th foot, Brevet Lieut-tenant-Colonel Pulleine; 2nd battalion, 24th foot, Lieutenant-Colonel Degacher, C.B.; No. 1 squadron Mounted Infantry, Lieutenant-Colonel (loc. r.) Russell, 12th lancers; Natal Mounted Police, Major Dartnell; Natal Carbineers, Captain T. Shepstone; Newcastle Mounted Rifles, Captain Bradstreet; Buffalo Border Guard, Captain Smith.

3rd Regiment Natal Native Contingent—Commandant Lonsdale; staff officer, Lieutenant Harford, 99th foot; 1st battalion, Commandant Lonsdale; 2nd battalion, Commandant Cooper; No. 1 company Natal Native Pioneer Corps, Captain Nolan.

Sir Evelyn Wood.

No. 4 Column.

Commanding, Brevet-Colonel Evelyn Wood, V.C., C.B., 90th foot.

Staff—Orderly officer, Lieutenant Lysons, 90th foot; principal staff officer. Captain Hon. R. Campbell, Coldstream Guards; for general staff duties, Captain Woodgate, 4th foot; for transport duties. Captain Vaughan, R.A.; senior commissariat officer. Commissary Hughes; commissary of ordnance. Assistant Commissary Phillimore; sub-district paymaster. Paymaster MacDonald; senior medical officer, Surgeon-Major Cuffe.

Corps—Royal Artillery, six 7-pounders, Major Tremlett, R.A.; 1st battalion, 18th foot, Lieutenant-Colonel Gilbert; 90th foot. Brevet Lieutenant-Colonel Cherry; Frontier Light Horse, Brevet Lieutenant-Colonel Buller, C.B., 60th foot; Wood's Irregulars, Commandant Henderson.

No. 5 Column.

Commanding, Colonel Rowlands, V.C., C.B.

Staff—Principal staff officer. Captain Harvey, 71st foot; district adjutant. Lieutenant Potts, 80th foot; senior commissariat officer, Assistant Commissary-General Phillips; commissary of ordnance. Commissary Wyon; sub-district paymaster, Assistant Paymaster Burgers; senior medical officer, Surgeon-Major Johnson.

Corps—80th foot, Major Tucker; Schutte's corps. Captain Schutte; Eckersley's contingent. Captain Eckersley; Ferreira's Horse, Captain Ferreira; Border Lancers, Lieutenant-Colonel Weatherley; Transvaal Rangers, Captain Raaff; one Krupp gun and two 6-pounders, Armstrong.

LINE OF COMMUNICATIONS.

Pieter Maritzburg — Grey Town — Helpmakaar.

Commanding, Brevet Lieutenant-Colonel Hopton, 88th foot.

Staff—District adjutant, Lieutenant Morehead, 24th foot; commissariat officer. Commissary Furse; commissariat (ordnance), Commissary Moors; district paymaster, Paymaster Bacon; senior medical officer, Surgeon-Major Ingham; commanding general depot, Brevet-Major Chamberlin, 24th foot. One company 88th foot, Fort Napier.

Grey Town and Middle Drift.

Commanding, Brevet-Major Blake, 2nd battalion, 4th foot.

Grey Town—One company, 2nd battalion, 4th foot.

Helpmakaar — Rorke's Drift.

Commanding, Colonel Bray, C.B., 4th foot.

Four companies, 2nd battalion, 4th foot.

Stanger —Lower Tugela Drift.

Stanger—Commanding, Brevet-Major Walker, 99th foot.

One company 99th foot.

Fort Pearson —Detachment Naval Brigade.

Base of Operations, Durban.

Commanding, Major Huskisson, 56th foot.

Staff—For general duties. Captain Somerset, R.B.; for transport duties, Captain Spratt, 29th foot; senior commissariat officer. Deputy Commissary Granville; commissary of ordnance. Assistant Commissary de Ricci; senior medical officer. Surgeon Jennings. One company 99th foot.

***

Large stores of everything necessary for an army in the field had been got together and sent up to the advanced depots, while oxen and waggons for transport were bought and hired wherever possible, with conductors, drivers, and leaders. Officers were sent to the Cape, Orange Free State, and Transvaal to buy horses and mules, and a large remount depot was formed at Pieter Maritzburg. So that, almost in every respect, the General commanding was as fully prepared as was possible under the circumstances. In the meantime the members of his Staff and Intelligence department were not idle. Information on every subject in connection with Zululand and its inhabitants was obtained from the most reliable sources; the outcome of which was the issue in November, 1878, of a small pamphlet, entitled the "Zulu Army," published for the information of those under his command by the direction of the Lieutenant-General commanding. The following is the descriptive portion, which is of sufficient interest to merit reproduction here:—

"The Zulu army, which may be estimated at from 40,000 to 60,000 men, is composed of the entire nation capable of bearing arms.

"The method employed in recruiting its ranks is as follows: — At short intervals, varying from two to five years, all the young men who have during that time attained the age of fourteen or fifteen years are formed into a regiment, which, after a year's probation (during which they are supposed to pass from boyhood and its duties to manhood) is placed at a military kraal or headquarters. In some cases they are sent to an already existing kraal, which is the head-quarters of a corps or regiment, of which they then become part; in others, especially when the young regiment is numerous, they build a new military kraal. As the regiment grows old it generally has one or more regiments embodied with it, so that the young men may have the benefit of their elders' experience, and, when the latter gradually die out, may take their place and keep up the name and prestige of their military kraal. In this manner corps are formed, often many thousands strong, such, for instance, as the Undi.

"Under this system, then, the Zulu army has gradually increased, until at present it consists of twelve corps, and two regiments, each possessing its own military kraal. The corps necessarily contain men of all ages, some being married and wearing the head-ring, others unmarried; some being old men scarcely able to walk, while others are hardly out of their teens. Indeed, five of these corps are now composed of a single regiment each, which has absorbed the original but practically nonexistent regiment to which it had been affiliated.

"Each of these fourteen corps or regiments have the same internal formation. They are in the first place divided equally into two wings—the right and the left—and in the second are subdivided into companies from ten to two hundred in number, according to the numerical strength of the corps or regiment to which they belong, estimated at fifty men each, with the exception of the Nkombamakosi regiment, which averages seventy men to the company.

"Each corps or regiment, possessing its own military kraal, has the following officers: one commanding officer (called the induna, yesibaya 'sikulu), one second in command (called the induna yohlangoti), who directly commands the left wing, and two wing officers called the induna yesicamelo yesibaya 'sikulu, and the induna yesicamelo yohlangoti. Besides the above there are company officers, consisting of a captain and from one to three junior officers, all of whom are of the same age as the men they command, while in the case of a corps the C.O. of each regiment composing it takes rank next to its four great officers when he is himself not of them.

"As to the regimental dress and distinguishing marks, the chief distinction is between married and unmarried men. No one in Zululand, male or female, is permitted to marry without the direct permission of the King, and, when he allows a regiment to do so, which is not before the men are about forty years of age, they have to shave the crown of the head, and to put a ring round it, and then they become one of the "white" regiments, carrying white shields, &c., in contradistinction to the "black" or unmarried regiments, who wear their hair naturally, and have coloured shields.

"The total number of regiments in the Zulu army is thirty-three, of whom eighteen are formed of men with rings on their beads, and fifteen of unmarried men. Seven of the former are composed of men over sixty years of age, so that, for practical purposes, there are not more than twenty-six Zulu regiments able to take the field, numbering altogether 40,400. Of these, 22,500 are between twenty and thirty years of age, 10,000 between thirty and forty, 8,400 between forty and fifty, and 4,500 between fifty and sixty years of age. From which it will be seen that the mortality in Zululand is unusually rapid.

"Drill—in the ordinary acceptation of the term—is unknown among the Zulus; the few simple movements which they perform with any method, such as forming a circle of companies or regiments, breaking into companies or regiments from the circle, forming a line of march in order of companies, or in close order of regiments, not being deserving of the name. The officers have, however, their regulated duties and responsibilities,

"Cetewayo"

according to their rank, and the men lend a ready obedience to their orders.

"As might be expected, a savage army like that of Zululand neither has nor requires much commissariat or transport. The former consists of three or four days' provisions, in the shape of maize or millet, and a herd of cattle, proportioned to the distance to be traversed, accompanies each regiment. The latter consists of a number of lads who follow each regiment, carrying the sleeping mats, blankets, and provisions, and assisting to drive the cattle.

"When a Zulu army on the line of march comes to a river in flood, and the breadth of the stream which is out of their depth does not exceed from ten to fifteen yards, they plunge in, in a dense mass, holding on to one another, those behind forcing them on forward, and thus succeed in crossing with the loss of a few of their number.

"In the event of hostilities arising between the Zulu nation and any other (unless some very sudden attack were made on their country), messengers would be sent by the King, travelling day and night if necessary, to order the men to assemble in regiments at their respective military kraals, where they would find the commanding officer ready to receive them.

"When a corps or regiment has thus congregated at its headquarters, it would, on receiving the order, proceed to the King's kraal. Before marching, a circle or umkumbi is formed inside the kraal, each company together, their officers in an inner ring —the first and second in command in the centre. The regiment then proceeds to break into companies, beginning from the left-hand side, each company forming a circle, and marching off, followed by boys carrying provisions, mats, &c. The company officers march immediately in rear of their men, the second in command in rear of the left wing, and the commanding officer in rear of the right.

"On arriving at the King's kraal each regiment encamps on its own ground, as no two regiments can be trusted not to fight if encamped together. The following ceremonies are then performed in his presence:—All the regiments are formed into an immense circle or umkumbi, a little distance from the King's kraal, the officers forming an inner ring surrounding the chief officers and the King, together with the doctors and medicine basket. A doctored beast is then killed, cut into strips powdered with medicine, and taken round to the men by the chief medicine man, the soldiers not touching it with their hands, but biting a piece off the strip held out to them. They are then dismissed for the day, with orders to assemble in the morning. The next day early they all take emetics, form an umkumbi, and are again dismissed. On the third day they again form an umkumbi of regiments, are then sprinkled with medicine by the doctors, and receive their orders through the chief officer of state present, receiving an address from the King, after which they start on their expedition.

"Previously to marching off, the regiments re-form companies under their respective officers, and the regiment selected by the King to take the lead advances. The march is in order of companies for the first day, after which it is continued in the umsila (or path), which may be explained by likening it to one of our divisions advancing in line of brigade columns, each brigade in a mass, each regiment in close column; the line of provision-bearers, &c., moves on the flank; the intervals between heads of columns vary according to circumstances, from several miles to within sight of each other; constant communication is kept up by runners. The march would be continued in this order, with the exception that the baggage and provision-bearers fall in rear of the column on the second day; and that the cattle composing the commissariat are driven between them and the rearmost regiment until near the enemy. The order of companies is then resumed, and, on coming in sight, the whole army again forms an umkumbi, for the purpose of enabling the Commander-in-chief to address the men, and give his final instructions, which concluded, the different regiments intended to commence the attack do so.

"A large body of troops, as a reserve, remains seated with their backs to the enemy; the commanders and staff retire to some eminence with one or two of the older regiments (as extra reserves). All orders are delivered by runners.

"It is to be noted that although the above were the ordinary customs of the Zulu army when at war, it is more than probable that great changes, both in movements and dress, will be made consequent on the introduction of firearms among them."

In addition to this valuable information, the formation of attack by the Zulu army was shown on a plan; and a photograph of a sketch map of Zululand, and the adjoining country, issued by the authorities at home, was also given. At the end of the work there were tabulated forms giving the details of how the Zulu army of 40,400 men was made up, including the names of the corps having a military kraal, regiments composing such corps, English meaning of name, by whom raised, name of commanding officer, name and position of military kraal forming the head-quarters of corps, age of men, number of men in regiment, total number in corps, distinguishing regimental dress and marks, with numerous valuable notes and remarks in the margin.

This pamphlet was followed by a small work entitled "Regulations for Field Forces in South Africa," which, by a general order, was drawn up and promulgated to the forces in this command, for the guidance of all concerned. Its contents included general regulations, rules as to encampments, regimental, general depot, commissariat, transport, ordnance store, field hospitals, sanitary precautions, horses, sick horse and remount depot, postal arrangements, commands and relative ranks, cattle and other prizes, local forces, Natal Native Contingent, and correspondence. In the appendix, forms, returns, conditions of service, general instructions, and tables of transport for every branch of the service were annexed, and an almanack for 1879 with several blank pages completed this handy little book.

Lastly, another small pamphlet was also issued, containing "Suggestions for the general Management of Horses and

Mules, while on Field Service in Natal and the Neighbouring Countries, with Notes concerning their more Common Ailments" which was drawn up by Veterinary Surgeon Glover, R.A., who appended to the work a list of prescriptions for use in various emergencies.

I think I have thus given as concisely and completely as possible an epitome of the preparations made, and of the state of affairs in Natal at the end of 1878. It only remains to note that H. E. the High Commissioner had sent to the Zulu King, as the sequel and conclusion of prolonged antecedent negotiations, an ultimatum, comprising a series of stipulations, unconditional compliance with which was prescribed. These demands related to the most objectionable features of the Zulu government and military system, such as the prohibition against the young men marrying; as also to the surrender of the sons of the Zulu chief Sirayo, and others, who at an earlier period had been concerned in the abduction and murder of some fugitive Zulu women who had taken refuge over the Border, in Natal. A delay of thirty days had been allowed, within which these several conditions were to be fulfilled by Cetywayo, if he were really desirous of maintaining peaceful relations with the Colony and the British; and it had been decided that in default of full satisfaction during that interval, the matter should pass into the hands of Lord Chelmsford, in order to compel submission by force of arms. The date of the expiration of the thirty days allowed in the ultimatum was the 10th of January, and I started away from Maritzburg on my first journey in December, so as to have a short tour of inspection before the day came for opening the campaign. The proper account, therefore, of my personal experiences will commence in the next chapter.

CHAPTER II

I LEFT PIETER Maritzburg on Tuesday, December 17, 1878, intending to ride through Grey Town, and along the Border as far as Helpmakaar, where the Head-quarters camp of the 3rd Column, under Colonel Glynn, was formed, which Column I intended accompanying into Zululand, my object being to see how far matters were in progress, and to get some idea as to the plan of the campaign, and what would be wanted. I purposed returning to Pieter Maritzburg in time to have my Christmas dinner at home; after which I should leave again for good, and remain with the Column until the Zulu question was settled. The old saying that "Man proposes and God disposes" was never more truly realised than in this case; for how many of us were there who thought that we should so quickly, as events proved, be only too glad to find ourselves back again safely over the Border into Natal!

There were only two ways of travelling optional to me—riding or driving; and after much consideration I decided upon the former, as being the more independent, and likely to prove also the more convenient in journeying over the rough Zulu country. Another reason was that fresh horses would always be procurable, but if any accident happened to the carriage I should be " stuck" at once. My kit was not a large one, and considering that I and my groom carried all we wanted upon our saddles, I think every one will admit that we were not heavily burdened with luggage, or likely to be stopped by want of transport. Grey Town, my first halt, is only forty-five miles almost due north of Pieter Maritzburg; but I was not able to get through in one day, owing to my being caught in one of the thick fogs which are so prevalent in that district. I took refuge for the night at Seven

Oaks, ten miles short of my destination, and reached the camp of the 2-24th Regiment just in time for breakfast next day.

On the road up, which is through Umvoti county, one of the finest in the colony for grazing and agricultural purposes, I was much struck by the appearance of the numerous farms, few of which showed any signs of ploughing or other agricultural operations being in progress. This apparent apathy on the part of the farmers was, however, due, as I found, in a great measure to the high rates given by Government for transport, which induced the men to take their waggons and spans of oxen, obtain loads for various places, and thus neglect their crops and farms. I could not help thinking at the time that this would not pay in the long run; and I felt sorry to see the colonists neglect their main support for the sake of a little temporary speculation in transport. Between Pieter Maritzburg and Grey Town alone, in those two days, I passed more than fifty waggons on the road up with Government stores for Grey Town, Pots Spruit, near Fort Buckingham (where there was a camp), and Helpmakaar. The rates per cwt. were about 5s. to 6s. from Pieter Maritzburg to Grey Town, 10s. to 15s. to Helpmakaar, and from 6s. to 8s. from Grey Town to Pots Spruit, which was a route over very bad country. The other roads were over a fair country, and kept in excellent repair. It will, therefore, easily be seen how profitable transport-riding was, when each waggon could take from sixty to eighty cwts., and travel at the rate of fifteen miles a day. Some men that I knew, neither farmers nor transport-riders, caught the infection, sold out of other businesses, bought a waggon or waggons as they were able, and went to work on the road.

When I reached the camp I was most cordially welcomed by Captain Symons and his subaltern, poor Franklin, whose bones now lie in the little cemetery at Helpmakaar, where he died of fever, shortly after our return from Isandwhlana. My horses were put up, and I came in for a share of a most excellent

General Plan of the Operations in Zululand, 1879

breakfast. Afterwards I had a stroll about the camp, and was introduced to Major Dunbar and the other officers, of whom Charlie Pope, Austin, Dyer, Griffiths, and Bloomfield, are now sleeping their last sleep in Zululand, under the shadow of a mountain whose name will always be associated with one of the greatest disasters that ever occurred to British troops. With Pope I was most charmed, and I enjoyed an hour spent in his tent, looking over his sketches, while the conversation was never allowed to flag by Austin and Franklin, who were in the tent with us. The camp itself was pitched on a slight hill, about three-quarters of a mile before Grey Town, on the right-hand side of the road, and was very comfortably arranged. Besides the tents of the soldiers, there was a large iron store recently built for the Commissariat and Transport Department. Altogether, there were six companies of the 2-24th, the other two of which were at Pots Spruit, from which they were ordered into Grey Town just as I left; and one company of the 1-24th and Major Harness's Battery of the Royal Artillery, consisting of six guns. Colonel Degacher was in command, with Captain Harvey, who had just got his company, as district adjutant. The health of the camp was exceedingly good, and only about one per cent, were in hospital. Athletics of every kind were encouraged, and all the men under fifteen years' service ran a thousand yards every morning before breakfast. Although the men were paraded daily, and went through the ordinary drill, they were not overworked, and had plenty of leisure time. I found both men and officers on the qui vive to hear the order given for a march to the front, and although comfortable where they were, they would willingly have crossed the Border at a day's notice.

Owing to heavy rains, the road farther up was almost impassable and delayed the waggon-convoys as well as myself very considerably. The road beyond Grey Town is very lonely, and, being close to the Border, is never a very safe one to travel during any disturbance; I was, therefore, fortunate in being introduced to a companion, a young Civil Surgeon. I mean, by that, one of those medical men, not belonging to the Army Medical Department, who were engaged by the Government at home and sent out there to assist. His name was Beresford, and he told me that he had seen a good deal of service in the Russo-Turkish war of 1877.

Anyhow, he was proceeding to Sand Spruit (marked Wilson's on Jeppe's map), having been attached to the 3rd Regiment of the Natal Native Contingent, then being formed at that station; and as I was also desirous of staying there for a few days, we were both very glad at our meeting. Before leaving Grey Town I proceeded to the office of my friend Warneford, the District Commissary, whose good offices were necessary to make our way smooth en route, as without special permits no one was allowed to draw forage, &c., from the depots established along the road, and there was no other similar accommodation. A few lines from him "did the trick," and thenceforth I must admit my journey along that road was made easy and pleasant. Beresford and I left at ten on Thursday morning, and after a five-mile pull up one of the stiffest hills in the colony, we reached "Burrup's," eight miles from Grey Town, before noon, where we "off-saddled" and fed both ourselves and our horses. We fell in here with a patrol of the Natal Hussars, established in a rough shanty, called the "Vultures' Nest," on an adjacent high hill, and who had a large stretch of country (including "Burrup's") to patrol. We left at about 2.15 p.m. in a heavy rain, and arrived at Mooi River, a distance of twelve miles, at 3.45, after passing through such a storm as I never had been out in here. We were simply wet to the skin; and, utterly heedless of the height and torrent of the swollen river, we plunged in harum-scarum, got through to the other side safely, and reached the accommodation-house on the other bank. Here the doctor and myself, wringing wet, tired and hungry, were received by the proprietor in the most surly manner; and, in fact, we had almost determined to push on to the Tugela, when, after a little indaba, we found out the sore spot, and succeeded in obtaining the needed shelter. We left next morning as early as we could, after feeding our own horses (to do which, as we had undressed to dry our clothes, we were obliged to go out barefooted and with only rugs around us, a ludicrous scene, better to be imagined than described), and cutting up the forage ourselves, as no one else would do it. We got to the Tugela Drift, another eleven miles, at 8.45, but were unable to ford it, as the river was too high. We were therefore obliged to cross on the punt. Several waggons were on the other side, unable either to cross the drift or get on to the punt, as the river had brought down such large quantities of sand and mud that the punt could not get near enough to the bank. At the Tugela we were obliged, though hungry as hunters, to content ourselves with sardines, dry bread, and coffee; it being absolutely impossible to get either meat, mealie-meal, or fowls, for love or money. We left for Sand Spruit at noon, and arrived there at 5 p.m., having done sixteen miles in four hours, outspanning once on the road; and very glad we were to reach the camp of the 3rd N.N.C. We both had letters to some and knew others of the officers; and I was anxious to see the work of the organisation of native levies. We were also rejoiced at the change in the country, which was there green, open, and flat; for, after leaving "Burrup's," the road through the "Thorns," which lasts until within six miles of Sand Spruit, is very trying in every way; nothing but up and down hill, bad roads, thorns on the right of you, thorns on the left of you, and no traffic, make it altogether one of the worst and most wearisome roads I have ever travelled on; and I have been over some bad ones. The heat and glare on a hot day were something to dread; it was always necessary to have your horses shod all round, and in wet weather it was really wet, and kept so longer than on the hills around. At one place, it is true, there is a most splendid view, reminding one of the Western Ghauts in India, and this is at the top of the steep ascent from Mooi River, as nearly as possible half-way to the Tugela, which from this point you can see, miles away, winding through hills, with nothing but range after range, and mountain after mountain, in front and on both sides. The cutting by which the road descends the hill to the Tugela is a really fine piece of work, principally scarped out of the sides of the hills, and winding prettily all the way down. Its gradient, although steep, is the same throughout, and the whole work reflects great credit on the Colonial authorities, who carried it out. The description of Sand Spruit camp and the events which occurred during my stay fully merit a chapter to themselves.

CHAPTER III

THE SITE of the camp at Sand Spruit, which stood a little way off on the right of the road, was not in any way suited for the purposes of organising such a large number of men; and a much better one could have been chosen farther on under the hills. The supply of water, certainly the prime consideration at all times, was small, uncertain, and of a very bad quality; and the position of the camp was altogether too much exposed, both to the hot sun, in the daytime, and to the heavy rain and wind storms which came down almost nightly from the hills to the S.E. However, such as it was, we found it on our arrival, and we were not long before we had quarters assigned to us, and every arrangement made for our comfort that was, under the circumstances, possible. The doctor had a tent to himself, and I shared the Commandant's, who, with his officers, was most anxious that I should remain with them throughout. Being pleased with what I had already seen, and naturally thinking that, wherever there was any fighting, the native regiments would surely be in the van, I promised that I would go in with them; only stipulating that I had to ride back to Pieter Maritzburg for my Christmas dinner, and would then rejoin them at once. This settled the matter. I sported the red puggaree, joined the senior mess, and in fact soon came to be looked upon as "one of them."

The experiment of raising the three native regiments was entirely an idea of the General's, and was carried out much against the wishes of our Lieutenant-Governor. But the only mistakes that I can even now see in the whole thing were, firstly, that Kafirs were called out from farms who were working as servants, whereas there were over 200,000 other natives, living on locations in the colony under our protection, from whom the entire number necessary ought to have been drawn; secondly, that they were not all armed with guns; and, lastly, that many officers were appointed to commands in the regiments who knew nothing of service, and still less of the natives, their customs, and language. Otherwise the scheme was an admirable one; and had it not been for the "scare" which our native allies received at Isandwhlana, I feel certain that they would have accomplished much more than they were subsequently found capable of. From these remarks I entirely except the mounted natives, who throughout did most excellent service, and completely proved the justice of the General's scheme. But then it must be remembered that they were all armed with breech-loading rifles; and this, together with the fact of their being mounted, gave them the confidence which the others always lacked. Of the organisation of the 1st and 2nd Regiments, N.N.C. I know nothing; but I was in action with the latter at Gingihlovo, and I saw a good deal of one battalion of the former while stationed at Fort Bengough, and later on in Zululand. The 3rd Regiment N.N.C. was commanded by Commandant Rupert La Trobe Lonsdale, formerly of the 74th Regiment, an officer who had seen much service in the late Cape war at the head of a large Fingo levy, and who was therefore justly considered as being "the right man in the right place." The regiment was divided into two battalions of about 1,000 men each; the first being under the command of Commandant G. Hamilton Browne, who had been through the New Zealand campaign, and the second of Commandant A. W. Cooper, late of the 95th Regiment, who had also served throughout the Cape war.

The natives from whom the 3rd Regiment Natal Native Contingent was to be composed had previously arrived, to the number of about 1,700, under the charge of Mr. Chadwick, the Assistant Magistrate for Weenen County, and were gathered from Pagadi's and other neighbouring tribes, among which I may specially name those belonging to Umkungu and Isikotu, two brothers of Cetywayo, who escaped with their mother from Zululand, at the time of the massacre of Umbelazi and his followers. Umkungu, the eldest, was not there himself, being too corpulent to march far, but his son was present in his place. The other brother, Isikotu, accompanied his men into camp, and was on the Staff of the Commandant. Isikotu is a fine looking man, for a Zulu, stands over six feet high, well made, and has a pleasant though indolent-looking countenance. The men belonging to his tribe, as also those of his brother's, seemed only too anxious to get into Zululand, and have a brush with their soi-disant and blood-thirsty relatives, Cetywayo and his warriors. In the morning, just before my arrival in camp, Mr. Fynn, the Resident Magistrate of the Umsinga Division, had come over and addressed the whole body of natives, more than 2,000, including many relatives and friends, not actually joining the regiment.

After lunch I expressed my intention of going on to Helpmakaar for a short visit, to see the camp there, and meet many old acquaintances from our city in the Natal Carbineers; and, fortunately, was again able to secure company, in the person of Mr. Chadwick, the gentleman who had brought down the Kafirs to Sand Spruit, and who, having a short holiday, also wanted to go up to Helpmakaar. We reached the top of the Biggarsberg in two hours, having passed on the road several Dutch waggons loaded with excellent coal from the Dundee District, en route for Pieter Maritzburg. We had not proceeded more than about three miles along the top of the hills, when we saw lying in front of us the tents of the troops at Helpmakaar, on about the same level, but separated from us by a deep valley, and connected only on the right by a small neck of land to the range we were on. This sight hurried us on wonderfully, and we were not long in getting over the distance between the two ranges. The part of the road where it passes over the connecting neck of land, with a valley on each side sloping downwards to an enormous depth, on the right to the Buffalo and on the left in the direction of Sunday River, reminded me much of a similar bit of road on the Inchanga, between Pieter Maritzburg and Durban; and went far to prove the great altitude (over 4,000 feet, I believe) at which the camp lies. The tents of the Natal Mounted Police (150), under Major Dartnell, were nearest to us; then came, with a short interval only between them, those of three corps of Mounted Volunteers, viz., the Natal Carbineers (60), under Captain Shepstone; the Newcastle Mounted Rifles (80), under Captain Bradstreet; and the Buffalo Border Guard (22), under Lieutenant Smith. About half a mile farther on was the camp of the 1-24th Regiment, under Colonel Glynn; only four companies of which were there; the others being—two in Pieter Maritzburg, one at Durban, and one at Kokstadt. The health of this camp had been fairly good, although they had heavy rains every day, and most of those men who were on the sick list were so from dysentery. Horses, however, felt the severe weather much, and several died; and if the rain continued they were likely to do so, until a move was made. On this afternoon, Colonel Glynn, Major Dartnell, Captain Shepstone, and Mr. Mansell had ridden over to Fort Pine, about eighteen miles on the road to Dundee, and did not return until late. Fort Pine is a new fort half-way to Dundee, constructed by Captain Hime, R.E., the Colonial Engineer, and Major Dartnell, the Commandant of the Natal Mounted Police, out of the grant of £1,000 for Police Barracks; and it is surprising how such a substantial place could have been erected there for that money. The walls are of stone, about twelve feet high, and broad in proportion, with double-storied towers at two of the opposite corners. There is accommodation for twenty-five officers and men, stabling for thirty horses, storerooms, offices, and magazines, and in fact everything necessary for a permanent station or temporary laager. A small detachment of the Natal Mounted Police was to be stationed there regularly. The whole place seemed strong enough to keep out all Cetywayo's army, and would stand some knocking about even at more civilized hands. There is another laager in the neighbourhood, but it is a private one, about seven miles away between Helpmakaar and Rorke's Drift. It is also of stone, with walls seven feet high, and the size of it is fifty feet square. Rorke's Drift is only twelve miles beyond Helpmakaar, to the right of it, and was the scene of operations carried out by the Native Pioneer Company under Captain Nolan. The 2-24th, under Colonel Degacher, were also to come to Helpmakaar; and Major Harness's Battery of six guns R.A. When this Column under Colonel Glynn advanced into Zululand, a coincidence occurred, such as I believe never before happened, viz., two battalions of the same regiment were side by side in action, and both commanded by brothers, Captain Degacher, of the 1-24th, being the senior officer left when Colonel Glynn gave up his regimental command for that of the Column. The commissariat arrangements at the camp were everything that could be desired, and, through the able superintendence of Sergeant-Major McLoughlin, A.S.C., since promoted, gave general satisfaction. A field-oven was started, and, in spite of the rain, the troops were enabled to have splendid bread every other day. There were three large commissariat stores of wood, roofed with galvanised iron, containing groceries, biscuits, ram, &c. &c., and five large wildebeest huts were also erected, in which were stored the mealies, oats, oathay, &c. &c., required as forage. There were large quantities of stores, almost enough for a year's campaign, and they were being increased every day. We had a very heavy storm with severe lightning during the night, but 1 slept soundly in the dispensing tent throughout.

In the morning, after seeing Captain T. Shepstone and other old friends, we left again for Sand Spruit, as there was more doing in that camp likely to be of interest. We arrived in time for Church Parade, held by a neighbouring Missionary, and then spent the rest of the afternoon in writing. The members of the mess had intended having a great feed that evening, having been successful in getting a buck and other little niceties; but just as the cook was preparing the savoury viands down came such a storm of wind, followed immediately by heavy rain, as not only to put out fires, but even to blow over some tents, and quickly flood us all out. The Commandant and myself bore it patiently for some time, but when things began to float about and small streams to flow through our tent, we thought the time for action had commenced; so divesting ourselves of some of our clothing, we put on our waterproofs, made a rush to the nearest tent for spades, came back and commenced to dig a good-sized trench outside the tent, so as to direct the water into some other channel. In this we succeeded, after everything was wet through, and then, as our misery was at its height, we made a journey through the camp to see how others had fared. The result proved that there were many worse off than even we were; and, for my part, I took credit that, like Mark Tapley, I was jolly under those circumstances.

One tent, in particular, had been erected over a pathway, and it was really a sight worth seeing to witness how—notwithstanding that the occupants had dug a deep trench round it— the stream, unchecked almost, poured through the tent and over its contents. A small stream, percolating through the sand, close by one side of the camp, soon became a roaring torrent, and not only carried away our only barrel (sunk to get decent water) but also upset the whole engineering scheme of one of the Captains, who had sunk several wells close to the stream in order to get water. These were now entirely filled up with soil, sand, and gravel. The last seen of the unfortunate barrel was a few of its staves floating down the stream some miles off. Altogether, when the storm ceased at eight o'clock, we were certainly sadder if not wiser men; and during the evening doubtless many of us had plenty of time to cogitate on the instability of mundane affairs. The attempt at a dinner which we had in a tent late that night may be left to the imagination, and I need hardly say that the buck and other luxuries were completely spoilt. However, after an extra "tot" to keep us warm, we turned in and slept till daylight. After breakfast at eight, I found that as the regiment would not be ready to move for more than ten days, I could easily run down to Pieter Maritzburg for my Christmas dinner, and yet get back in time to advance with the Column on the 10th; so I arranged to leave that morning, and had as many commissions given me to execute as would have required twenty men to fulfil. My previous companion again accompanied me to the Tugela, when he left to return to Estcourt, and I got on that night to "Burrup's" where I met a lot of men, two of whom I found out were special service men, and the others were subalterns for the Frontier Light Horse, the Adjutant of which —Captain Hutton, who served with distinction in the Cape and New Zealand wars—was coming up with a lot of recruits and six mule-waggons of stores, ammunition, &c., to join the headquarters near Utrecht, and had left Pieter Maritzburg on the previous Thursday. I left "Burrup's" early next morning, and half-way down the hill to Grey Town, met the rest of the F.L.H. party coming up, having been detained by the bad weather on the preceding evening.

When I reached Grey Town, I heard with regret that, owing to a message which had come in from the Border, to the effect that Cetywayo was calling in his men for the different regiments. Colonel Degacher had decided on sending four companies of the 2-24th to Helpmakaar at once, instead of waiting over

Christmas Day, permission for which had been granted by the General. The order was not unexpected, and therefore not badly received, and, thanks to the energy of Lieutenant Michel, 57th Regiment, Director of Transport for the Grey Town District, who succeeded poor Griffiths when he joined his regiment, the waggons were got ready in good time with serviceable oxen, and, headed by their band, the four companies, under Major Dunbar, marched out of town at 11.30. A Rocket Battery on led mules, under Captain Russell, R.A., came into camp during the morning, and encamped close by the Artillery. They were destined for Krantz Kop, to form part of Colonel Durnford's Column, and, I said at the time, would rather astonish the Zulus when in action. I cannot, however, proceed farther without bearing my testimony to the first-class way in which all the commissariat arrangements had been made, calculated, and carried out for that district; and notwithstanding the heavy call made upon the department and its head (Commissary Warneford), and the difficulties of transport, everything was completed up to time, and there were absolutely no arrears anywhere.

On my road down, I passed at "Purcell's" a troop of the Mounted Native Contingent; they were fifty strong, under Lieutenant Davies, who had been under Colonel Warren in Griqualand, and all of them Makolwa Kaffirs from Edendale. The men all found their own horses and saddles, the rest of their kit being found by Government. They were armed with Martini-Henrys and did good service. They carried their own tents and everything with them, and were not only fine-looking men, but, what is of more importance, well mounted. Five of these troops were to be formed, and join Durnford's Column. Farther on, at "Cremer's," I fell in with the officers and non-coms, of the two first battalions of the 1st Regiment N.N.C., under Commandants Montgomery and Bengough. Owing to their waggons having stuck repeatedly, they had been delayed much on the road, and did not expect to reach Grey Town for three days. The natives for those two battalions were to be at Grey Town that week. Another troop of the mounted N.N.C. was also with them, under Captain Barton, but did not look as smart as Lieutenant Davies's troop. I arrived back in Pieter Maritzburg without farther events, and after making my arrangements for a lengthened absence, left again for the front the ensuing week. From what I heard, the Lower Column, under Colonel Pearson and Major Graves, were to cross the border on the 4th, and those from Krantz Kop and Helpmakaar on the 10th.

CHAPTER IV

I LEFT PIETER Maritzburg again on New Year's Day, 1879, in a pouring rain, which did not improve as I got farther on. My road was the same as before, but on this occasion I fell in with companions earlier on, at a place called "Cremer's," a well-known hotel about twelve miles from town, and prettily situated near what are called the Lower Falls of the River Umgeni. My two fellow-travellers had reached this place just before me, and had already baited their horses and drunk their "tots." My horse being a good one, I did not care to stay and off-saddle so soon, and therefore was ready to proceed at once. One of them, Mr. L, X. Byrne, I had known previously in Pieter Maritzburg, where he held some Government appointment; he had now, however, given that up and joined the Commissariat Department, so as to get a chance of proceeding to the front. The other, Mr. Dalton, was also in the Commissariat Department, and had come up from the Cape Colony, where he had done good service. The names of both these men afterwards became famous, in connection with the gallant defence of the post at Rorke's Drift, to which both contributed materially, and where poor Byrne lost his life, being shot through the head while giving a drink of water to a wounded soldier.

The rain increasing, and a thick fog again coming on, we could only manage to reach "Purcell's" at Seven Oaks, and were very glad to be under shelter. In the afternoon an ambulance arrived, on its way down to Pieter Maritzburg, containing Brevet-Major Much, 1-24th (whom I had known before at Cape Town), and Civil Surgeon Hartley, both invalided home, and rather "down in the mouth" in consequence.

When we reached Grey Town, which we did next day after

The British army on the march in Zululand, engraving c.1879

breakfast, I found the whole place in a great state of excitement in consequence of a mounted messenger having arrived early that morning from the Border with news that Cetywayo had refused all demands, and had 8,000 men on the Border near the Lower Drift, and that other large bodies were assembling opposite each of our other Columns. Lord Chelmsford, accompanied by Lieutenant-Colonel Crealock, Major Gossett, Captain Buller, and Lieutenant Milne, R.N., had arrived the day previous from the Lower Tugela, en route for Helpmakaar, with their camp equipage and baggage. The troops here were also ordered to move up at once, and the Mounted Infantry, under Major Barrow, left Pots Spruit for the Lower Tugela that day. The three battalions of the 1st Regiment N.N.C. were still to remain for organisation at Krantz Kop, which place was the head-quarters of Colonel Durnford. I at once went over to the camp of the 2-24th, and remained there, accompanying them thence on their march to the front. The General and Staff left that morning in front of our four companies, and Major Harness's Battery R.A. followed. We all encamped at "Burrup's" that evening, where His Excellency entertained several officers at dinner. Next morning at daybreak the Headquarters of the Staff left, but the 24th were delayed until the afternoon on account of the oxen, which required a good feed before proceeding through "the Thorns." I forgot to mention that a mounted orderly arrived just after midnight with important despatches from Helpmakaar, and the General was roused in consequence. The intelligence was connected with the presence of several thousand Zulus near Rorke's Drift. When we marched on again the artillery remained behind for another day, waiting for some waggons which had been delayed. Mooi River was reached that afternoon, and after much hard work the waggons were all got through the Drift; the men being punted over. As it was a fine night, and Major Black, commanding Left Wing 2-24th, wanted to get on quickly, we bivouacked in the open. At daybreak next morning we proceeded, and reached the Tugela in five hours. We again bivouacked, but on this occasion we were not so lucky, as a heavy thunderstorm came on in the evening, and wetted us all thoroughly. The men were walking about all night trying to keep themselves warm, and then at daybreak we resumed our trek. Our next halt was at a spruit about nine miles on, where breakfast was served out. At this place I left the 2-24th, as I wished to push on so as to reach Rorke's Drift in time to cross over with the 3rd Regiment N.N.C., which I learnt had been sent on in front; and I was accompanied for the rest of my journey by Mr. Cooke, of Estcourt, who was proceeding with the final batch of Kafirs for Commandant Lonsdale's Regiment. It is really astonishing how these Kafirs can march. Very few horses can walk with them, and it is capital fun marching with a lot, as they are not only amusing in their manners and speech, but are also constantly enlivening the march by war songs, extempore and otherwise.

We got to Sand Spruit, where the 3rd Regiment N.N.C. had been encamped for some weeks, in a very short time, and made a halt for feeding purposes. While here, I noticed a lot of over 800 Kafirs being marched off towards the Border, and, on enquiry, found that these men were part of the reserves being called out, to act as a Border Guard, and were going on to the Buffalo to be distributed along its banks as sentries. I found that this system extended from Helpmakaar right down to the Tugela, so that those who were in fear of a Zulu invasion had no need to be afraid of not receiving timely notice. These reserves are placed in parties of 800, under an officer who speaks the language, and comes from the same district. The scheme is one that recommends itself, and adds another to the many proofs (if needed) of the careful and skilful manner in which this expedition was carried out by His Excellency the General and those under him. We were constantly on the alert on this part of our journey between Sand Spruit and the camp, as a dense fog prevailed all the way, and our Kafirs were rather apprehensive of meeting any large body of Zulus who might perhaps have crossed over the Border and be prowling about. When we arrived at Helpmakaar we were given quarters and rations, and then had to do the best we could for ourselves. The cold during the night was intense, and we all suffered from the want of sufficient blankets. Great changes had been made here. All the Volunteers had left, and were stationed between this and Rorke's Drift; but their place in camp was occupied by one squadron of the Mounted Infantry, who had been brought up from Pots Spruit. Two companies of the 1-24th had left the previous week for Rorke's Drift, and four companies of the 2-24th, being the right wing, left on the morning of my arrival.

 The scene at Helpmakaar presented a very different appearance on my arrival to what it did when I last visited it. The camp was very much larger in extent, and also slightly changed in aspect. The Head-quarters-staff camp was pitched to the right of all the others, almost in the centre. The Union Jack was flying in front of the tent of the General, and his mule-waggons were placed in position behind; otherwise there was nothing to show the difference between it and the other camps.

Next morning, Monday, January 6th, I proceeded at once to the Drift. About four miles on the road, just after beginning to descend from the Biggarsberg Range, upon which Helpmakaar is situated, there is a little Dutch farmhouse called "Vermaaks," from the name of the owner, rather prettily situated on a ledge, and close by I found the Natal Carbineers encamped. They had been sent there some days previously as a kind of advanced guard, and also because, from the prominent position, although unseen themselves, they could overlook a large portion of the Zulu country opposite. I stayed to lunch with the officers, Captain T. Shepstone and Lieutenants Royston and Durrant Scott, who, poor fellow, died a gallant death at Isandwhlana, with many of those other brave colonial lads who followed him from Pieter Maritzburg in the same corps. We lunched right royally, as, being yet in Natal, privations and "short commons" had not yet commenced. Beacon-fires had been seen every night across the Border, and it had been noticed that whenever more troops came down the road towards the Drift a signal was also made from a kraal on our side about two miles off up the valley. So Captain Shepstone had caused it to be surrounded a few evenings before my arrival, and captured the male inhabitants, sending them back to Helpmakaar as spies. They were the first prisoners taken in the war, and turned out to be some of Sirayo's people. Our feast being disposed of, I started, and after a tedious ride down a very winding road reached the valley below. Thence I made haste along the flat to Rorke's Drift, where I found the 3rd Regiment of N.N.C. encamped, with a company of Native Pioneers who had been preparing everything for the punt. The right wing of the 2-24th arrived there also that afternoon, and encamped close by. The house of the Missionary, De

Witt—who and which subsequently acquired notoriety on the worthy man's visit to England—was about half a mile farther away from the river, at the foot of a high mountain, and was being converted into a commissariat store; another smaller one adjoining it was made into a hospital. Next day, Tuesday, January 7th, we got pretty well settled down and comfortable. I took up my quarters with Commandant Lonsdale, and had a tent next to his. Our mess-house was sunk about two feet in the ground, and the sides were built up with sod walls four feet high, with a tarpaulin stretched over some poles as a roof, and some empty boxes, with the bottoms knocked out, let into the walls for light and ventilation. This did very well in fine weather, but on the next evening, while it was raining heavily, the roof not having slope enough, a quantity of water accumulated on it, the weight of which broke the not over-strong supports, and down came the whole lot upon us, tarpaulin, poles, and water, greatly to the detriment of our dinners and our tempers. Added to this, our cooking operations were of necessity carried on in the open air, and were likewise liable to be affected by the weather. It may, therefore, easily be imagined that we got very little dinner that evening. Later on we succeeded in setting matters somewhat straight. Several mounted men were seen, during the day, watching our position and movements from the hills opposite, but they took good care to keep out of rifle range. Drill went on regularly at every available moment, and I noticed with pleasure much improvement, in the execution of the few movements necessary, since I had last parted with the regiment at Sand Spruit. The Pioneers, assisted by some Royal Engineers, commenced building the punt, which had been brought up in pieces ready to be put together. A kind of pontoon on barrels was also made, and the preparations were progressing well for our expected crossing on the 11th.

During the afternoon of Wednesday the camp was startled

by a sentry sending in the news that several mounted men were coining down to the river from the Zulu side, and, at that distance, it was impossible to distinguish who or what they were. All turned out and hurried down to the Drift, where the punt was working, and it was then discovered that the visitors were not Zulus at all; but that the party consisted of Captain Barton and Lieutenant Baron von Steitencron, of the Frontier Light Horse, with an escort of one corporal and three men, who had made a most adventurous ride from Colonel Wood's Column, which we learnt had crossed the Blood River on the previous Monday morning, and were encamped a few miles in Zululand. Captain Barton had been out exploring roads, &c., and meeting with no opposition had penetrated right through to our camp, a distance of over thirty miles. The Kafirs all along the road had been friendly, and gave them information and milk. The only place where they heard they were likely to be annoyed was at a kraal of some mission Kafirs, so they kept away. As it was very late when they arrived at our camp, it was considered dangerous for them to return, so they waited with us till morning, and then left on their journey back. We heard afterwards that they reached Colonel Wood's Column safely. The day following, the whole of the Head-quarters Column was moved down from Helpmakaar, including a large commissariat convoy, and it was then seen that the state of affairs was serious, and fighting was meant. This rejoiced the hearts of nearly all, for many had grumbled because we did not advance ten days before, when the twenty days expired which had been given for the surrender of Sirayo's sons and a fine of cattle, Cetywayo not having deigned to take the slightest notice of these demands. Next day, which was Friday, the last of the thirty allowed in the ultimately it became known with certainty that we were to cross the Border in the morning, and our spies brought in news that no large body of the enemy was near, as they had all taken their departure to assemble in their different regiments at Ulundi before the King. About noon the General and Staff arrived, and an inspection was held of the 3rd Regiment of the Natal Native Contingent. The General seemed much pleased with the two battalions, and addressed the Kafirs, giving them good advice—saying that no prisoners, women, or children were to be injured in any way. After dismissal, every one was busy getting ready for the morrow's work, and as reveille was to be sounded at 2 a.m. few of us slept that night, the time being short, and the excitement of the impending issue arousing natural feelings, not devoid of uncertainty and anxiety even in those most "eager for the fray."

CHAPTER V

FROM SATURDAY, January the 11th, dates the real commencement of the war, and although no bloodshed occurred, the fact of our intention to "fight it out" was fully brought home to the minds of the neighbouring Zulus by a large capture of arms and cattle, both of which are almost as dear to them as life. Our successful crossing was unopposed, notwithstanding all their previous boasting about the resistance they would offer. Preparations for crossing the river had been completed the night before, and the state of the river was such as to make it possible for the Native Contingent, mounted men, artillery, and waggons to cross easily at the ford. The weather remained fine until after reveille sounded at 2 a.m., but between that time and half-past four, when all were in readiness to cross, a thick fog came on, accompanied by drizzling rain, which made operations rather more uncertain and difficult. However, all passed off without a hitch. In our part of the camp tents were struck and the different regiments in their places ready to cross at 4.30. The first battalion of the 3rd Regiment N.N.C. was ordered to cross at the Drift itself, which was broad, deep, and with a heavy current, but there was a small island in the centre which helped to facilitate the transit. The entire Cavalry Brigade, under Lieutenant-Colonel Russell, deposited their arms, &c., on the pontoon, and then rode back to follow the 1-3rd N.N.C. at the Drift. The 1-24th Regiment, under Captain Degacher, crossed at one of the ponts, and the 2-24th, under Colonel Degacher, C.B., at the other; while the 2-3rd Regiment N.N.C. crossed at a drift higher up the river. The Artillery, six guns, under Lieutenant-Colonel Harness, were in position on a slight rise at the camp, to protect the movement, but did not follow until the next day. Having previously arranged to accompany the 3rd Regiment N.N.C. throughout the campaign, I went down to the Drift with them; and, with Captain Krohn, led the way over, arriving first on the other side, so that, I may say, as far as our Column was concerned, I was actually the first man in Zululand after war was declared, and the troops moved over. The crossing at this drift was executed under the eye of the General, and was most successfully carried out; as, although several minor accidents occurred, neither horse nor man came to much grief. The river came up to the men's necks in places, and ran at the rate of over six knots an hour; this will show how difficult it must have been with a very stony bottom. One mishap took place, which might have ended fatally: a man of the Mounted Infantry was swept from his horse, and would have been carried away by the stream had it not been for the gallant conduct of Captain Haves, 1-3rd N.N.C, who jumped into the river and succeeded, at the risk of his own life, in getting the man across all right. This act was witnessed by all, and drew a highly flattering mention from the General, which afterwards appeared among the Column Orders. The two line regiments crossed all right at the two pontoons, and with the 3rd N.N.C. took up a position on the opposite side, ascending the hill in skirmishing order. The line, when opened out in skirmishing order, was quite three miles long, and was formed as follows: — Beginning from our right, the 1-3rd N.N.C. commenced from the bend of the river, having four companies skirmishing, and the rest in reserve on the extreme right flank, then some companies of the 1-24th, also with a reserve. The 2-24th followed in similar order, and the line was ended with the 2-3rd N.N.C, five of whose companies were extended, the others forming a reserve placed on the extreme left flank. The whole force was advanced a few hundred yards, and then halted until the fog lifted. After a short time the Cavalry Division came through our ranks with his Excellency Lieutenant-General Lord Chelmsford and Staff in the centre, and proceeded at a smart trot some way inland to meet Colonel Wood, as arranged.

After the party had passed some distance onward the mist lifted, and the advanced guard were able to capture an armed Zulu and a small herd of cattle. A good deal of excitement was prevalent during the reconnoissance, for it was not positively known whether the Zulus under Sirayo's sons would be met with or not, as they had declared they would fight us. However, nothing was seen of them, except a few scattered Zulus, and the troops rode steadily on until they were met at 9.15 a.m. by Lieutenant-Colonel Buller, commanding the Frontier Light Horse, who had ridden out to conduct them to the camp of Colonel Wood's force, which had crossed over the Blood River, and was stationed in Zululand about thirty-two miles away from our Column. Herds of cattle, sheep, and goats, all captured from the enemy, were seen in every direction about Colonel Wood's camp, and proved that his Irregulars were splendid foragers. After staying there about two hours, Lord Chelmsford returned, and instead of coming back direct they went away to some kraals on their right, where Zulu herds of cattle were seen. These were captured by the Natal Mounted Police and the Natal Carbineers without any resistance being offered, and the inhabitants of the kraals had their guns, ammunition, and assegais taken from them. Nothing else was taken or injured. Camp was reached in the afternoon, and great were the rejoicings at the news of our having successfully opened communication with Wood's Column, and at the capture of over three hundred head of cattle, several horses, and a number of sheep and goats.

In the meantime, while this was being done by the cavalry, the greater portion of our waggons, oxen, ambulances, &c., were being got across on the pontoon, and this work tried to the utmost the powers of all concerned, but resulted most successfully and creditably to those in command. At any rate, by evening enough were got over to enable us all to encamp. Piquets were sent out, sentries posted, strong cattle-guards appointed, and other arrangements made for the safety of the camp, but nothing was attempted in the shape of a "laager" or shelter trenches in front of our position. How indispensable these were was not found out until the lesson had been taught by bitter and costly experience. We had a thunderstorm that nighty and retired to rest with the pleasant consciousness that at five the next day (Sunday) a reconnoissance in strength was to be made by the whole column to Sirayo's mountain-stronghold. The tired men grumbled, but were pleased at the prospect of meeting the enemy.

At 3.30 a.m. reveille sounded, and the different regiments were paraded as follows: the 1st Battalion, 3rd Regiment N.N.C., 860 strong, under Major Black (Commandant Lonsdale being still ill), and Commandant Browne; four companies of the 1-24th, under Captain Degacher, 100 Mounted Infantry under Captain Brown, 100 Natal Mounted Police, under Inspector Mansell, 60 Natal Carbineers, under Captain Shepstone, and 86 Newcastle Mounted Rifles and Buffalo Border Guard, under Captain Bradstreet. The whole Column was under the personal command of Colonel Glynn, C.B., and Lieutenant-Colonel Russell had charge of the Cavalry Division. There was also a reserve force formed of the 2-3rd N.N.C, under Commandant Cooper, and the 2-24th, under Colonel Degacher, C.B., which started three hours after we did, and passed the scene after the action was over. They were, however, of great service in thoroughly clearing the valley, burning Sirayo's great kraal, and capturing about 200 head of cattle which were escaping from our men. We started punctually at five, and rode about nine miles, with the Carbineers thrown out in skirmishing order, and vedettes of the Mounted Infantry on each flank. When we arrived on the other side of the hill, where it begins to descend into the valley in which Sirayo*s kraals were, we heard a war song being sung, as it seemed, by a large body of men, and we could also distinguish moving forms on the top of the Ngnutu Hill opposite, as well as among the rocks up a steep and stony krantz. The lowing of cattle was also noticed, and proved to us distinctly that those men— having doubtless heard of our having captured cattie the day previous—had driven their cattie up among the rocks, and established themselves up there in caves, &c., &c., determined upon resistance. This knowledge served to redouble both our vigilance and eagerness to get at them. At the bottom of the Valley a small spruit divides it, and we were halted on the side while the General and Colonel Glynn made their observations and consequent plan of attack. Some little time elapsed before this was done, and then the cavalry were first sent over to go round the hill on the right, and try to outflank any that might escape, and also to get up to the top for the same purpose. The main attack made upon the centre of the krantz itself was conducted by the men of the l-3rd N.N.C., led by Commandant Browne, under the command of Major Black, 2-24th, and four companies of the 1-24th, under Captain Degacher.

This force was immediately extended in line, with orders to advance straight up to that part of the ravine where the Zulus were hidden. This was done steadily, although great difficulty was found in keeping the line unbroken, owing to the rough nature of the ground, and several very awkward gullies intervening. As we approached to within about 600 yards, a voice was heard asking "By whose order the white Impi had come there, and whether they were enemies?" To this no answer was given, and we again advanced. Major Black in the meantime sent down for orders as to when to open fire, and permission was given to fire only after they first fired at us. Shortly after, at about 7.30, the first shot was fired from behind a large rock, and injured a Kafir belonging to the Native Contingent. After that a constant fusilade was kept up until the cattle were taken with a rush, made by No. 8 Company under Captains Duncombe and Murray, led by Commandant Browne. The Zulus then became desperate, and retreated to their caves, pouring in a heavy fire from behind rocks. This had the effect of breaking our line, and many of our natives turned and ran. However, owing to the exertions of the officers leading the first four companies, and notwithstanding the fact that some of the enemy began to throw down heavy rocks on the advancing men, they succeeded, after a severe hand-to-hand fight, in shooting nearly twenty men, taking four others prisoners as well as many women and children.

In this last hand-to-hand fighting Captains Haves and Hicks greatly distinguished themselves, and Lieutenant Harford of the 99th Regiment, attached as Staff Officer, performed a most plucky action in advancing to the mouth of a cave out of which many men had been shot, and succeeding in inducing four men to come out, deliver up their arms, and give themselves up as prisoners. His revolver had been emptied at the time, and he might easily have been shot by any of them, as they came out one by one. The loss on our side was two natives killed, and eighteen wounded, including Lieutenant Purvis (shot through the arm) and Corporal Mayer (with a bad assegai wound in the leg). All the other casualties were of minor importance, and occurred exclusively among the Native Contingent.

In the meantime, two companies under Captains Harber and Hulley on the extreme left had, with the four companies of the 1-24th under Captain Degacher, advanced along to the left, and succeeded in getting round over the point of the ravine on to the other side, so as to prevent any escape, and gradually mounted higher, until they reached the top. This was done well, and several fugitives were shot and horses taken. In many places an exchange of fire was made, with no loss on our side, but about six of the enemy were killed. The top was reached through a tremendous defile, and just on the other side they captured three horses. When on the top several fugitives, on foot and mounted, were seen, away in the distance, making round the base of another hill, rising from the top of that they were on. But the Zulus were too far off for anything to be done. The sight obtained was magnificent. Looking north, down a precipitous cliff, a splendid valley extended for miles, rich in verdure, covered with deserted kraals, and bounded on each side by high mountains; while to the south the Buffalo and the Natal mountains were seen in the distance, with our camp at Rorke's Drift looking like a tin miniature soldier's camp. To the eastward, the Isipezi Hill rose in the air with its curious-shaped head, and close by it was our road to Ulundi. Altogether, it was a sight worth seeing. The Cavalry Division, in getting round the right flank, up the valley, were followed along the heights by several of the enemy, in number about thirty, under a younger son of Sirayo. These Zulus constantly taunted the cavalry, and at last fired on them. Colonel Russell then ordered Captain Shepstone to send forward eight of his men to draw their fire, and although within point-blank range, they never flinched or wasted a shot, and fortunately not one was hit. A general advance was then made, the men being dismounted, Major Dartnell accompanying them in a gallant way. They succeeded in killing three, wounded others, and the rest fled, among whom were some on horseback. The Mounted Infantry and N.M. Police had also ascended, the one on the left and the other on the right, and by a combined flank movement were able to cut off the retreat of the others, who had fled, and obliged them to cross over an exposed plateau, where six were killed outright, including the son of Sirayo. The whole Division then went up to the top, and halted for a short meal. They afterwards went on farther to the hill beyond, accompanied by some of the native levies, and examined a large kraal on the top. The troops then came back by the same way, and through heavy thunder storms returned to camp. Several guns were taken, many assegais, and much sour milk and other Kafir produce. None of the guns were modem, but consisted of old Tower muskets and carbines. A large quantity of ammunition was found, including several hundred rounds of Westley-Richards ammunition, and a new waggon of Sirayo's. The cartridges were brought away, but it was impossible to get the waggon down at that time.

Just as this engagement was finished the second force, consisting of the 2-24th and the 2-3rd Natal Native Contingent, under Colonel Degacher, C.B., which had started some hours after us, came up and were taken on farther up the valley to Sirayo's principal kraal, called Loxie, the General accompanying them. The place was deserted, though it had been prepared for a defence. The walls of the cattle kraal, which were strongly built up of stone, had been loopholed, and a large cave at the back had a stone fortification round the mouth, so that the position would have been a strong one if well defended. The surrounding huts were at once burnt and everything destroyed that was possible. Some old women were found in a cave and they told as that the men had intended fighting, but when they saw our force the day before they had taken their cattle and women, and left for inland. The fruits of the day's proceedings, as far as loot was concerned, consisted of over thirty horses and ponies, about 400 head of cattle, and several goats and sheep. Altogether the result of the action gave great confidence to our native allies, camp followers, &c. I learnt from a wounded prisoner that Sirayo himself, his eldest son, and his brother and his sons were all some distance off with a small Zulu Impi. Sirayo's eldest wife and daughter were taken prisoners, with many other women and children, but were all sent back to their kraals by order of the General.

His policy in so doing was not approved by the officers who best understood the native character, and who could not see the wisdom of allowing men and women to come into camp either as prisoners or to surrender themselves, and then to be fed well, treated kindly, and allowed to go when and where they liked. Considering the experience we had in the last Cape war, surely this should not have been permitted.

CHAPTER VI

WE RESTED a day for cleaning up arms and accoutrements after the rain; and on Tuesday morning, at five a.m., a detachment, consisting of the left half battalion of the 2-24th under Major Dunbar, a Pioneer company under Captain Whitfield, and the l-3rd N.N.C. under Commandant Browne, moved off and marched across the Bashee close by the scene of operations on the previous Sunday. A rough encampment was made, and then we settled down to work, making, or rather repairing, roads.

On Sunday the 19th rumours had reached us that a night attack was to be made on us by a large Zulu Impi under Sirayo, and consequently, for the first time, some small entrenchments were formed just outside the exposed portions of our camp. We remained at the Bashee Talley until Monday, the 20th January, when, as all the roads were completed, we moved on to our next camp, at Isandwhlana, being joined, or rather overtaken, by the rest of the third Column from Rorke's Drift, leaving only one company of the 2-24th, under Lieutenant Bromhead, some Engineers, and a few natives to guard the drift, look after the pontoons, and garrison the commissariat store and hospital. The post was left under the command of Major Spalding, D.A.Q.M.G.

The entire force then proceeded together to the now ever-memorable and unfortunate camping ground at Isandwhlana (or the Little Hand Mountain), which we reached that same evening. The new camp was distant about eight miles from the Bashee Valley, almost due east, and on the left-hand side of the road we were pursuing to reach Ulundi from the Drift. After first leaving the Bashee Valley, we had to make a slight ascent

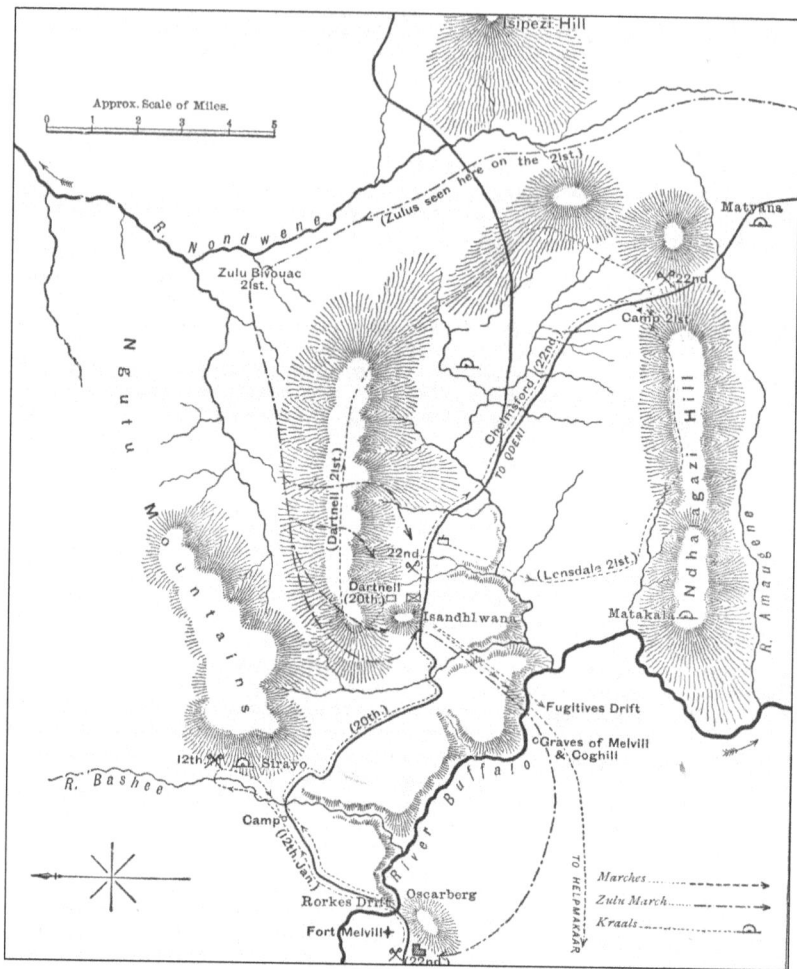

Plan of the Marches near Isandhlwana Between January 12th and 22nd, 1879

over a neck of land connecting the Ngnutu and another smaller hill, and then the road continued over a few miles of plain grass ground, intersected here and there by small streams and waterwashes, running north and south, until we came to another neck of land, from which point the hills again recede, those on the right breaking into steep ravines and rocky krantzes, running parallel with the Buffalo for miles, and those on the left making a semicircle from the Ngnutu to the mountains on the other side of which we encamped. The road up to this point was in fair condition, and needed little doing to it to enable the waggons to pass. After we had descended from the second neck of land into the valley below, it was quite a different matter, and large working parties of the 3rd Regiment N.N.O., and also of the 24th Regiment, had to be sent forward to prepare the way. This they did speedily and well, and at a difficult crossing of a small but rocky stream which runs down the Talley half-way between the plain above and the Isandwhlana Mountain, a smart piece of road-making and repairing was successfully completed, and that without detaining the column more than an hour. Immense boulders had to be moved, chasms filled up with rocks, the approaches on each side cut away and levelled so as to render easy what must have always hitherto been a most dreadful bit of road for waggons to cross through; and the manner and rapidity in which this was done reflected the highest credit on Major Black, of the 2-24th, who was directing operations, and also on those officers of the 3rd N.N.C. who superintended the different portions of the work. During the passage of the waggons through the drift the assistance rendered by Captain Krohn and Lieutenants Vane and Campbell, who did the whole of the driving themselves, enabled the convoy to pass through without any accident, although there was a nasty turn just in the centre, with one boulder sticking out, which could not be easily removed. The drivers and leaders were in a most helpless state of confusion, and had they been left to themselves would not only have entirely blocked up the road for hours, but also most probably have smashed up several waggons and their contents completely.

From this drift the road wound up a hill slightly covered with bush on our left, and thickly studded with rocks on the right, until the summit was reached, and we looked down on another large grass-covered plain with hills on the left and on the right; and the Malakata and Inshlazagaze Hills, some ten miles in front of us. At the spot where our road crossed this position we had a small kopje on the right, and then about fifty yards to our left rose abruptly the Isandwhlana Mountain, to the height of several htmdred feet above the level of the hill we were on. It was entirely unapproachable from the three sides nearest to us, but on the farther side, that to the north, it sloped more gradually down, and then connected with the large range of hills on our left, by another broad neck of land. We just crossed over the bend, then turned sharp to the left, and placed our camp facing the valley, with the eastern precipitous side of the mountain behind us, leaving about a mile of open country between our left flank and the hills on our left. The right of the camp extended across the neck of land we had just come over, and rested on the base of the small kopje abovementioned. That was the exact position of our third camping ground in Zululand—a spot which will not only be remembered with the saddest emotion by all South African colonists, as being the death-scene of so many of her noble sons, but will also be noted in the future history of the British nation as a place where a massacre of British officers and men took place, such as has never previously occurred so suddenly, completely, or with such a heavy loss of camp equipment, arms, guns, ammunition, waggons, oxen, horses, and colours.

The camp was pitched during the afternoon in the following order:—Beginning with the extreme left, we had the 2-3rd Regiment N.N.C., 1-3rd N.N.C., R.A., 2-24th, Volunteers, and Mounted Infantry, the Natal Mounted Police, and the 1-24th on the right. The waggons were all placed between the camp and the hill at the back; and behind them, immediately against its base, the Head-quarters tents were pitched, with their waggons beside them; the hospital being dose by on the neck. I may here mention that at our previous camping ground in the Bashee Valley, although reports came in to us that a large force of Zulus was approaching, yet, as our mounted patrols did not corroborate this statement, no defences or entrenchments of any kind were put up around it until the evening previous to our departure, when for some cause or another a small stone wall was built along two sides of the camp, one feuding the road we were going, and the other fronting the country between us and the Buffalo. This was all that was done at that camp; and, notwithstanding the clear and distinct orders given and published in an official book called "Regulations for the Field Forces in South Africa," not a single step was taken in any way to defend our new position in case of a night or day attack from the enemy, either by forming the waggons into a laager or by erecting a shelter trench round it. And it is to this error of judgment that I cannot help attributing the awful result which awaited the return of the reconnoitring party, and which not only thoroughly crippled our offensive power for some months, but even placed the colony itself in great danger of Border incursions.

In the first place, it seems now pretty generally known that the Column itself was hardly strong enough to advance through the country, protect its camp, &c., keep open its rear, and at the same time send out strong parties to reconnoitre and also to attack the different surrounding Zulu haunts; and as the General had repeatedly asked for more reinforcements, I must come to the conclusion that while so far away from Colonel Wood's or Colonel Pearson's Column, we were proceeding with too much confidence and with greater celerity than was consistent with safety. I had throughout always asserted that it would take longer time than people expected to get to the King's kraal, much less conquer the country; and also that the mere fact of finding all the younger Zulus retreating in front of us, and proceeding to join Cetywayo, boded a heavy attack upon one Column, and should have put us on our guard against the specious reports given by some of the old chiefs who submitted to our advance. However, it is no use crying over spilt milk, sentries, and of all the other arrangements, such as they were, which had been made for the general safety of the camp. This was also the last time I saw him alive. Many of these little incidents, however trivial at the time, recur to one's memory with awful force and vividness after the occurrence of such a dreadful disaster as that which unfortunately befell nearly all those we left behind us in camp next day.

Everything having been arranged overnight, punctually at 4.30 a.m. we started with eight companies of the 1-3rd N.N.C., under Commandant Browne, and eight companies of the 2-3rd, under Commandant Cooper; the whole being commanded by Corps-Commandant Lonsdale. As will be noticed, two companies from each battalion were left in camp for regimental and other duties.

How well I remember that morning, and the dejected aspect of those officers belonging to the four companies N.N.C. detained by duty at the camp! Young Buée, the assistant-surgeon, started with us, but his pony went so lame that he was obliged to go back; unhappily, as it turned out afterwards, for he, too, was fated never to leave the camp again alive.

The cavalry force which followed us was commanded by Major Dartnell, Captain Shepstone, and Mr. Mansell, and was instructed to go round to the left of the Upindo and Isilulwane Hills, and then on the top, so as to cut off any people and cattle that might try to escape from the Native Contingent, which had to beat round the slopes to the right. After a march of three hours, we reached the banks of the Indawene stream, which flows from a kind of precipice and waterfall in the middle of hills and vallies, both sides of which are magnificently covered with foliage, dotted with Zulu kraals and mealie fields. Upon arriving at the stream, the 1-3rd advanced on its left bank, up towards its source, in open skirmishing order, and, although no Zulus were seen, several head of cattle were taken at the second kraal we came to, and traces were found of recent occupation. The 2-3rd kept on the other bank in the same direction, and when both battalions were a few hundred yards off the waterfall, the first was ordered to right-turn, cross the stream, and ascend the steep height on the opposite side, and then proceed on the top of the mountains, right round the edges, keeping parallel with the 2-3rd, which was then wheeled back, and sent in skirmishing order round the base and sides to the right, through the great Thorn Valley of the Malakata, which is the western portion of the Indhlazakazi range. In going round we had some Tory difficult ground to get over, which seemed to try the powers of our non-coms.—who were not mounted—very considerably. In fact, it is not to be disputed for one moment that white men cannot keep up with a Kafir in a day's march over stony and hilly country, and, therefore, every white officer and non-com. should have been mounted. About noon a halt was made, and an al fresco sort of lunch partaken of. In the meantime the l-3rd N.N.C. had proceeded quicker along the top, it being good ground, and were now seen approaching us from the east, coming down an easy slope on the hills some distance off with a lot of cattle, which they had captured in some hollow on the top. Shortly afterwards two more companies of the same battalion also turned up with more cattle, and announced that they had seen many more cattle in the direction of the Buffalo, from which, at the place where we halted, we were only three miles distant. A short rest benefited us much, and after having captured so many cattle we started off again with renewed energy, and still proceeded in an easterly direction, but gradually working our way round and up the mountain side. At about 4 p.m. we reached the top, and then saw all the cavalry up there, but some distance off. We were again halted, and our Commandant and Harford, his Staff Officer, rode off to Major Dartnell to hear what they had done. A long time seemed to elapse before Harford came back with the important news that the mounted force, accompanied by Major Gossett, A.D.C., had come across a large body of the enemy (considerably over 1,600) on a neck of the Upindo Hill, due east from us, where they held a very strong position in a krantz, taunting our few mounted men, who, of course, without infantry could do nothing. They therefore rode back to the Indhlazakazi, and met the Natal Carbineers, and later on our two battalions. A hasty council of war was held by the various commanding officers, and as it was thought that either the body of Zulus were the advance-guard of a larger force, or proceeding to assist those hidden in the various caves and krantzes around us, it was decided to advance our whole force to the edge of the range (only separated by a small valley from the hill occupied by the Zulus), to send the mounted men to reconnoitre, and ascertain the strength and exact position of the enemy, and then to bivouac that evening close by, so as to prevent any farther hostile advance during the night. The news that we had still to go on a few miles was not well received, but after much grumbling, for the men were tired and hungry, and a long way from camp, we marched across the top to the other (North-Eastern) edge, and could then see on the next range, three miles off, a large body of Zulus, about 2,000 strong, who were massing, and seemed inclined to come down to attack the cavalry which had descended across the valley to reconnoitre, and were halted about a mile from them. We waited very patiently, and then saw a small body of Volunteers detached and gallop up to within about 800 yards of the Zulus, when instantly, and with beautiful precision, two companies of the enemy opened out into skirmishing order, the flanks at a double, and tried to surround the party, although they did not fire a single shot. Our men, acting up to their instructions, had seen enough, wheeled round, and joined their main body again. The

'The Battle of Isandhlwana' from the Illustrated London News and The Graphic

Zulus did not follow far. As it was now late, nearly six o'clock, Major Dartnell deemed it advisable not to attack, and came back to us with orders to bivouac that night where we were, and attack them the first thing in the morning. Just previously to this the Major had sent in for some blankets and provisions, to be sent out that night for our use, and had also stated the above facts to the General, asking for reinforcements. Loud, deep, and Sequent was the grumbling among some of the officers of the Natal Native Contingent at having to bivouac out there, tired, and without blankets, food, or forage; and two Lieutenants, Avery and Holcroft, without orders, left to return to the camp at Isandwhlana, and were in consequence among the killed next day. We bivouacked that night in a hollow square, three sides of which were formed of the 3rd N.N.C. two companies deep, and the other by the Mounted Police and Volunteers, the officers sleeping in the rear near their companies, with all the horses ringed in the centre.

About midnight—fires having been seen all night on the

opposite hill, where the Zulus were—a few shots were fired by the outlying piquet, and (for what reason will never be known) one of our corners, No. 1 Company 1-3rd N.N.C, gave way and fled across the centre of the square, trampling over their officers and causing a general stampede of the horses; until, upon being met by the men of the other battalion on the opposite side, who stood firm and freely used their assegais, the torrent was stemmed and the alarm found to be false. I was trying to sleep, in the centre, near the Commandant, at the time, and we were both dozing off, when the first thing I remember was being trod upon by horses, then a hoarse shout arose, and several dusky forms, naked and with brandished weapons, ran over me, at which, waxing wroth, and very naturally imagining the Zulus were come, I "up with" my rifle and clubbed one man down, and then went to try and find my horse, which I did not do for some time. I was coming back with revolver in hand prepared for anything, when I recognised the red strip on some of the men's heads, and then knew they belonged to the Contingent. They were soon, however, reformed, owing to the active exertions of their officers. I had, however, had enough of them that night, and afterwards went and lay down among the Mounted Police and Carbineers, who at the first alarm lay down in line with bayonets fixed and cartridges inserted, after having told off a guard for the horses, in the most quiet and soldierlike manner; the officers all walking about cheering the men and keeping them acquainted with what was passing. After this it was useless trying to sleep, as we felt sure there would be another false alarm, if not a real one; and I therefore did like the rest, not forgetting to saddle my horse, which was found for me, and hold his bridle in one hand ready for any emergency. A trying three hours brought daylight, during which we did have one more false alarm, but it was not taken much notice of this time. I should mention that just after dark Lieutenant Walsh, with twenty Mounted

Infantry, arrived after a tedious and plucky journey from the camp, during which he met with small bodies of the enemy, and brought four pack-horses with some few blankets, tea, sugar, biscuits, and tinned meat. This was distributed among us, as far as it would go, and did a little to make us more comfortable. This officer also brought the news that the General would be with us at daylight, and that reinforcements in strength were to come up in the morning, so as to assist in the attack on the body of Zulus we had seen that evening. He also stated that Captain Browne, of the Mounted Infantry, had been out reconnoitring towards the Isipezi hill on our left front, and had not only seen several large bodies moving in an easterly direction, but when returning had fallen in with eight mounted Zulus and thirty footmen, with whom, as they attempted to cut his party off, he had an engagement, ending in the death of two Zulus and two of their horses, without any casualty on our side. The Zulu firing was stated to be most erratic. Besides this, one or two mounted bodies of Zulus had been seen hovering about, particularly on our left front. So that altogether things looked cheering, and the chance of measuring our strength against the enemy seemed to be rapidly drawing near.

CHAPTER VIII

Dawn broke next day, Wednesday, January the 22nd, with heavy mists on the tops of the Indhlazakazi, Upindo, and Isilulwane Hills. Before daylight our party fell in and stood to their arms, awaiting the promised arrival of the General and reinforcements, who came up shortly afterwards. This force had left the camp at Isandwhlana at 8 a.m. and consisted of a squadron of Mounted Infantry, seven companies of the 2-24th Regiment, and four guns under Colonel Harness, R.A. Lord Chelmsford accompanied the relieving force in person, and was attended by his usual Staff and several other officers not specially on duty in camp that day, who had just come out for a ride. In the meantime orders had been sent back to Rorke's Drift, to Colonel Durnford, R.E., to bring up his 800 mounted men at once, as also his rocket battery. Having been unable to cross at the Middle Drift, his Column was divided and coming slowly up to unite with ours. As daylight progressed we could see that the main body of the enemy had left the hills in front of us, but their scouts were visible here and there; so the following preparations were made for surrounding the position. The Natal Carbineers and Mounted Police under Major Dartnell were started off to get round on the right flank between the position of the enemy and Matyana's stronghold; while the two battalions of the 3rd Regiment N.N.C. were ordered to advance across the valley and sweep right over the hill in front (Isilulwane), which was evidently the key of the position.

In going up, we could notice that the Mounted Infantry under Colonel Russell, four guns under Colonel Harness, and seven companies of the 2-24th under Colonel Degacher, C.B., were steadily proceeding up the valley on our left along the road which led from our camp farther into the country, with the intention of taming the enemy's right. An ambulance and one other loaded waggon accompanied this force. When the two battalions of the Native Contingent reached the top of the hill after a hard pull up, and no success in "finding ebony" a halt was called, and then within a very few minutes sharp firing was heard, away on the Upindo hill to our right; and upon turning that way, we saw—not two miles off—a lot of our mounted men chasing some Zulus over the hill in a direct line for us. So the double was sounded, and away we went to help cut them off. Seeing this, those of the enemy who were not shot left the top of the hill, ran down the sides and took refuge in the caves and rocks abounding. We soon arrived at the spot, and after three hours' work routed all the rest out of their hiding places, shooting many and assegaing others. Lieutenant Harford, 99th Regiment, staff officer to Commandant Lonsdale, again distinguished himself by going in alone under a nasty crevice in some stones, shooting two men and capturing another. This officer did the same thing at the attack on Sirayo's strongholds, and would seem to have a charmed life. "May he long keep it!"—was our wish at the time.

The two battalions were then got together, and prepared to march back to the camp, having killed about eighty men. At this point I left them, and galloped across to where the cavalry had re-united, and there heard the history of the whole of their morning's work. It appears that after leaving us that morning they saw a body of the enemy away still farther on the right, among whom were some mounted men, and Major Dartnell gave orders for the Carbineers and Mounted Police to ride after them. This they did, and began to open fire (greatly to the astonishment of the Zulus, who stood jeering at them) at eight hundred yards—and even at that distance succeeded in killing one or two. Seeing this, the enemy fled up the hill as hard as they could; but, as it turned out, not fast enough to escape the

Battle of Isandhlwana (1879). Painting by Charles Edwin Fripp (1854-1906)

men of the Carbineers, who, putting their horses to full speedy gained upon them and shot many running. Indeed, I was told by an eye-witness that dead shots were made in this manner at over six hundred yards. Three horses were captured, and the stem chase continued until they met the men of the Native Contingent, when they returned, leaving it to their sable allies to finish up the business. Over sixty were then killed, and we only know of one man who escaped. Matyana himself was nearly caught by Captain Shepstone, N.C., who chased him for miles on horseback, and was close to him, when he jumped off his horse and dropped over a steep krantz. The horse was brought into camp. The mounted men under Major Dartnell then had tea and biscuits, and awaited the coming up of the General and Staff for farther orders. As scattered bodies of the enemy, apparently falling back on their main supports, had been seen by the other attacking parties, a general advance was ordered by Lord Chelmsford, who remained with the infantry and guns, which continued advancing up the valley to the left of the Isilulwane hill; while Colonel Russell with the Mounted Infantry went on still farther to turn the right of the Isipezi hill, and then to act as circumstances might require. The idea did not seem to have occurred to any one that the enemy were carrying out a preconcerted plan. At ten o'clock the General and his Staff made a halt at the top of the valley for breakfast; and shortly afterwards Captain Buller, Rifle Brigade, A.D.C., rode up with the information that the mounted men were engaged on the extreme right; at the same time the news first arrived that large bodies of the enemy were seen on the left of our camp. The General then ordered the 1-3rd N.N.C., under Commandant Browne, to retire on the camp, and scatter any small bodies of the enemy that might be found hovering about between us and the camp. At 11 a.m., Lord Chelmsford then rode away towards the right, sending two companies of the 2-24th over the hill; and the rest went back by the road they had come, until they arrived at the place where it branched off to the site of our proposed new camping ground, to which they at once proceeded, as escort to the guns. Those officers who had accompanied the General for a ride only here left him, and unfortunately for themselves returned to camp. An escort of ten mounted infantry went with these officers, among whom were Captain Allan Gardner, 14th Hussars, Lieutenant McDougall, R.E., and Lieutenants Dyer, 1-24th, and Griffiths, 2-24th. After passing over the Isilulwane hill, the General proceeded along the Upindo until he came up with the Mounted Police, Natal Carbineers and Native Battalion, who had been engaged with Matyana and his followers.

The General only remained for a short time, to receive from Major Dartnell his report on the morning's work, and then left us, with instructions to return two miles farther back, to the head of the Amange gorge, and there remain; his intention being that the camp at Isandwhlana should be struck that afternoon (Wednesday), and the entire force moved forward to the spot selected as our halting-ground. This intention, it is almost needless to add, was unhappily never carried into effect. But our orders were at once acted upon, and on our arrival we found the Staff already there, looking through their field-glasses at some large bodies of Zulus, who were about ten miles away, massed in proximity to the camp. This was at about half an hour past noon; and it was then that the first uneasy suspicion was aroused in our minds, that some important, possibly sinister, events were perhaps in progress at the camp. Mr. Longcast, the General's interpreter, learned from one of the prisoners that an immense army had been expected to arrive that very day from Ulundi; and from the enumeration of the different regiments composing it, the numbers of that force were variously estimated, by those familiar with them, at from 20,000 to 25,000. Suddenly, during his cross-examination of other prisoners, the sound of artillery-fire was distinctly heard in the direction of the camp; and the Zulus immediately said, "Do you hear that? There is fighting going on at the camp."

This was at once reported to the General, who was by this time some way down the hill, towards the spot, near the Amange stream, where the Mounted Police and Carbineers were already off-saddled. Remaining there only for a very few moments, he passed on to the lower part of the Amange, where the road crosses, to select a site for the new camp. At this juncture one of our mounted natives came galloping down from the opposite ridge, whence the camp could be seen, and reported to a Staff-officer that an attack was being made on the camp, as he had seen heavy firing and heard the big guns. On this being reported to Lord Chelmsford he at once galloped up to the crest of the hill, accompanied by his Staff, and on arrival every field-glass was levelled at the camp. The sun was shining brightly on the white tents, which were plainly visible, but all seemed quiet. No signs of firing, or of an engagement could be seen, and although bodies of men moving about could be distinguished, yet they were not unnaturally supposed to be our own troops. The time was now 1.45 p.m. and not the faintest idea of disaster occurred to us. It was believed that an attack on the camp had been made and repulsed, as those who knew the arrangements previously made for its defence had every right and reason to assume. Some time was passed on the ridge, and it was not until a quarter to three that the General turned his horse's head downwards to the Amange stream. After some time had been passed on the site marked out for the new camping ground orders were given for Captain Shepstone and his Volunteers to return to the camp and ascertain the position of affairs there, and what had occurred.

I joined them, and we had not proceeded very far on the road when we met a mounted messenger, who had been sent off by Colonel Pulleine with a note to Lord Chelmsford, to inform him that the camp was attacked by large numbers of Zulus, and requesting him to return at once with all the forces at his command. Upon this we halted to await the arrival of the General, who quickly came up with us, accompanied by the Mounted Infantry, and proceeded up the valley with us to reconnoitre. At this time we had travelled about three miles on our return, and had passed Colonel Harness with his four guns, accompanied by a detachment of the 2-24th, the ambulance and a waggon, and the main body of the Mounted Infantry, all on their way to the new encampment. At this moment a mounted man was seen approaching, and speedily recognised as Commandant Lonsdale, who proved to be the bearer of the most dreadful news. Those who were present when he told his terrible tidings to Lord Chelmsford will never forget the scene, nor their feelings at the time, as they exchanged looks of amazement, grief, and horror.

It appeared that in pursuing a mounted Zulu he had become separated from his corps, and had therefore ridden quietly back to the camp at Isandwhlana. On arriving within 800 yards of it, at about 2 p.m., he found large masses of the enemy surrounding it, and in conflict with our troops. He had but just time, on discovering the state of matters, to turn and fly for his life: several shots were fired after him, and he was chased by many Zulus. But owing, fortunately, to the stoutness and pluck of his well-known little pony, "Dot," he succeeded in escaping the pursuit, and rejoined his regiment, also marching back in false security, and utter ignorance, like all the rest of us, of the frightful catastrophe which had occurred not five miles away. For although, as stated, the sound of artillery-fire, and even the rattle of musketry, had been heard during the morning, yet they were attributed to some skirmishing only, and no one even had a thought of the fatal truth.

So soon as Commandant Lonsdale's tale was told, orders were sent back, by Major Gossett, A.D.C., for the rest of the Column to return at once; and meanwhile we halted, awaiting their arrival with unspeakable impatience and anxiety. In order, if possible, to gain farther information, mounted patrols were detached, in skirmishing order, to the crests of the adjoining ridges, to watch the progress of events. As they came in, we could only learn that the enemy were rapidly increasing in numbers, and seemed to have beaten our troops, and to be burning the tents and taking away large quantities of stores, waggons, oxen and horses. This news served to increase our maddening impatience, and the miserable anxiety with which we awaited the on-coming of our supports. This was further enhanced by the report of a small scouting party of mounted men, who were sent forward with orders to approach as near as possible to the camp. On their return, they brought the intelligence that nearly all firing had ceased, and everything was in possession of the enemy, who held in great force what was almost our only road back to Natal. It was universally felt that to attempt an advance with only two battalions of the Native Contingent and a few jaded cavalry would be rash and foolhardy in the extreme. At

Isandhlwana: the dash with the colours

the same time the news was scarcely accepted as true; or at least we hoped it might prove to be only partially so; and that our troops had simply been driven to fall back on Rorke's Drift, by the superior numbers of the enemy.

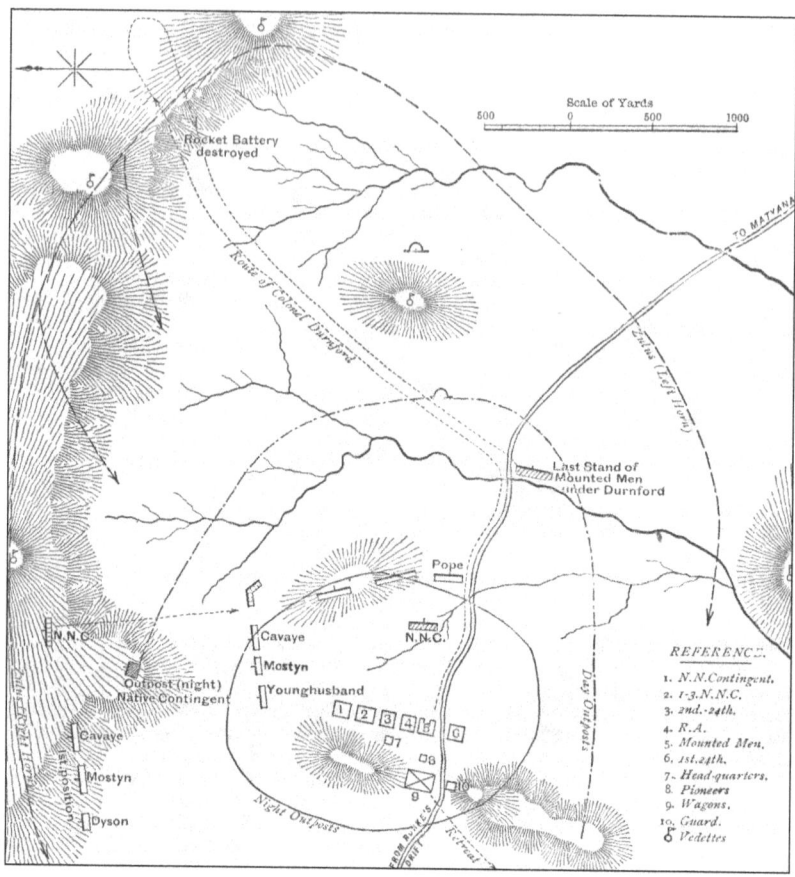

Plan of the battle of Isandhlwana January, 22, 1879

It was quite four o'clock when the rest of our reconnoitring Column rejoined us, and the order of march for our whole force was established as follows:—The four guns were placed in the centre, with a half battalion of the 2-24th extended in line on each flank, that on the right being commanded by Colonel Degacher, that on the left by Major Black; on either side of them were eight companies of the 3rd N.N.C.; and the cavalry outside of all, on the flanks; Major Dartnell, in command of the Mounted Police and Volunteers, on the left; and Colonel Russell, with his Mounted Infantry, on the right. The ambulances and waggons followed the guns, with a small guard closing up the rear. Before the march was commenced the General briefly addressed the men, saying that the camp had fallen into the hands of the enemy, who had captured it in overwhelming force during our absence; but that he relied upon them to retake it, and so reopen our communications with Natal. Then the advance was made in the above order —with fear in our hearts as to the events that might have taken place, but nevertheless with a stem determination to recapture the position, even in the increasing darkness, and whatever might be the cost.

When we arrived within two miles of the camp, advanced guards were sent forward, but nothing was seen of the enemy. Our route was continued in the same order and with all precautions; the daylight dying away more and more, until, when the water-wash to the south of the camp was crossed, it was as dark as it ever became throughout that memorable night. At a distance of within a mile, where the ground rose to the site of the camp, we could see, by the shadows against the horizon, on the top of the neck of land, where our road ran back to the Bashee Valley, and so on to Rorke's Drift, that the enemy had dragged numerous waggons, so as to place a sort of barrier across our only road back. And from behind this we thought we could hear the hoarse cries of the enemy, and the rattle of their knob-kerries and assegais against their shields. A halt was therefore made to allow the guns to pour four rounds of shrapnel into the barricade, when the advance was resumed. Meanwhile Major Black received orders to gain possession, at all risks, of the kopje on the left of the ridge; as those holding it would then be enabled to protect our flank effectually, and to command the ridge itself with a destructive fire. As the gallant Major moved off in the dark on this hazardous errand, apparently one of almost certain death, I heard him call out to his men, "No firing, but only one volley, boys, and then give them the cold steel." After a short advance by the main body a second halt took place, and the shrapnel-fire was repeated. Afterwards all was silence, and we resumed our onward march. The 2-24th on the right were ordered to fire a few rounds, with the object of drawing the fire of the enemy, if any, but fruitlessly; and then, in silence and darkness, we moved on once more.

A little farther on, and we began to stumble over dead bodies in every direction, and in some places, especially where from the formation of the ground there was a ditch or anything like shelter, the men were found lying thick and close, as though they had fought there till their ammunition was exhausted, and then been surrounded and slaughtered. When within a few hundred yards of the top of the ridge, with the large and grotesque form of the Isandwhlana Mountain looming up in front of us, and showing clearly against the sky in the dusk of evening, we heard a ringing British cheer from hundreds of throats. We thus learnt that Major Black and his men of the 2-24th had gained the kopje without any resistance, and therefore that the enemy had retired still farther, though between us and Rorke's Drift. It was 8 or 9 p.m. by the time our little force had ascended the ridge: we received orders to bivouac where and as we were, on the field of slaughter, and only to move forward by daylight in the morning. Such precautions as were possible were taken to guard against a surprise; for it was known that a large force was following in the rear; and the victorious enemy were believed to be in close proximity to our front and flanks.

But oh! how dreadful were those weary hours that followed! while all had to watch and wait, through the darkness, with what patience we could muster, for the dawn of day; with the knowledge that we were standing and lying amid and surrounded by the corpses of our late comrades—though in what fearful numbers we then but little knew. Many a vow of vengeance was breathed in the stillness of the night; and many and deep were the sobs that came from the breasts of men who, perhaps, had never sobbed before, at discovering, even by that dim light, the bodies of dear friends, brutally massacred, stripped of all clothing, disembowelled, mutilated, and in some cases decapitated. How that terrible night passed with us I fancy few would care to tell, even if they could recall it. For my own part, I felt both reckless and despairing—reckless at the almost certain prospect of an overwhelming attack by the enemy, flushed with victory—despairing, because of the melancholy scene of horror which I felt awaited us at daybreak. During the night we noticed fires constantly burning on all the surrounding hills; and in particular one bright blaze riveted our attention throughout, as it seemed to be near Rorke's Drift, and we feared for the safety of those left in that small place, knowing how utterly powerless we were to aid them in any way before morning. Happily, in this instance, our fears were vain.

After lying down for a while close to the General and his Staff, I arose at about an hour before daylight, for the purpose of taking a quiet look around, to see the state of matters for myself, and recognise what bodies I could. Nothing but a sense of duty could have induced me to undertake the task, or sustained me in its execution so as to go through with it. Not eyen on the recent battle-fields of Europe, though hundreds were lying where now I saw only tens, was there over a more sickening or heart-rending sight! The corpses of our poor soldiers, whites and natives, lay thick upon the ground in dusters, together with dead and mutilated horses, oxen and mules, shot and stabbed in every position and manner; and the whole intermingled with the fragments of our Commissariat waggons, broken and wrecked, and rifled of their contents, such as flour, sugar, tea, biscuits, mealies, oats, &c., &c., the debris being all scattered about, and wasted as in pure wantonness on the ground. The dead bodies of the men lay as they had fallen, but mostly with only their boots and shirts on, or perhaps a pair of trousers or a remnant of a coat, with just sufficient means of recognition to determine to which branch of the Service they had belonged. In many instances they lay with sixty or seventy empty cartridge cases surrounding them, thus showing that they had fought to the very last, and only succumbed and fallen, after doing their duty without flinching, and when all means of resistance were exhausted. It seemed to me, at the time, that it was really wonderful that so small a force had been able to maintain such a desperate resistance for so long. There were, indeed, only about 900 men in camp, exclusive of our natives, who ran away, and of Colonel Durnford's mounted men, under Captain Barton; and yet, fighting in the open, without defensive works, protection or cover, they kept at bay for hours the almost overwhelming army of Zulus, by whom they were attacked and surrounded. Captain Barton subsequently told me that his mounted men really fought well at their first charge, and until all their ammunition was exhausted; they were then compelled to fall back on the camp, where they sought for a fresh supply of ammunition. Unfortunately, this was refused them by the officer in charge, who said it would all be required by the infantry themselves. This was assuredly a fatal error of judgment, inasmuch as a large quantity of ammunition unused fell into the hands of the enemy, together with more than 1,000 Martini-Henry rifles and carbines. Perhaps, however, though the defence might have been prolonged, the disastrous issue could not have been averted, considering the strength of the enemy. So far as I could judge, from what I saw through my field-glass, combined with all the reliable information which could possibly be obtained at the time, and careful computation, the line of Zulu warriors, which came down from the hills on the left, must have extended over a length of nearly three miles, and consisted of more than 15,000 men. And another large body, of at least 5,000, was held in reserve, remaining on the crest of the slope and taking no part in the first onslaught. They took part in the work of spoil and plunder at the camp, and aided in driving off the captured cattle and such waggons as had not been wrecked. Most of the bodies of their dead were also removed by them in the waggons, so that not many were found by us on the field; this makes it difficult to form any accurate estimate of the total loss on their side, which must have been considerable. Assuming that our troops had seventy rounds each, and allowing for the effective execution of many rounds of shrapnel and case from the two guns, as well as the rockets, discharged into the dense masses at close quarters, I think the Zulu loss may fairly be set down at not far short of 2,000, an estimate which has been considered low by military men well qualified to judge.

I had scarcely returned from my melancholy round, when, just as daylight began to appear, preparations for the advance were completed, and the word was given to march. Formed in fours, not in line this time, we proceeded rapidly on our return route, with strong advanced and rear guards, and feeling well on our flanks. On nearing the farther side of the plain, where the neck of land gives access to the Bashee valley, we saw in the distance on our left a returning Zulu impi, numbering many thousands. Judging from the numerous evidences of burning kraals bordering the Buffalo river itself, we concluded that this was a part of the victorious army which had set out from Isandwhlana, attacked the post at Rorke's Drift, and were now on their way back to Ulundi, after raiding the Border. This sight served to intensify our anxiety, and caused us to hurry onwards. We quickly reached the brow of the hill overlooking the Buffalo river and Rorke's Drift, with our previous camping ground on the opposite bank; but the sight of buildings in flames at the station by no means allayed our fears. Before we quite reached the river I carefully examined the house at Rorke's Drift through my field-glass, and thought I could distinguish the figures of men on parts of the wall and roof of the large building, and one of them seemed to be waving a flag. The attention of the General having been called to this. Colonel Russell, with some of his mounted infantry and myself, at once crossed the river and galloped up to the station at full speed. Much to our delight and relief, we were greeted with a hearty English cheer, showing that here at least no irreparable disaster had befallen. We quickly dismounted, and found the place had been temporarily defended by a barricade of empty biscuit-boxes and mealies in sacks, while outside numerous bodies of dead Zulus were lying all around. The little garrison, it appeared, had received timely warning from the fugitives escaped from the camp at Isandwhlana, and they were thus enabled to make some slight preparations for the anticipated assault, so that they successfully withstood, and repulsed with severe loss to the enemy, a body of over 4,000 Zulus, that had commenced the attack on them at five on the previous (Wednesday) evening, and continued almost unintermittently till daybreak, only retiring upon the approach of our little column. The small garrison consisted of only about 130 men, under Lieutenant Chard, R.E., and Lieutenant Bromhead, 2-24th. Major Spalding, D.A.Q.M.G., had been left in command of the post, but had gone away to Helpmakaar late on the Tuesday afternoon preceding. The following officers were also present at the post and rendered material aid in the defence: Dr. Reynolds, 1-24th, Lieutenant Adendorff, 1-3rd N.N.C., Messrs. Dunne, Dalton, and Byrne, of the Commissariat Department, as also the Rev. Mr, Smith, Protestant Chaplain to No. 8 Column.

It seems that several parties of men, escaping from the scene of the massacre at Isandwhlana, some of them strong in numbers, passed by Rorke's Drift; but it mast be said, much to their discredit, they would not remain to aid the little garrison, but continued their flight to Helpmakaar. The conflagration which we had seen was in a detached building, used as a hospital, at

Engraving of Lieutenant John Rouse Merriott Chard (1847-1897) who commanded the troops at Rorke's Drift, where he won a VC.

some little distance away from the house; this, though at first defended, could not be held, and had therefore been evacuated. The loss sustained by the Column at Isandwhlana is given in Appendix A, and the official report of the subsequent attack on Rorke's Drift by the officer in command, Lieutenant, now Major, Chard, V.C, will be found in Appendix B.

The rest of the Mounted Infantry, and the General with his Staff, speedily also arrived at the station; and the gallant defenders, on relating the particulars of their heroic resistance, were warmly commended and deservedly congratulated. The remainder of the Column in the meantime crossed the river and encamped temporarily close by. Shortly afterwards, by the General's orders, the entire force was set to work to dear the

Engraving of Lieutenant Gonville Bromhead (1845-1892) who was second in command at Rorke's Drift where he won a VC.

ground around the station of all cover for an enemy's attack, to reconstruct and strengthen the barricade, and to mount the four guns, one at each corner. The roof of the house, being of thatch, was also stripped from it, to prevent farther peril of fire. The two battalions of the N.N.C. were posted on the large hill at the back, to prevent any enemy occupying it to fire down on the station, and also to keep guard on the river. These preparations were necessary, as precautions against any possible attack, as the General had decided to remain for the time at Rorke's Drift; and they occupied the whole morning. Not till they were completed were the rations served out. It will readily be conceived what a boon this was at last, to men who had been out for two days and nights, who had had during that time absolutely nothing to eat but a little biscuit and tinned meat, and nothing to drink except bad water, while undergoing the fatigues of marching and skirmishing, and the wretched anxiety of such a miserable bivouac as our last. Colonel Russell was then sent on, with a mounted escort, in order to see if the road was open up to Helpmakaar, and to learn what had been and was being done there. During his absence, however, three officers arrived, belonging to the 1st N.N.G. under Major Bengough (part of what had been Colonel Durnford's force;. They had ridden down from Helpmakaar, and found the roads open and clear of the enemy. No attack had, up to that time, been made upon that station, which was well guarded, a laager having been formed. Small parties and scouts of the enemy had been seen in the vallies below and on the surrounding hills. We also learnt, half-an-hour later, that the country to the north was free of the Zulus, a party of the Buffalo Border Guard having ridden over from Fort Pine. Trivial as these items of intelligence may now appear, they were at the time significant and useful to us, by restoring hope to our hearts, as indicating that no attack by any overwhelming force of the enemy was to be apprehended, and that there would be time to reorganise the Column and repair our loss of men and means.

For my part, on considering the serious nature of the reverse which our troops had suffered, and the great importance of transmitting full and correct particulars, I at once resolved to start that same evening, and ride straight back to Pieter Maritzburg, so as to be in time to telegraph the news to Cape Town, for despatch by the mail-steamer for England of the following Monday. This I was happily enabled to effect, and so give the colonial people the earliest trustworthy intelligence as to the list of killed and missing from the Head-quarters Column. Having made my determination known, undertook to be the bearer of any despatches, messages, or telegrams, and received a great many from all ranks, from His Excellency downwards. I made all my preparations as rapidly possible, as reports had

The defence of Rorke's Drift 1879. Oil painting by Alphonse de Neuville in 1880

come in from some of Commandant Lonsdale's native scouts to the effect that Zulus were crossing le river at a point lower down, and it was considered possible at the station at Rorke's Drift might again be attacked in force that night. I therefore took my leave of Lord Chelmsford—who, in spite of his grief at the recent disaster, was still thoughtful enough to devote a few friendly words to me—and saying good-bye to all those who had happily come out of that "Valley of Death" with me, I galloped off. Though sore at heart at parting from those with whom I had gone through so much, I was not sorry to find myself on the road to Pieter Maritzburg, with news of importance to all interested in the officers and men of our Column.

I may appropriately close this narrative of our mischance by a quotation from the letter of a Staff-officer, written on these events:—

"There was reason to believe that the Zulu army consisted of the Undi corps, including the Tulwana, Nkonkone, Ndhlonhlo, and Ndhluyengwe regiments, about 4,000 strong; the Umcityu, including the Unqakamatye and Umtulisazwe regiments, about 6,000 strong; the Nkobamakosi regiment, about 4,000 strong;

the Inkulutyane, including the Umzikaba and Unddududu regiments, 2,500 strong; and the Nokenke, 2,000 strong; or an aggregate of about 18,500 men in regiments. Besides this there were at least another 5,000 men belonging to various tribes and head men, making the whole force employed against No. 8 Column on the 22nd inst. about 23,000 to 24,000 men. Of this number the last named were ordered to show themselves as much as possible, and induce as many of our troops to go in pursuit of them as they could, avoiding at the same time actual fighting—this they did to perfection. A force of some 15,000 men was moved up from the Ibabinango mountain during the night of the 21st inst., a distance of about 25 miles, not en masse, but in small parties. On arriving to the left of our position they lay down as they were, fires and speaking being strictly prohibited. Another body, about 8,000 or 4,000 strong, was ordered to watch the road to Rorke's Drift, and follow up all those who might escape that way, and I believe that had our men followed the waggon road instead of going straight across country, hardly one would have come out alive. We know how well carried out, tactically speaking, were the Zulu Generals' strategic arrangements. In the attack on the camp there was no hurry or excitement on their part. They first outflanked and surrounded it, and then, and not till then, did they give way to their natural impetuosity and charge with the assegai. No soldier can, I think, fail to admire and respect the soldier-like qualities thus displayed by the enemy, much as his hatred and contempt may be excited by the brutal and savage characteristics they otherwise exhibited, and in the future the Zulu army will command that amount of precaution and respect which is necessary before it can be conquered."

CHAPTER IX

CHARGED WITH many commissions and letters, I started, all alone, from Rorke's Drift for Helpmakaar, at 3.30 p.m. on Thursday, the 23rd of January, with two tired horses, which I rode and led alternately. At Helpmakaar I found that a laager of waggons had been formed around the store, and everything was arranged to offer a stout resistance to any attack by night or day. As I was most anxious to prosecute my journey that same night, I tried in vain to obtain a fresh horse, but unfortunately none was to be had; so that I was fain to stop there the night to give my jaded animals some rest. The little garrison comprised about 160 men, reliefs for the 24th Regiment, and about thirty others, who had been successful in effecting their escape from the massacre at Isandwhlana on the previous day. Among them I recognised several well-known faces of the Carbineers, and I learnt that some few of the survivors had gone on direct to Pieter Maritzburg. It was with heartfelt pleasure that I was enabled to strike all these names out of the long official list of the missing which had been entrusted to me. Though not given to fault-finding, I cannot, however, refrain from commenting on the treatment which I met with at the hands of the garrison generally. I was—as was well known to all—a man who had suffered in the recent trouble, lost all he had with him at the camp, thankful for his escape from the slaughter, but hungry, weary, and worn out, having been three days in the saddle and two nights almost without sleep. Yet nothing in the shape of hospitality, kindness, or civility was shown me by any of the officers or others, except a few of the fugitives in similar case. All that I wanted to supply my needs I had to look after and obtain for myself, without aid or courtesy being extended to me. Such

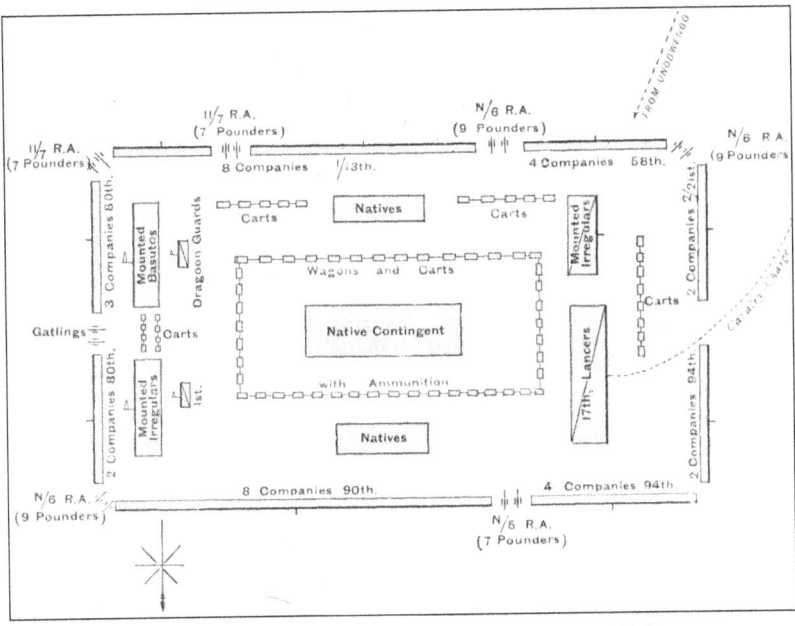

Plan of the Defences at Rorke's Drift (January 22, 1879).

conduct was neither manly nor soldierlike.

Leaving at daybreak, I reached Sand Spruit after a smart trot in the early morning, and heard a rumour on the way that the Zulus had again attacked Rorke's Drift on the preceding night, and been beaten off. At Knox's I met Lieutenant Shepherd, of the 2-4th King's Own Regiment, who told me that there was a valuable convoy of thirty waggons of stores and ammunition at the adjacent unprotected Court House, which he, together with Colonel Bray, Captain Middleton, two non-commissioned officers, and twenty men, had to guard as best they could against possible attack by the Zulus, who were reported to be in small parties in the vicinity. As they had women and children with them, he urged me to tell the officer in command of the next detachment of troops that I might meet, to hurry on to their assistance. This I willingly undertook to do, and we parted with all friendly assurances of sympathy. I accomplished the fifteen miles thence to the Tugela with some difficulty, as my horses were nearly done up, and here I halted, and had my first good meal of meat, bread, and tea since leaving the camp on Tuesday; and I need scarcely say I enjoyed it heartily. During my stay, Colonel Law, R.A., and Captain Jones, R.E., arrived with many waggons, and on receiving my message, determined to leave the waggons, and press forward with the escort. Resuming my route, after two hours' rest, I next met Major Grenfell, D.A.A.G., and explained the position of affairs to him, and he gave me a note to the officer in command of the 2-4th, who were not far behind, to hurry their advance, also light and without waggons. It appeared that Major Grenfell had been on the way up to join the General, in company with Colonel Bellairs, but on receiving Lord Chelmsford's first despatch (sent by a mounted policeman), announcing the loss at the camp, the Colonel had returned alone to Pieter Maritzburg, to make all arrangements necessary under the circumstances, and especially to order all the troops at command to be sent on from Cape Colony to Natal at once.

At Mooi River I found a large number of Government and hired waggons, carrying stores, &c., but all stuck there, because neither drivers nor leaders would go forward, owing to the alarming reports brought down the road by the fugitive Kafirs of the Native Contingent. The fact was, that these runaways had created almost a panic along their road of flight. For my part, I consider that every native that had fled from Helpmakaar deserved to be shot, and certainly every white man that had left our outposts at Rorke's Drift and Helpmakaar should have been tried by court-martial for cowardice. As far as I could ascertain, those who thus took refuge in flight had spread the most extraordinary tales about their miraculous escapes. But inasmuch as many of them passed Helpmakaar early on the day of the 22nd, and as the conflict at the Isandwhlana camp, fifteen miles away, had only terminated about 4 or 5 p.m., it seems to me that they could have seen very little of the fatal fight, and could have known nothing positive about the disastrous result. These doubtful points remain to be cleared up. Between Mooi River and Burrup's I met the detachment of the 2-4th, and gave my note from Major Grenfell to the commanding officer. Before reaching Burrup's I was caught in one of the most severe storms of thunder, lightning, and rain that I have ever seen; indeed, the horses could not be got to face it, and there was nothing for it but to halt and submit to the drenching. Arrived at Burrup's, I got rid of my wet clothes, rolled myself in some blankets, and after taking some hot tea—the only thing to be had—I slept the sleep of the tired, "if not of the just." The following morning early, though weak and weary, I pressed on to Grey Town, which I reached at 7 a.m. All my old friends were rejoiced to see me alive, having been led to believe that every one with the Column, except the fugitives who had passed that way, had been slaughtered. I was glad to be able to contradict all these sensational reports, and to give the latest authentic news, painful as that was. At Mrs. Plant's, where I breakfasted, there were a number of officers of the 2-4th, who listened with breathless interest to my details, and to the list of killed and missing. One of the officers of the King's Own, Lieutenant Penrose, made a sketch of the scene, which appeared subsequently in the Graphic. I had an order on the resident magistrate for fresh horses, but by this time I was so thoroughly exhausted that I could not continue my journey in the saddle. I accordingly changed my mode of travelling, and completed the rest of the distance by the post-cart.

At Pieter Maritzburg I found the most intense excitement prevailing, owing to the many alarming rumours that had been spread, and the absence of all reliable intelligence. The streets were thronged, and on our arrival at the post-office I was at once recognised and most heartily welcomed; indeed, ill as I was, I was quite unable to get away until all my news had been made public. The Natal Times, with great promptitude and enterprise, immediately published an "Extra" with the full particulars; and although some of those too clever people, who are never lacking, pretended to throw doubts upon the accuracy of my account, it was afterwards officially corroborated in almost every particular. I had every reason to feel flattered with the need of recognition and praise generally awarded to me for my long and arduous journey to bring early and correct tidings of such deep interest and importance to the people of Pieter Maritzburg and the Colony. My duty did not end therewith, for I was specially charged with letters to His Excellency Sir Bartle Frere, and many other officials, all of which I made an effort to deliver that same day, before returning home to enjoy well-earned and much-needed repose. Of the list of those missing from the fatal field of Isandwhlana, which I had myself compiled with no small trouble, and brought down so quickly, I may say that it proved too mournfully accurate; unhappily of all the brave fellows, whose names were there enumerated, not one has been heard of alive since then.

The state of consternation and excitement which had prevailed in the city for the two preceding days was unprecedented and indescribable. It was on Friday, the 24th of January, that their Excellencies the High Commissioner and the Lieutenant-Governor had issued, for the information of the public, a brief account of the reverse, as given by Captain Stafford and Lieutenant Davis, the substance of the news being already known. But the public in general seemed actually to be so staggered at the gravity and painful character of the intelligence that they seemed utterly unable to give credence to the facts. A state of the utmost and most anxious suspense ensued, which increased to such a pitch as at one time almost to threaten violent measures against those who had brought the news, for it was even rumoured that, on comparison and cross-examination, such discrepancies had been found in their statements as to throw doubts on their truthfulness. This was of course quite unfounded. But before the Government were able to issue any reliable details, the excitement and anxiety for more news reached such a climax that a deputation of the citizens had an interview with His Excellency the Lieutenant-Governor (on Saturday) to request him to allay public anxiety by publishing without delay all that was known. Late in the afternoon a summary of Lord Chelmsford's despatch was posted on the notice-board at the Colonial Secretary's office; but great disappointment was felt when it was seen that this gave no detailed account or list of the severe losses. My arrival, about 5 p.m., enabled this deficiency to be supplied; but the fuller knowledge thus given of the extent of the calamity only served to deepen and intensify the public feeling. Crowds gathered about the newspaper office, eager to scan the printed list and see whether any of those known and dear to them were among the lost, and the scene was sad and striking for those who witnessed it. Amazement, yielding to rage and grief, was eventually succeeded by vague feelings of alarm, and the public mind was rapidly disquieted by uneasy rumours of all kinds respecting the position of affairs at the front. It need scarcely be said that these fears were identified with the probability of a border-raid by the victorious Zulus in overwhelming strength, extended possibly to the chief towns, Durban and Pieter Maritzburg. The citizens went about with anxious countenances, whispering gloomily at street-corners, and crowds thronged around the Colonial Office and the newspaper offices, eager for the smallest item of news. Meanwhile, the subject of the defence of the city was discussed at a meeting of the Town Board, and a memorandum, with some hints to the people as to what should be done in the possible contingency of their being required to go into "laager" was issued by the Commandant, Colonel Mitchell. This led to the conclusion, erroneous as it proved, that the Government was in receipt of some further information of an unfavourable character. All suitable preparations were made by the authorities. At the Court House and Colonial Office wells were dug, and at the former a supply of ammunition, under a guard, was stored in the magazine. All through the Sunday waggons were engaged in removing stores to the depots. Parties of men were employed on the construction of barricades with boxes filled with earth in the open street-spaces around the Court House, the windows of which were made secure by fitting stout wooden shatters to them. These operations were superintended by Volunteers of the Rifle Corps; the new Town Guard and the Volunteers commenced patrolling the city, and other precautions were taken to meet all possible dangers. Instructions were given to the members of the various households to have provisions ready, and be themselves prepared to go into "laager" at short notice, for which the alarm would be given by the ringing of the bells. After-events may have tended to show that these preparations, and the species of panic in which they originated, were somewhat exaggerated, and possibly too late to have been of any value if there had been any existing cause for them. But at the moment it cannot be doubted that the danger was substantial, and the necessity real.

Many reasons have been assigned for Cetywayo's unaccountable withdrawal and inaction after that memorable 22nd of January; but it will always remain a subject of wonder that he did not at once launch his victorious and elated army upon the colony of Natal, which undoubtedly for the moment lay defenceless, and powerless to make any effectual resistance against a rapid and well-organised raid, for which the opportunity had come and the way then lay open. Some persons agree with Bishop Colenso in attributing this abstinence to the Zulu King's sincerity in his previous peaceful professions. But it must be admitted as a preferable explanation, to attribute it to a combination of other causes, such as the sanguinary loss to themselves by which the victory of the Zulus was attended; the farther severe check and ultimately disastrous repulse inflicted on their forces on the ensuing night at Rorke's Drift, and lastly, the division and disposal of the spoils and plunder of the camp, and the necessary removal of the guns, rifles, ammunition, and waggons which were captured. Be that as it may, the opportunity speedily passed away, with the merely defensive preparations which were at once set on foot along the frontier line and in the colony itself, which thus was happily spared what might have been a terrible calamity, attended with great loss of property and cruel slaughter.

On the Sunday evening (Jan. 26) Lord Chelmsford, with some of his Staff, arrived in Pieter Maritzburg, having ridden down, via Helpmakaar and Ladysmith, the Border road, by which I had ridden alone, being then considered unsafe. The news they brought was most reassuring, to the effect that the Zulus had all retired inland, and had been followed up by our Border Kafirs, who attacked straggling bodies of the enemy and killed many, thus restoring complete confidence along the Border. The General came down only to consult with His Excellency Sir Bartle Frere, the High Commissioner, and send fuller accounts by telegraph and letter to England.

CHAPTER X

THE FOLLOWING are the best accounts yet given of the events of the 22nd of January at Isandwhlana, at which, fortunately for me, I was not present. But although I have therefore no personal knowledge of the facts, I need no apology for inserting them in my book, as they are essential to the history of the war.

A Government conductor of waggons has stated that—"Between 3 and 4 a.m. the General left the camp with a column to attack 'Matyana's' location, and there only remained in the camp five companies of the 1-24th Regiment and one of the 2-24th, numbering with the Staff and others about 800 Regulars, two field-pieces with the requisite artillerymen, and some mounted men. At 8 a.m. we heard firing in vollies from the General's direction, south-east of the camp. At this time we perceived the Zulus collecting in force to the north of the camp. Our small force was ordered under arms at once, but dispersed again shortly afterwards, and the cattle belonging to the camp were directed to be brought into camp and inspanned; this was done by half-past ten. The Zulus were then seen coming in force over a ridge about a mile and a half distant. At eleven Colonel Durnford came into camp with 860 mounted men of the Native Contingent, and formed in front of the two guns. He advanced two miles on the left flank of the approaching Zulus, out of sight of the camp, and after a heavy fire retired, the Zulus coming on in an extended line two miles from end to end. Two companies of the 1-24th marched forward to attack the right wing, supported by a few of the mounted natives, while Colonel Durnford attacked the left wing, and the Infantry cheeked the progress of the Zulus for about an hour, but were forced to fall back on the camp, as the Zulus had got in among them from the rear, and were fighting hand to hand. The two field-pieces were in the centre, firing shot and shell, and cutting up the Zulus by scores, but every gap made by them was filled up immediately. At half-past twelve the enemy's line had extended to about three miles to surround the camp, which they had already entered from the rear, and the officer in command of the two field-pieces was stabbed in the set of trying to spike his guns. At one o'clock the Union Jack in front of the General's tent was pulled down and torn to pieces; but a general panic had already commenced, and I then retired from the camp in company with one Carbineer (name unknown), and one Army Staff sergeant. We galloped as fast as our horses would carry us, straight to the Buffalo, through the retreating body, consisting of Native Contingent and such of the Regulars as had escaped, all of whom were subjected to a galling fire from the Zulus on both sides, who followed us closely all the way. On reaching the Buffalo, at a spot where there was no drift, all rushed in helter-skelter, and many men and horses were drowned, while bullets were flying in all directions. On the Natal side of the Buffalo, Captain Essex, who had joined our party, took command, and led the white men to Helpmakaar, where laagers were formed with waggons, the coloured men escaping to Sand Spruit and the Tugela. The attacking party of Zulus consisted of about 20,000 men, and they took possession of everything in the General's camp. The officers and men of the 24th Regiment stood their ground, and were killed in the ranks; not one of them is supposed to have escaped, as none had arrived at Helpmakaar by seven on Thursday morning. The spot crossed by the retreating party is about five miles below Rorke's Drift. I did not see the attack made on the small detachment stationed there in charge of the hospital and commissariat stores, but I saw fire there between eight and nine in the evening. When I left the camp Colonel Durnford was still alive, as well as a small remnant of the Regulars, but they were so hemmed in that escape was impossible, and their ammunition seemed expended, for artillerymen were trying to break open the cases on the waggons to supply them, but it was too late."

Another remarkable account, subsequently given in Durban by Meshla Kwa Zulu, the captured son of Sirayo, is the most detailed in its statements, and fully corroborates the preceding account of Isandwhlana. It also gives an admirable summary of what occurred at Rorke's Drift, Zlobani Mountain, and Kambula. It says:—"We slept the night before the battle in a Talley rising from the Ngnutu range, and running eastward towards the King's kraal. It abounds with scrubby bush and small stones. We did not see Lord Chelmsford's army leave the camp on the day of the battle, but heard the report of firearms, and saw him returning. No orders were given as to the attack; it was not our day. Our day was the following day: it being the new moon we did not intend to fight. Our intention was to attack the camp next day at dawn, but the English forces came to attack us first. Three mounted troops —white and black—attacked us first. The Zulu regiments were all lying in the valley I have mentioned, but the Umcityu made their appearance under the Ngnutu range, and were seen by the mounted men of the English forces, who made at the Umcityu, not seeing the main body of the army. They fired, and all at once the main body of the Zulu army arose in every direction, on hearing the firing. The attention of the English mounted troops was drawn to the few men who had exposed themselves under the range, and before these mounted men knew where they were the main body of the Zulus got up and swarmed in every direction. On their seeing we were so numerous they retired, and the Ukandapemyu regiment fired. The mounted men retired very slowly on seeing the Zulu army. On seeing the English troops retiring the Ukandapemyu regiment, called also the Umcityu, advanced. The mounted men retired and advanced four times; we just went on, and they retired before us, our Zulu army appearing to become more numerous every moment; we never stopped in our advance. There is a little red hill which overlooks Isandwhlana, within sight of the camp, and there the Ngobamakosi, to which I belong, came in contact with two companies of mounted men. This was on the left, and about as far from the camp as the Court House is from Fort Napier; but we were on the height looking down. Some of these mounted men had white stripes up their trousers (Carbineers); there were also men dressed in black, but none of the Native Contingent on the brow of this hill. The Ngobamakosi and Uve regiments attacked on this side. The English force kept turning and firing, but we kept on; they could not stop us. But on the side of this little hill there is a donga, into which the mounted men got, and stopped our onward move there: we could not advance against their fire any longer. They had drawn their horses into this donga, and all we could see were the helmets. They fired so heavily we had to retire; we kept lying down and rising again. The Edendale men were in this donga, but we did not see the Basutos. The former were mixed with the Carbineers. At this time the wings of the Zulu army were running on both sides above Isandwhlana, and below towards Rorke's Drift; the men in this donga were firing on the chest of the army. Then, when the firing became very heavy—too hot—we retired towards the left wing, towards Rorke's Drift, and they then withdrew. On seeing us retire towards the Buffalo, they retired on the camp, fearing lest we should enter the camp before they could get to it, and that the camp would not be protected. All the troops had left the camp to come and attack us, but on seeing us retiring on the camp as we did, they also retired on the camp. The soldiers were sent out in small companies in various directions, and caused great havoc among the Zulus. The Carbineers on entering the camp made a strong stand there, and their firing was very heavy. It was a long time before they were overcome—before we finished them. When we did get to them they died in one place all together. They threw down their guns, when their ammunition was done, and then commenced with their pistols, which they used as long as their ammunition lasted; and then they formed a line, shoulder to shoulder, and back to back, and fought with their knives. At this time many of the soldiers had retired from the positions where they had gone to attack ns, and the Ukandapemyu and Umbonambi regiments were killing them from the end of the Camp. The Carbineers and others were in the rear of the camp, the soldiers in the front part. The Zulu army first entered the front, where the soldiers were. When the soldiers retired on the camp, they did so running, and the Zulus were then intermixed with them, and entered the camp at the same time. The two wings then met in the rear of the camp, and those who were in the camp were thus blocked in, and the main body of the Zulu army was engaged in chasing and killing the soldiers. When the Zulus closed in, the English kept up a strong fire towards the Buffalo. They were concentrated near the rear of the camp, and the fire was so heavy as to enable them to make an opening, and thus a great many of the mounted men escaped through this opening. The attention of the Zulus was directed to the killing of men in the rear, and so they did not attend to the closing up of this opening, and thus let the mounted men oat. There was a mixed medley, of white men, Edendale Kafirs, and others, who managed to get out in the direction of the Buffalo. They made an opening across the neck, crossed the stream and then made for the Buffalo. This stream is that which goes through my father's kraal. The ridge on this side is what we call the neck, the camp was on the other side.

"The resistance was stout where the old Dutch road used to go across; it took a long time to drives back the English forces there;

they killed us and we killed them, and the fight was kept up for a long time. The British troops became helpless, because they had no ammunition, and the Zulus killed them. There were cannon fired at this place where the opening was; they were left in the camp. I first saw the cannon when the soldiers left the camp and came to attack us in front. There was one drawn by mules (the rocket) and two by horses. They commenced firing as we came over the small hill looking down upon the camp, and before we had entered the camp at all. They came to assist the Carbineers in the donga, and fired in the same direction from near the donga into the body of the Zulu army. Four shots were fired at the Ngobamakosi; they then turned and fired at the Umbonambi also. I don't know how many shots they fired at them; they fired very quickly, not at one, but at all three regiments; they must have fired from ten to twenty shots; they commenced firing when we were a long distance away—we had not got near the camp, it was as far as the Willow bridge from this Court-house, and we had to ran all that distance to the camp. There was something wrong with the rocket battery. Two of the mules got on the top of a boulder, and were thrown over and killed; two mules then were left, but the man could not fire it. When we really saw rockets fired was at Kambula. The cannon did not do much damage. It only killed four men in our regiment, the shot went over us. None were killed by the Zulus between the top of the hill and the donga; our firing was bad. When they were in the donga with the police we had to retire, because we found our losses were so heavy. When they were rising out of the donga and retreating on the camp, we shot two Carbineers, and so got from the donga to the tents. They mounted their horses, which they had drawn into the donga with them. The Carbineers were still fighting when the Edendale men got into the camp. When the Carbineers reached the camp they jumped off their horses, and never succeeded in getting on them again.

They made a stand, and prevented our entering the camp, but things were then getting very mixed and confused; what with the smoke, dust, and intermingling of mounted men, footmen, Zulus, and natives, it was difficult to tell who was mounted and who was not. The soldiers were at this time in the camp, having come back from the front, all but two companies, which went on to the hill and never returned—they were every one of them killed. They were firing on the wings of the Zulu army, while the body of the army was pushing on, the wings also succeeded, and before the soldiers knew where they were, they were surrounded from the west, attacked by the wings from the right, and the main body from the back. They were all killed, not one escaped; they tried to make an opening towards the camp, but found the Zulu army was too thick; they could not do it, it was impossible. We searched the pouches of the men; some had a few cartridges, most of them had none at all; there were very few found. Some had cartouche-boxes, others cartridge-belts: the belts were all empty, but a few cartridges were found in a few of the cartouche-boxes. I did not see the soldiers fix bayonets. They could not have done so; they were retiring with the waggons. They turned the oxen and were going towards the drift, and were crossing the neck and making for the waggon-road. These waggons were without tents, and the soldiers were on each side of them. But the bayonets of the men of the two companies who were killed were fixed, and the men formed back to back. Some Zulus threw assegais at them, others shot at them; but they did not get close—they avoided the bayonet; for any man who went up to stab a soldier was fixed through the throat or stomach, and at once fell. Occasionally when a soldier was engaged with a Zulu in front with an assegai, another Zulu killed him from behind. There was a tall man who came out of a waggon and made a stout defence, holding out for some time, when we thought all the white people had been driven out of camp. He fired in every direction, and so quickly as to drive the Zulus some in one way, some in another. At first some of the Zulus took no notice; but at last he commanded our attention by the plucky way in which he fought, and because he had killed so many. He was at last shot. All those who tried to stab him were knocked over at once, or bayoneted; he kept his ground for a very long time. When I came up he had been stripped of his upper garments. As a rule we took off the upper garments, but left the trousers, but if we saw blood upon the garments we did not bother. I think this man was an officer; he had gaiters on, but I did not see his coat. His chin was shaved. He was killed immediately under the Isandwhlana hill. Only two cannon were taken to Cetywayo; the two in the front part of the camp were sent. The cannon remained on the field for a long time, and at last Cetywayo sent for them; he directed Mtembu, who lived near, to remove them. Each Zulu helped himself to watches, and such other property as they could lay hands upon and carry away. All the dead bodies were cut open, because if that had not been done the Zulus would have become swollen like the dead bodies. I heard that some bodies were otherwise mutilated. There was a man whose head was cut off at the entrance of the camp, where the white people held out, and formed back to back. The dead Zulus were buried in the grain siloes in two kraals; some in dongas, and elsewhere. Zulus died all round Isandwhlana.

"The men who fought at Rorke's Drift took no part at Isandwhlana; they were the men of the Undi regiment, who formed a portion of the left wing. When the camp at Isandwhlana had been taken, these men came up fresh and pursued the fugitives right over the Fugitives' Drift into Natal. There was a long line of stragglers, as we supposed, making for Jim's house. The other reserve regiments, intending to cut them off, crossed the Buffalo at the point where the Bashee

The Defence of Rorke's Drift

flows into it, and came round crossing the road near the kraal of Inswarele. These reserves complained that they had had no opportunity of taking part in the battle of Isandwhlana, and therefore they went on to Rorke's Drift, and fought there. These were men with rings. We who had fought at Isandwhlana were as tired as the Englishmen, and many more of the English forces would have escaped if the reserve regiments had not come up.

"About Zlobani and Kambula I commence at Zlobani. The English forces went up the mountain and did not see us; we came round the mountain. Those who were on the side of the mountain where the sun sets succeeded in getting out quickly; those who were on the side where the sun rises were driven the other way, and thrown over the krantzes. There was a row of white men thrown over the krantzes, their ammunition was done, they did not fire, and we killed them without their killing any of our men; a great many were also killed on the top; they were killed by the people on the mountain. We did not go up the mountain, but the men whom the English forces had attacked followed them up. They had beaten the Maqulusi, and succeeded in getting all the cattle of the whole neighbourhood which were there, and would have taken away the whole had we not rescued them. We encamped for the night, and then in the morning we went to attack the Kambula camp. When we were a long way from the camp we saw it, and it appeared as if an entrenchment had been made. When we got as near to the camp as the Victoria bridge is from this Court-house the white people came towards us on horseback. They commenced firing first; we did not commence there. We fired and they fired; they retired, and we followed them. That was the Ngobamakosi regiment. We thought the Zulu army was not far off, but it appears that at this time the main body had not got up, I mean that portion of the army which subsequently rose in the rear of the laager. The horsemen galloped back as hard as they could to camp; we followed and discovered ourselves almost close to the camp, into which we made the greatest possible efforts to enter. The English fired their cannon and rockets, and we were fighting and attacking them for about one hour. I mean the Ngobamakosi regiment. Before the main body of the Zulu army came up, we, when the Zulu army did come up, were lying prostrate—we were beaten, we could do no good. So many were killed that the few who were not killed were lying between dead bodies, so thick were the dead. The main body of the Zulu army attacked the camp from the rear, and tried for a long time to get in. The Nkenke regiment succeeded in getting into the cattle kraal. The Umbonambi regiment suffered much loss; indeed, the last two-named regiments were almost annihilated. It was unfortunate for the Zulus that the Ngobamakosi regiment should have marched quicker than was expected; we had no intention of attacking the camp, but were drawn on to do so by the mounted men before the main body of the Zulu army came up. The regiments were anxious to attack, but we went there cross, our hearts were full, and we intended to do the same as at Isandwhlana. At the Ondine battle (Ulundi), the last, we did not fight with the same spirit, because we were then frightened. We had had a severe lesson, and did not fight with the same zeal. At Kambula the Ngobamakosi suffered the most. At the conclusion of the fight we were chased by the English forces over three ridges and were only saved from entire destruction by the darkness. I myself only just managed to escape. Night came on, and they left off following ns. Had we all come up and attacked the Kambula camp at the same time we should have entered the camp on that day; it is at any rate probable if the attack had not been spoiled as I have said. Umnyanian was the chief in command; Tshingwayo also commanded under him. The Zulu plan was determined on by Cetywayo, whose orders were not to attack the entrenchments, but pass them by. If they attacked us we were to attack them; if they remained in their laager, then we were to pass on into the Transvaal territory, and that would bring the English forces out. But as it happened, we found ourselves by accident in action with the English forces. Cetywayo was very angry with us, and said we had no right to attack the laager. He blamed, and said he would kill the officer in command, but he did not. We acted contrary to instructions at Isandwhlana, and were successful; and then we acted contrary to instructions at Kambula. The attack at Rorke's Drift was led by Dabulamanzi and Vumangwana. Dabulamanzi is not a good general; he is too hasty. He commanded the lower column at Gingihlovo. Gwelegwele and Umbulwana commanded at Inyezane. We do not know how it is the Coast Zulus did not fight better. We looked down upon them, and complained that they fought so badly."

Such is the account given by an intelligent Zulu of these various affairs, and it will be found interesting from its minuteness and accuracy.

During the week following my journey back to Pieter Maritzburg I drew out a rough sketch-plan of the camp at Isandwhlana and the surrounding country from memory, showing the positions of our various forces in the camp itself as well as indications of the defence made by its holders. This was not only published in the colony, by my permission, from the original map drawn for the London Standard (which appeared in its columns on the 6th of March, 1879), but was also copied wholesale by other papers both in South Africa and in England, without any acknowledgments of its source, or recognition of its compiler.

My opinion of the disaster was written at the same time, and appeared in the same issue as the plan. And as, even now, with my more intimate knowledge of what really did occur, I find nothing to alter therein, the reproduction of a short extract will not be out of place or valueless:—

"A Court of Enquiry is now sitting here on the loss of the camp at Isandwhlana, and until its verdict is given it would be obviously unfair of me to lay the blame on any one individual; but whatever may be the result, the Home Government are undoubtedly to blame for having refused Lord Chelmsford's request to them to send out a regiment of cavalry; as nothing is more certain than the fact that to carry on a campaign quickly and successfully in Zululand large forces of mounted men are necessary, not only for fighting, but principally for mounted patrol and vedette work, combined with despatch-carrying and keeping open communications. It is universally admitted that what irregular cavalry we had behaved splendidly, both volunteers, police, and mounted infantry, but still we had not enough of them.

"Each successive account given by those who escaped seems to bear out more fully the opinion I expressed in my letter describing the whole affair—that, had the force in camp either acted purely on the defensive, or sent out part to keep back the onslaught until a waggon laager or entrenchment was made, not only could they have held out until the General arrived, but most probably they would have beaten off the enemy long before the evening. That this fact must be obvious to any one may be seen from the following:—About 100 men, with a slight temporary fortification of biscuit-cases and sacks of mealies, kept off 4,000 Zulus for one whole night at Rorke's Drift, killing over 400 and wounding many hundreds more; if similar tactics had been carried out at Isandwhlana, the 900 white men, with artillery, plenty of ammunition and stores, could surely have kept off the 20,000 who attacked the camp. And if seems to us here plain that some officer in command of the camp that day not only neglected his duty by not fulfilling the orders given, but also forgot the most simple military rules laid down for warfare against the Zulus in a book published officially, entitled 'Regulations for Field Forces in South Africa.' The real full truth of what did take place on that 'black Wednesday' will never be known, as not only are all the executive military officers dead; but, of the fugitives who escaped, not one was in a position to say what orders were given or from whom they were received, as they either belonged to the native infantry or cavalry, and were therefore fighting outside the camp.

"Of course, although the reverse was a most serious one in every way, it can hardly be said to have been a defeat of one of our Columns; but as the Zulus are sure to make light of the number of their own dead—and prisoners say their losses were awful—and equally sure to exaggerate the loss on our side, the gain in prestige to our enemies amounts to something considerable. Through the arrival of the 2-4th Regiment, who have been hurried up to the front, the Head-quarters Column is now quite as strong as it was before; and the loss of camp equipments, waggons, stores, &c., can easily be made up in a few weeks, so that, if it were thought necessary, we could again recross and commence our march afresh, were it not for the danger of leaving a large disaffected native population close on our borders, and our inability to prevent raids being made into Natal by the small tribes of turbulent Zulus adjacent to the Tugela. Therefore, all we have to do is to remain carefully on the defensive until the arrival of our reinforcements from home, and then we shall be able to leave a sufficient force in the Colony itself, as well as increase the strength of each Column by two regiments. After what has occurred it is useless to deny the fact that the native contingents are a failure, except those who are mounted. Therefore, when the campaign is recommenced, no dependence should be placed on them for any other purposes than scouting, fatigue parties, and cave and bush hunting."

Note. —I have somewhat anticipated events by giving Meshla Kwa's brief accounts of the subsequent battles at Zlobani and Kambula, hereinafter to be described. But I deemed it preferable to leave the Zulu's description, mainly of Isandwhlana, complete as given.

CHAPTER XI

I MUST NOW, however, show what had occurred elsewhere, in the meantime. While the Head-Quarters No. 8 and No. 2 Columns were going through such vicissitudes, the other Columns, Nos. 1, 4 and 5, were carrying out their preconcerted plans. To begin with No. 1, viz., that under the command of Colonel Pearson. The first care was to establish a frontier post at Fort Pearson, on an almost inaccessible height on the Natal side of the Lower Tugela River, about four miles from its mouth. Several days were then spent in making the necessary arrangements for crossing into Zululand. On January the 11th a punt was got ready and communication thoroughly established with the other side; but owing to the state of the river, and some difficulties about the waggons, two days, the 12th and 18th, were occupied in getting the two Divisions of the Column across. This was done entirely without opposition of any kind being offered, although the enemy were close by, in parties of varying strength. Another small earthwork, named Fort Tenedos, was then established on the Zulu bank of the river, and the leading Division started off on its first march into the enemy's country on Saturday, the 18th, being followed next day by the rear part of the Column, leaving only a detachment of the Naval Brigade to garrison the forts. Cavalry reconnoissances were made daily, and the ground in front was thoroughly felt before each advance. The Inyoni, a small stream about ten miles off, was reached on the first day, and the Umsindusi, which flows into the Amatikulu river nearer the sea, on the second. The third day's march brought the Column to the Amatikulu, where the bushy country commences; and greater care was then taken, as it was known that a large force was marching from the King's kraal to that of Sequakeni, near Etshowi, ta oppose their farther advance, and that it numbered from 6,000 to 10,000 fighting men. Early on the morning of the 22nd (the same day that was so fatal to No. 3 Column) the head of the first Division had just crossed the Inyezane river, and was proceeding with breakfast, during a short halt, when they were attacked by a large force of the enemy, who, having chosen their position, were lying in wait for our advance. The various descriptions given of this fight differ so materially that I content myself by referring to Colonel Pearson's official reports. (Vide Appendix C.) At any rate, the result was that the enemy were thoroughly beaten, and fled in all directions. It appeared from the statement of a captured prisoner—a High Chief of Cetywayo's—that a Zulu impi of 6,000, consisting of the Umxapu, Umdhlanefu, and the Ingulubi regiments, and several small tribes of the district, had received orders to watch the crossing of the Tugela by the British troops, and then to draw them on to a place called Inyezane (where they had always been victorious hitherto), beyond which they were on no account to allow the troops to pass. They acted up to their instructions, so far as to allow the troops to get to the chosen spot, but then, unfortunately for their little scheme, Colonel Pearson and only part of his Column beat them completely on their own ground, under every disadvantage, in two hours and a half, killing over 350, and wounding hundreds besides. On the same day that this was taking place, a large Commissariat reserve of eighty waggons left Fort Pearson, escorted by three companies of the 99th Regiment, under Colonel Ely; but they were halted on the Amatikulu a few days afterwards, to await the coming of a further escort, sent down by Colonel Pearson from Etshowi. The gallant Colonel had decided upon entrenching himself for the present at the mission station of that name, and was there encamped with his whole Column, having entered the place on the day after his successful engagement at Inyezane.

Colonel Ely reached Etshowi in safety, and on the 27th an escort of two companies 3rd "Buffs," two companies 99th, and one of the N. N. contingent, under Major Coates, with fifty waggons, having been sent back, arrived on the Tugela. They reported the road quite clear; but that there were numbers of Zulus in the bush surrounding Etshowi. The news of the disaster to the third Column reached Colonel Pearson on the 28th; and next day it was decided to hold the position, and send back the mounted forces and Native Contingent. Thus the food and other supplies might be made to suffice, so as to enable Colonel Pearson to hold the place, even if besieged, for at least a period of two months. At midnight on Wednesday, the 29th, the natives and mounted forces reached the Lower Tugela Drift on their return, having come through in one day by a forced march. Some, in fact, took only nine hours. A good deal was said, and is still thought, about the extraordinarily loose way in which this march was conducted, which made it resemble a retreat more than anything else. As indicative of this I give the following extract from a letter which is most interesting:—

"Lower Tugela Drift, Thursday, Jan, 30, 1879.

"Here we are back in Natal, minus all our baggage, pots, clothes, and food. In fact, we have nothing but what we stand up in. On Tuesday, at twelve a.m., news reached Etshowi that the whole Zulu army might be expected to attack the Column at any moment. Colonel Pearson decided to send back all the mounted troops, under Major Barrow, and the Native Contingent, and to hold the Etshowi Fort. The waggons were placed inside the entrenchments, all our ammunition, with the exception of seventy rounds per man, was handed over to the Infantry, and we left six companies of Buffs, four companies of the 99th, the Royal Artillery, Naval Brigade, and Engineers, four guns, Gatling, and rocket apparatus, in all about 1,200 men. The fort would be finished in twenty-four hours after we left,

Cetewayo, chief of the Zulus.

and every effort was being made to strengthen it. They have two months' food in hand. 'We were sent back; first, to protect the banks of the Tugela; second, because our horses could not be taken into the fort; and lastly, because of the difficulty of feeding the Native Contingent, and supplying the mounted troops with forage for horses. The spare stock of forage and tent bags, &c., was taken to strengthen the fort. The whole Zulu army won't take it, nor do I think they will try. We made a forced march, leaving Etshowi at 2.15 p.m., and reaching the drift at 10.30 p.m. No enemy had appeared before Etshowi. If the Mounted Police troops and Native Contingent had left together at 5 p.m., properly organised, and marched in proper order, our natives would have better understood the meaning of the movement. After the battle of the Inyezane, they were full of confidence, and ready to do anything; but such a march as theirs of Tuesday night was calculated to create an erroneous impression in their minds, and it will take some time to reassure them. In their present disorganised state there will be a little trouble to get them together again, and a longer time still to inspire confidence. The volunteer corps also feel the effects of the forced march. Barrow's horse came with us, and we are about 330 strong. There are no Zulus within miles of the Lower Drift. In my opinion they are concentrating their forces on the Columns. There was a large body of Zulus in the Umhlatuse Bush and Valley; we reconnoitred them, and saw every sign of such being the case."

After this time the Zulus of the neighbouring tribes, strengthened by a small impi from the King's kraal, surrounded and laid a kind of siege to Etshowi, rendering communication difficult. Only native runners were able to have even the slightest chance of getting through; and even these became very chary of offering to make the attempt after several had tried and been killed. It was not until the system of flashing signals by the Heliograph was arranged at both ends that anything like constant communication could be maintained. A full account of what occurred at this fort between the arrival of the Column in Etshowi and its relief on April the 6th will be found farther on, in the chapter following my account of the march and doings of the relief column which I accompanied.

CHAPTER XII

THERE REMAIN now only two other Columns, the movements of which have to be accounted for: No. 4, under Colonel Evelyn Wood, V.C., C.B., and No. 5, commanded by Colonel Rowlands, V.C., C.B. Of the latter, as it was intended to keep Secocoeni and other neighbouring predatory petty chiefs in order, and protect that part of the Transvaal against any inroads of the Zulus, it will suffice to say that its Head-quarters were at Derby, with a detachment at Luneburg; and that it did not advance from these posts, excepting to prevent disturbances in the district. It consisted of the 80th Regiment, the Swazie Levy, under Captains Fairlie and MacLeod, and several irregular corps of horse and foot. In regard to No. 4, Colonel Wood, having formed his Column at Utrecht by the first days of January, established a camp and laager at Balte's Spruit, about six miles from the Blood River; and then moved on to the boundary on Saturday, January 4th, leaving two companies of the 18th and two guns at Balte's Spruit, where large Commissariat stores were being established. The river being too high to cross, and the drifts requiring repair, a camp was formed near Conference Hill (destined to remain until the end). On their arrival everything seemed still, and nothing was to be seen but a few Zulus and some cattle on Bemba's Kop. On the following Monday, January 6th, the troops crossed in two divisions, the 18th Regiment, two guns Royal Artillery, and Native Contingent at the new drift, and the 80th, with the Frontier Light Horse and the Dutch Volunteers, at the upper one. A patrol was sent inland, and saw great numbers of cattle, herded by bodies of armed Zulus; information was also obtained of large numbers of the enemy being en route for the King's kraal. Nothing of importance occurred there until the 10th, when all the mounted men and natives were ordered out, under the Brigadier, to open up communication with our Head-quarters Column, which was effected next day. They found all kraals deserted, and few Zulus about; they succeeded in capturing on their return about 4,000 cattle, 2,000 sheep, goats and several horses. These were sent on to Utrecht immediately after they reached the camp at Blood River; where, meanwhile, on the 8th, news had been received that the Zulu King had refused to take any notice of the ultimatum, and that large forces of the enemy were assembled near Sirayo's and the White Umvoloosi, to oppose the further advance of Nos. 8 and 4 Columns. During the next few days Umbemba, a neighbouring chief, surrendered with his family and cattie, and was removed to Utrecht. Messages were also sent to Seketwayo and Oham, to obtain their submission, but with no result. Operations in woodcutting were also carried out daily by large fatigue parties, as firewood would be very difficult to obtain along the route intended to be taken by No. 4 Column. On the 15th a large cavalry patrol went out towards the kraals of Seketwayo, Bouza and Umnatie, situated between the White Umvoloosi and Bevaan Rivers. Their kraals were found entirely deserted, but at Bevaan the patrol came suddenly upon a large impi of the enemy, about 8,000 strong, and had to retire after an exchange of shots. Next day, being reinforced by 250 of the Frontier Light Horse, a reconnoissance in force was made to the position held by the enemy, and after a good deal of skirmishing, in which several Zulus were killed, the party returned unmolested to camp, having seen nothing of the impi itself, except their spoor leading to the Bagulusini military kraal. On the 17th the Column was moved on to Wolf Spruit, having several skirmishes with small bodies of the enemy along the road; and thence marched on to Tinta's kraal, where a fort was built near the White Umvoloosi. A small force having been left here as a garrison, Colonel Wood moved on farther to the Zuinguin Nek, and reported officially on the 23rd as follows:—

"Lieutenant-Colonel Buller, with Mr. Piet Uys, reconnoitred the Zuinguin range on the 20th, but were unable to reach the eastern end, near Umbemba's kraal, being opposed by about 1,000 Zulus. That day No. 4 Column reached the Umvoloosi, and Tinta, uncle of Seketwayo, came to me out of a cave to which I had gone, about six miles east of Umvoloosi River. In the evening I sent back Tinta's people, with a convoy of waggons, about seventy, escorted by one company 90th L.I. Later, hearing more Zulus had crossed the Umvoloosi, I reinforced the escort. On the 21st we built a stone laager fort; left all superfluous stores over one week's supply, and crossing the river halted (m the left bank, and at midnight on the 21st and 22nd, leaving one company 1-18th L.I. and the company 90th, which had just arrived from Blood River (marching 34 miles in 25 hours), at Fort Tinta, we started on patrol; Colonel Buller, with the Dutchmen and two guns, marching up the right bank of the Umvoloosi, while the 90th and 1st Battalion of Wood's Irregulars made direct for the range of the Zuinguin, so as to strike it about three miles from the Umvoloosi. Though until 3 a.m. it was very dark, and we passed over difficult country, guided by some Dutchmen, the 90th arrived at the summit about 6 a.m., just as Colonel Buller ascended by the Gaz-Tad line. After resting for two hours we moved towards a few hundred Zulus who were on the south-eastern summit of the range. These retired hastily, leaving about 250 head of cattle and 400 sheep and goats, which were brought back into a camp which had been formed by Colonel Gilbert, who marched at 3 a.m. on the 22nd from the Umvoloosi River. From the eastern extremity of the range we saw under the Zlobani Mountain, near Umbemba's kraal, about 4,000 Zulus drilling: they formed a circle, a triangle, and a square with a partition. They were moving later, so far as we could see in the dusk, up the Zlobani Mountain. The patrol reached camp at 7 p.m., having been under arms, the infantry carrying 100 rounds, nineteen hours. One gun-limber was broken, it being let down by ropes over a heavy steep hill, but we hope to repair it today. Our movements could not be possible without the aid of Mr. Piet Uys and his men, whose local knowledge is invaluable. I propose to move on to-morrow, weather permitting, towards the Bagulusini kraal, about eighteen miles distant. The Zlobani Mountain is part of the Ityentika range."

After this no news was received from No. 4 Column until the 26th, when it was known that a Zulu army had been sent against it, and after a short though sharp engagement had been beaten and retired precipitately, about 600 of our men being engaged against 6,000 of the enemy. Colonel Wood also reported that he had heard during this engagement of the disaster that had occurred to No. 3 Column, and he was retiring in consequence to Kambula, a position at the foot of the Ingata-Ka-Hawane Mountain, so as the better to cover Utrecht, and yet enable him to make raids to the north-east when necessary. It did not take long for the Column to establish itself there, and then the old routine of patrols and harassing the enemy recommenced. On February 1st Lieutenant-Colonel Buller, C.B., with a force of eight officers and 106 non-commissioned officers and men of the Frontier Light Horse, under Captain Barton, Coldstream Guards, and 88 Dutch burghers, under Mr. Piet Uys, advanced, by a forced march, attacked and destroyed the Bagulusini military kraal, consisting of 260 huts, and captured 270 head of cattle. The Zulus occupying it fled in all directions, with a loss of six killed, and the force travelled sixty miles that day. Colonel Wood attached great importance to this action, as that kraal had been a rallying point for the enemy for some time past.

As their stay at Kambula was likely to be prolonged, until the 3rd Column was reinforced and able to assume the offensive again. Colonel Wood strengthened his position by moving higher up and constructing a new strong earthwork fort on the top of a conical hill, commanding the approach to the camp (which was by a small narrow ridge) and a view of the country for twenty miles around. The angles were also bastioned to mount artillery, and the guns then commanded three sides of the position. At the same time a strong waggon laager was made a short distance off. Meanwhile, the little force was not idle, but constantly scoured the country, and harassed the people for twenty-five miles round. The effective strength of Wood's brigade was at that time:—Royal Artillery, 105; Royal Engineers, 11; 13th Regiment, 540; 90th Regiment, 704; Frontier Light Horse, 212; Mounted Infantry, 8; Burgher Volunteers, 51; Native Escort, 19; Native Contingent, 1,065—total 2,715. Subsequently to the destruction of the camp at Isandwhlana, it was decided to strengthen Wood's Column with the greater part of Rowland's force, consisting of the 80th, Weatherley's, Raaf's and Ferreira's Horse, and the Kaffrarian Riflemen; which was done by the end of the month. Colonel Rowland going back to Pretoria, as commandant in the Transvaal. An important patrol went away on the 11th February, consisting of 70 Frontier Light Horse, under Captain Barton, 30 Burghers and 300 of Wood's Native Irregulars, under Piet-Uys, senior, Lieutenant Colonel Butler, C.B., commanding; and succeeded in capturing five hundred head of cattle, after a slight engagement. Several other patrols were made to Makatee's Kop, and Luneberg, all resulting similarly in the dispersion of the enemy and capture of cattle. The Zulu chief, Oham, after long and troublesome negotiations," surrendered to Captain McLeod, at Derby early in March, and was brought home to Utrecht. Nothing else of interest occurred until the 12th March, when news of the disaster at the Intombi River startled every one. From the report of Lieutenant H. H. Harward, who escaped and rode into Luneberg with the news, leaving his men to follow afterwards, it appeared that being awake during the night, he heard a shot fired in the distance; he got up and ordered the sentry to arouse the detachment on the side of the Intombi Drift nearest Luneberg, and to apprise Captain Moriarty of the &c., and ask for his orders; these were that the escort should remain under arms. He afterwards found that this shot was fired about 4 a.m. He then retired to his tent close by, waited, dressed, and about an hour afterwards heard, " Guard turn out." He instantly turned out and saw, as the fog lifted, a dense mass of Zulus about two hundred yards from the waggon laager, extending all across the valley with a front of some two or three miles apparently. His men (35 of all ranks) were at once put under a waggon near the tents, and directed their fire on the flanks of the enemy, who were endeavouring to surround the waggon laager on the other side of the river. He next observed that the enemy had gained full ' possession of the camp, and were driving off the cattle. The remainder of the escort were retiring on the river, which was full of human beings. On seeing this he directed the fire entirely with the view to covering the retreat of the men. This fire was well sustained, and enabled many to get over the river alive. The enemy were now assegaing the men in the water and also ascending the banks of the river close to them; for fear, therefore, of the men being stabbed under the waggon, and to enable them to retire before their ammunition should be exhausted, he ordered them to retire steadily, and only just in time to avoid a rush of Zulus to their late position. The Zulus came on in dense masses and fell upon the men, who being already broken gave way, and a hand to hand fight ensued. He then endeavoured to rally his men, but they were too much scattered, and finding re-formation impossible, he mounted his horse and galloped into Luneberg at utmost speed, and reported all that had taken place. The strength of the enemy was estimated at not less than four thousand men.

The sketch attached to Lieutenant Harward's report shows the position of the camp on either side of the river, indicating tents, waggons, &c. The cattle were inside the laager.

Major Tucker, 80th Regiment, commanding at Luneberg at the time, sent in the following official report on this affair:—"I have to report, for the information of His Excellency the Lieutenant-General Commanding, that on the 7th instant a party consisting of 104, all ranks, under command of Captain D. B. Moriarty, 80th Regiment, left Luneberg with a view of escorting and bringing into Luneberg eighteen waggons, variously loaded, on their way from Derby. Some of these waggons were reported as broken down on little Intombi River, and Captain Moriarty's orders were to bring these waggons or their loads into Luneberg, but if this was impossible, owing to the fearful state of the road, he was to laager his waggons at the Intombi River and wait until he should be able to cross. Daring the 8th, 9th, and 10th, the river was so very high from the constant rains, that nothing could be done. On the 11th the river lowered some four feet, but the stream was so rapid nothing could be got across. A light raft consisting of planks and empty barrels had been made, but would carry very little weight. On the morning of the 12th about 6.30 Lieutenant Harward arrived at Luneberg from the Intombi River, reporting that the camp and waggons were in possession of the enemy.

"As I had no mounted men under my command, I at once ordered all the horses belonging to the officers of the regiment to be saddled, and proceeded to the camp at the Intombi River, leaving orders for 150 men of the 80th Regiment to follow. On approaching Meyers' Mission Station we observed, extending for about two miles under the brow of Umbeline's Hill, a long thick line of Zulus making their way eastward. I computed the body of the enemy in view at not less than four thousand; there were undoubtedly many more; as we could see no cattle being driven, these Zulus were evidently making a hurried retreat.

Arriving at the Intombi River, I found the laager completely wrecked, the cattle being taken and the contents of the waggons strewn about the place, and from the bank of the river we could see the dead bodies of our men lying about on the opposite side. On the arrival of the 80th from Luneberg, the bodies were collected and interred on this side of the river.

"I regret to report that Captain D. B. Moriarty was killed, together with Civil Surgeon Cobbin. Out of a total of one hundred and four officers and men of the 80th Regiment, forty are known to be killed, twenty are still missing, and forty-four have escaped to Luneberg—one man slightly wounded. In addition to the above, Mr. Whittington, waggon conductor, a volunteer named Campbell, late of Ferreira's Horse, and a native driver, have been killed. With regard to the twenty men reported missing of the 80th Regiment I fear most of them have been drowned or assegaied in the river, which was running swiftly, and was exceedingly high at the time. A list of the waggon-employees will be sent as soon as possible.

"It is impossible to ascertain the loss of the enemy. Twenty-five bodies were found at the scene of action, principally on the bank of the river, and doubtless many more were drowned. Two Zulus have been taken prisoners, both wounded severely. Prom one I gathered the information that the 'Impi' which attacked the laager was headed by Umbeline, who was instigated to bring this force by Manyanyoba. This prisoner distinctly stated twice that there were nine thousand Zulus present, and that they were collected from all parts of the surrounding country; he further stated that Umnyamana was asked to assist, but refused to send his men.

"From all information I can gather on the subject, the camp was evidently surprised, the enemy taking advantage of the mist to approach the camp unseen. I consider the men fought well and bravely, but were completely outnumbered. The small party under Lieutenant Harward, on this side of the river, rendered to a hopeless cause valuable assistance, in covering the retreat across the river of such men as were able to reach it; and I am of opinion that but for those on this side of the Intombi River, not one man would have escaped, and that had the escort been double its number, the result would have been the same. The river having subsided about mid-day, I was enabled to bring across the rockets, ammunition and powder, untouched by the enemy." Major Tucker's official return of killed and missing is given at Appendix D.

The news of this reverse, as may be supposed, coming so soon after that of Isandwhlana, made the column at Kambula doubly careful, and more than ever anxious to get a fair chance at the enemy. In order the more effectually to complete their line of communication and check the inroads of marauding parties of Zulus, Commandant Schermbrucker and his corps of Kaffrarian Riflemen were sent to Doom Berg about equidistant from Dundee and Balte's Spruit, and so in direct communication with Helpmakaar and Ladysmith. On March 23rd, over a hundred men of Baker's Horse arrived with a large convoy from Utrecht; and a large mounted force of over four hundred left the camp for a visit to the Intombi district, and with the intention of hunting up Umbeline and Manyanyoba. A contingent of Wood's Irregulars and one hundred of Oham's men accompanied them. Colonel Wood himself commanded, and was accompanied by Colonel Buller and Mr. P. Uys, senr.; and this brings us up to the disaster which ensued at the Zlobani mountain; subsequently followed by the brilliant success at Kambula camp itself. The events of these two engagements were not thoroughly known for some time afterwards, and only reached Lord Chelmsford just after his victory at Gingihlovo. I will, therefore, leave the account of both events until I have brought my own personal experiences up to that date.

CHAPTER XIII

After Lord Chelmsford had made the best arrangements possible under the circumstances for the organisation of the Head-quarters Column, and the protection of the Border; and the towns of the colony had each done what they could towards preparing themselves for any emergencies; there was nothing else to be done, but patiently await the arrival of the reinforcements which had been sent for at once. As it was evident there would be little chance of any effective operations being undertaken for nearly two months by the Head-quarters Column, to which I had hitherto attached myself throughout the campaign, I resolved to turn my attention elsewhere, and make myself as far as possible personally acquainted with the movements of the other Columns; and also to make a rapid run through the frontier districts, in order to see for myself the actual condition of matters along the Border. As events occurred, however, I was only enabled partially to realise this projected trip. My first point was Etshowi, for a visit to Colonel Pearson's Column No. 1: and this arrangement of my route was primarily induced by the fact, that Lord Chelmsford himself had preceded me, with a similar object in view. I left Pieter Maritzburg for Durban, on Friday, 7th February. At Pine-town—the sanatorium of Natal, beautifully situated about twelve miles inland from Port Durban—I noticed a very significant indication of the feeling of insecurity which was so generally prevalent during the first few weeks after the disaster at Isandwhlana. Steps were being taken, under official orders, for converting the hotel into a laager in case of a Zulu raid. An entrenchment was being constructed and an outer barricade or stockade, formed of railway sleepers, by way of temporary fortification. This precaution was un-questionably prudent and wise, though happily, as it turned out, superfluous, owing to the inaction of the Zulus. I found Durban full of up-country people, many of whom even took their departure subsequently by the mail-steamers for Capetown. An epidemic of this kind was very infectious about this period; but he would have been a bold man who should have ventured to assign a cause in the scare about Zulu raids. As a matter of course, the most prominent subject of interest was the reinforcement of our troops and a material change had come over the views as to the best mode of effecting that desirable object, arising mainly out of the distrust in our native levies. Colonel Lonsdale, having disbanded his 3rd Regiment, N.N.C., had gone to Cape Colony, with some of his officers, in order to raise in their stead five troops of white volunteers and three of Fingoes as being far more reliable. Active measures were also in progress to obtain mounted men for Captain Baker's Light Horse, and especially for the Head-quarters Column. The U.R.M.S, Natal brought from the Cape small drafts for the 2-4th, 88th, and 99th Regiments, all of whom were at once sent up to the front. It will readily be understood that the time was too early to expect the arrival of any large bodies of troops as reinforcements. It is, however, singular to note that a rumour was current that two British regiments had left England on the 15th of January. This was of course without foundation— excepting in so far as the "wish was father to the thought"—for there could be no reason to suppose that reinforcements had been specially requested, or would be despatched by the Home Government, prior to the arrival in England of the news of the disaster at Isandwhlana. That, as I calculated, would take place on Saturday, 8th February; and even then some tune would necessarily be required for preparations and outfit of the troops and transports, &c., intelligence of which could only reach us by telegram about a fortnight later at the very earliest.

Of the naval squadron on the coast, the Tenedos had gone to Simon's Bay for repairs, leaving her Naval Brigade for frontier defence; and the Active, with Rear-Admiral Sullivan, C.B., on board, was away up the coast of Zululand, towards St. Lucia Bay. H.M.S. Boadicea, recently arrived at the Gape from Home, was on her way to Natal, to land a Naval Brigade for service with the troops. The latest news from Colonel Pearson was under date the 8th February, and reported him to be comfortably established at Etshowi, with a force numbering 1,785 in all, of whom 1,860 were combatants. The Kaffir runners, who had come through with this news, reported that large bodies of the Zulus were being massed together between Etshowi and the Tugela. This showed that there would be great difficulty in keeping open the communications, even with mounted men, still more with runners only; or unless the heliograph were established; and so it proved subsequently. As regards the remainder of our Columns I may note that Colonel Wood's strength was reported as consisting of 89 officers and 1,668 non-commissioned officers and men, with 750 native levies, making a total of 2,507 of all arms. The remainder of Colonel Glyn's Column, No. 3, divided between Helpmakaar and Rorke's Drift would number nearly 2,000 white troops, all the natives, as stated, having fled or been disbanded.

The General, in person, attended by Colonel Crealock and Major Gossett, left Durban on Tuesday, 11th February, en route for Fort Pearson and the Border, in order to complete the arrangements then in contemplation to re-open communications with Colonel Pearson, and to despatch a relief-convoy of provisions, stores, &c., for Fort Etshowi. It was officially understood that Colonel Law, R.A., had been ordered down from Helpmakaar to take the command, and that a dash might be made to relieve Pearson. This intelligence hastened my movements, as I was anxious to get to the front and accompany the relief-column. I therefore started on the 12th, and was two days on the road, noting the defensive preparations made at various points. Thus, crossing the Umgeni River, four miles out, and the Umhlanga River, ten miles farther, I found the residents all prepared for concentration to combine in resistance to any Zulu inroad. Three miles farther at Verulam, a pretty strong laager was formed. At the crossing of the Tongaati River, eight miles off, and the Umslahli River, another eleven miles, where John Dunn has his settlement, similar arrangements prevailed, and frequent communications were maintained. At the Umvoti river, six miles farther, the American mission station is the centre of a flourishing district; here, the church, over-looking the Drift, and a large sugar mill on the opposite bank, were put in a tolerable state of defence. This place would have been rather exposed in case of actual attack; as it is near the fork, where the bye-road branches off to the left to Thring's Post on the Tugela (and formerly the only road to Mapomulo) by which a Zulu force might have entered the colony without approaching Fort Pearson and Stanger. This point, it struck me at the time, had been somewhat overlooked and neglected. It is true that the Natives Border Guard, under Captain Lucas, were extended along the banks of the Tugela from Kranzkop down to its mouth; and they would have been the first to run And give the alarm if a crossing were attempted, whereby at any rate timely notice of danger would have been given.

Stanger, forty-six miles from Durban, is the most important station on the coast-road. Here everything was in readiness; a strong laager had been formed, surrounding the Government buildings, and one of the commissariat buildings, in a very commanding position to the right of the road, had also been fortified; both were well-provisioned and provided with everything requisite for a prolonged defence, in case of attack. The garrison comprised two companies of the 88th, just arrived from Durban, relieving two of the 99th, sent on to Fort Pearson; and with them were also the Isipingo Mounted Rifles. Moreover a building occupied by Surgeon-Major Tarrant and his medical staff, as a base Auxiliary Hospital, and situated on a hill a little way out of Stanger on the Tugela road, had also been fortified, and was held by a half company of the 88th.

The crossing of the Monoti river, about eight miles from Stanger, was assigned to the 2nd Regiment, N.N.G. as a recruiting station, and for the organisation of the natives for the defence of the frontier. Eleven miles farther on, or sixty-four miles from Durban, the Lower Tugela Drift was commanded by Fort Pearson on the Natal side and Fort Tenedos on the other. I found on my arrival that Lord Chelmsford, on his inspection of the latter, had condemned it as untenable and ordered it to be evacuated. But as it was subsequently found that it could be made secure by throwing up traverses and other defensive works, Fort Tenedos was re-occupied, and garrisoned by two companies of the 3rd Buffs, under Captains Wyld and Macclear, the Tenedos Naval Brigade, and twenty mounted infantry, under the command of Lieutenant Kingscote, R.N. Fort Pearson was held by seven companies of the 99th Regiment, under Major Coates, one hundred mounted infantry, under Major Barrow, and the men of the commissariat and transport corps. On the Tugela itself, besides the Native Border Guard, distributed along its course, there were at MacDonald's Farm, about eleven miles up, the Stanger Mounted Rifles; and the Natal Hussars, with the Durban, Victoria, and Alexander Mounted Rifles, stationed at the important drift or crossing known as Thring's Post, twenty-three miles away, and about half the way to Kranzkop, which is forty-five miles from Fort Pearson. Such was the disposition of the frontier defence, during the critical interval that elapsed before the arrival of adequate reinforcements. All the reports from the Border were to the effect that large bodies of die enemy were encamped behind the hills on the Zulu or left bank of the Tugela; and it frequently occurred that parties came down to try the depth of the river, and ascertain if it was low enough to permit of a crossing; and they would even carry on a running conversation with the Border Guard Natives on the Natal side, chaffing them and saying "they meant to come down and pay John Dunn a visit, and eat sugar at Umvoti." By Monday the 17th February several doubtful questions were cleared up, so that I found a change in my own plans would be necessary.

Lord Chelmsford saw reason to abandon for the time all idea of sending a relief-column to Etshowi, considering the difficulties of the road, the strength of the intercepting enemy, and the inadequacy of our own force. This project—which had, by many experienced men, been deemed impracticable from the first—was therefore reluctantly postponed until the arrival of the expected reinforcements, a delay of at least a month, and, indeed, longer as it turned out. The General consequently resolved to return to Durban; but before his departure he held an inspection of all the troops in garrison at the two forts; and in the course of a brief address he took occasion to refer to the recent disaster at Isandwhlana; stating it as his "firm conviction that the troops there present would have been more than sufficient to have repulsed the attack of the 18,000 or 20,000 Zulus reported to have been engaged in the attack, if only they had been kept together, and had not lost their formation, when at a distance from the camp, where they could not renew their ammunition when exhausted; but even then, they had their bayonets and knew how to use them. To that alone, he thought, must be attributed the sad loss, and entire slaughter of so many companies of the 1-24th and 2-24th, than, whom Her Majesty the Queen had never possessed better or braver soldiers. He therefore exhorted the troops he was addressing never to underrate or despise their enemy, but to stop their advance by close, accurate and steady firing; and on no account to break their ranks, but to maintain their ground and formation, fighting it out, if need be, back to back with the bayonet. They were doubtless eager to advance and meet the enemy, but he must ask them to be patient, as they could not have the opportunity just yet awhile." Immediately after the review, Lord Chelmsford left for Durban, attended by Colonel Crealock and Major Gossett.

The General's policy of inaction at this period, remaining quietly on the defensive, and merely making all such arrangements as were best calculated to secure the Border against serious danger from hostile incursions, was subjected at the time to a good deal of adverse criticism; but I am thoroughly convinced by all I saw and heard that it was, under all the circumstances the best possible course. "Why this cowardly inactivity!" was the common remark, our force being still not much inferior, numerically, to that with which the campaign had been commenced. This counter-opinion, as will be admitted by all who knew the facts and were qualified to judge, was equally devoid of good foundation and mischievous, as tending to prevent that full and implicit confidence in our commander that was so essential on the part of all the troops, regular and colonial, under his command. The defeat of Isandwhlana had rendered it doubly necessary to avoid any rash or inadequate steps, and to provide that all future movements should be so organised, and carried on with such numerical strength, as to avoid any similar check, and to ensure success. Hence the wisdom of being contented simply to hold the positions already taken up, to guard the Colony against Border raids, and wait until the reinforcements on the way should have rendered it possible to raise the Columns to such a strength as should surely overcome all possible resistance of the Zulu enemy—a policy which was afterwards crowned with success.

CHAPTER XIV

DURING MY stay on the Tugela, on this occasion, I was able to make excursions on horseback to various districts in the vicinity of the frontier, and among others to MacDonald's Farm, and the month of the Nonoto River. This river is about one hundred and twenty yards wide and deep in proportion; the estuary is a fine expanse of water, running some distance inland, but there is an immense sandbank forming a bar at the entrance. The banks are very fertile, but show in places the devastation caused by the nightly visits of hippopotami, which frequent this place. These amphibians are now very scarce in Natal, and indeed I only know of one other locality where they are still to be found. Alligators swarm everywhere; and one such very large and ancient saurian had for many years past frequented the drift on the Tugela road, snapping up such unconsidered trifles as dogs, sheep, and even an occasional Kafir; he had, however, departed this life, but little regretted, some short time previously to my visit. On my journey I passed Fynney's and John Dunn's huts; and at Stanger, while at "tiffin" with Major Walker, 99th Regiment (in command of that post), I was fortunate enough to fall in with that much maligned and little understood individual, John Dunn himself. He is of medium height, strongly built, forty-five years old, and has all the appearance of being just what he is, a thoroughly seasoned colonist. His manner is inclined to be abrupt, and at times he is absent-minded, as even while his eyes seem intent on your face, his thoughts appear to stray elsewhere. He had at that time, of course, a heavy responsibility on his shoulders, and for him much depended on the course and issue of the war. He had but just undertaken to give the General every assistance in his power; and in consequence, so soon as the reinforcements arrived, and the relief-column started for Etshowi, John Dunn was officially appointed chief of the Intelligence Department attached to that force, and placed in fall command of a body of Native Scouts, raised from among his own followers. We had a long and interesting conversation on the situation of affairs in general, and on the protection of the frontier in particular. An account having recently appeared of statements made by him when interviewed by a colonial newspaper correspondent, he admitted to me its substantial accuracy, but said he had not intended it to be made use of as coming from him. At partings he promised to communicate with me occasionally; and, indeed, I afterwards obtained from him much useful and interesting information.

I may here note, that throughout my border peregrinations I found, to my surprise, that there was far less scare on the subject of Zulu raids than prevailed farther inland and at the chief towns, Durban and Pieter Maritzburg. Most of the families of farmers and planters within a few miles of the Tugela were living quietly, pursuing their ordinary avocations. They were certainly prepared for active resistance or flight, if rendered necessary; but they not only felt pretty sure of receiving ample and timely notice of any attempt by the Zulus to cross the river in force; they were also full of confidence in the security afforded by the disposition of our troops all along the front line. In one case, at Darnell, situated on the short cut from Stanger to the Drift, I found my friend away on active service with the Mounted Volunteer Corps, to which he belonged. His wife, however, with her six children, the eldest a girl of sixteen, with two boys next in age, remained at home all through the war, although there was not a white man about the place, and no males but Coolie servants and the Kafirs on the farm. Once only were they frightened into taking refuge in the laager at Stanger, but happily the alarm turned out to be false.

'A sketch from Fort Ekowe'. The Graphic, May 24th 1879

My stay at Fort Pearson and on the frontier was cut short by the receipt of a telegram, which compelled me to give up my intended Border trip and return as quickly as possible to Pieter Maritzburg. Before leaving I learnt that a point higher up the river, Kranzkop, had always been regarded as the weakest along the frontier line of defence. Close at hand is the only drift across the Tugela in that vicinity, and it has always hitherto been a favourite crossing-place with the Zulus. Here were encamped the remainder of poor Colonel Durnford's Mounted Native Regiment, under the command of Captain Cherry, in a position quite the reverse of safe; but an earthwork, named after him, had recently been constructed, giving greater security, so that, with the 250 mounted men at Thring's Post, lower down, it would be impossible for the enemy to cross with impunity or unobserved, or to remain long unattacked. There can, however, be little doubt that whatever other motives might have actuated the Zulus in their abstention from an attack in force upon the Colony, one contributory cause was certainly the fear of being thus cut off; superadded to which was also the variable character of the river and the known uncertainty of crossing at the drifts. Floods are very sudden and rapid, and the water will frequently rise several feet in a few hours, so as to render the drifts impassable. Doubtless, these considerations, together with the threatening position held by Colonel Wood's column on the Blood River, the strong defence of Colonel Glyn's column at Helpmakaar and Rorke's Drift, and the inroad of Colonel Pearson, located at Fort Etshowi, all combined to influence the result, by which the Colony was left unassailed.

I remained in Maritzburg, well occupied with my letters and telegrams, until March 5th, when, having attended to everything of moment, and brought all my work up to date, I thought I would have another run up the old road to Helpmakaar and Rorke's Drift, and get as much farther as I could, until recalled to meet a confrère Mr. MacKenzie (sent out to represent the Standard with another Column), who was daily expected by the U.R.M.S. German at the Cape. His departure had been telegraphed to me previously, and I had made the necessary arrangements for him to join Colonel Wood's column as soon after his arrival as he could. This was one of the things that had brought me back from Fort Pearson so quickly, much to my regret, although of course in the interests of the paper I represented, and, for my own sake, I was glad to know another "Special" was on his way out, and would relieve me of part of the work at any rate.

CHAPTER XV

Leaving Pieter Maritzburg on the 5th I reached Grey Town next day, and went the whole way without passing a single waggon, and did not even meet any horsemen or foot passengers. The farms all seemed deserted—at any rate of their female inhabitants—but the laager at the Umvoti, although empty, bore traces of recent occupation. At "Purcell's" I fell in with Captain Ayliff, of the Native Horse, who was returning to Kranzkop with a troop of mounted natives which he had recruited from among Jantje's men at the Ixopo, a district in the S.E. of Natal, near the Umzimkulu river. They were a very serviceable-looking body of men, well mounted, and fairly equipped; and, under the immediate control of Jantje's eldest son, seemed likely to prove their worth. On my arrival at Grey Town, where I found everything perfectly quiet, I at once proceeded to the laager, and there found a change for the better in the shape of an earthwork, which had been constructed in front of one end of the laager (that facing the north), and surrounded by a deep ditch, thorn and wire entanglements, and in fact all the necessary adjuncts for receiving and treating the wily Zulu with that care and attention which is his due. This earthwork had been constructed entirely by the men of the three companies of the 4th King's Own quartered there at the time, under Major Twentyman, and reflected great credit on them, as also on the officer who superintended its erection. The laager itself had been improved by adding another layer of sand bags to the height of its original wall. They were also loopholed, and thus gave additional opportunity for treating any enemy to a warm reception. At the Commissariat and Transport Offices I found the same activity as of yore, continuing; but I missed sadly one familiar face, that of poor Griffiths (killed at Isandwhlana), who was foremost in the work of his department when I was last going that road.

At Grey Town I was joined by Commandant Cooper and officers of the 3rd N.N.C., returning to Rorke's Drift from leave at Pieter Maritzburg. We left early on Saturday, March 8, and after a short stay at Burrup's—still deserted by its owner and his family—we reached Mooi river that evening. The roads were in a dreadful state, and we had to cross the river in the punt, as it was impassable, owing to the heavy rains. Early next morning we resumed our journey, and reached Fort Bengough in the evening. This fort had been built since the affair at Isandwhlana, to strengthen the position, by the men of the 1st N.N.C. Regiment, under Major Bengough, after whom it was named. It occupied the top of a high stony kopje, about a mile off the road on the left of our old camp at Sands Spruit. The fort was oval in shape, and covered about an acre. The walls were built of stone, loopholed, and from ten to fifteen feet high. Two flanking projections were thrown out on each side from the centre, and the fort was divided internally into three divisions, each being practically impregnable. The magazine, in the centre, a fine square stone building, was erected by Captain Dellamore, R.E. The Kafirs occupied one of the end divisions, and the officers the other; but many of the latter had grass huts on the flat below, for messing and living in by day, which materially conduced to their health and comfort. Patrols from this force were constantly sent down to the Tugela river, some ten miles distant, sometimes crossing; and skirmishes have occasionally taken place in which a few Zulus were killed.

On the 10th we journeyed on to Helpmakaar, where we stayed an hour and a half for lunch. Throughout the entire route I could not help remarking the immense change that was apparent since my previous journeys up and down. Formerly, the road was lively with a crowd of traffic; it was now all but deserted. This began to be noticeable after leaving Pieter Maritzburg, and became still more so farther on; while, when once past Grey Town, there was as little traffic or company on the road as if one had been in Zululand instead of in Natal. It resulted mainly from an incident that had occurred some short time previously: in consequence of some sadden scare about a Zulu raid, all the drivers and "foreloopers," in charge of the waggons then on the way up to Rorke's Drift, deserted and fled en masse, and the Government was put to endless trouble and expense by the resulting confusion, so in order to set matters straight again they closed this route for their own use. All Government waggons thereafter proceeded by the direct route to Ladysmith, and thence through Dundee to Helpmakaar and Rorke's Drift, a considerable distance farther round. The border-road was consequently left to solitude, and used merely by officers and men on leave, going to or returning from town. Helpmakaar, like other places, was also greatly changed. I found that the old temporary fortification of mealie-sacks, biscuit-boxes, &c., &c., had given place to a strong earthwork erected round the commissariat stores, with four guns, 7-pounders, mounted on the parapets at the angles. There was a pretty large force there still, under Colonel Glynn, C.B., who had Major Clery as Staff Officer. It consisted of two companies of the 1-24th, Bainforth's and Upcher's; Colonel Harness's Battery, No. 5 Brigade, R.A.; one company of the Royal Engineers, under Captain Jones; seventy-five men of the Natal Mounted Police under Major Dartnell, and twenty-five Natal Carbineers. As we were to leave again at 8 p.m., I had not much time to spare; but I made a point of going to the little graveyard, not far distant from the fort, to look at the last resting-places of poor Franklyn of the 2-24th, and young Hay, of the Carbineers, who had only been dead a few days. There were many other graves there, all kept neatly and in good order, as well as could be done by kind hearts and willing hands, under the circumstances.

We reached Rorke's Drift early in the evening, and I felt myself again quite at home among the officers of the 2-24th, and those of the 3rd Regiment, N.N.C., among whom, I saw with pleasure, Harford, of the 99th, still remained, and be was the first to welcome me again. How that evening passed away, in talking over the past events of the campaign, may readily be imagined; and although tired, I sat up a long time with Major Black, "yarning." Our chief topic was the recent wonderful recovery of the bodies of Lieutenant Goghill, A.D.C., and Adjutant Melville, 1-24th, as well as of the missing Queen's Colour of that regiment. The Major, who had himself taken the principal part in the exploit, gave me very willingly the details of it as follows:—On the 4th of February, Major Black, accompanied by Commandant Cooper and several other officers of the Natal Native Contingent, went out in search of the body of Adjutant Melville, who was reported to have had the colours of the 1 -24th with him when last seen to cross the Buffalo. About 800 yards on the Natal side of the Buffalo river they found the bodies of Adjutant Melville and Lieutenant Coghill, A.D.C., lying among some boulders, where they had fallen. In the Buffalo river, some distance ahead (about 300 yards). Major Black recovered the colours, with the staff broken in a rather dilapidated condition. The bodies of the two late gallant officers, who had so nobly fallen and had preserved the colours, were buried, and the services of a clergyman to read the burial service were obtained. The spot where they lie side by side was then marked with a heap of stones. Major Black and his Staff of N.N.C. officers then returned to Helpmakaar, and reached that place on the night of the 4th of February. On the morning of the 5th of February a general parade was ordered, and the recovered colours were trooped in front of a general parade at Helpmakaar, when Colonel Glynn, C.B., in most touching and affectionate terms, addressed his men, and informed them that through the gallant and most praiseworthy efforts of Major Black, 2-24th Regiment, the colours of the 1-24th had been found in the Buffalo river, and that the bodies of Lieutenant Coghill and Adjutant Melville had also been recovered, and had had a most respectful burial. He said they had to thank Major Black for the recovery of their colours. The men, hereupon, burst out with acclamations, and three cheers for the gallant major, who, in reply, addressed Colonel Glynn, C.B., and the men, and said they were giving him too much praise; they had not only to thank him, but the officers of the Natal Native Contingent who accompanied him, and who also gave him most valuable assistance in recovering the bodies of his two brother officers, as well as the colours of their own gallant regiment. He said, in conclusion, he had simply done his duty. The men were then dismissed, and this episode, so gratifying to the regiment, thus ended. After this, I of course rode down next day to see the spot and to visit the graves of these two young but courageous officers, who, even in death, had shown their spirit and gallantry. Their name and fame will long dwell in the memory of their comrades and survivors, and be enshrined in the history of their country.

As at Helpmakaar, the temporary fortification, hastily erected after Isandwhlana, had been replaced by a large and strong stone wall, surrounding the whole of Rorke's House, and taking in the cattle-kraal. It seemed quite impregnable, and was loopholed all round. At the back, facing the hill, the wall was carried up two stories high, and a balcony of planking had been erected for the soldiers to stand upon. The roof had been taken off the house, which was only covered in roughly with tarpaulins. The troops then at the Drift consisted of the 2-24th, under Major Black, a detachment of Royal Engineers, ten Mounted Police, and the officers and non-commissioned officers of the two battalions of the 3rd Regiment, N.N.G., the whole were encamped outside during the day-time; but all came inside the fort after sundown, and found it close quarters. Most of the men had to lie down on the bare cold ground, and the others had nothing except tarpaulins arranged as best they could to cover them. The officers lay down under the veranda, but the house itself was used as a hospital and for the protection of the stores. When I arrived there I found over fifty men in hospital, and forty sick, while eight had died since its occupation. This did not surprise me, knowing the place as well as I did. The only wonder to me was that more had not died, especially considering that ever since the 29rd of January and up to the time of my visit, the officers and "non-coms" of the 3rd N.N.C., had been simply bivouacked out on the ledges behind the fort, without tents, tarpaulins, clothes, and even in some cases with no blankets. They had lost all their baggage and effects at Isandwhlana; and the stores for their re-equipment, by some mischance, had never reached Rorke's Drift.

Many messes had not a cooking utensil between them, therefore it may easily be imagined what grumbling there had been among these officers and men, since their natives had been disbanded, and they were kept idle all the time, and not allowed to leave the Drift, except in small parties, on leave for a few days. I was pleased to hear that some alterations were about to be made to remedy all this, and even before I left, all those among the "non-coms" who could speak the Kafir language, along with a few officers, were drafted off to form a mounted corps in connection with Wood's Column. A new stone fort was in course of construction on a slight eminence overlooking the punt, and it was being hurried on so as to provide a change of quarters, as the old place was becoming very unhealthy. This new fort was called Fort Melville in memory of the officer of the 1-24th of that name, who died so gallantly trying to save the colours of his regiment. From this station there was no difficulty in perceiving that all the waggons at Isandwhlana were not yet removed. And hopes were freely expressed that a party might soon be made up to penetrate to the scene of the disaster. Every one was willing to go, but orders had been given that no one was to attempt it without permission.

The day following my arrival I received notice of the German having reached the Gape, and as it would take me as long to get to Durban by road, as the steamer would take coming round by sea, if not longer, I had no option but to again hurry off. Before leaving I bespoke a kind reception for my confrere, who would ride that way on his road to Colonel Wood's Column; and then, receiving many commissions of all sorts and sizes for execution at Pieter Maritzburg and Durban, I started back on Tuesday morning before breakfast, haying the pleasure of Captain Symons' company as far as Helpmakaar. We took the short cut up the mountain, past Vermaak's, and rode the distance in two hours, which was very good work. On my arrival I made straight for the camp of the "Natal Carbineers" lunched with Lieutenant Royston, and then went round to the different tents and chatted with my many friends in the corps. Many of the members were very discontented at haying to remain there idle, and the fact that their captain, T. Shepstone, junr., had been taken away and sent to the Orange Free State to raise a troop of mounted Basutos added not a little to their discontent. Owing to the lack, I suppose, of something better to do, tales were bruited about little to the credit of those interested. In particular, mention was made about the conduct of one officer who escaped from Isandwhlana and, neither stopping at Rorke's Drift nor Helpmakaar, took some mounted men from the latter station on to Dundee. This and other similar cases were severely animadverted upon, and I have little doubt but that by-and-by more will come out than is generally known about many of them. Waggons were busy bringing in wood, which had to be cut and brought some distance off down in the valley below the range. This was the only work I saw done at the camp. Just previous to saddling up again, I went inside the fort to a large marquee, in which, fastened to one of the poles, I found the missing colour of the 1-24th, recovered by the party under Major Black. It was very little damaged, and, I should say, will be more valuable than over to the regiment in its present state. Three p.m. found me going down the Biggarsberg Range, and a sharp trot brought me to Fort Bengough at five, where I dined and slept that night. Major Bengough, the commandant, was away at the time with two of his companies, and Major Dartnell and some Natal Mounted Police. They were out for a two days' patrol along the river. Next morning I was early on the road again, and managed to get into Grey Town by 8 P.M., haying passed one company of the 4th Regiment, under Captain Moore, at Mooi River, where they encamped that night. I had a few minutes' chat with him, and learned that they were going to Utrecht. This information was given with a dismal countenance, and as he had no subaltern, and the road is not a nice one at any time, I did not wonder at it. Sleep, long and sound, refreshed me, and, my horses being tired, I left them to follow, and took the post-cart down to Pieter Maritzburg, getting in by 6 p.m. on Thursday, March 13.

CHAPTER XVI

MY HOME-STAY at Pieter Maritzburg was limited to one day, and I went on at once to Durban, where I arrived just in time to meet the as. African with my confrère, Mr. Mackenzie. Having paid our respects to the General and other military officials, who, notwithstanding its being Sunday, were very busy, owing to the arrival of reinforcements, we made the best of our way to Pieter Maritzburg again, where I assisted my colleague in his arrangements, gave him all necessary introductions and instructions, and despatched him on his way to join Colonel Wood's Column. My own time was very short, as I was anxious to get back to Durban, where I was specially interested in the preparations then actively in progress for the formation of a Column for the relief of Pearson at Etshowi. The 57th and 91st Regiments had already arrived, and the General only awaited the arrival of another Infantry battalion, which was expected to be the 3-60th, to complete his arrangements and effect a start. My intention was to accompany the relief-column, and I could not afford to lose a day. The next day, therefore, found me en route for Durban once more.

Affairs in general seemed to be brightening up everywhere, and great hopes were expressed as to the result of the impending march to Etshowi. We had learnt, by signal from there, that a large force of nearly 20,000 Zulus had passed within sight of the place, and we trusted to be able to give such an account of them as would once and for all settle the point of supremacy, in the coast district at any rate. Another good piece of news had also just come down from Rorke's Drift, to the effect that, two days after I left, a party under Colonel Black had volunteered, obtained permission, and actually visited the scene of the disaster at Isandwhlana.

An eye-witness gave the following account of the patrol:—"On Friday, the 14th of March, a party of volunteers, under Lieutenant-Colonel Black, 2-24th Regiment, consisting of Captain Symons. Captain Harvey, Lieutenant Banister, and Sergeant Tigar, of the 2-24th, Commandant Cooper, and twelve officers of the Natal Native Contingent, and ten of the Natal Mounted Police, left Rorke's Drift, at 7 a.m., crossed the Buffalo on the pont, and rode through the Bashee Valley to make a reconnoissance of the camp at Isandwhlana. The scouts in advance saw fires burning in the kraals in the Bashee Valley, and disturbed three armed men with guns near the drift at the foot of the Isandwhlana Hill, who ran off at the approach of the party. Arrived on the now well-known and oft-described 'ridge,' a horrible scene of desolation was spread before them, and the still highly-tainted air filled their nostrils. After posting vedettes on all sides to guard against a surprise, they proceeded systematically to examine the whole of the battlefield. Some thirty Zulus were seen running from the kraal in front of the camp, and when out of sight they fired several shots, with the intention, no doubt, of giving the alarm, and shortly afterwards signal-fires were seen burning on the hills. The Guard-tent of the 2-24th Regiment was first searched, in hopes of finding some trace of the two colours of the regiment, which had been left there on the morning of the 22nd of January last. The tent, colours, and belts had all been taken away. They next searched each camp in detail, and afterwards rode down by the side of the 'donga' that ran in front of the camp; and then still farther afield, where the different incidents and phases of the terrible battle were supposed to have taken place, and observed the following: The Zulu dead had all been removed. The waggons to the number of over 100 were uninjured, and stood for the most part where they were left. All the tents had been burnt,

'The Field of Isandhlwana Revisited'. This sketch shows General Marshall's first arrival at the scene of the slaughter in May 1879. Published in the London Illustrated News, July 12th 1879.

cut up and taken away, the poles only being left. Everything of value had been looted, and what had not been taken away had been stabbed with assegais. Sponges, boots, brushes of all descriptions, quantities of books, papers, photographs, gaiters, and various other articles were scattered about. Horses and moles were lying still tied to the piquet-ropes and waggons, and a good many skeletons of oxen were scattered here and there. The bodies of our poor brave soldiers showed where the fury of the enemy had overtaken them. They were all in and about the camp, or down the path the fugitives took; not a dozen could be found in the whole surrounding of the camp, nor in the 'donga' bearing out the testimony of survivors, who relate that while the soldiers held the donga they suffered no loss. The greatest number counted lying together within a very small compass was sixty-eighty and these were in the left rear of the 1-24th, near the officers' mess-tent. The majority were 24th men, but there were some of other arms as well. As regards the state of the bodies, a subject of morbid but painful interest, they were in all conditions of horrible decay. Some were perfect skeletons; others that had not been stripped, or only partially so, were quite unapproachable, and the stench was sickening; with but few exceptions, it was impossible to recognise any one, and the only officer that was seen was discovered by his clothes. It was considered that it would be three to four weeks before the bones could be collected and buried. Were an attempt to be made to do so now nothing could be done but to throw earth over the corpses. Close to the small heap of dead bodies before mentioned, the colour-belt of the 1-24th Regiment was found by Corporal Ghroschky, Natal Mounted Police; it was the most interesting thing found, though not perhaps the most valuable, as Captain Symons found a large bundle of cheques belonging to him that had not been opened. Having thoroughly searched the camp, they proceeded to look for the two guns. One limber was found on the road leading down the valley towards the Izipesi Mountain, about a quarter of a mile to the front of the camp. The other limber, much broken, was found lying in the ravine where Lieutenant Curling, R.A., described the guns as having been upset and lost; and the team of six horses, all harnessed together, was lying by it; the ravine was so steep that one or two of the horses were suspended by the harness over the stream; both the guns and carriages had been removed. This ravine is about half a mile from 'the ridge' and numbers of bodies were lying between the two. On the order to retire being given, the party returned by the same road, being twice fired upon, without effect, by two small parties of natives; once as they were leaving the ravine, and the second time from the 'krantzes' above the Bashee Valley."

Some important information, based on good authority, derived from a high and reliable native source, had also been received in relation to affairs in Zululand. There were said to be only forty Government waggons at Cetywayo's kraal, and he had sent a force to Isandwhlana, during the preceding week, to fetch away the remaining waggons and the two field-pieces which had been left behind at the camp. There were no white men captives at the King's kraal, as had been reported. A few prisoners had originally been taken alive, but they were killed on the field of battle. Cetywayo had called up his people, but found much difficulty in getting them together; they would not re-assemble as heretofore. In fact, they were becoming tired of fighting, and began to feel that their cause was hopeless and the Zulu power broken, as the effect of their serious losses and reverses, even in spite of their triumph at Isandwhlana, which had cost them so dear. Colonel Pearson was stated to be safe from attack at Etshowi; but a large Zulu impi completely surrounded him to cut off all supplies; nevertheless, it was said, if the supplies were sent forward with an escorting column of adequate strength capable of defeating all the attacks of the enemy, and cutting its way through, the Zulus would become quite demoralized. All this was confirmed by what we knew, and was regarded as most satisfactory and encouraging; and it was in the main amply corroborated by after-events.

Of the reinforcements, H.M.S. Shah was the first to arrive (on March 6th), and that most unexpectedly. It appeared that she was on her way home from the Pacific Station, where she had been the flag-ship; and then, stopping at St. Helena, her captain heard of the disaster at Isandwhlana, and on consultation with the Governor of that island, it was determined to change the route of the vessel, although homeward bound after three years' service; and taking all the available troops from the island, to bring them on at once, in order to be able to render speedy and effective assistance to the imperilled colony of Natal. This most praiseworthy, manly, and responsible course met with the highest admiration and appreciation of the colonists, and afterwards came in for eyen higher praise from the Lords of the Admiralty and the Government at home. The Shah brought over 100 officers and men of the 88th Connaught Rangers, under Captain Baldwin and Lieutenant Wyncow, and a detachment of the Royal Artillery belonging to No. 8 Battery 7th Brigade, numbering over fifty non-commissioned officers and men, commanded by Major Ellaby, who had with him Captain Cooke and Lieutenant De Lisle. It was also determined to land a strong naval brigade from the ship itself. It numbered 894 officers and men, and was the largest naval brigade landed on these shores. The brigade was composed of naval seamen, Royal Marine Artillery, and Royal Marine Light Infantry; and the men were all fine specimens of English sailors. Commander Brackenbury took charge of the brigade, and the names of the other officers accompanying it were Lieutenants Lindsay, Drummond, Henderson, and Abbot; Sub-Lieutenants Hamilton and Smith-Dorrien; Doctors Shields, Sebbold, and Connell; Mr. Cooke and Mr. O'Neil (gunners), and Mr. Chappie (clerk). The R.M.L.L were under Captain Phillips, and the B.M.A. under Captain Burrows. The General and Bear-Admiral Sullivan, C.B., were present at their disembarkation, and expressed much pleasure at their opportune arrival. Two nine-pounder guns, one Gatling gun, and two 24lb. rocket tubes were also landed with the brigade. This force left for the Lower Tugela on March the 10th, four days only having elapsed between their disembarkation and departure inland. On the same day H.M. troopship Tamar was signalled as approaching the port, and by 1 p.m. she was at anchor, having brought the 57th Regiment from Ceylon. She landed half the regiment next day, and the rest on the day following. The Lieutenant-Governor and other colonial authorities were present to receive the regiment on its landing, as also large crowds of people of every colour, age, and sex. The 57th (West Middlesex) Regiment is better known as the "Die-hards," and, as consisting of nearly all long-service men, much was expected from it.

On March 14th, Durban, for the first time in the history of Natal, since the British flag was hoisted at Pieter Maritzburg, became the headquarters of the military in South Africa; and as it was the base of the leading operations then occurring, such a transfer was absolutely necessary. News from Etshowi was in the meantime communicated daily, when the weather was fine; and on the 16th Durban rejoiced over the receipt of the following telegram from Lieutenant-Colonel Law, at the Lower Tugela:—

"Just received a message from Colonel Pearson, dated 16th March, 1879. He has made a road from the fort to join the main road to Inyezane, shortening distance three miles, and avoiding the Hinza Forest. It was made under fire. Lieutenant Lewis, 3rd Buffs, being slightly wounded. Pearson went, on the 1st March, to destroy Dabulamanzi's kraal, six miles off; surprised them, and returned skirmishing all the way. No casualties on his side. One of the native messengers who had got through safely insisted on going back to Etshowi, and he deserves much credit for his desire; but I have not allowed him to go, as we can now communicate everything by signal."

This proved fully that Colonel Pearson and his force were not idle, or incapable of moving out of Etshowi, for a short time if necessary; and as it was known that their stock of food would last until the beginning of April, our hopes of a speedy reunion rose higher and higher. Just after the receipt of the above news, the U.R.M.S. Pretoria arrived with the 91st Regiment (Princess Louise Argyllshire Highlanders) on board. This was the first arrival of troops despatched from England as reinforcements; and much credit was given to one of our local lines for their steamer having made the fastest passage over here, beating several other reported "crack" ships. The march of this regiment (which is not a kilted one, but wears the clan tartan "trews," and have their pipers dressed in full Highland costume), as they proceeded from the Point to the camp in Durban, seemed greatly to amuse the native population, and drew forth remarks in the Kafir tongue more peculiar and forcible than polite. On Tuesday, the 18th, another naval brigade was landed from H.M.S. Boadicea, which had lately arrived to take her place as flag-ship of the Cape Station, instead of H.M.S. Active, ordered home; and on the next day the 57th and 91st Regiments both sent off large detachments en route for The Lower Tugela. They proceeded by rail to Saccharine Station, as far as the coast-line then extended, a distance of about twelve miles from Durban, and thence marched the rest of the way (fifty-two miles.) Thursday saw the departure of the naval brigade of H.M.S. Boadicea in a pouring rain. It numbered 238 men, who had with them one Gatling gun, and one field-piece, the men being armed with Martini-Henry rifles. They were, as most men of all the naval brigades are, a fine, sturdy lot of fellows, and left in the highest of spirits. Lieutenant F. B. Carr was in command, and the other officers were Lieutenants E. C. Hobkirk, J. B, Benett; Sub-Lieutenants H. F. Lyon, H. Coachworth; Midshipmen Warrener, Hon. Colville, Hewitt, and Cruikshank. The 3-60th arrived in the C.R.M.S. Dublin Castle during the same day, and the whole battalion were landed soon afterwards, excepting about 200 men, who were on their way out in the ss. Russia, then on the voyage with the 58th Regiment on board. The hired transport ss. Manora was the next to arrive, two days afterwards (on Saturday the 22nd); and she brought the first battery of artillery, including three English horses. This steamer was a very fine one, and on her passage over from England had beaten the celebrated ss. City of Paris, which left Southampton on the same day that the Manora left the London Docks. The troops which arrived by her formed M Battery 6th Brigade Royal Horse Artillery. The officers who landed were Lieutenant-Colonel Browne, Major Sandham (commanding M Battery), Captain and Adjutant Alleyne, Captain Legard, Lieutenants Shiffner, Jarvis, and Thompson, and Captain Vibart, N Battery 5th Brigade (who came out to join his battery, already on service, in the place of poor Stuart Smith, killed at Isandwhlana), Captain Spinks (Army Service Corps), and Captain Molyneux, 24th Regiment (one of the General's A.D.C.'s). There were altogether 165 non-commissioned officers and men, and ninety-two horses of the Royal Horse Artillery. It appeared that only two horses died on the voyage, but they were replaced at Simon's Bay. The Artillery had with them six seven-pounders, several of the new tip-carts and Kaffrarian carriages. They also brought four Gatling guns for the Commissary of Ordnance, and a supply of camp-equipment for the same department. They drew their rocket equipment from the Commissary of Ordnance at Durban. The men carried Martini-Henry carbines, and the drivers were armed with swords. The whole battery was fully equipped before leaving England. The horses were all very powerful animals, and the men a smart lot of fellows, most of them having seen service in India. The entire landing operations were from first to last most successfully carried out. There were also landed from this steamer thirty-two non-commissioned officers and men of the Army Service Corps, commanded by Captain Spinks.

CHAPTER XVII

I ARRIVED IN Durban on the evening after the Manora anchored in the bay, and speedily made myself acquainted with the arrangements in progress. In the town itself, in preparation for the absence of the troops, an Indian Contingent had been raised to do garrison duty, and the Volunteer, Rifle, and Artillery Corps were called out.

I spent three more days in Durban until the 26th of March, and then left for the Lower Tugela. During that time nothing of much importance occurred, except the arrival of the sailing ship Umvoti from the Mauritius, bringing 103 men of the 88th Foot, under Captain Bowen and Lieutenants Moore and Webb, and sixty men of the Royal Artillery, with their 7-pounder guns, commanded by Captain Maclean and Lieutenant Evans. The people in that island had felt great sympathy with the Colonists of Natal, and Lady Barker, the wife of the Colonial Secretary of the island, and the Hon. F. Napier Broome, lately Colonial Secretary in Natal, had offered to organise an association of volunteer nurses to tend the sick and wounded in Natal; while Mr. Carmichael, the editor of the English newspaper there, immediately organised a volunteer corps of sixty men, mostly Europeans, whom he placed at the disposal of the Mauritius Government for service in Natal. General Murray, commanding the troops in the island, however, had thought fit to decline the offer, much to the regret of all. These two instances, however, prove what practical sympathy was evinced by the people of Mauritius.

Within the month, many accessions had been made to the noble army of "Specials," and I was, I think, the last to leave Durban for the front. I found that I had been preceded by

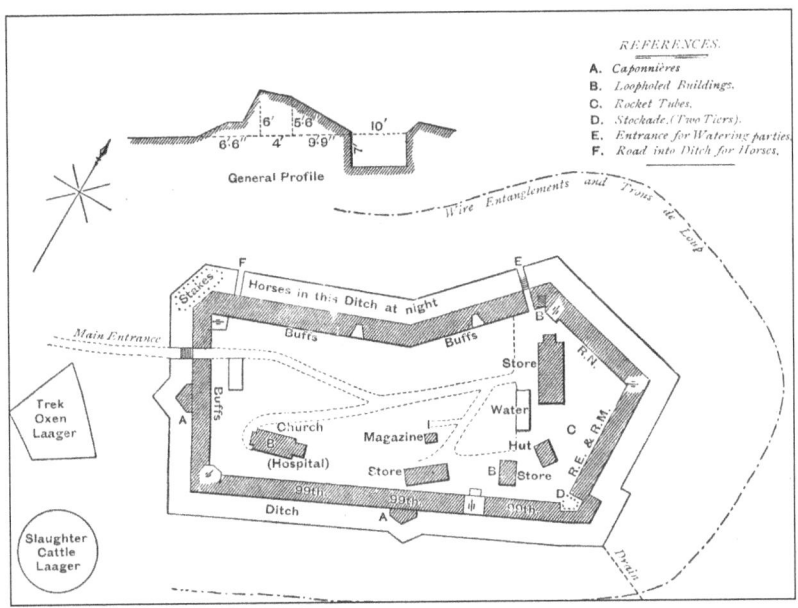

Plan of the Fort at Etschowe.

Mr. Francis of the Times, Melton Prior, Illustrated London News, Fripp, the Graphic, Dormer, Cape Argus, and Mr. W. Peace, who represented the Daily Telegraph until the arrival of Mr. P. Robinson from Afghanistan. Other English, Colonial, and Provincial papers were also represented. Some of them, however, did not accompany us past the Tugela. I arrived at Fort Pearson by 8 p.m. on Friday, the 28th of March, and found that the Column was under orders to march on Saturday at daylight. With that intent all the troops, except the 3-60th, had already crossed the river, and were bivouacked around Fort Tenedos. The two forts, Pearson and Tenedos, had been so much strengthened, as to be practically impregnable to any enemy without artillery; and I may here note, that at various points along the coast-road, leading by Stanger to the Tugela, old positions had been greatly strengthened, and new defensive works added. On the Zulu bank of the river a strong advanced position had been taken up and fortified at the St. Andrew's American Missionary Station, about five miles from Fort Tenedos, on the road to Etshowi. Extraordinary efforts had also been made for many weeks past in arranging the Transport and Commissariat Services necessary for a large force. These branches, at that time and in that country, were all important; inasmuch upon their efficiency success or failure depended quite as much as on mere generalship, tactics, or strategy in the handling of the troops. Nothing was subsequently found wanting, afterwards, in these two services, in any material respect. The General's orders were that, to save transport, no tents should be taken with the Column, and food, consisting of biscuits, tinned meat, and tea, only sufficient for ten days; nothing else being allowed, except the special stores and supplies for the relief of the force at Etshowi. Even thus limited, the convoy consisted of 122 waggons and carts, occupying a line two and a half miles in length at the least, and under the most favourable circumstances.

Before proceeding with the details of events on the now memorable march to Etshowi, I now give a list of the troops forming the Column, as well as the distribution of the various commands. To commence with: His Excellency Lieutenant-General Lord Chelmsford commanded the whole force in person, with Colonel Crealock, M.S., as his Staff Officer, and Captain Molyneux and Lieutenant Milne, R.N., as A.D.C.'s. The Column consisted of two Divisions, the advance being under the command of Colonel Law, R.A., who had Captain Fitzroy Hart, 31st Foot, as Staff Officer; and the rear Division of Colonel Pemberton, of the 60th Rifles, with Captain Buller, A.D.G., as Staff Officer.

Advance Division: The 91st Regiment under Major Bruce; five companies of the 99th, and two of the 3rd Buffs under Major Walker of the 99th; the Naval Brigades of the Shah and Tenedos under Captains Brackenbury and Kingscote, who had with them two 9-pounder guns, two 24lb. rocket tubes, and one Gatling; the Mounted Infantry and Volunteers under Major

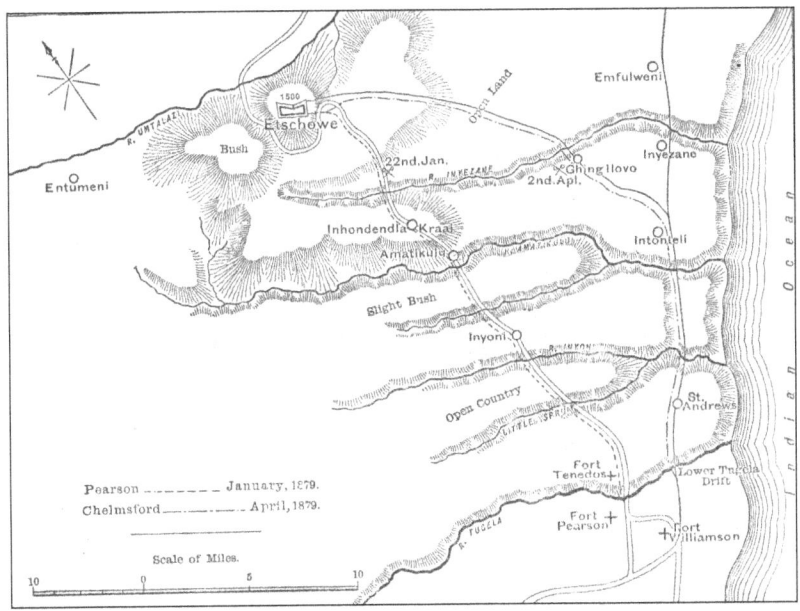

Plan of the Marches of Pearson (Jan., 1879) and of Chelmsford (April, 1879) to Etschowe.

Barrow, 19th Hussars, with Captain Courtenay, 20th Hussars, as second in command; Jantje's troop of mounted natives under Captain C. D. Hay, and the 5th Battalion of the Natal Native Contingent under Commandant Nettleton. Added to these there were 150 of John Dunn's men, who under his own personal supervision, aided by his head man Moore, acted as scouts with great service throughout the whole march. These brought the number of men in the Advance Division to 3,350 fighting men, of whom 1,870 were Europeans.

The Rear Division under Colonel Pemberton consisted of the 57th Regiment under Colonel Clarke, the 3rd Battalion of the 60th Rifles under Colonel Northey, the Naval Brigade of the Boadicea under Lieutenant Carr, R.N., and a portion of the Marines of the Shah and Boadicea with one Gatling and two 24lb. rocket tubes. The 4th Battalion Natal Native Contingent under Captain Barton, another troop of mounted natives under Captain Nourse, and a splendid troop of mounted whites nnder

Captain Cook, completed the Division and brought its numbers up to 2,270 fighting men, of whom 1,470 were whites.

The grand total of the fighting men of the Column was therefore 5,620 men, of whom 3,840 were Europeans. All the natives were, however, on this occasion armed with rifles, mostly of the Martini-Henry pattern, and this put them more on a footing of equality with the enemy, and certainly gave them more confidence and pluck. In addition to the above forces we had a large Medical Staff under Surgeon-Major Tarrant; and, with the officers and men employed in the Commissariat and Transport Departments, both under the control of Deputy Commissary-General Walton, our strength was in round numbers nearly 6,000 men. Colonel Hopton of the 88th Regiment, much to his regret, was left behind at Fort Tenedos in charge of the Lower Tugela, with about 500 men of all arms, but consisting principally of those from his own regiment. The new Commodore of the Cape Station, Captain Richards, R.N., of the Boadicea, also accompanied the expedition with Lieutenant Preedy, R.N., as A.D.C., the principal reason of this step being the natural anxiety of the Commodore to see the brave Naval Brigade of the Active under Captain Campbell, which was shut up in Etshowi.

CHAPTER XVIII

THE ENTIRE Column, having crossed the River Tugela on Friday evening, spent a most miserable and trying night in bivouac, on very bad ground, in a heavy rain, and without shelter. This might well have been avoided, without disadvantage from the point of view of military efficiency; for there were plenty of tents at Fort Pearson, which might have been erected for the shelter of the men and left behind. There is nothing so trying to troops as lying out in the open all night in wet weather. Be that as it may, however, punctually at 5 a.m. on Saturday, the 29th of March, reveille was sounded and by six the advance guard was en route for Etshowi; at 8.30 the last waggon left Fort Tenedos. The General, Commodore, and their Staffs, crossed over at eight, shortly followed by John Dunn and his men. The direct road, which had been followed by Colonel Pearson, was quitted shortly after passing the St. Andrew's Mission Station, for one diverging to the right, nearer the sea-coast, which passed through a more open country. The first day's march ended at the Inyoni, where, not unmindful of the neglect which had proved so disastrous at Isandwhlana, a proper laager was formed and entrenched. The waggons were drawn up as nearly as possible in a hollow square, with the front towards the river, and the rear facing Natal. All the troops bivouacked outside the laager, each regiment along one face, with the Naval Brigades, guns. Gatlings, and rockets distributed at the angles. Outside of the troops, about twenty yards away from the waggons, a light shelter-trench was dug all round. The cattle, horses, and mules were brought inside the laager during the hours of darkness. Mounted patrols were sent out in every direction for four or five miles, immediately on our arrival at the Inyoni; and an inner cordon of piquets was formed at a distance of about a mile and a half, with outlying natives; the sentries were formed in groups of four, also with natives, about half a mile from the laager, and each regiment kept one company on guard all night, relieved every hour. These precautionary dispositions were not the less expedient because daring the march no sign of the enemy had been seen, nor were there any alarms daring the night. On Sunday morning, after the mounted patrols had again scoured the country and the cattle had been allowed to graze, the march was resumed at 10.30 a.m., in the same order as on the preceding day. The Inyoni Drift was crossed with some little trouble, and the route being devoid of other incident, after a good day's march, the Column reached the banks of the Amatikulu at 2.30. Here our laager was formed on a somewhat more extended scale, so as not to be cramped for room, and the same precautions were adopted for the security of the camp against attack. We learnt during the evening that large bodies of the enemy had been seen from the Middle Drift and other places on the Tugela border, coming down through the bush country on the Zulu bank of that river, as if concentrating for an attack. As the drift at the Amatikulu was a most difficult crossing, which would take us nearly all the day to get over, special arrangements were made on Monday to prevent any successful attack on the convoy in the act of crossing. The troops were, therefore, formed in order of battle. The advanced guard crossed early, and took up a strong position to the left of the road, commanding the bend of the river, and any hostile advance from that quarter. They were supported by one Battalion N.N.C. and their own detachment of the Naval Brigade. A hill on the left of the laager, commanding the drift below, and the valley terminating the Amatikulu Bush, was held by the 57th Regiment, in extended order, supported by part of the other N.N.C. Battalion, and flanked to right and left by the Naval Brigades of the Shah and Boadicea, with a Gatling and rocket battery. The 60th protected the laager itself, and provided a rear guard in conjunction with a detachment of mounted men and natives. Fatigue parties aided in the actual work of getting the waggons over the drift, the approaches being steep, and the stream deep and strong; and the crossing was successfully effected in six hours, from 7 a.m. to 1 p.m. In all these precautions may be seen the fruits of the severe lesson of the past. Upon this occasion, also, their efficiency was not practically tested; for only small bodies of Zulus were seen during the day by the mounted men, and those all fled when discovered. Major Barrow himself went to a distance of twelve miles, and visited Umaquendo's kraal, and several large kraals were burnt by Jantje's Native Horse. Captain Hay and others saw signal-fires in several directions, noticeably on the hills about three miles on this side of Etshowi. The camp and laager on Monday evening were formed at a place only two miles beyond the river Amatikulu, and, as regards the laager, on a somewhat different plan. The waggons, instead of being placed side by side diagonally across the boundary line, were drawn up, end on to each other, overlapping, one inside and the next outside of the line.

The distances traversed up to this time were, approximately: —From Fort Tenedos to the Inyoni river, ten miles; thence to the Amatikulu, nine; and three more to the third laager, making in all twenty-two miles, which was excellent work to have been accomplished in three days, as it was over a new road, and across two rivers. The march recommenced on Tuesday, the 1st of April, at 7 a.m., the 57th Regiment leading the way, as, by way of equitable apportionment of the duties on the road, an exchange of place was now made between the rear and advanced guards. The aspect of the country now began to change. Hitherto, the Column had traversed rolling grassy plains, with gentle slopes, wooded knolls, and small streams at intervals, diversified with an occasional deserted kraal and patch of cultivated ground. We now entered on a more wooded country, with large patches

The Ekowe relief force crossing a stream. By William Heysham Overend, c1879

of the high and strong Tambookie grass bordering the road, and many treacherous boggy places, which had to be crossed or circumvented as best could be done. On this day's (Tuesday's) march it was found necessary to make occasional halts, to allow the Column and convoy to close up, and on two occasions the regiments in front were sent out in extended order to sweep through the long grass and clumps of bushes, so as to avoid any ambush or attack, and Barrow's mounted men were patrolling some distance ahead, on the high hills overlooking the Inyezane valley. The site selected for our new laager—now become famous by the name of Gingihlovo —was on the summit of a slight knoll, upon the slope of hills on the hither side of the River Inyezane, whence it was distant about a mile and a half. This spot was reached by the advance about half an hour after noon, and the laager was carefully constructed. Colonel Crealock had determined, from the previous experience on the road, that if made about 130 yards square, the laager would give us sufficient room for the cattle and waggons, and space for the native troops inside the Europeans, who would then have two men to the lineal yard of our outside line of defence. The front of the laager overlooked the Inyezane river towards Etshowi, with its rear towards the sea, an old military kraal, burnt some time since, on the right flank, and the Amatikulu Bush, at some miles distance, on the left. Darkness set in just as the work was completed, but before it was possible to do anything towards cutting down the high grass and clumps of bushes by which, at about 100 yards distance, the laager was encircled. This, as matters chanced, was unfortunate, as it gave the enemy a better chance, in the subsequent attack, than they would otherwise have had. During the afternoon we received from the Tugela news of the affairs at Zlobani Mountain and Kambula Camp, with Wood's Column, but the details were vague, and we could only understand clearly that in the end Colonel Wood had been victorious, inflicting severe losses on the Zulu army, but at a comparatively high cost of officers and men. About 7.45 p.m. we had a false alarm, but nothing farther occurred throughout the night. Several large fires were seen, away in the distance, at the top of the valley on our left front, which were the night-fires of the force by which we were attacked on the following day.

On Wednesday morning, April 2nd, our scouts and mounted natives were sent out on patrol at sunrise, shortly after five. Rising at 5.30 a.m., I fancied I heard a few shots in the distance, but paid no particular attention to it; and meanwhile, preparations were made for grazing the cattle and getting breakfast, as the General had decided that the Column should remain encamped all that day, and that on the day following he would take a part of the Column and make a march on Etshowi, to bring away Colonel Pearson's forces to our camp; Etshowi Fort was to be evacuated as being difficult of access, and out of the line of the proposed subsequent march. About six, as I was stationed on a waggon at the left front corner of the laager, I saw large bodies of Zulus swarming over the hills beyond the Inyezane, and heard several shots in succession. This I reported to Colonel Crealock, and the attention of the Staff was drawn to the position of affairs; when it at once became evident that we were in for a fight, and that the enemy were advancing direct on our camp in force, driving in our scouts and mounted natives before them, seeking to repeat the tactics which they had found so successful at Isandwhlana. Preparations were speedily completed to give them a warm reception. The 60th Rifles held the front face, with the Marines and a Gatling at their right-hand corner, and the men of the Boadicea and two rocket tubes at the left angle. The 57th defended the right flank, towards the old military kraal, having some of the Naval Brigade and a Gatling at their right-hand in the rear corner. At the left rear corner were the rest of the Naval Brigade with two 9-pounders; the 91st were aligned along the rear face of the laager, and the 99th and 3rd Buffs on the left flank. All the mounted men were assembled behind the regulars close by the waggons, at the right and rear of the laager, while the N.N.C. regiments were located at the left rear angle, by the guns. The conductors, and all non-combatants who could obtain a rifle, placed themselves on the top of the waggons, whence many an effective shot told on the on-coming Zulu ranks. Just after 6 a.m. two strong columns of the enemy crossed the Inyezane, and two smaller ones advanced simultaneously, from the direction respectively of the Amatikulu bash and the old military kraal. Within ten minutes' time the leading men of the hostile columns had deployed into the valley, and the right and left horns were at once sent forward at the doable, according to custom, to surround our position. While thus deploying in masses, the time seemed to me favourable for rocket-fire, but no orders being given Lieutenant Carr had to wait. The engagement was begun by the Gatlings at 1,000 yards range, and when the enemy closed to within 800 or 400 yards the firing on both sides became incessant. The enemy

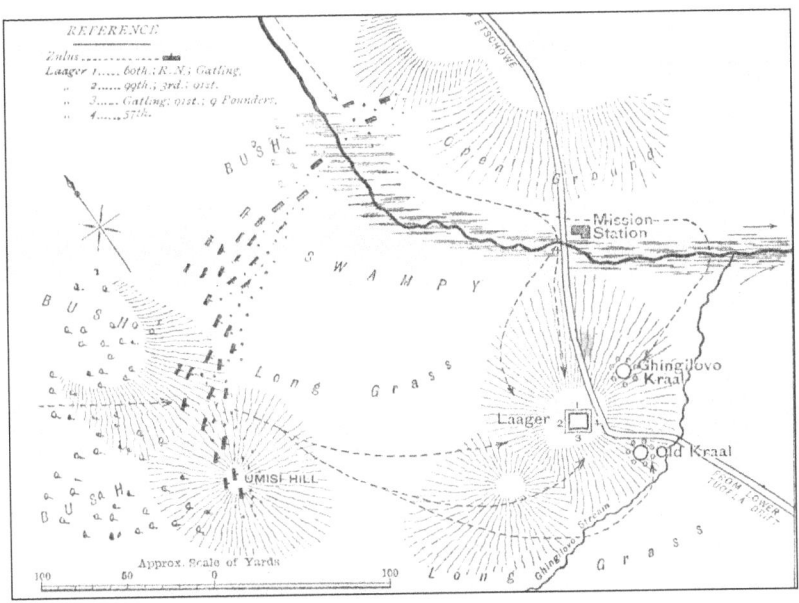

Plan of the Battle of Ghingilovo (April 2, 1879).

advanced well, under cover of the long grass and bushes, but their progress was for some time arrested at the edge of the cover, as our fire was too hot to allow them the chance of a rush. Shortly, however, a most determined attempt was made to break in upon the right front corner, and another on the rear face; some of the Zulus succeeded in getting even as far as within twenty-five yards of the trench, but the withering fire of the defence effectually stopped them, and they were compelled to desist from the effort. Steady firing on both sides ensued, and several of our men and officers were hit. Colonel Northey was one of the first to fall, badly wounded, and Surgeon-Major Longfield fell next, both hit in the left shoulder. Captain Hinxman was shot in the leg, and poor Johnson of the 99th, Instructor of Musketry, fell dead, being shot right through the breast within a yard or two of his commanding officer and myself. The General and his Staff were omnipresent; Lord Chelmsford on foot, with his red nightcap on, encouraging the men, directing their fire, and instructing them to fire low and steady. The Staff were mounted and had some narrow escapes, many of the horses being killed or wounded under them; Colonel Crealock and Lieutenant Milne were slightly hit in the arm.

During this time I and a friend of mine named Palmer, who had accompanied the expedition as conductor, with a lot of waggons, had each got a rifle and were steadily taking pot-shots, at any native who made himself visible, from the top of the waggon, which position gave us a great advantage. Palmer (who is a crack shot, having hunted large game in the interior for years) brought several to the ground. One shot in particular was a great success; about a hundred yards off,—straight in front of as, three Zulus had managed to gain the shelter of a thick bash, whose roots formed an impenetrable barrier to even our hot fire, and it was from this bush that the shot was fired which killed poor Johnson. His death was, however, quickly avenged, as we both arranged to wait quietly until the Zulus fired again, and then taking good aim we fired together just as two of them bad raised themselves on their knees to get a fair aim. The one aimed at by Palmer sprung up high in the air, with outstretched arms, and fell backwards dead, shot clean through the forehead, as we found out afterwards. The one I aimed at was only wounded, but in a little while both he and the third Zulu were killed by some of the 99th. After the battle the three were found close together, and Palmer and I took and divided the trophies of war, including their native dress, arms, and accoutrements; and we keep them yet, as most prized and hardly-won spoils. Every now and then I left my post of vantage and took a stroll around, to see what was occurring elsewhere. My groom, a cockney lad who had probably never seen a shot fired in earnest before in his short life of seventeen years, was coolly engaged after having saddled my horses, in making me a stew for breakfast, and preparing coffee as a precursor. He seemed to watch the engagement throughout without any signs of fear, and amused us much by the droll remarks he made.

At about 6.45 there was a slight lull in the firing, just after the enemy had been foiled in a desperate attempt to storm the rear of the position with a rush. Orders were then given for Major Barrow to charge the enemy in that quarter. Taking out his Mounted Infantry, the gallant Major led the charge in person, having formed his men in two lines, with instructions to the rear rank to protect any of their comrades in the front rank, who might fall, from being surrounded and assegaied by the Zulus. After a few shots, the Zulus turned and fled, but were quickly caught up and despatched by the sabres of the men. Major Barrow was slightly wounded in the thigh, but the casualties were surprisingly few. Then came the turn of the N.N.C., who were also ordered out, and charged the enemy, led by Commandant Nettleton and Hart, on foot. The Zulus fired one volley and then fled precipitately. The firing then also ceased on all sides, and the enemy joined in the flight on the front, right and left flanks, under a hailstorm of rifle bullets, shells and rockets. The N.N.C. made their charge from the rear a little after 7 a.m., and in half an hour's time not a Zulu was to be seen for miles in any direction, except the wounded, most of whom were unfortunately killed by our natives; their officers were only able to save the wounded Zulus in a few instances, as these latter when overtaken would turn and attempt to slay their pursuers.

Two large bodies of Zulus had remained in reserve on the hills at the other side of the Inyezane, but they also retreated when they saw their men beaten and put to flight. A number of those who escaped on the left gathered on a hill a mile and a half off towards the Amatikulu; but they were speedily dislodged and scattered by a few shells from the 9-pounders, which plumped into the mass and did considerable execution, as we subsequently saw, on visiting the spot. Thus terminated the engagement at Gingihlovo, in which our casualties were, one officer killed and three badly wounded; four men killed and about twenty-five wounded; and of our natives, about seven killed and ten wounded. Of the wounded, Colonel Northey subsequently died, as did also some of the men. The official return is given in Appendix E. The firing in our ranks was throughout very fair, taken all in all, and considering the many young soldiers. Though in some cases the number of shots fired per man in a company ran up to fifteen, yet the general average would not much exceed seven or eight; the 67th Regiment, however, were as low as five rounds per man on a flank where a most determined fire had been maintained by the enemy from a good and fairly secure position. The officers were specially earnest in restraining the men from too rapid firing; and in one case an officer (Kennedy of the 99th) sprang out in front of the trench itself, to enforce strict obedience to his commands. This was the very acme of courage and coolness, and naturally produced a wonderful effect. I may also note that John Dunn himself was firing from a waggon, and afterwards issued with his own men in pursuit of the flying foe, doing great execution, as they scoured the country for miles around. It was impossible for a long time to form any estimate of the enemy's loss, which must have been heavy. It was thought that only 600 or 700 had fallen, as only 473 bodies were found and buried within 500 yards of the laager. But this was afterwards seen to be an under estimate, as not only was the whole valley strewn with dead bodies, but numbers who escaped died of their wounds many miles away. Ultimately, as many as 1,100 corpses were found, in all, and hundreds more must have been wounded, more or less seriously. At any rate the lesson was severe, and the rout complete. The Zulus threw everything away, guns, assegais, and shields, to lighten themselves in their flight; and a large number of guns was afterwards found in the river Inyezane, which was crossed by the greater part of the fugitives. The crushing nature of their defeat was also evidenced by the bet that during our farther advance to Etshowi and return thence, not a single Zulu was seen, excepting those found at Dabulamanzi's kraal. No praise can be too great for the wonderful pluck displayed by these really splendid savages, in making an attack by daylight on a laager entrenched and defended by European troops with modern weapons and war appliances. This fully confirmed the opinion I had never failed to express, that they would fight us again and again, no matter how often they were beaten, as soon as any trusted Chief could assemble some thousands of them.

From the prisoners we learnt that the King Cetywayo had sent this Impi down to attack us, under the command of Dabulamanzi and Somayo. It numbered 115 companies, of over 100 men in each, equal to nearly 12,000 fighting men, belonging to five of their best regiments, viz., the Uve, Tulwana, Umcityu, Umbonambi, and Ukobamakosi. Their object was to prevent the relief of Colonel Pearson, and they had marched for two days without food, until they had arrived at a spot on the old Inyezane road, about six miles from our laager, and hidden from it by intervening hills. Arriving so late, they had been unable to send out scouts, and were, therefore, ignorant of our strength. Some difference of opinion had arisen among them as to whether the attack should be made at once that (Tuesday) evening; but Dabulamanzi favoured the plan of having food and a night's rest before attacking in the morning; and this was ultimately decided on, partly on account of our having sent up a rocket-signal at 8 p.m. of which they did not understand the meaning. The fighting men belonging to the district in our vicinity were stated to be away in the Engoa Forest, farther up the coast, together with their women and children.

At about half-past 8 a.m. our attention was attracted by flashing from Etshowi, so a party was told off to receive and transmit messages by signal. Colonel Pearson's first message congratulated Lord Chelmsford on his victory, adding that they had been able plainly to see the whole engagement. We were also informed of Wood's recent conflicts; and that another Zulu Impi of some 20,000 men was approaching the river on the Border, of which advice and warning had been given to our troops and stations at Helpmakaar, Newcastle, and Utrecht. We then informed Colonel Pearson that part of the Column would come through on the ensuing morning, and would expect to be met by him outside the fort. The rest of the day was devoted to the care of the wounded, the burial of the dead at noon, and the requisite arrangements for the despatch of the flying column to Etshowi. The laager, it was decided, should be made smaller, protected by an encircling sod-fence, and left in charge of five companies of the 99th, two of the 3rd Buffs, and two of the 91st; also a part of the Naval Brigade, with one troop of Mounted Horse, the guns, a Gatling, and rockets, and both battalions N.N.C.; the whole force being under the command of Major Walker. During the day, about noon, while dinner was being cooked, there was a false alarm; and we were roused by another at night, about 4 a.m., when all stood to their arms till daylight at 5.30: but fortunately nothing came of them. At 7.30 a.m., on Thursday the 3rd of April, the flying column started in the following order: John Dunn's scouts, a troop of Mounted Infantry, 60th Rifles, part of the Naval Brigade with Gatlings and rockets, some waggons of the relief convoy, the 57th Regiment, six companies 91st, more waggons, and strong rear-guard. The route followed was by the valley to the left, with the intention of hitting off Colonel Pearson's old road, just by the first crossing of the river Inyezane. The work of patrolling was carefully executed, and Major Barrow's men specially covered the hilly ground on the opposite bank of the river, by which the enemy had advanced to the attack, and retreated on the previous day. On the way, a messenger from the laager overtook us, to announce that Colonel Pearson had flashed a message for 400 trek-oxen with all appurtenances to enable him to bring away all his waggons. Orders for these to follow were given by the General, and Jantje's Horse, under Captain Hay, were told off as an escort. A little farther on we came across the "spoor" of the Zulu army, on its march to the attack. There were eight tracks side by side, very distinct, and giving evidence of a numerous host. The Inyezane was crossed about 11.30, and a halt was called, during which a mounted orderly brought a despatch from Major Barrow, who was then on a hill right in front of us, overlooking Pearson's battle-field of the Inyezane. He reported that on both banks of the river numbers of Zulu arms and equipments had been found, betokening their complete rout and headlong flight; also that no enemy was to be found on our right flank, so that we only need guard our left, towards the bush. During the halt I rode on to inspect the site of the battle of Inyezane, which I recognized at once, from having seen the sketch-plan by an officer who was present. Looking at it, I felt surprised that so small a force, as those then engaged, should have been able to beat off so large a body of the enemy with such trivial loss. After the inarch was resumed, about 8 p.m., we passed the spot where our killed had been buried. The grave was under a large mimosa tree, and had evidently remained untouched. The small wooden cross, with the names of the dead roughly cut in it, marking the last resting-place of brave Englishmen, was still there. At some places the Zulus had evidently dug the road away to render it impassable; and John Dunn pointed out to me, in a gorge in the middle of a large forest, what had been for some considerable time the encampment of an impi or regiment, apparently in wait for Pearson's force, if it had issued from Etshowi, to waylay it in the defiles. Still farther on we came upon the remains of a number of waggons which had been left on the road up, by Colonel Eley's convoy.

It was now 4.30 p.m., and as we were nearing Etshowi, I rode off to the front to get ahead, and first into the fort, if possible; remembering that Colonel Pearson had made a new road, shortening the way, and avoiding the vicinity of the Hinza Forest. Profiting by this short cut, I had the pleasure of being the first man of the Column to shake Colonel Pearson by the hand at the relief of Etshowi. Two other "specials"—Francis, of the Times, and Dormer, of the Cape Argus —had already left us, and I saw them, racing each other for the honour of being first in, along the broad road, a mile in front. They found out their mistake, when they saw the gallant Colonel at the head of 500 men, coming down by the new road from Etshowi. They then tried to cut across the country to attain their end; but it was too late, and the last I saw of them, on that occasion, was that one was "bogged," and the other's horse, already pumped out, could not be got over a nasty spruit. Leaving Colonel Pearson to proceed and meet the General and relief column, I galloped on to the fort, where I had a most cordial welcome all round. After exchanging the news, I went out to watch the arrival of our troops, which lasted from 7.30 p.m. till midnight. Colonel Pearson speedily returned to make all necessary arrangements for the encampment of the flying column outside the fort. The scene which occurred as the troops came up, the shouts, cheers, and congratulations on all sides, would beggar description. When the General and Staff came up, the ramparts were manned, and three hearty British cheers hailed their arrival; great enthusiasm was also manifested when the 91st came in with their pipers playing.

It was late before the rear-guard arrived, and all the weary soldiers were enabled to rest, after the fatigues of a long march of twenty miles. For my part, I was only too glad to accept the offer of a shakedown in the waggon of Father Walsh, the Roman Catholic Chaplain; and was speedily in the arms of Morpheus.

CHAPTER XIX

REVEILLE SOUNDED at 5 a.m. next morning, Friday, April 4th, and I spent the early hours in getting all possible information about the fort, and the enforced sojourn of its defenders since their occupation of the station, as related in Chapter XI. These particulars will be found of sufficient interest to merit reproduction here. Colonel Pearson reached Etshowi on the 23rd of January, the day after the engagement at Inyezane. The N.N.C. regiments and mounted troops having been sent back to the Tugela, the little garrison consisted of the following:— Colonel Walker, C.B., Scots Fusiliers, Staff Officer; Captain MacGregor, 29th Regiment, Q.M.G., and Lieutenant Knight, 3rd Buffs, A.D.C.; 3rd Buffs, 550 men, under command of Colonel Parnell; 99th Regiment, 330 men, under Colonel Wellman; Captain Wynne, R.E., and 96 men; Captain Campbell, R.N., with Active Naval Brigade, 165 men; Captain Beddoes, Natal Pioneers, and 100 men; and Lieutenant Lloyd, R.A., with 30 men; making altogether about 1,300. The other officers holding appointments were—Staff-Surgeon Norbary, R.N., Senior Medical Officer, Surgeon-Major Fitzmaurice, and Surgeons Thompson, R.N., Wilson, A.M.D., and Giles, civil; Assistant-Commissary Heygate; Captain Pelly Clarke and Lieutenant Thirkill, 88th Regiment, Transport Officers; Lieutenant Rowdon, 99th Regiment, with 12 mounted men, and Captain Sherrington, N.N.C.

I made a sketch of the fort at the time from personal observation, aided by the notes of Captain Campbell, R.N. The position was not favourable, being completely overlooked and commanded all round by hills not 300 yards away. But that could not be avoided, as the existing buildings were there: however, as time went on the defensive power of the place was increased by raising the parapet, and forming various traverses, so as to render it, in the end, practically almost impregnable. In point of size the periphery was nearly 500 yards, and outside there was a fosse 10 feet deep and 15 feet wide, with stakes in the bottom, and caponniers run out in the centre of the sides, flanking the whole ditch. The four 7-pounder guns were mounted at the angles, and sod parapets were formed to protect the gunners. At one of the corners a Gatling was also in position, and at the southern apex two 24-lb. rocket-tubes were located near one of the guns. In the front there was a large drawbridge, for waggons, which was raised every night; and there were also two small foot-bridges, one being called the Engineers' Gate, and the other the Water Gate, as being close to the stream of water, which flowed past the lower end of the fort, having its source in a spring a little way off. No difficulty was ever experienced with the supply of water, as the stream was effectually commanded by the guns. Inside the fort, on the right hand, was the neat little church with its iron roof and small belfry. It had been used as a hospital, and loopholed all round for defence: surrounding tents were occupied by the medical staff, and other patients. Close by the church a small enclosure contained the graves of Missionary Robertson's wife, and of three men, wounded at Inyezane, "nobly doing their duty," as inscribed on the wooden cross which is their memorial, and died here of their wounds. Beyond this were two buildings used as stores, and another long low building occupied by the commissariat, with a veranda, which became the headquarters, mess-room, and dormitory of the officers of the Naval Brigade. These were the only permanent erections in the place. The artillery had built for themselves a wooden house; and the rest of the large garrison were provided with sheltered sleeping accommodation among the waggons and tents arranged over the vacant spaces of the enclosure. In point of supplies, their condition had not been so bad as was expected, owing to the extreme care with which the provisions had been husbanded. In fact, at the time of our relief Column arriving there were still fall rations for the force for a week. Medicines were scarce, and there were no provisions suitable for the sick and convalescent. The force therefore suffered in point of general health. Dysentery and typhoid fever were the principal maladies. We found 84 men in hospital and 70 outside patients. Many of the officers, although recovered from absolute disease, were nevertheless so reduced and weak that but for our arrival they must shortly have succumbed to the want of such food as they could eat. Among those who were in such a state of weakness may be named Captain Jackson, Lieutenant Thirkill, Captain Wynne, and Lieutenant Hughes; and of these, the first and last alone survived ultimately, as both Wynne and Thirkill unfortunately died not long after their return from Etshowi. In the little cemetery outside the fort were the last resting-places of four officers and 23 men. This "God's-acre" was enclosed by a railing of rustic woodwork, and most beautifully kept: the graves were laid out regularly in rows, each having a cross or memorial with an inscription cut on it, and covered with shrubs and flowers.

One of the officers showed me his diary of the occurrences of their stay during two and a quarter months. From the 23rd of January they were much harassed by the enemy on the hills, firing down on the camp, and attacking vedettes, cattle-guards, and stragglers; and they were busily engaged throwing up earthworks for protection. On the 28th January a message was received from the General, saying that Colonel Pearson was either to return to the Tugela, or do the best he could for the safety of No. 1 Column, as the whole Zulu army was reported to be coming against him. A discussion arose among the officers as to what was the best to be done, but it was ultimately decided to remain and make every preparation so as to enable all to be quartered in the fort; also to send back all the mounted men and native troops, being short of provisions and ammunition. Colonel Eley arrived in the evening with a convoy of both, and made things look more cheerful. On the 80th three messengers were sent to the Tugela, but could not get through farther than the Inyezane, as they reported that the Zulus were "like the grass"; 650 oxen were also sent back under the charge of some natives, who returned at 4 p.m., having had the oxen captured, and only just managed to save their own lives. Next day, the 31st, the Zulus were all round the fort, in parties of forty to fifty. They occupied the stony hill or look-out, but were shelled off. February 1st, the outposts exchanged shots with Zulus, and the men were busy all day at the fort. More messengers were sent off. This sort of thing continued all through February. On February 11th, messengers were received from the General, saying that he should not be able to make an advance for six weeks, if even then, and ordering the surplus troops to be sent back to the Tugela, as he had no troops to relieve us with. It was proposed to take three companies of the 99th, half of the Engineers, Naval Brigade, and N.N. Pioneers, to march by the short route, start in the middle of the night carrying 130 rounds, and reach the Tugela next morning. This proposition was deferred, and met with the disapprobation of the council of commanding officers. On the 16th sickness began to break out, and owing to want of medicines and comforts increased rapidly; one man died. On February 21st a force of 200 men went out with rockets to beat up the covers where Zulus had been annoying cattle-guards, but with no success. Very violent thunderstorms became constant about this time, making the men very miserable, and the fort wet and dirty. From this date parties were out daily, collecting mealies and pumpkins, and burning the surrounding kraals. Another month commenced with an account of a big expedition which started off on 1st March. It consisted of 500 men, with one gun. They marched off at two in the morning, with the intention of reaching and burning a big military kraal belonging to the King, seven miles off. They arrived there at daylight, surprised the Zulus, and put them to flight. The force then burnt the kraal, and got back safely to the fort at 10.30 a.m. The next day, 2nd of March, flashes were perceived from St. Andrew's mission station. This was repeated next day, and the signal made out to be "Expect 1,000 men on the 12th inst.; meet us at Inyezane." All the looking-glasses in the fort were got together, the best chosen, and a good deal of ingenuity shown in patting the thing in working order. On the 5th another message was received from Colonel Law to Colonel Pearson, "By General's order I advance to your support with 1,000 men, besides natives, as far as the Inyezane; be prepared to sally out to meet me with surplus garrison." Two days later a vedette was attacked by eleven Zulus, who surrounded him, and, although shot in four places and assegaied in others, as was also his horse, he succeeded in getting away, and most gallantly galloped in. This man (Carson), of the 99th, never moved a muscle, and bore the pain most wonderfully. On examination he was found to be shot through both thighs, the two middle fingers of his right hand were hanging by the skin, and he had other wounds of a slighter nature. While galloping away, a shot hit the breech of his rifle, which he had slung at his back, and thus saved his life, but the shock was tremendous. The brave fellow recovered, and I saw him walking about quite unconcernedly. The new short-cut road was first started on the 6th, and on the 10th, whilst the road party were at work, the covering party had a sharp skirmish with the enemy. Next day half the garrison went out to fix the portion of the road right through into the old one. They had several brushes with the enemy, and Lieutenant Lewis had a bullet pass through his helmet, grazing his forehead, and making a severe indent on the skin. On the 18th satisfactory signals made out that a permanent relief force of 4,000 men and 2,000 natives would leave the Tugela on the 1st of April. This relieved the minds of all the garrison wonderfully, who had up to that time been living under a dread of having to march in, which could only have been done at a dreadful sacrifice of life, more especially of the wounded, if any engagement took place, as, having no carts, they could not have been removed. Two days after this, on the 15th, large bodies of Zulus were seen marching to the northwards, and were variously estimated at from 10,000 to 20,000 men, so that if Colonel Law had tried to get through with only 1,000 men, they would have been cut off to a certainty. On the 17th another vedette was surprised and assegaied in eighteen places. The body was afterwards rescued by a party and buried. It appears he was surrounded by the Zulus, who crept up unnoticed through the long grass, and he was shot before they assegaied him. On 23rd March two spies from the King arrived with a white flag. They were seized and questioned outside, blindfolded and brought in and then ironed, because of discrepancies in their statements. The one said that he had been a messenger from Cetywayo to Bishop Schroeder at Krantzkop to ask why the British were making war on him, as they had always prevented him doing so with other people. The Governor had answered that he was abiding by the Tugela Convention, and the King had now sent them to us, and offered a free and unmolested passage to the Tugela, if we did not burn their kraals and destroy the gardens. This messenger stated that he was sent on by the Bishop, whose daughter had sewn on the white flag to the stick. This likely tale did not go down, as we were too old hands to be caught by such chaff. The other Zulu who accompanied him stated that he joined the messenger from the King by command of Dabulamanzi, who instructed him to tell the impi that had been lying in wait for us not to harm us if we agreed to the message. Both these artful gentlemen were kept along with another man who had brought a message from Colonel Law to Colonel Pearson, but had been thirteen days on the road, and when he arrived said he had lost his Martini-Henri rifle, had been chased by the Zulus, and accounted for wearing a 2-24th great coat by saying that he found it. The last entry in the diary was made on the 26th, and mentions that a messenger was sent to the Tugela for a little medicine, and arrived back with a little, and some few papers on this date.

As likely to be of interest to the relatives I herewith give copies of the inscriptions placed on the crosses above the graves of the four officers below-mentioned who died at Etshowi.

The first is:— "Sacred to the memory of Lieutenant A. S. F. Davidson, Adjutant, 99th (Duke of Edinburgh) Regiment, who died in Etshowi on the 27th March, 1879, aged 24 years. 'Thy will be done.'" The second is, "In memory of Lewis Cadwallader Coker, midshipman, Naval Brigade, H.M.S. Active, who died at Etshowi, March 16th, 1879, aged 19 years." Underneath this is a circle with a broken anchor carved within it. The third is, "Sacred to the memory of 2nd Lieutenant George B. Evelyn, 'The Buffs,' who died at Etshowi on the 30th March, 1879, aged 21 years;" and the last is, "In memory of Captain H. J. N. Williams, 'The Buffs,' and late 4th 'King's Own,' who died at Fort Etshowi, 12th March, 1879." This memorial has a beautiful wreath of leaves carved out in relief just underneath the inscription. All four are the work, lovingly done, of Captain Gelston, "The Buffs." The official list of all those who died at Etshowi is given in Appendix F.

On Friday, April 4, Colonel Pearson's Column started, with 116 waggons, on their return to the Tugela. Their route was by the same road as on the march out, and they arrived safely at Fort Tenedos early on the ensuing Monday morning, the journey not having been marked by any special incident worthy of record.

On the morning of their departure from Etshowi the General sent off a detachment of his flying column—consisting of John Dunn's scouts. Captain Beddoe's Native Pioneers, and the mounted men—on an expedition to Dabulamanzi's kraal a few miles away, which was successfully destroyed. The flying column, in its turn, evacuated Etshowi on the same day and rejoined the rest of the relief column at the laager of Gingihlovo. Thence a transfer was made to a new entrenched permanent station called Fort Chelmsford, at a site near the Inyezane, in which position a portion of the force was left in garrison, consisting of the 57th, 60th, and 91st Regiments, with one battalion N.N.C., the Mounted Infantry, and the Naval Brigade. The rest of the relief column returned subsequently with the General to Fort Pearson for farther service in the campaign against Ulundi. Their homeward march was only marked by one noteworthy, though painful, incident, arising out of one of those unaccountable scares from night alarms. About 8.30 a.m. a piquet of the 60th fired a shot at some imaginary foe, and Dunn's scouts, who were in front, took fright and rushed back, carrying with them the entire piquet of the 60th, in a complete state of disorganisation and running over their own officers. The trench-guard, also of the 60th, under the impression that the Zulus were attacking, fired among the fugitives, killing and wounding five of the 60th and eight of Dunn's scouts. The whole affair was inexplicable and disgraceful. The colour-sergeant of the 60th, in charge of the piquet, was immediately tried by Drumhead Court-martial and sentenced to five years' penal servitude and to be degraded to the ranks. On the journey home, I may say, memorial crosses were erected to mark the burial-places of our comrades who had lost their lives in previous engagements at Gingihlovo and the Inyezane. The latter of these had been specially prepared with suitable inscriptions by Captain Gelston, and only completed on the last night of our stay at Fort Etshowi. Many traces were seen on the road of the large Zulu Impi which had attacked and been defeated by the relief column at Gingihlovo, and one large encampment, with a grass hut, evidently where Dabulamanzi, Somayo and the other chiefs had rested. It may also be noted that during the absence of the flying column at Etshowi, the remainder of the force left in laager at Gingihlovo, had scoured the country for miles around, the two battalions of N.N.C. being chiefly employed on this service. Five hundred more dead bodies had been found (besides numbers seen on the way by Colonel Pearson's Column) and about as many guns, comprising old muskets and Enfield rifles, a few Martini-Henry rifles, and several of French and German patterns. A number of prisoners had been taken (although no large body of the enemy had been encountered), and these unanimously described their late defeat as severe and crushing, but they said the young men would again assemble and still fight. One of the prisoners spoke English well, having travelled as servant to an Englishman, and he averred that he had seen three white men living as prisoners at the King's kraal, and they were officers.

So ended the memorable and successful relief of Colonel Pearson and his Column at Etshowi.

CHAPTER XX

Leaving the Tugela, Mr. Francis, the Times Special, and I returned to Durban, where I left him and proceeded to Pieter Maritzburg in order to obtain fuller particulars of the eventful engagements which Colonel Wood's, or No. 4, Column had had at the Zlobani Mountain and Kambula Camp, brief accounts of which had reached us on the march for the relief of Etshowi. The description of these affairs which was obtained from a captive Zulu, who was present thereat as well as at Isandwhlana, has appeared (though somewhat out of its proper place) in a previous chapter and may advantageously be compared with the following official details.

The first information received in the colony of the former conflict—which was a disaster almost as lamentable as that of Isandwhlana, and more so than that at the Intombi river—came by telegram to the Colonial Secretary from Ladysmith, dated March 29, as follows:—

"The Zlobani Mountain was successfully attacked, and a large number of cattle captured on the 28th; but a force of 20,000 Zulus coming from Ulundi surrounded the mountain while our force was at the top. In an action which ensued, nearly all the cattle were recaptured, and there was considerable loss on our side. The Zulu army attacked Colonel Wood's camp at 1.30 p.m. on the 29th. Fought most courageously until 6.30, when they were driven off and pursued a considerable distance to eastward. The loss on our side about seven officers and seventy men killed and wounded."

Colonel Wood's official report followed on the 30th with full details of the whole affair.

"From Colonel Evelyn Wood, commanding No. 4 Column, to

the Deputy Adjutant-General.

"Kambula. Camp, Zululand, March 30,1879.

"Sir,—I have the honour to report that the Inzhlobana Mountain was successfully assaulted, and its summit cleared at daylight on the 28th, by Lieutenant-Colonel Buller, C.B., with the mounted riflemen and the 2nd battalion of Wood's Irregulars, under the command of 2nd Commandant Roberts, who worked under the general direction of Major Leet, commanding the corps. I joined Colonel Russell's Column at dusk on the 27th inst., at his bivouac, about five miles west of the Inzhlobana Mountain. I had with me the Hon. B. Campbell, district staff officer to No. 4 Column; Mr. Lloyd, political assistant; Lieutenant Lysons, 90th L.I., orderly officer; and my mounted personal escort, consisting of eight men of the 90th Infantry and six natives under Umtonga, one of Panda's sons. Soon after 3 a.m. I rode eastward with these details, and at daylight got on Colonel Buller's track, which we followed. Colonel Weatherley met me coming westward, having lost his way the previous night, and I directed him to move on towards the sound of the firing, which was now audible on the north-east face of the mountain, where we could see the rear of Colonel Buller's column near the summit. I followed Colonel Weatherley, and commenced the ascent of the mountain immediately behind the Border Horse, leading our horses. It is impossible to describe in adequate terms the difficulty of the ascent which Colonel Buller and his men had successfully made, not without loss, however; for killed and wounded horses helped to keep us on his track where the rocks afforded no evidence of his advance. We soon came under fire from an unseen enemy. Ascending more rapidly than most of the Border Horse, who had got off the track, with my staff and escort I passed to the front, and, with half-a-dozen of the Border Horse, when within a hundred feet of the summit, came under a well-directed fire from our front and both flanks, poured in from behind huge boulders of rock. Mr. Lloyd fell mortally wounded at my side; and as Captain Campbell and one of the escort were carrying him on a ledge rather lower, my horse was killed, falling on me. I directed Colonel Weatherley to dislodge one or two Zulus who were causing us most of the loss; but as his men did not advance rapidly, Captain Campbell, Lieutenant Lysons, and three men of the 90th, jumping over a low wall, ran forward and charged into a cave, where Captain Campbell, leading in the most gallant and determined manner, was shot dead. Lieutenant Lysons and Private Fowler followed closely on his footsteps, and one of them, for each fired, killed one Zulu and dislodged another, who crawled away by a subterranean passage, reappearing higher up the mountain. At this time we were assisted by the fire of some of Colonel Buller's men on the summit. Colonel Weatherley asked for permission to move down the hill to regain Colonel Buller's track, which he had lost, and by which the latter gained the summit without further casualties. At this time he had lost three dead, and about six or seven wounded. Mr. Lloyd was now dead, and we brought his body and that of Captain Campbell about half-way down the hill, where we buried them, still being under fire, which, however, did us no damage. I then worked slowly round under the mountain, to the westward, to see how Colonel Russell's force had progressed, bringing with the escort a wounded man of the Border Horse, and a herd of sheep and goats driven by four of Umtonga's men. We stopped occasionally to give the men stimulants, unconscious of the fact that a very large Zulu force was moving on our left across our front. We were about halfway under the centre of the mountain when Umtonga saw and explained to me by signs that a large Zulu army was close to us. From an adjacent hill I had a good view of the force. It was marching in five columns with 'horns' and dense 'chest,' the Zulu normal attack formation. The Ulundi army being, as I believe,

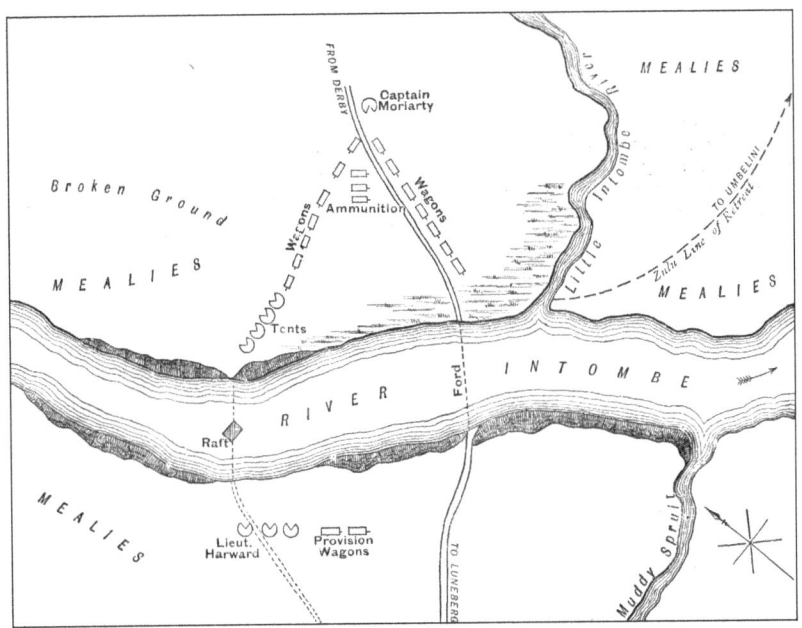

Plan of the disaster on the Intombe River (March 12, 1879

exhausted by its rapid march did not close on Colonel Buller, who descended, after Oham's people, the western point of the mountain, and thus he was enabled, by great personal exertions and his heroic conduct, to bring away not only all his men who had lost their horses, but also all his wounded who could make an effort to sit on their horses. Seeing from the Zinguin Neck, where I had gone with an escort and some of Oham's men, that although the Ulundi army did not come into action, yet some two or three hundred Zulus were pursuing our natives, who still maintained possession of some hundreds of cattle, I sent an order to Colonel Russell, who was then ascending the western end of the range, to move eastward and cover the movement of our natives to the camp. This he did, but before he could arrive some of the natives were killed. We reached camp at 7 p.m., and Colonel Buller, hearing that some of Captain Barton's party were on foot some ten miles distant, at once started in heavy rain with led horses, and brought in seven men, as we believe, the sole survivors of the Border Horse and Captain Barton's party, who, being cut off when on my track, retreated over the north end of the Ityntecha range. While deploring the loss we have sustained, it is my duty to bring to your notice the conduct of the living and dead. In Mr. Lloyd, Political Assistant, I lose an officer whom I cannot replace. In writing to Sir Bartle Frere, on the 26th inst., explaining that the success I had hitherto obtained was in a great measure owing to my subordinates, I penned the following lines: 'I need not trouble you with the names of my military staff, but I am anxious to bring under your notice the name of Mr. Lloyd, who has been of the greatest assistance to me. To personal courage and energy, he adds a knowledge of the Zulus, their language and character, and every attribute of a humane English gentleman.' Yesterday he showed great courage and devotion. His Excellency knew Captain the Honourable B. Campbell. He was an excellent Staff Officer both in the field and as regards office work, and having shown the most brilliant courage, lost his life in performing a most gallant feat. Though he fell, success was gained by the courageous conduct of Lieutenant Lysons and Private Fowler, 90th Light Infantry. Captain Barton, commanding Frontier Light Horse, was always forward in every fight, and was as humane as he was brave. On the 20th of January, one of Umsabe's men, whom Captain Barton wished to take prisoner instead of killing him, fired at Captain Barton within two yards, the powder marking his face. When last seen on the 28th inst. he was carrying on his horse a wounded man. Lieutenant Williams, 58th Regiment, who came out for transport duties. I nominated him as Staff Officer to Wood's Irregulars, and he evinced on this as on previous occasions marked courage. Mr. Piet Uys gave on the 28th a fine example to his men, as he always did, and remaining behind to see them safe down the mountain, was surrounded and assegaied. On the eve of the engagement I undertook in the name of the Imperial

Government, that if Mr. Uys fell, I would watch over the interests of his children. I trust that his Excellency the Lieutenant-General and in Zululand will thoroughly support my promise. Colonel Buller naturally says nothing about his own conduct, but I hear from the men that it was by his grand courage and cool head that nearly all the dismounted men were saved. His services to this Column are invaluable. I desire to bring to the notice of His Excellency the General Officer Commanding the names of those officers Colonel Buller mentions. I append a list of the killed and wounded as far as I have been able to obtain the particulars, and I will forward a corrected list later."

The full returns of the killed and wounded in this action, as well as in the following one at Kambula, will be found in appendix G.

The official report of the latter action was as follows:—

"From Colonel Evelyn Wood, Commanding Column No. 4, to the Deputy Adjutant-General:—

"Camp Kambula, March 30th 1879.

"Sir,—I have the honour to report that the camp was vigorously attacked by Zulu regiments from 1.30 to 5.30 p.m. The chief command was exercised by Nymani, who did not come under fire, and Syingwayo. The army left Ulundi on the 24th inst., with orders to repeat the attack of the 22nd of Jan-nary, near Rorke's Drift. On the 24th inst., four regiments were left near Etshowi, and four at Ulundi. Early in the afternoon, Captain Raaff, who was out reconnoitring, sent in one of Oham's men; he told me that he was behind with the captured cattle; he put his head-badge into his pocket, and was recognised by a friend, who was ignorant of his haying joined ns; he marched with the Zulu army to the Umvolosi.

"At daylight he went out drinking, and persuaded his companions that they were recalled, ran away to Raaff's men and told them how the attack would be made at dinner-time.

About 11 a.m. we saw approaching dense masses in five bodies to the Zungani range of mountains, near the Umvolosi. Two companies which were out wood-cutting were called in; the cattle brought into laager, with the exception of about 200 which had strayed away in the direction of the natives from the two whose duty it was to herd them. At half-past one o'clock the action commenced. The Mounted Riflemen, under Colonels Buller and Russell, engaged an enormous crowd of men on the north side of the camp; being unable to check them the men retired inside the laager, and were followed by the Zulus until they were within 300 yards, when their advance was checked by the accurate firing of the 90th L.I., and the Zulus spread out to the front and rear of the camp. The attack on our left had slackened, when at 2.15 p.m. heavy masses attacked our right front and our right rear. The enemy, well supplied with Martini-Henry rifles and ammunition, occupied a hill not seen from the laager, and opened so accurate an enfilade fire, though at long ranges, that I was obliged to withdraw a company of the 13th posted at the right rear of the laager. The front, however, of the cattle laager was stoutly held by a company of the 13th; they could not, however, see the right rear, and, the Zulus coming on boldly, I ordered Major Hackett of the 90th L.I., with two companies, to advance over the slope, the companies moving down to the rear of the cattle laager guided by Captain Woodgate, and well led by Major Hackett, who, with Captain Woodgate standing erect in the open under a heavy fire, showed a fine example to the men, as did Lieutenant Strom, who, sword in hand, ran well in front of his company. The Zulus retired from their immediate front, but the companies being heavily flanked, I ordered them back; whilst bringing them in Major Hackett was dangerously, and, I fear, mortally wounded. In any case I doubt his being able to serve again, and he will be a heavy loss to the regiment. The two mule guns were admirably worked by Lieutenant Nicolson, R.A., in the redoubt, until he was mortally wounded. Major Vaughan, R.A., director of transport, replaced him and did good service. The horses of the other four guns, under Lieutenants Biggs and Herde, were sent under the laager until they came within one hundred yards of them, but these officers with their men, and Major Tremlett, R.A., to all of whom great credit is due, remained in the open the whole of the engagement. In Major Hackett's counter attack. Lieutenant Bright, 90th Light Infantry, an accomplished draughtsman, and most promising officer, was wounded, and he died during the night. At 5.30 p.m., seeing the attack slackening, I ordered out a company of the 1-13th to the right rear of the cattle laager to attack some Zulus who had crept into the laager, but who had been unable to remove the cattle. I took Captain Ley's company of the 90th Light Infantry to the edge of the Krantz on the right front of the cattle laager, and they did great execution among the mass of retreating Zulus. Commander Raaff, at the same time, ran on with some of the men on the right rear of the camp, and did similar execution. I ordered out the mounted men who, under Colonel Buller, pursued for seven miles the flying Zulus retreating on our left front, chiefly companies of the Maqalusini Kafirs, under Umsirayo, killing great numbers, the enemy being too exhausted to fire in their own defence. From prisoners we have taken it appears that the column which attacked our left, and then being repulsed, moved round to our front rear, and right rear were composed of the Nokenki, the Umbonambi, and Nampumino Regiments. The Maqalusini under Umponyo attacked the front, the Undi the right front, and the Ikobamakosi the right. I append a list (not enclosed) of our casualties and we are still burying Zulus, of whom there are five-hundred lying close to the camp. I cannot yet estimate their entire loss, which is, however, very heavy. Three-hundred firearms have already been picked up close to camp, several M.H. rifles being amongst them. I received every assistance from the officers commanding, Lieutenant-Colonel Gilbert, Colonel Buller, Major Tremlett, and Major Rogers, and from the following officers of my staff:—Captain Woodgate (who evinced great courage, for which I in vain recommended him for promotion after the Ashantee expedition), Captain Maude (who, while replacing temporarily the late Captain the Hon. B. Campbell, rendered me very great assistance). Lieutenants Smith and Lysons, orderly officers, who, with Captain Woodgate, carried in a wounded soldier of the 13th, who was lying under fire. Li doing so Lieutenant Smith was himself wounded. The wounded were cared for most promptly by Surgeons O'Reilly, Brown, and staff, generally under fire."

The following remarks, written by my colleague upon his arrival at Kambula, two days after the fight, are most interesting, and need no preface. After giving a short description of the fight at the Zlobani Mountain, he continues:—

"If the Inzhlobane affair stood by itself, people both in the colony and in England would begin to think the campaign was fitted to be disastrous; but happily it was followed by the Zulu attack on this camp, and by so decided a repulse of the enemy that it must have the effect of raising every one's spirits, and of showing that the redoubtable warriors of Cetywayo are not invincible. The action was fought with several advantages in favour of the defenders. First, the presence of the enemy was perfectly well known, and his approach was seen in the form of long black lines, like dense cloud shadows creeping down the sides of the Zuinguin Neck two hours before the first shot was fired. There was, therefore, ample time to fetch the woodcutting parties that were out, and to drive in and laager all the cattle and horses that were out feeding on the veldt. Everyone, from the gallant Colonel Wood downwards, felt perfect confidence in being able to beat off the attack, formidable as the Zulu host undoubtedly was in point of numbers; and, every man, knowing his duty, did it with a coolness and devotion which were sure auguries of success. All the points round the camp had been carefully measured, and, as a consequence, from the moment the enemy reached these points and fire was opened, the artillery and infantry shot with the certainty that they were not wasting their ammunition. Admirable judgment was shown also in precipitating the Zulu right attack by sending out all the mounted men to engage them the moment they came up. These fine fellows did their work well, bullying the Zulus so effectually that they lost their temper, and in driving in the swarm of wasps who were stinging them so sharply, they advanced almost unconsciously under the fire of the camp. Once engaged there was no retreating, and they pushed home their attack vigorously. A sharp half hour's fighting, however, showed that they were not going to be successful from the north. They lost enormously, and at their nearest point, being under the fire of men who were resting their rifles, and were so cool that many of them were smoking their pipes, scarcely a shot failed to take effect. Decidedly sickened by their first essay, the fighting line took ground to their own left, and sought the cover of out-cropping rocks to the east, to join the masses that were now gathering along the front, the right, and the right rear of the camp. These seemed to rest for a short time before attacking, as if to take food, and then swarming down the slope opposite in successive waves, they dipped into the deep hollow sluit bed which covers the right of the camp, and practically disappeared, hiding themselves in a marvellous way. From here successive lines of skirmishers poured up the steep ascent to the ridge on which the camp is situated, and a furious fire was poured into the fort and the exposed faces of the cattle and the main laagers. It was well replied to both by artillery and rifle fire, again with immense loss to the assailants, and though they fought with a pluck and a determination that is the admiration of all military men here, they never succeeded farther than to effect a lodgment for a brief period in the cattle laager, which was only garrisoned by one company 1-13th, and was never considered tenable. Our loss would have been much less severe than it was but for the fact of many of the Zulus being armed with the Martini-Henry rifles which were captured at Isandwhlana and the Intombi River. Parties of the enemy armed with these splendid weapons finding cover under the rocks to the east and in a fold in the ground to the west kept up an enfilading fire from 600 to 1,000 yards, which inflicted all the serious damage of the day. Major Hackett, when gallantly leading a couple of companies of the 90th over to the reverse slope, where a more than usually severe attack was developing, was struck by one of these bullets, which cut out both eyes. The brief hold of the cattle laager was the one Zulu success of the day, but the murderous fire by which it was immediately swept from the fort and from four guns under Major Tremlett, which worked in the open during the best part of the day, made the place untenable. The Zulus, however, stuck to it like men, and one of them charged out when the company of the 18th, which had been defending it, retired, and assegaied a fine fellow who was the last to leave, and who had just before saved the life of his own sergeant. From the waggons of the laager they kept up a good fight for some time with the whole camp, including Colonel Wood and his Staff, who, posted in the ditch of the fort, set the men an example, not merely of cool courage, but of good shooting. Colonel Wood himself shot three running Zulus in successive shots, stopping a rush from the laager to cut off his staff, who went to the rescue of a wounded man who would otherwise have inevitably been assegaied. The gros of the Zulus lay in the body of the spruit, waiting evidently to make a rush in force directly their men got into the fort and main laager. Their chance, however, never came, and when, after repeated attacks, all most bloodily repulsed, they gave up the business and began to retreat in the most orderly and leisurely style, such a cheer rose from the beleaguered garrison as has never before been heard in South Africa. They did not waste much time, however, in rejoicing. Infantry and artillery fell to again, plying the retreating masses with shells and storms of bullets, while the bugles sounded to horse, and every mounted man, except the mounted Basutos, who had remained out the whole day annoying the rear of the enemy, saddled in hot haste and started in pursuit. The flying horsemen turned the retreat into a rout, slaying without resistance the flying savages, until darkness put an end to the pursuit. Many were shot, but many also fell stabbed with their own assegais, the horsemen arming themselves with these weapons, and using them as if giving point with a sabre. Many of the Zulus simulated death, others tried to hide in ant-bear holes, and one or two prayed for mercy, but as a rule they met their fate silently and with the stoicism of the valiant savages that they are. Some 800 bodies were buried round about the camp, and the most modest estimate is 800 killed in the pursuit, but the dead are lying about all over the country in the line of the retreat, and I have no doubt if the kloofs and spruits were searched the bodies of many a mortally stricken man, who had crawled there to die, would be discovered. I think that to say 1,200 were killed would be quite within the mark, and if we assume the usual proportion of wounded it will be seen that the Zulus have received a lesson which may not be without its effect on the issue of the campaign."

These are all the principal extracts from official and other sources, and I think they will be found quite sufficient thoroughly to explain the engagements at Zlobani and Kambula. From which time until the Columns were reformed nothing of importance occurred.

CHAPTER XXI

THE EVENTS described in recent chapters, namely the relief of Etshowi, in the south, and the Zulu effort to dislodge and crush No. 4 Column, in the north, occupied the earlier part of the period of comparative inaction, which —spending the arrival of farther reinforcements—did not terminate with them. The earliest arrivals were despatched to Etshowi; and during their brief campaign, ship after ship, and regiment after regiment, continued to arrive at Durban, until the full quota of the reinforcements, so speedily and vigorously despatched from England by the Home Government, had reached Natal. I need not here advert, with anything more than the briefest notice en passant, to the mingled feelings of dismay, regret, and indignation with which the news of the disaster to the British arms at Isandwhlana had been received in Great Britain, early in February. The results, as manifested by the active preparation and speedy despatch of forces, adequate to ensure a successful termination of the war, are all that this account is alone concerned with. The Queen Margaret was the first to arrive after the Umvoti, subsequent to the departure of the relief column for Etshowi. She brought 223 men of the Army Service Corps and 236 horses and mules, and arrived at Durban after a passage of thirty days, on Thursday evening, the 27th March. The whole of the horses and mules were landed that night. The following officers arrived by the Queen Margaret: —Commissary-General Long, Assistant-Commissary-General Smith, Sub Assistant Commissaries Delisle and Nichols, Conductors Field and Riley, and Veterinary Surgeon Morgan, R.A. Two days afterwards the City of Venice arrived, bringing the 3rd and 4th companies of the Army Service Corps, mastering about 200 men, and they had with them 150 horses. She brought the following officers:—Deputy Commissary-General Long in command. Deputy Commissary Noake, Assistant Commissaries Armstrong, Phillips, Joyce, Surgeon-Major Elgie, Veterinary Surgeon Killick, and Paymaster Hains. The City of Venice was afterwards made the flag ship at Durban and remained the Head Quarters of the Naval Transport officers until after the arrival of Sir Garnet Wolseley and the battle of Ulundi. During the next day, Sunday, H.M.S. Tamar and the hired transport Olympus both arrived. The Tamar brought the 2nd Battalion 21st Royal Scots Fusiliers, who had been trans-shipped from the hired transport City of Paris at Simon's Bay. The City of Paris, it will be recollected, touched the Roman Rock as she was entering the bay, and, as it was not deemed safe to allow her to proceed with the troops, she was detained in order that a thorough examination might be made as to the injuries she had received. The Tamar brought also the following officers of the Army Medical Department—Deputy Surgeon-General J. L. Holloway, Surgeon-Major H. Lamb, Surgeon-Major D. A. Leslie; Surgeons L. Townsend and H. Jagoe, and Lieutenant J. D. Marshall, A.H.C., making a total of thirty officers. Early the following morning, the hired transport Olympus made the anchorage. She had on board 11 officers, 189 non-commissioned officers and men, and 140 horses, of the Royal Artillery. The following were the officers' names:—Major F. Le Grice, Captains H. H. Crookenden, H. B. Z. Arowne, Lieutenants W. L. Davidson, J. H. Woodhouse, E. H. Elliott, F. J. A. French, W. J. B. Blake, C. J. T. Munro, Surgeon J. M. Jones, and Veterinary Surgeon W. Haggar. The next day, two companies of the 3rd-60th Rifles also arrived by the U.R.M.S. Danube, which brought Prince Louis Napoleon. On April 20th, the China followed, bringing the 94th Regiment, and two companies of the 57th. The officers of the 57th detachment were Major Tredennick, Captain Phillips, Captain Hughes Hallett,

Captain Lord Gifford, V.C. (Sir Garnet Wolseley's A.D.C.), and Lieutenants Sutton-Jones and Litton. In addition to these officers there were also on board Captain Chater, 91st Regiment, aide-de-camp to the Princess Louise and the Marquis of Lorne, Surgeon-Major Wallis and Surgeon-Major Smith. The s.s. Russia, another of the Cunard liners, arrived the next day with the 58th Regiment, and drafts for other Regiments, consisting of Colonel Reilly, C.B., one officer and two men, R.A.; Colonel Whitehead, 28 officers, 900 non-commissioned officers and men 58th Regiment; two surgeons, one chaplain, four officers 21st Regiment; one officer, five non-commissioned officers and men A.H.C., and seven horses. The Palmyra followed, with the 30th Company Royal Engineers, consisting of Brevet-Lieutenant-Colonel Harrison, Lieutenant Colonel Stewart, 7 officers, 195 non-commissioned officers and men; one officer, fifty noncommissioned officers and men of the Army Hospital Corps and fifty horses. Another day elapsed, and then the s.s. England brought part of the 17th Lancers. Her arrival had been eagerly looked for, and much excitement was shown when it became known that she was actually anchored in the Bay. She brought the Head-quarters, 28 officers, 820 men, and 240 horses, under command of Colonel Drury Lowe. The rest of the regiment had embarked on board the France and were due within a few days' time. Major-General Marshall commanding the cavalry, and Major-General Clifford, subsequently at the head of the base of operations, were passengers by the England. There were also on board Captain Lord Downe, A.D.C., Captain Stewart, 3rd Dragoon Guards, Brigade Major; and Captain Heneage of the Royal Engineers, extra A.D.G. to General Marshall.

On April 4th a telegram from the Cape was received to say that the troopship Clyde, with a large detachment for the 1-24th Regiment, had gone ashore, and struck on the Gaza Rock, between Dyers' Island and the mainland, on the previous day. It was reported that the weather at the time was foggy but fine. The discipline on board was perfect; boats lowered, men lauded, and horses saved. The boat conveying news of the accident palled to Simon's Bay, 70 miles, in fourteen hours. The Tamar went on to bring up the men to Natal, and left Simon's Bay with the troops on the 8th April.

H.M.S. Encounter, which had just previously arrived, left also for Natal direct, calling on her way up at the wreck of the Clyde with divers. That vessel had, however, become a complete wreck. She was sunk in seven fathoms of water inside the north-west corner of the island. One and a half million rounds of Martini-Henry ammunition were spoilt through this accident.

H.M.S. Tamar arrived at Durban again on Friday morning, April 11th, bringing the troops and horses from the Clyde. The troops consisted of drafts, a number of men being intended to fill up the vacancies in the 24th Regiment. There were altogether on board 15 officers, 4 staff sergeants, 2 officers' servants, and 528 privates, making a total of 549. The following were the officers on board:—Brevet-Colonel H. F. Davies, Grenadier Guards; Captain W. M. Brander, 24th Regiment; Captain F. Glennie, 24th Regiment; Lieutenant F. S. Halliday, 24th Regiment; Captain Sir W. G. Gordon Cumming, Bart., Scots Guards; Captain the Hon. B. S. G. Stapleton Cotton, Scots Guards; Captain the Hon. G. A. V. Bertie, Coldstream Guards; Lieutenant the Hon. B. C. G. Carrington, Grenadier Guards; Lieutenant W. D. McFarrer, Grenadier Guards; Lieutenant the Hon. C. B. W. Colville, Grenadier Guards; Captain M. Stourton, 63rd Regiment; Lieutenant J. B. Carey, 98th Regiment; Lieutenant G. S. Nicholson, 1-7th Regiment; Captain F. Coppinger, A.P.D.; and Surgeon-Major E. Ward, A.M.D.

Two of the finest vessels that have ever floated in the waters of the Indian Ocean anchored in the Durban roadstead on Wednesday, April 9th, bringing with them one of the most distinguished regiments of Her Majesty's army. Both the Spain and the Egypt (hired transports) of the National line, were seen at the anchorage early in the morning, and the fact of their having the 1st Dragoon Guards and their horses on board was sufficient to attract a large number of persons to the Point. The Spain left Southampton on the 27th February; touched at St. Vincent on the 16th March; and arrived at Capetown on the 6th April. She had on board 312 troops and 286 horses. There had been no sickness at all on board during the voyage, and all the horses, both officers' chargers and troopers, were reported to be in first-class condition.

In addition to the Dragoons, the following were on board the Spain:—91st Regiment: Second-Lieutenants Dixon and Lane-Fox; Lieutenant Wyllie, 21st Regiment: Second-Lieutenant Fienais. Army Medical Department: Surgeon-Majors De Hodgson and G. H. Giraud. Civil Service: Mr. Dogherty, interpreter. Colonel Alexander was in command of the Dragoons, and Captain Willow came out in the place of Captain Underwood, an exchange having been effected some time prior to the regiment having been ordered to Natal. Lieutenant Leslie, whose name appeared in the list of officers, remained at the depot. The Egypt brought 20 officers, 300 troops, and 300 horses.

The steamship France, with the rest of the cavalry reinforcements, consisting of 311 men and 288 horses of the 17th Lancers, arrived a few days afterwards; and this concluded the total number of transports despatched from England, with the exception of the steamship Andean, one of the East India and Pacific Company's vessels, which had only the reserve ammunition column on board. She arrived on the 15th, and brought an augmented battery of artillery, O Battery, 6th Brigade, under Major Duncan, who rendered valuable service in the Ashantee campaign. The train consisted of six small-arm ammunition carts, six ammunition and store waggons, and a limber forge waggon. All the vehicles were mounted on the special Kaffrarian plan, each provided with the Cape brake, and all constructed for bullock-draught over rough roads or tracks. There were on board altogether 300 men, who had been quartered on the main decks fore and aft. The main object of this train was to keep the column supplied with ammunition, and two magazines were brought out by the Andean with an aggregate capacity of 200 tons.

When all were landed, the Royal Artillery, Army Service Corps, and Cavalry were despatched to the cavalry camp prepared for them at Cato's Manor, and on Saturday the 12th were inspected by the General, Lord Chelmsford, attended by Major-General Clifford and Colonel Crealock.

The Infantry had been sent off to join their respective columns as quickly as possible, so that no great show was possible, but in order to gratify the people of Durban, and show the "natives" a sight. General Marshall ordered the cavalry out on Monday the 14th for a march through the town. Both regiments turned out their full strength, in light marching order, and the scene as they passed through the crowded streets of Durban will never be forgotten. The Dragoons all carried the Martini-Henri carbine, in addition to their swords. The Lancers carried their lances, Martini-Henri, and sword. General Lord Chelmsford and Major-Generals Clifford and Marshall, with their Staffs, and many other officers, witnessed the sight en passant.

CHAPTER XXII

THE ARRIVAL of all these reinforcements and the three new Major-Generals brought the total number of the British Army in Natal to a considerable strength. The campaign was accordingly arranged on a new plan. In the first place, the numerous Columns were done away with, and the following were adopted as the designations of the forces in the field, under the Lieutenant-General commanding, viz.:—1st Division South African Field Forces: Major-General Crealock, C.B., commanding, consisting of all troops on the left bank of the Lower Tugela. 2nd Division South African Field Forces: Major-General Newdigate commanding; consisting of all troops in the Utrecht District, other than those attached to the flying column under Brigadier-General Wood, V.C., C.B., which was designated as "Brigadier-General Wood's Flying Column." Major-General Marshall assumed command of the Cavalry Brigade, and Major-General the Hon. H. H. Clifford, C.B., V.C, took up the command of the base of operations and superintendence of the lines of communication.

The whole of the forces were divided as follows:—

First Division (General Crealock's) Lower Tugela Command.
- Naval Brigade: 800 Officers and Men
- M Battery 6th Brigade Royal Artillery: 90 Officers and Men
- Detachment 11-7th Royal Artillery: 25 Officers and Men
- 2-3rd Regiment: 836 Officers and Men
- 57th Regiment: 830 Officers and Men
- 3-60th Regiment: 880 Officers and Men
- 88th Regiment: 640 Officers and Men
- 91st Regiment: 850 Officers and Men

- 99th Regiment: 870 Officers and Men
- Mounted Infantry, 2nd Squadron: 70 Officers and Men
- Army Service Corps: 50 Officers and Men
- Army Hospital Corps: 20 Officers and Men
- Royal Engineers 150 Officers and Men
- 8-7th Royal Artillery: 80 Officers and Men
- O 6th Royal Artillery: 50 Officers and Men
- Lonsdale's Horse: 84 Officers and Men
- Cooke's Horse: 78 Officers and Men
- Colonial Volunteers: 105 Officers and Men
- Native Contingent:—
  Foot: 2,556 Officers and Men
  Mounted: 151 Officers and Men
- *Total Strength, Effective and Non-effective: 9,215 Officers and Men*

Second Division (General Newdigate's).
- 1st Dragoon Guards attached to 2nd Division: 650 Officers and Men
- 17th Lancers attached to 2nd Divpsion: 626 Officers and Men
- N-5 Royal Artillery: 76 Officers and Men
- N-6 Royal Artillery: 80 Officers and Men
- 10-7 Royal Artillery: 70 Officers and Men
- 10-6 Royal Artillery: 30 Officers and Men
- Royal Engineers: 60 Officers and Men
- 2-4 Regiment: 790 Officers and Men
- Detachment 1-13 Regiment: 63 Officers and Men
- 2-21 (2 Companics at Maritzburg): 820 Officers and Men
- 1-24 Regiment: 530 Officers and Men
- 2-24 Regiment: 586 Officers and Men
- 58th (1 Company at Durban): 906 Officers and Men
- 80th (several Companies in Transvaal): 300 Officers and Men
- 94th (1 Company at Grey Town): 870 Officers and Men
- Army Service Corps: 60 Officers and Men

- Army Hospital Corps: 30 Officers and Men
- Grey Town District Colonial Volunteers: 139 Officers and Men
- Natal Mounted Police: 75 Officers and Men
- Natal Carbineers: 27 Officers and Men
- Newcastle Mounted Rifles: 18 Officers and Men
- Buffalo Mounted Guard: 20 Officers and Men
- Native Contingent:—
   Europeans: 41 Officers and Men
   Natives (foot): 3,128 Officers and Men
   Natives (mounted): 243 Officers and Men
- *Total strength Effective and Non-effective: 10,238 Officers and Men*

General Wood's Flying Column.
- 11-7th Royal Artillery: 87 Officers and Men
- Royal Engineers: 13 Officers and Men
- 1-13th Regiment: 721 Officers and Men
- 90th Regiment: 823 Officers and Men
- 1st Squadron Mounted Infantry: 103 Officers and Men
- Army Service Corps: 9 Officers and Men
- Army Hospital Corps: 13 Officers and Men
- Frontier Light Horse: 173 Officers and Men
- Baker's Horse: 179 Officers and Men
- Transvaal Rangers: 141 Officers and Men
- 1st Battalion Wood's Irregulars:—
   Europeans: 14 Officers and Men
   Natives: 377 Officers and Men
- 2nd Battalion Wood's Irregulars:—
   Europeans: 5 Officers and Men
   Natives: 355 Officers and Men
- Natal Native Horse:—
   Europeans: 4 Officers and Men
   Natives: 75 Officers and Men
- *Total strength Effective and Non-effective: 3,092 Officers and Men*

Grand Total.
- 1st Division: 9,215 Officers and Men
- 2nd Division: 10,238 Officers and Men
- General Wood's Flying Column: 3,092 Officers and Men
- *Total Effective and Non-effective, namely, Europeans 15,660, and Natives 6,885: 22,545 Officers and Men*

Out of this grand total there were above 400 sick and noneffective with the 1st Division, 300 with the 2nd Division, and 600 (including some of Wood's Irregulars absent and not accounted for since the 28th March) with Wood's Flying Column. So that altogether, deducting say 1,500, Lord Chelmsford had at his disposal from the middle of April, a total of 21,000 troops, of which over 15,000 were Europeans. Colonels Pearson and Wood were made Brigadier-Generals; and the former was to command No. 1 Brigade, 1st Division, and Colonel Pemberton, 3-60th, the other. They both, however, had to give up their commands through sickness, and Colonels Rowlands, V.C, C.B., and Clarke, 57th Regiment, succeeded them.

Major-General Clifford, V.C., C.B., had the following Staff for the management of the base of operations, and the maintenance of the lines of communications between Zululand and Natal:— Lieutenant Westmacott, 77th Foot, Aide-de-Camp; Major W. F. Butler, C.B., Assistant Adjutant and Quartermaster General, stationed at Durban; and Captain W. B. Fox, Royal Artillery, Deputy Assistant Adjutant and Quartermaster-General.

At the same time it may be noted that Prince Louis Napoleon had volunteered for service, and arrived by the U.R.M.S. Danube, being shortly afterwards appointed extra A.D.G. to Lord Chelmsford; and he accompanied him on his journey to inspect the 2nd Division and Wood's Flying Column. His Imperial Highness arrived on the 31st March, and met with a most enthusiastic reception.

Lord Chelmsford left Durban during the second week in April, and after a short stay in Pieter Maritzburg, left for Dundee and Utrecht on Tuesday, the 22nd, accompanied by Colonel Crealock, C.B., Major Gossett, and Captains Molyneux and Bailer. Prince Napoleon, extra A.D.C., and Surgeon-Major Scotty late 18th Hussars, then recently attached to His Excellency's Staff, did not leave until the following Friday, on account of the indisposition of the Prince. Lieutenant Milne, R.A., A.D.C., who had been very ill since his return from Etshowi, was unable to get away for some time after. Major-General Newdigate, with the various officers connected with his Staff and Division, also left during the week for Landmann's Drift and Doornberg, where the Second Division was to be organised; and Colonel Bellairs, D.A.G., Major Grenfell, D.A.A.G., and Major Spalding, D.A.Q.M.G., also left Pieter Maritzburg with the Head-quarters for Utrecht. General Crealock proceeded to the Lower Tugela shortly after his arrival, and at once began his preparations for an advance early in May. General Marshall went up to Pieter Maritzburg, and with his staff awaited the arrival of the Cavalry Brigade, which was marching up in four wings. Among the many other officers who volunteered or came out on special service, at this time, I may name Lord William Beresford, who came over from Khiva, and who was at once appointed staff officer to Brigadier General Wood, in the place of the late Captain the Hon. R. Campbell.

On the march up the Head-quarters and right wing of the 17th Lancers were the first to arrive at Pieter Maritzburg, on Wednesday 23rd, and were followed by the 5th Battalion Naval Brigade, Royal Artillery, under Major LeGrice, and the Army Service Corps Companies. The Dragoon Guards came next, and the left wing of the 17th Lancers brought up the rear of the Cavalry Brigade a few days afterwards. They were all marched off as soon as possible in wings, in the order they arrived at Pieter Maritzburg; and on Wednesday the 30th, General Marshall with his aide-de-camp. Lord Downe, A.D.C., Major Stuart, Brigade Major; and the Honourable Guy Dawnay, left town for Dundee, whither the left wing of the Lancers and the Army Service Corps followed. The same day Commissary-General Strickland and Staff arrived in Maritzburg.

The town was full of "Specials," all attracted north-westwards; and during the last few days of April, and the first few in May, Archibald Forbes arrived for the Daily News, leaving Mr. Collins to remain with the Coast Division; also Francis Francis of the Times, which paper was ably, though officially, represented with General Crealock. They were followed by Mr. Philip Robinson, of the Daily Telegraph, who remained at Pieter Maritzburg, sending Hon. A. Bourke, with Head-quarters, and Mr. Capel H. Miers, to the First Division. Messrs. Fripp, of the Graphic, and Melton Prior, of the Illustrated, also went up towards Dundee, and I followed with M. Paul Deléage who had come out to represent the Paris Figaro. As he was unable to speak English, I was glad to offer him my assistance and company en route. We were nearly the last to leave and had arranged to ride the whole way; but as he wished to push on and I wanted to keep with the left wing of the 17th Lancers, whom I caught up a few miles out of Pieter Maritzburg, we parted after the first day's journey, and I saw him no more for some time.

CHAPTER XXIII

A CONSIDERABLE PERIOD now elapsed, in which the troops were on the march, for concentration at the positions taken up as Head-quarters of the various Divisions. My notes of the occurrences connected with the movements of the Cavalry Brigade, interesting enough at the time, would now be deemed monotonous and trivial. The route was diversified by a few false alarms, which kept the men on the alert, but were fortunately, otherwise unattended by evil results; as also by sundry rumours of fighting on the frontier, and even of Zulu raids across the Buffalo River, either actual or prospective. One of these was caused by an error of an officer of the King's Dragoon Guards, who was out scouting on the River bank, and reported that a body of about 1,000 natives had crossed or bivouacked in Natal. The supposed enemy, however, turned out to be only Major Bengough's Battalion, N.N.C., on its march from the Umsinga to Landmann's Drift, which had made a reconnoitring incursion into Zululand and burnt several kraals. Landmann's Drift was the Head-Quarters of the 2nd Division of the British South African field-force, under Major-General Newdigate. The camp itself was situated about 600 yards on the Natal side of the river, on the right hand side of the road leading down to the Drift. Three earthwork forts had been built end on to each other, in a kind of echelon, with about fifty yards between each. The Cavalry and Artillery camp were placed between two of them, and the cattle laager, made of waggons, in the other space, thus bringing them well under shelter of the guns and amply protected by flank-fire on each side. Major-General Newdigate's Staff consisted of Captain Lane, Rifle Brigade, and Sir W. Gordon Cumming, A.D.C.'s, Major Robinson, Rifle

Brigade, A.A.G., Major Gossett, 54th Regiment, A.Q.M.G., and Lieutenant-Colonel Montgomery, Scots Fusilier Guards, D.A.A.G., and Q.M.G. There was a large hospital, with Surgeon-Major Semple as P.M.O., and the Rev. Mr. Smith (of Rorke's Drift notoriety), and Father Bellord, respectively the Protestant and Roman Catholic chaplains. Colonel Tatton Browne commanded the Royal Artillery, and Captain Anstey the Royal Engineers. At Doornberg, seven miles away, there were also a fort and a laager, being the post commanded by Major Tucker, 80th Regiment. Farther on, another twelve miles, our most advanced spot. Conference Hill, was commanded by Colonel Davies, Grenadier Guards, who had with him six companies of the 94th Regiment, Bettington's troop of Natal Horse, a detachment Royal Engineers, and Shepstone's mounted Basutos. For their defence there was another fort and laager. While eight miles farther on towards the north-east was Brigadier-General Wood's new camp at Magwechana, close to the Sand Spruit, one of the sources of the White Umvoloosi.

It was during this interval of preparation that a second visit to the fatal field of Isandwhlana was made from Rorke's Drift, of which I subsequently received an account from some of the officers present. The party consisted of seventeen volunteers, mostly officers, under Colonel Black, 2-24th; among whom were the Hons. G. Bertie, Coldstream Guards, and the Master of Colville, Grenadier Guards, Captains Symons, Bannister, Wrench, Bell; Lieutenants Mainwaring, Logan, Phipps, and Lloyd. They started at 4 a.m., every precaution being taken to guard against surprise, and after a brisk ride through the Bashee Valley, the ridge overlooking the battle-plain of Isandwhlana was reached just at sunrise. Vedettes were posted, and the ground was carefully examined, but little of value being found. Nearly 100 waggons and other vehicles were still left, mostly in good condition. The only discovery worthy of note was that of Lieutenant Pope's diary, in which the latest entry was as follows:—

"22nd January, 1879—4 a.m.— A, C, D, E, F, H Companies of ours—1,2,3 N.N.C.—mounted troops and four guns off.

Great Firing.

Relieved by 1-24th.

Alarm.

3 Columns Zulus and mounted men on hill E.

Turn Out. 7,000 (!!!) *more* E.N.E., 4,000 of whom went round Lion's Kop.

Durnford, Basutos, arrive and pursue.—Rocket Battery.

Zulus retire everywhere.

Men fall out for dinners."

In returning, the party followed the Fugitives' path, which was easily traced by the debris and dead bodies; crossing, with some difficulty, the ravine, where the two guns had been abandoned and captured, another quarter of a mile brought them to a watercourse with steep banks, and here the party were fired upon by a small party of Zulus on the hills above, who kept well under cover and fired several shots.

The precipitous rocky bank of the river lay three miles farther on, over a very rough road and broken ground. Here the party divided and a careful search was made for the body of Major Smith, R.A., who lost his life in the vicinity. Lieutenant Mainwaring, fortunately, soon came upon the body, nearly concealed by the rank growth of grass, and clearly recognisable by the uniform. Captain Symons after a steep bit of climbing reached the top of the cliff, finding numerous bodies of men and horses, where they had crashed headlong down, sorely pressed by the pursuers. While in the act of giving a rough burial to the remains of poor Major Smith, they were again fired on by Zulus. Hastening up the river, they were enabled to get safely across at the Drift, where a company of the N.N.C. had been sent by the forethought of Major Bengough, and drove off the thirty or forty Zulus who had followed up, hoping to take the party at a disadvantage while crossing. The principal object of the expedition, namely, to search the Fugitives' path had been thoroughly carried out. A report had reached the officers of the 2-24th, that in the flight, a tall officer, on a chestnut horse, with a colour, had been seen between the battle-field and the river, on the 22nd of January; but no trace could be seen of the officer or colour, supposed to have been Lieutenant Dyer, the Adjutant of the 2-24th. The look-out men at the signal station reported that some small bodies of Zulus, some of them mounted, had come into view at Isandwhlana, after the party had quitted the field, and had come down the Bashee Valley, whereby a rencontre, and perhaps loss of life was avoided.

On the Saturday following, May 17th, the camp was thrown into a state of great excitement, by the announcement that the General, after consulting General Newdigate, had determined to start on the Monday morning with all the cavalry for Isandwhlana, via Rorke's Drift, in order to visit the camp, bury the dead and bring away the waggons and any relics that might be found. Accordingly, on the 19th an early start was made, the Army Service Corps, waggons, and mounted Native scouts leading the way, followed by the two regiments of Dragoon Guards, and the Lancers bringing up the rear. Strong advanced and rear guards, and flanking patrols a mile away, provided full precautions to secure our march. After bivouacking one night on the road, at Dill's House, the brigade reached Rorke's Drift between three and four, and were there joined by the Natal Carbineers, and Colonel Harness, R.A., with two guns. No very strong body of the enemy had lately been seen anywhere in the neighbourhood; but the presence of an Impi of 2,000 or 8,000 Zulus near Matshana's stronghold was reported.

All the arrangements having been completed over night,

General Marshall led the reconnoitring force across the river at day-break on Tuesday, having with him one regiment each of the Lancers and the Dragoon Guards, Natal Carbineers, Mounted Police, Rangers, and Scouts, and two guns, with the Anny Service Corps and seventy-pairs of led horses. The advance was made in open order, no signs of the enemy being visible until close upon our destination. Then signal-fires were seen on the hills to the right, and spread quickly along the course of the river, to the Inshlazagaze mountains. In the meantime, Colonel Drury Lowe had gone in advance of us, with the other regiments of Lancers and Dragoon Guards, and some Carbineers, and scouts, in order to make a circuit to the left, round Sirayo's Kraal, and intercept any Zulu force in that direction. Bengough's N.N.G. battalion followed in their route, and Colonel Black, with four companies 2-24th, took up a position on the rising ground at the head of the Bashee Valley, to protect our rear, and frustrate any attempt to cut us off. The N.N.C., and Lowe's Cavalry Brigade were to meet us at Isandwhlana; and as we progressed we were able to trace their advance by the smoke from the kraals to which they set fire. Away in front of us our own scouts were racing to reach the scene first. Pushing on steadily and carefully we reached the plain of Isandwhlana between 9 and 10 a.m.

I found the whole site of the conflict over-grown with grass, thickly intermixed with green and growing stalks of oats and mealies. Concealed among these, lay the corpses of our soldiers, in all postures and stages of decay; while the site of the camp itself was indicated by the debris of the tents, intermingled with a heterogeneous mass of broken trunks, boxes, meat-tins, and their contents, with confused masses of papers, books, letters, etc., scattered in wild disorder. The sole visible objects, however, were the waggons, more or less broken up, and the skeletons of horses and oxen. All else was hidden from view, and could only be found by a close search. I had the melancholy satisfaction of discovering my own tent, or rather the disjecta membra of what had once been mine; and immediately behind it were the skeletons of my horses, with the bodies of my servants, just as I had left them picketed on the 22nd of January, when I accompanied the reconnoitring force with Lord Chelmsford. But I could find nothing of any value remaining; my papers, letters and books were lying about, torn up. I found, and brought away with me as mementoes, some of my wife's letters, a book of some of my MS. stories, and a photograph that had reached me just two days before the massacre.

While the work of harnessing the horses to the best of the waggons was being actively prosecuted, all the men, except those on duty as vedettes or otherwise, were permitted to wander over the scene of the disaster; and various interesting relics were found and brought away. In some cases letters from those who were among the slain, addressed to their relatives at home, were obtained complete, and these would doubtless be treasured by the recipients, notwithstanding the painful re-opening of wounds scarce healed. Captain Shepstone, with the Carbineers, after some search, came across the corpses of Colonel Durnford, R.E., Captain Bradstreet, N.M.R., Lieutenant Scott, N.C., and all their slain comrades, except London, Bullock, and the few who were killed on the Fugitives' path. Poor Durnford was easily recognisable, as he had on his mess waistcoat, from the pocket of which Shepstone took a small pocket-knife with his name on it; two rings were taken from the dead man's hand, and preserved with the knife, for transmission to his family. The body of Durrant Scott was found, hidden partially under a broken piece of waggon, evidently unmutilated and untouched. He had his patrol jacket buttoned across, and while the body was almost only a skeleton, the face was still preserved and lifelike, all the hair remaining, and the skin strangely parched and dried up, though still perfect. All these lay together, and, judging from their position, these brave young colonists must here have made their last gallant stand, and all perished together. Standing by one another to the last in life, without attempt at flight, so we found them still associated in death. Peace to their ashes! Having known them all well, I felt quite unequal to a minute examination, and quickly quitted that part of the field. Colonel Durnford's body was wrapped in canvas and buried in a sort of waterwash. The others were covered over with stones, in default of better burial or subsequent removal, and their names written in pencil on wood or stone close by, a too transient memorial, but all that was possible. The Royal Artillery, and Natal Mounted Police buried all the bodies of their slain comrades to be found. But those of the 2-24th alone were left untouched, at the express desire of Colonel Glynn and the officers of the regiment, in the hope that they might themselves be enabled some day to render these last sad honours to their dead comrades. This feeling, even if a mistaken one, merits respect and consideration. No other bodies of officers were recognised, so far as I could learn, except those of Lieutenants Gibson and the Hon. S. Vereker, N.N.C. The General being anxious, for many and obvious reasons, not to delay our return, a start was made as soon as the waggons were ready, and we reached Rorke's Drift at 8.30 p.m., without any incident. Among the forty waggons brought away there were two water-carts, three Scotch carts, one gun-limber, and a rocket-battery cart; about twenty were left behind in a more or less disabled condition, unfit for removal; consequently, some sixty or seventy more waggons were missing, and must have been removed by the enemy at different times. Among the kraals which were burnt that day, one contained signs of very recent occupation, and the staff of the Queen's Colour of the 1-24th was found there. In another, about two miles away from the camp, many skeletons of Zulus were found, and in another direction some large Zulu graves were discovered; showing that the enemy, as I conjectured at the time, must have carried away many of their dead and wounded in our waggons.

On the morning after our expedition, a squadron of Lancers, with some Artillery under Colonel Harness, went down our side of the river, and crossed over at the Fugitives' Drift, returning in the afternoon, after having duly effected their object; which was to give burial to the remains of Major Stuart Smith, found, as previously narrated, by Colonel Black and his party on the 15th May.

CHAPTER XXIV

IN THE meantime, however, the authorities were actively engaged, with the other branch of Her Majesty's Service, and in another quarter. For a long time, almost in fact from the beginning of the war, hopes had been expressed of its being possible to find a landing-place on the Zulu coast, somewhere between the month of the Tugela and St. Lucia Bay; as it was thought, very naturally, that if we were able to form a station easily accessible from the sea in the enemy's country itself, a great deal of time and money might be saved; and it would effectually obviate all the evils of the heavy, slow, and cumbersome ox-transport in such a deadly district, and over such heavy roads; and at the same time prevent the necessity of continually sending detachments to escort convoys between the Lower Tugela and Fort Chelmsford, which, more than almost anything else, told so heavily on the troops engaged in that unpleasant duty. H.M. ships Active and Tenedos were the first sent up to regularly explore the coast, and did good service until the Tenedos got ashore on a reef hitherto unknown, or at any rate not marked down on any of the charts in its right position. The crew of the Active, although shorthanded, under the splendid example and direction of Lieutenant Marrack, worked hard for nearly thirty-six hours in assisting their consort off the reef, and fortunately their efforts were rewarded by success. But as the Tenedos had to proceed to Simon's Bay for repairs, it was deemed better to await the arrival of H.M. gunboat Forester, then on her way out, than to risk a large ship like H.M.S. Active on that coast again. The Tenedos had, some months previously, put ashore a Naval Brigade of sixty men, under Lieutenant Kingscote; and, after the arrival of the Shah and Boadicea, it was found possible to allow them to rejoin their ship at Simon's Bay, so that she should not have to sail home shorthanded. They, therefore, left Durban in the middle of May, in the hired transport steamship Andean for Simon's Bay. These men had done a good deal of work in connection with the campaign. They helped to make the pontoon bridge at the Lower Tugela, garrisoned Fort Tenedos for a long time, and then rendered important service in Zululand.

Towards the middle of April, H.M.S. Forester was sent up on her first trip of exploration along the coast from the Lower Tugela to Point Durnford, a stretch of about forty-five or fifty miles. She returned with a satisfactory report, and paid a second visit on the 23rd to take soundings. On the 24th the men engaged in this service, with the boats inshore, were fired upon by a large body of Zulus, who suddenly made their appearance on the beach. The fire was returned, and the boats at once taken out to sea to rejoin the ship; no casualties occurred, fortunately, though the boats' crews had a very narrow escape. The Zulus retreated into the bush, and their cover was shelled with considerable effect. A third trip resulted in the selection of a possible landing-place near the outlet of the Umlalaas, a blind river, of which the water is discharged into the sea by percolation through the sand. This site was about ten miles south of Point Durnford, and received the name of Port Durnford. The coast is of course very exposed, necessitating the use of steamers and surf-boats; and even then, as the result showed, landing might not always be practicable. Nevertheless, it was the only suitable site, and bad might be regarded as better than none.

On shore. General Crealock was busy with the organisation of his (No. 1) Division, and accumulating at Fort Chelmsford sufficient stores to enable him to make an advance up the coast to the river Umlalaas, so as to occupy an entrenched station there for the purposes of the projected landing, which it was decided to effect. While the necessary boats and equipment were being provided, the Forester made another trip along the coast. The Zulus were seen in considerable numbers, on the hills and beach, and were again shelled with considerable loss. but the information derived cast some doubt on the prospects of an effectual landing being made, and showed that the difficulties were numerous.

All these reports having reached the public, and much importance being attached to the scheme of the naval authorities for establishing a landing place at Port Durnford, I was summoned down by telegraph from Rorke's Drift to proceed at once to Durban, and take a passage on board any of the steamers going thither. The summons was so peremptory that it left me no option but to give up all hopes of going in with the cavalry; and I said good-bye to my numerous friends, feeling myself to be a much ill-used and disappointed man. The telegram was sent on from Ladysmith and reached me on the day after my second visit to Isandwhlana. On Thursday, May 22, I again turned my horse's head eastward. Coming down the Border-road on this occasion I passed plenty of loaded waggons on the way up, and the grass was good all along. Ample preparations had been made for the defence of the Border-line, and from Helpmakaar, where Tateleka's Mounted Natives were stationed, down to opposite Grey Town, large bodies of natives were posted at intervals. Patrols into the enemy's country were of constant occurrence. Near Fynn's (the magistrate) house 1,500 of the Native Reserve were encamped, under Commandant Reynolds; while lower down came Mr. Knight with 900, Mr. Frankish with 350, and De Boor with 250.

At Grey Town the good people of the town had had a scare the night before my arrival; and I found this sort of thing was of constant occurrence, partly, no doubt, in consequence of the numerous raids made from Grey Town to Kranzkop in the adjoining Zulu border country. Orders, however, were soon afterwards received to stop all border-raids; and considering that our farmers, living near the Buffalo or Tugela, had everything to lose, and the Zulus nothing (for they could easily move their cattle farther away, and rebuild their kraals elsewhere), it must be admitted that our best policy would have been to keep strictly on the defensive. I reached Pieter Maritzburg the same evening by post cart, and found that neither H.M.S. Forester nor the two transports would leave for at least another week.

In consequence, however, of a farther probable detention of the expedition to Port Durnford, owing to the land forces not being moved up with sufficient rapidity, I found that there would be time for me to run up to the Lower Tugela and back, before the ships sailed. I, therefore, determined to make the journey pro bono publico, by inspecting on my way and reporting upon the hospital arrangements made at the base and front for the reception and recovery of the numberless convoys of wounded sent down from the coast-column. For although every one who knows the coast-country at all had expected that the list of sick and wounded would be very heavy, yet no one for an instant supposed that the number would be so great as it was; and, therefore, it was suspected that either lack of medical men, or want of proper hospital accommodation and treatment, might have something to do with the great increase, or else that some other cause must have largely contributed to it. Having, therefore, a little time at my disposal, I determined to judge for myself as to the accuracy of public reports.

I first visited the three principal Military Hospitals at Durban, where I had many conversations with the medical officers about the reports prevalent with regard to the failure of medical arrangements at the front, and even at Fort Pearson; and there can be little doubt that in the earlier part of the campaign our forces were miserably deficient not only of medical officers, but also of proper supplies of medicines, instruments, and all the numerous paraphernalia necessary to render the surgeon's aid valuable in the field. We need not go farther for an example of this than the instance shown so clearly, but sadly, in the account of the besieged at Etshowi, or the well known scarcity of quinine and instruments, &c.

The new system, however, has also much to answer for; and from what I have seen during this campaign I feel assured that many improvements will have to be made before it can equal or supersede the old regimental system. Of course field and base hospitals are very necessary, but it must be clear to the meanest capacity that it is much better, in time of active warfare, for each regiment to have its own medical aid attached to it than have to depend on strangers, whether belonging to the A.M.D. or merely civil surgeons. Towards the latter end of the war, however, great amelioration was effected; and subsequently, during my two months with Sir Garnet Wolseley in Zululand, I particularly noticed that the medical arrangements then in vogue were excellent.

While I was occupied in this investigation, the rumour reached Durban that the Prince Imperial had been killed by the Zulus while on duty in advance of the Head-quarters Column; but as nothing definite was known, and the report was contradicted in several presumably well-informed quarters, it was very generally disbelieved. Unfortunately, as all the world quickly knew, it turned out to be too true. I, therefore, proceeded on my tour of hospital inspection, as far as the Lower Tugela, visiting that at Harwen, near Stanger, on the way. As far as I could judge, the many complaints which had been made were not entirely well-founded; and the shortcomings which existed were mainly such as would be inseparable from the hospital service at the front, in such a country and under such conditions. They may partially also be attributed to the fact that no adequate estimate or allowance had at the outset been made of the large number of sick who were likely to, and did, come on the list: consequently, the medical staff originally sent out was insufficient, and the stores similarly deficient. Something may also be set down to the effects of climate along the coast-line. The principal diseases which prevailed were— enteric fever, dysentery, and coast fever which is of the type of low fever. Another thing worthy of note is that the proportion of young soldiers invalided was very great, indicating that raw recruits and short-service men are not the best fitted for a campaign in such a climate. The proportion of the sick was nothing like so great among the older men who had seen service elsewhere, or regiments which had been any length of time away from England.

From the purely military point of view I found great changes had been made in the way of new defensive works, and considerable progress had been made in the organisation of the 1st Division, by Major-General Crealock, as well as in the transport of stores to the front, and their accommodation at Fort Chelmsford, as the base of the forward movement against Ulundi from the coast, in co-operation with the other Divisions from inland. To facilitate these essential operations temporary bridges across the Lower Tugela were constructed. Two convoys were sent forward weekly, under escort of a strong force, of never less than 1,000 men, two guns and some mounted men; the General being determined to exercise caution, and run no risk of disaster happening unexpectedly. It must be admitted that the commanders on land were disposed to expect but little from the naval scheme of landing stores, &c., at Port Durnford, and, therefore, were anxious to forward as large stocks as possible by land, so as to be comparatively independent for supplies, in case of emergency during active operations early in June. At this time provisions for six weeks were already in store at Fort Chelmsford, and another month's supply was on the road up. The naval expedition, it was expected, would land a six weeks' supply, and might, if requisite, land stores for two months more. As a necessary preliminary to any such enterprise being successfully carried out. General Pearson's first duty was to advance from Fort Chelmsford across the river Umlalazi and establish the depot at Fort Durnford, these two depots becoming the bases of a rapid march upon the King's kraal. And this was effected in due course. The Staff of the First Division of the British South African Field Force, under Major-General Crealock, consisted of Major Walker, 99th, A.A.G.; Captain Garden, D.A.Q.M.G.; Captain Murray, D.A.A.G.; Captains Byng and Button, 60th Rifles, A.D.C.'s; Sub-Lieutenant Coatsworth, Naval A.D.C.; Colonel Law, C.R.A.; Captain Blood, C.R.E., with A.C.G. Healy; Major Barrow, commanding mounted troops, and Captain Campbell, the Naval Brigade.

Colonel Walker, Scot's Guards, was Commandant at the Lower Tugela. Colonel Rowlands, V.C., C.B., commanded the 1st Brigade, with Captain McGregor as Brigade-Major; and Colonel Clarke, 67th Regiment, was at Fort Chelmsford in command of the Second Brigade, and had Captain Hart for his Brigade-Major.

Meanwhile I returned to Durban, having had a cabin on board the Forester placed at my service by Commodore Richards, to enable me to accompany the sea expedition. And I arrived in time to be present at the ceremonials which attended the funeral cortege, conveyance, and embarkation of the body of the unfortunate Louis Napoleon, late Prince Imperial of France.

CHAPTER XXV

THE DEATH of the Prince Imperial, considered per se, can only be regarded as a minor episode of the campaign, especially from the merely military standpoint. But various causes— his rank and misfortunes, his connection with the British army, the actual incidents of the fatality, arising out of the duties of the expedition, and lastly, the subsequent proceedings in connection with the inquiry by court-martial—combined to invest it with a special pathos and interest, almost world-wide. At first, great uncertainty prevailed as to the exact circumstances under which the Prince met with his death. The first version made public was that of the official telegram as follows:—

"Commandant Ladysmith to General Clifford, Pieter Maritzburg.

June 2.

"Account of the Prince's death from Itelemie Hill this morning. The Prince and Carey, 98th Regiment, were at a kraal, twelve miles from Itelemie Hill. When mounting to return, the Zulus jumped out of the grass and fired, missing the lot. Prince and two Europeans rode into donga. Zulus were hidden there. Assegaied the three. Had they ridden in a different direction, probably they would have escaped."

Another despatch, of June the 6th, varied somewhat in its details from the above account, stating that "the Prince rode ten miles from General Newdigate's camp with escort of Captain Carey and six men of Bettington's Horse, and one Basuto. Off-saddled close to a mealie field. Suddenly attacked by twenty Zulus. Horse being restive. Prince unable to mount, fell underneath, and was kicked and then killed, with one trooper and Basuto. Body found next day with twenty assegai wounds."

The death of the Prince Imperial, by Paul Jamin (1853-1903). c.1882

The real facts of the case, as will be seen, were slightly different.

The result was to some extent influenced by the anomalous position held by the Prince, and the independence of his peculiar non-official connection with the expedition. His application for a regular commission having very properly been refused by the military authorities at home, he was only present as a volunteer; nevertheless, he held some kind of a recognised position as an extra aide-de-camp to Lord Chelmsford, who had given special instructions as to the duties on which he was to be employed, and the manner of their execution, with a view to prevent his rashly incurring unnecessary and unavoidable risks. These restrictions somewhat chafed the Prince, who seemed inclined to seek adventure and put himself forward, at any chance of having a brush with the Zulus. This led to his becoming in some way transferred or attached to the Quartermaster-General's Department, to which, from his thorough military education at Woolwich, he was considered a welcome coadjutor. At any rate, he was engaged on a reconnoitring survey on the 1st of June, when he met his death, and he was duly provided with an escort under Lieutenant Carey, whose special duty it was or should have been to secure his safety. The superior officer more immediately concerned and responsible in the matter was Lieutenant-Colonel Harrison, A.Q.M.G., with whom, personally, the Prince was believed by the Lieutenant-General commanding. Lord Chelmsford, to be. And it appears from the subsequent official despatch of Field-Marshal the Duke of Cambridge, Commander-in-Chief (reviewing the proceedings of the court-martial on Lieutenant Carey), that the Duke was of opinion that Lieutenant-Colonel Harrison had erred in "failing to impress upon the Prince the duty of deferring to the military orders of the officer who accompanied him, and the necessity of guiding himself by his advice and experience," as well as in that "his orders to Lieutenant Carey were not sufficiently explicit," and that he should have "displayed more firmness and forethought in his instructions to Lieutenant Carey and the Prince."

The special duty on which the Prince was employed was making sketches and to select a camp on the Ityotyozi River, and the escort provided consisted of six troopers of Bettington's Horse, under Lieutenant Carey, and a native guide. It has also been stated that there were to have been six mounted Basutos in addition, but these did not arrive in time. This, however, seems doubtful, and is of little importance. The reconnoitring party proceeded on their expedition, and in the afternoon halted and off-saddled at a deserted kraal on the banks of the Ityotyozi, surrounded by mealie-gardens and abundance of cover to conceal the approach of an enemy. It appears that the native guide had reported the presence of Zulus in the vicinity, and shortly afterwards, just as the Prince had given the order to mount, a sudden volley took them by surprise, and a body of Zulus rushed upon the party. There can be no doubt at all that it was sauve qui peut, and Lieutenant Carey and his escort mounted and rode off, each for himself, as best they could, without any attempt at defence or rallying. The Prince and two troopers unfortunately lost their lives, and were only missed when the party re-assembled. So far as can be ascertained, the Prince's horse was restive and startled by the volley, so that the Prince was unable to mount. The holster of the saddle seems to have given way, after the Prince had run a little distance with the horse, vainly attempting to get into the saddle. Thus he fell, and being surrounded by the Zulus was slain, with his face to the foe.

The escort, in their flight, fell in with General Wood and Colonel Buller, with a party also reconnoitring the road for the Flying Column, and the General gave very significant expression to his opinion of the whole affair. It was then 5 p.m., the mischief was done, and it was too late to do anything more that day. On the following day a strong cavalry detachment, under General Marshall, was sent out to visit the kraal and recover the dead bodies, which was successfully accomplished. The body of the Prince Imperial was found by Captain Cochrane, of the Natal Mounted Horse, lying in a donga, and appeared not to have been dragged after death, but to have fallen where he lay. He was lying on his back with the left arm across the breast, as if in self-defence. There were eighteen assegai-wounds, all in front, any-one of five of which would have been fatal; there was a wound through the right eye, the eyeball being out, but no bullet wounds, and there was the usual gash across the abdomen, exposing the intestines, as generally inflicted by the Zulus after death. The body had been stripped, but a fine gold chain remained round the neck, with a medallion and locket of the Ex-Empress Eugenie, his mother. The bodies of the two troopers of the escort who fell were found close by and were decently buried on the spot. The dead body of the Prince was

'Lord Chelmsford following the body of the Prince Imperial'.
Engraving from the Illustrated London News, July 1879

removed to the camp, where identification of the body was duly and formally completed—as subsequently attested in a statement signed by Major-General Clifford, Colonel Mitchell, Monsieur Deleage, special correspondent of the Paris Figaro, and Xavier Uhlmann, one of the deceased Prince's attendants, an old, faithful, and respected servant of the late Emperor Napoleon III.

The whole circumstances of the affair, the weakness of the escort, the rashness and neglect of due caution displayed all round, the headlong flight, &c., &c., became the subject of a good deal of discussion and no little animadversion, even amounting to strong condemnation for pusillanimity in many quarters. In the result, Lieutenant Carey was suspended from Staff duty on the 11th of June, and brought to trial by Court-Martial on the following day, for "having been guilty of misbehaviour before the enemy." The result of the deliberations is not quite clear. It was almost certainly adverse to the prisoner, who was sent home under arrest. But by the Horse-Guards' despatch from the

War Office, dated August 16th, Lieutenant Carey was "released from arrest, because Her Majesty had been advised that the charge was not sustained by the evidence," and therefore did not confirm the proceedings. But the Commander-in-Chief did not hesitate to say that "Lieutenant Carey, from the first, formed a wrong estimate of his position, and hence omitted to take essential measures of precaution," and to express, "with the voice of the army, his regret that, whether or not an attempt at rescue was possible, the survivors of this fatal expedition withdrew from the scene of disaster without the full assurance that all efforts on their part were not abandoned until the fate of their comrades had been sealed." Substantially, every one will endorse these opinions and sentiments. (A copy of the above despatch, and summary of the evidence given at the Court-Martial, will be found in Appendix H.)

It only remains to add that the body of the Prince was conveyed via Pieter Maritzburg to Durban, and placed on board the Boadicea for conveyance to the Cape, where it was transferred to the Orontes, and so brought back to England, and deposited in the Chapel at Chiselhurst. At all points of the transit of the melancholy cortege it was received with the deepest respect and sympathy, and honours almost regal. The details of processions and ceremonials observed, however interesting, would be too lengthy, and foreign to the object of this book.

CHAPTER XXVI

During the early part of the month of June, a very doubtful problem was solved, and a successful landing-place established at Port Durnford by the united efforts of the Coast Column and H.M.S. Forester with her convoy. Before giving the details of my sea trips in that gunboat, and the particulars of the actual landing, it may be as well to take a brief retrospective glance at the doings of General Crealock's Column from the end of April (after the relief of Etshowi) until its arrival in the Umlalazi Plains in June. After Fort Chelmsford was definitively fixed upon to be the main advanced depot for No. 1 Division of the South African Field Force, it was necessary to convey and store there, ready for use, at least two months, provisions for the whole force, before a general advance could be made towards Ulundi. With this view. Fort Crealock was established on the right bank of the Amatikulu, and another fortified position. Fort Walker, on the Inyoni River, for the purpose of protecting the convoys going and returning between Forts Pearson and Chelmsford, which usually took three days on the journey up, encamping each night at one of the two intermediate positions. These convoys, on an average, went up about twice a-week. The monotony of the month of May was varied by the surrender of Maquenda, a brother of the King—whose chief kraals were close by Fort Chelmsford—by the negotiations with Dabulamanzi and with other chiefs for their surrender, and the frequent rumours of attack. Envoys were also received from Cetywayo, but, as the bearers of these peace-overtures were men of no position, very little credence was given to their statements, and still less faith put in the King's so-called peaceful intentions. Great and increased precautions were taken against surprises either by day or night, at the forts or on convoys, as time passed, and nothing seemed certain as to the movements of the enemy, who only appeared in very small parties, and then rarely on this side of the Umlalazi. Early in June, things were so far advanced as to enable the 1st Division to move up to the front, which was done in two Columns, a few days only separating the advance of each. The field-telegraph had been established up to Fort Chelmsford, and upon the arrival of the whole Column at that position, it was intended to abandon all communication by road with Fort Pearson, and to rely entirely upon the two months' provisions stored at the depot, and the establishment of a landing-place on the coast. On the 20th June everything had been completed. Fort Crealock practically evacuated, and Fort Chelmsford made impregnable, with two months' provisions. On that day the forward movement was commenced, and by the end of the month the force was duly encamped on the sea-coast, at the spot selected for the landing-place. The crossing of the Umlalazi was effected by means of a pontoon-bridge, and all other difficulties of the road overcome. No serious opposition was encountered by the way. Some trifling skirmishes took place, but the Zulus of the district mostly retired towards the Umhlatoozi River as the Column advanced; and many submissions of chiefs and others took place. An entrenched position, called Fort Napoleon, was formed for the camp at the Umlalazi Siver, and a similar small earthwork, with shelter-trenches, was thrown up on a small eminence commanding the landing-place and its approaches, as well as the surrounding plains, at Port Durnford.

Meanwhile, in pursuance of previous arrangements, I had availed myself of the privilege offered me of a berth on board H.M.S. Forester, engaged on the naval duty of the expedition. The Forester, a composite gunboat of 455 tons, with engines of 60 H.P., was commanded by Lieutenant-Commander Sydney Smith, her armament being of four guns, namely, two

20-pounder breech-loaders fore and aft, and two 64-pounder converted 8-inch muzzle-loaders in centre of main deck, one forward, and the other abaft the mainmast, and her crew numbering 60 all told. Leaving Durban on the 19th June, she reached the selected site on the following day; but it was not till Monday, the 23rd, that the arrival of the Column took place, and communications were opened up with General Crealock. The Forester was then sent back to Durban, to prepare the transports and await orders for the final trips. These orders came on Sunday, the 29th, when the little squadron steamed off. There were, besides the gunboat, the steam-tug Koodoc, transport Natal, U.S.S., with Captain Twiss, R.N., as Chief Transport Officer, and the Tom Morton with mules and stores. Conspicuous among the accessories were two Algoa Bay surf-boats, specially purchased, at a cost of £1,000, and with crews complete. The landing operations, under the special supervision of the General in person and of the commanding naval officers, were commenced immediately after our arrival on the following day, when each surf-boat made two trips, landing about 80 tons of stores in all. The work was resumed next day, Tuesday, 1st July, but before noon the sea became rough, and the surf increased so that farther proceedings were impracticable, and all communication between the ships and the shore was cut off. This was of some practical inconvenience, as I and several others who had come on shore from the ships were unable to return on board or obtain any of our belongings; and we were thus cast on the hospitality of the officers in camp, notably of the 57th, or "Die-Hards." Similarly, officers from the camp, who had gone to visit the ships, were compelled to remain: and the situation was sufficiently embarrassing for all parties. But this inauspicious change in the weather and conditions bad, as will be seen, still worse effects, exemplifying in a remarkable way the difficulties and hazards of the landing-place on an open coast-line with a beach never free from surf.

News had been received that Sir Garnet Wolseley—who had just arrived out in Natal, having been sent out specially to take the command in chief of the British army and bring the war to a close—was coming up the coast on Wednesday, 2nd July, in H.M.S. Shah, in order to land at Port Durnford, and go up with the Column of the 2nd Division to Ulundi. We had also had the intelligence that Lieut.-General Lord Chelmsford, and Major-General Newdigate, and the 2nd Division, and Brigadier-General Wood's Flying Column, had already advanced to the vicinity of Ulundi, burnt a large kraal close by, and were expected to attack that stronghold of Cetywayo almost immediately. The prospect was disappointing for our Division, who would apparently not be able to get up in time to take any part in the decisive battle—as indeed turned out to be the case. In due course, however, the Shah arrived, with Sir Garnet on board, early on Wednesday morning; but unfortunately the surf, which had been running very heavily during the night, was still too high for a landing to be risked; and all preparations in honour of the Commander in Chief were made in vain. On the following morning there was a little better chance, but owing to some unaccountable delay in getting the party on board the tug, the surf having again increased, the attempt at landing proved abortive, although the hatches were battened down on the lighter, and the efforts were persevered in for more than an hour, until the conviction was forced upon all that the landing was not only dangerous but impracticable. In fact an accident occurred by the breaking of the tow-rope, which might very easily have had evil results. On Friday, however, no favourable change having taken place, the abortive attempt was given up, and the Shah steamed back to Durban with Sir Garnet Wolseley on board, his plans being necessarily changed by the contretemps, which compelled him to go up overland vid Forts Pearson and Chelmsford.

The monotony of camp-life was broken and varied by cavalry expeditions, in one of which, by a strong force, under Major Barrow and Lord Gifford, the large military kraal of Empangweni, one of Cetywayo's chief places, about fifteen miles away, was effectually destroyed, as well as all the kraals for six miles around. Some important surrenders of Zulu Chiefs and large numbers of natives, also occurred, and many cattle were captured and given up. As a matter of course, after the Shah's departure, the sea subsided, and landing operations were resumed, with much valuable work and results. After five days spent on shore, I was prevented by an unfortunate concatenation of circumstances from rejoining the Forester and my personal effects. So I went on board the Natal with Captain Brunker, D.A.Q.M.G., a companion in misfortune, and we reached Durban on Tuesday, July 8th. When we quitted the camp, they were momentarily expecting the arrival of Sir Garnet Wolseley; and in a state of excited preparation for a projected three days' patrol, with all the available cavalry, to try and open up communications with Lord Chelmsford near Ulundi. Before we left, however, the news arrived that Lord Chelmsford had defeated the enemy and destroyed Ulundi; and great was the disappointment as well as the rejoicing thereat. The prevailing sentiment was, that while regretting the 1st Division was not present at the battle, yet it was satisfactory that Lord Chelmsford had put the finishing stroke to the campaign before the absolute arrival of Sir Garnet Wolseley had finally taken the supreme command out of his hands. Just at starting a telegram advised us that Sir Garnet had at length reached the camp at Port Durnford from Fort Pearson.

CHAPTER XXVII

THE DELAYS and difficulties which had thus beset the establishment of a coast-depot, in connection with a sea-base of operations—together with the late arrival of the new Commander-in-Chief, Sir Garnet Wolseley, and his abortive attempts to effect a landing—combined to render the movements of the coast-column, or 1st Division, to which I had attached myself, comparatively ineffective in co-operating for the ultimate aim of the renewed campaign, namely, the destruction of the King's Kraal at Ulundi, and the capture of the Zulu monarch himself. The brunt of this part of the work consequently fell upon the Columns of Generals Newdigate and Wood, encamped—when last noticed in this history, vide Chapter XXII.—at Kambula and Landmann's Drift. It now becomes necessary to return to that time, and trace by what stages General Lord Chelmsford succeeded in bringing about the final battle at Ulundi, in capturing Cetywayo, and in completely breaking up the Zulu military power.

After it had been decided that General Wood was to retain the command of his own Flying Column, separately from either Division, no move was made by him until the beginning of May, when the Column marched south about fifteen miles, and encamped at a site just under Laguey's Kop, called Segonyamana Camp. On the preceding Saturday Lord Chelmsford and his staff, with the Prince Imperial, arrived in the camp, and they left again on the day the first move was made, being accompanied by General Wood as far as Conference Hill, from which place they rode back to Landmann's Drift. Lord Chelmsford, during his short stay, inspected the site of the camps and fight at Kambula, and also rode over to the Zuinguin, from which he had a good view of the Zlobani Mountain. Another move of a few miles in the same southerly direction followed a few days afterwards to a place called Magwechana; and then, on the 25th May (Sunday), the first real move towards Ulundi since the Flying Column had left Kambula was made. The new position then taken up was situated between the two mountains marked on the military map as Nkandi and Mundbla, where a fort was erected by Major Moysey, R.E. The force stayed here some days; and on the 28th, the 80th Regiment, under Major Tucker, joined the Column, and were quickly followed by Major Owens, R.A., with a battery of four Gatlings, and a company of Royal Engineers under Captain Jones. On June 1st, the Column again moved to a camp near the Itelezi, which brought them close to Newdigate's Column, upon whose left flank they were to operate. The next advance brought them to the Ityotyozi River, on June 2nd. (It was here that Prince Louis Napoleon lost his life.) On the following day they shifted camp just across the river, and although it was a short trek of only a mile, the task of crossing the stream involved a great deal of labour; and to effect the transit of nearly three hundred waggons, even through a good drift, is no easy work. It would have been an utter impossibility, on this as on many other occasions, had it not been for fatigue-parties of infantry and others being put on to help. Another short march of three miles was made on the next day, in which they crossed the Mangwini River, another affluent of the White Umvoloosi, and from there they went on and encamped at a place called Matyamhlopi, from a hill of that name on the left of the road the Column was pursuing; this was on the 5th, and on the same day the skirmish took place at the Ezunganyan, in which Lieut, Frith, 17th Lancers, lost his life.

This was the first hostile encounter of any moment that had occurred since the renewal of the campaign against Ulundi. Colonel Buller was in command of a cavalry reconnoitring party, comprising the Natal Mounted Natives, Baker's, Macdonald's, and the Frontier Light Horse. A small force of Zulus was observed in the vicinity of three large kraals under the Ezunganyan—a table-topped hill, rising 800 or 1,000 feet from the valley, very precipitous, with a considerable talus, dotted with thorns, and affording cover for skirmishers. The kraals were surrounded and burnt, with only trifling casualties, and the party returned, but were met by General Marshall, with the Lancers, and some Dragoons and Shepstone's Horse. The regular cavalry were sent to the front somewhat unnecessarily, as there was nothing useful to be done; and in the brief skirmish that ensued, on the return. Lieutenant Frith fell, shot through the heart by a stray Martini-Henry bullet, as the Zulus had taken advantage of a donga and spruit-bed to outflank them, which brought them to closer quarters. It was known that a large impi was at a military kraal in the neighbourhood, who it was hoped would be drawn into an attack, but they did not enter an appearance on this occasion, having been warned, as we learned from the messengers, not to attack us. Shortly after this skirmish a junction was effected between the hitherto separate forces of Newdigate and Wood, and the combined Divisions were commanded in person by Lord Chelmsford during the remainder of the march.

The 2nd Division, under General Newdigate, with which were Lieutenant-General Lord Chelmsford and Head-quarters, made the first movement of the final advance towards Ulundi on May 28th, the camp at Koppie-Allein being ultimately broken up on the 1st of June. At that time the Zulus of the border tribes were reported to be concentrating near Ibabanango and Inzayeni, and regiments from the King's kraal were also stated to have been sent by Cetywayo to assist their resistance to the advance of the British. Considerable delay, however, attended and retarded the forward march, the attendant column of store and baggage waggons being very large, and the transport service difficult, from the nature of the road and the necessity of guarding against attacks and surprises. One convoy alone numbered 600 waggons, and the Flying Column was specially detached to Conference Hill to escort its march forwards from Landmann's Drift—a quasi-retrograde movement which caused some surprise and dissatisfaction, as it was thought that a simpler and easier arrangement would have been to send a portion of Newdigate's Division (being eight miles in the rear of Wood) for this escort-duty. Some dissatisfaction also was felt at the apportionment of cavalry duties between the two chief regiments, the King's Dragoon Guards being split up into sections to keep open the communications to the rear, while the Lancers were sent to the front; whereas it was thought that a more equitable arrangement would have been to have taken one wing of each regiment for these services respectively. On the 4th, the camp at the Itelezi ridge was broken up, and a position assumed on the right bank of the Ityotyozi River. On this day, three Zulu messengers came in with a flag of truce, and it appeared that they had previously gone on a similar errand to General Crealock's Division at Gingihlovo, but were sent away, being told that Lord Chelmsford alone could treat with them, and receive any overtures on behalf of Cetywayo. The bona fides of these pretended messages being, as on three previous occasions, more than doubtful. Lord Chelmsford's reply was, that his advance would by no means be delayed, unless definite submission were made on the basis of the terms previously communicated to the King, especially as to the surrender of the captured guns. On the evening of the 6th occurred another of those unaccountable and discreditable "scares" in which the soldiers guarding the temporary laager opened fire before the piquets could all get in, and several casualties of killed and wounded occurred; and even two shots were fired by the artillery at this false alarm. Two strong stone forts were constructed at the camp on the Nongweni River, as protection for the large depot formed there for stores of provisions and forage.

The news of Sir Garnet Wolseley's proximate advent to take the Command-in-chief, received about this time, acted as a stimulus to a more vigorous and independent advance, and the project of diverging to Kwamagwasa to await the junction with Crealock's Division, supposed to have been entertained, was abandoned in favour of a direct advance. The line of march now came upon the forward continuation of the original route from Rorke's Drift, and a few days' march brought the forces (on the 19th June) to a position on the head-waters of the Upoko River, where also a new fort was at once constructed. On the 22nd the march was resumed, and Ulundi itself became visible from the new position on the Impugulyana ridge. Meanwhile, no direct or definite news had been received of Crealock's movements, unaccountably delayed; but it was rumoured that the 1st Division were at Entumeni on the preceding Wednesday (June 18th), which would render a meeting of the forces probable, somewhere about the junction of the road with that leading inland from the coast to Ulundi. The entire force was in excellent health and spirits, in spite of all delays and difficulties. Contrary to expectation, however, no hostile opposition had been encountered so far. The Zulus were only met with in small bodies, and the sole incidents of the advance had been an occasional skirmish and the burning of kraals by the patroling parties and scouts. On the 25th and 26th the camp was removed (some six miles) to Itukayo; and a very large Zulu Impi was seen at a distance on the banks of the White Umvoloosi, but the enemy took to flight on the advanced guard being reinforced. On the 27th a considerable distance (over ten miles) was covered, and the troops encamped at Magnibonium. Here, again messengers were received, with 150 oxen and two elephant's tusks. They bore with them Lord Chelmsford's ultimatum, sent from the

Nongweni River, still in the official envelope addressed to Cetywayo, with a note enclosed by a white man, C. Vynn, a trader, containing another unsatisfactory message on behalf of the King. Lord Chelmsford, in reply, said be could not accept the tusks, as all the conditions had not been complied with, but he would delay the crossing of the White Umvoloosi for another day, to enable the King to give final satisfaction and show compliance, by sending 1,000 men to make submission, and by delivering up the guns and rifles; otherwise, the oxen would be sent back to Ulundi, and the march at once resumed.

Both Columns halted on the 28th, and formed a large laager of waggons, to be left there, with a garrison of three companies of the 1-24th, and other detachments, altogether amounting to about 500 men, and on the day following the forces took up positions, still farther advanced, at Entonganeni, down in the valley below the heights of Magnibonium. Thence the Columns advanced, on the 30th, another five miles without tents, and with ten days' rations. Considerable bodies of the enemy were constantly seen near Ulundi. On the evening of that day Lord Chelmsford telegraphed to Sir Garnet Wolseley:—"Ten miles from Umvolosi River. King's messengers have just left with message from me. I must advance to position on left bank of river. This I do to-morrow, but will stop hostilities, pending negotiations, if communicated demands are complied with by 3rd July, noon. There are Indunas come with cattle and guns. I have consented to receive 1,000 captured rifles instead of a regiment laying down its arms. As my supplies will only permit of my remaining here until the 10th July, it is desirable I should inform you of the conditions of peace to be demanded. White man with King states he has 20,000 men. King anxious to fight; Princes not so. Where is Crealock's column? Signal."

The following official telegrams were also despatched on the 2nd and 3rd July:—

"Camp, Umvolosi River, July 2.

"Inform Sir Garnet Wolseley that on the 80th June I marched five miles. On the 1st July I marched nine miles. Formed two separate laagers about half a mile from Umvolosi; latter part of march through difficult country. Very large bodies of the enemy seen yesterday morning moving up from the river towards Ulundi and neighbouring kraals, from which they advanced towards the river again in the afternoon. Today I intend to join both laagers together, and to make one strong compact laager, capable of being held by one battalion. Unless King accepts the terms I have offered him as condition for treating, I propose at noon, 3rd July, to cross the river and make a strong reconnoissance in the direction of Ulundi."

(From Chelmsford to Clifford.)

"Camp, Umvolosi River, July 3.

"Commnnicate at once following reply to Wolseley's message of 30th:—

"July 8.—Your message of 30th received last night. Weather has prevented flashing since; communication by this means very uncertain. My force is concentrated, and will remain so, with exception of necessary post lines of communication, and am to-day making very strong laager of my waggons on right bank of Umvolosi. To-morrow I propose moving all available men up to Ulundi, and expect to fight with strong forces of the enemy. Endeavours to communicate with Crealock by native messengers have failed. I will try again when moving towards Kwamagwasa."

CHAPTER XXVIII

THE INCIDENTS of the 3rd and 4th July, ending in a complete victory over the whole Zulu Army, on their own chosen ground, and at their own selected time, fully deserve a chapter to themselves. The following record of the principal events is derived from the telegrams and letters of my colleagues, and the official reports:—

Upon the 1st and 2nd, the force remained quiet on the Umvoloosi Hill, hut the greatest excitement reigned in camp, as to whether Cetywayo would or would not send in the guns and rifles captured at Isandwhlana. The opinion at Head-quarters was that he would do so, and there his pacific intentions had all along been believed in; while, on the contrary, throughout the Column in general, opinions and hopes alike were that Cetywayo had only been trifling with and deceiving us.

On the evening of the 1st there was a false alarm. Some of Newdigate's men mistaking their own officer, while visiting his rounds, for a prowling Zulu, had fired upon him. The alarm spread in the camp, and there was immediately a cry of "stand to your arms," followed by a rush of men (who were bivouacking outside the laager, but within an abbatis of thorns) to gain the shelter of its wooden walls. Some came in minus their rifles, and were much bantered by their comrades, in consequence; they also received a severe rebuke from the authorities. The Native Allies were placed a little way outside, and had an entrance to themselves; and when the alarm arose, they also rushed in naked, making most hideous noises, and were actually taken for the enemy and received accordingly. Several were wounded but no other damage ensued. The other Division moved up closer together and laagered, the two enclosures practically joining and

Major-General E. Newdigate, C.B.

occupying a slope going down to the river, while the summit was crowned by a redoubt, formed of the angular boulders which are found strewn about the ground.

On the 2nd, as the day went on and no word came in from the Zulus, the spirits of the camp rose; and when it became known that some of the men going down to the river for water were fired at from the other side, there was general satisfaction, for there could then be no longer a doubt as to the hostile intentions of the enemy. The 3rd of July arrived; and as at twelve o'clock the time expired for the return of the guns, &c., and nothing had been done to comply with those demands, orders were at once issued for the herd of cattle which had been brought in on the 26th of June, to be returned, and sent across the river to the

King. Shortly afterwards Colonel Buller started with a Cavalry detachment, to effect a reconnoissance across the river towards Ulundi, feel for the enemy, and select the best route for the advance of the entire force on the morrow. This reconnoissance was very nearly brought to a fatal termination, as a strong force of the enemy had been detached to out-flank them and cut off their retreat, availing themselves of some dongas and spruits, which intersected the ground and enabled the wily Zulus to lie in ambush and effect a surprise from the cover. Colonel Buller, however, detected the artifice just in time to recall his men, and a safe retreat was effected, with only a few casualties, under cover of two parties of Baker's and Raaf's Horse, who had detected the Zulu scheme and placed themselves favourably to hold them in check. Some special acts of devoted gallantry occurred during this brush with the enemy. One mounted trooper was suddenly thrown, his horse being shot dead beneath him; but happily Lord William Beresford, seeing his imminent danger from the long line of Zulus not 150 yards away, galloped back and taking him up en croupe, rode safely with him out of the scrape. In another case. Commandant D'Arcy, of the Frontier Light Horse—who was recommended for the Victoria Cross, for having saved the lives of several wounded men in the unfortunate Zlobani affair — took a severely wounded man up behind him under a heavy fire. He had no sooner done this than his own horse was wounded, and threw them both, the Commandant being himself injured in the fall. Nevertheless, he succeeded in getting the wounded man safely away behind another trooper, before remounting and riding off in safety himself. Fortunately our loss in this affair was only three men killed and four wounded, the casualties to horses being more numerous, viz., thirteen dead and missing. In the evening the laager was strengthened, and additional protection obtained against surprise by cutting down the surrounding bush; as the Zulus were heard until a late hour, apparently congregated on the opposite bank, dancing and singing war songs; and an early morning attack would have been in consonance with their general mode of warfare. However, nothing of the kind took place.

On the 4th July, Colonel Bellairs, A.G., was left in command of the camp-garrison, comprising 900 white troops and natives; while the rest of the combined forces of Newdigate and Wood crossed at day-break, after breakfasting by moonlight, in pursuance of orders issued the previous evening. Buller and his mounted men led the way, vedettes in front, and on the right and left flank, feeling their way cautiously forward, without encountering any opposition or seeing the enemy. General Wood and Staff with his Division had the advance, as usual, the 80th Regiment escorting Major Owen's two Gatling guns, and Major Tremlett's Battery R.A. The passage of the river was made in excellent order, under the immediate supervision of Lord Chelmsford; and after passing the hill and dongas where the skirmish on the 3rd took place, the entire force took up the formation of a hollow square, for the order of march, which was preserved all through the subsequent battle; the Lancers brought up the rear. In this way the advance was steadily made until the Nodwengo Kraal (which is some 500 yards in diameter, and formed of several concentric rows of huts) was passed. Two strong Zulu columns had been seen coming down from the hills into the valleys on the left of the line of march, where they were lost to view; and another considerable Impi came direct from Ulundi towards the advancing column. These were quickly supplemented by others on different sides, converging upon the British position from all quarters, front, flank, and rear. After a brief halt, the hollow square of the British troops ultimately took up a favourable position to the north-east of Nodwengo, on the level top of a slight knoll, with the ground sloping downwards for several hundred yards away on all sides, and affording no cover from bush. Here the impending attack was

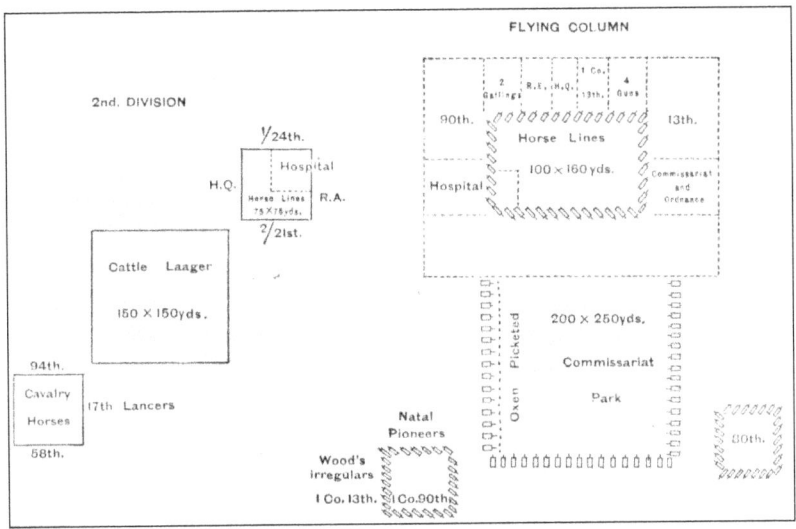

Plan of laagers on the march to Ulundi.

eagerly awaited; and the Cavalry were sent out in front in various directions, with the object of precipitating the enemy's assault. The front of the square faced towards Ulundi, to the south-east, and was defended by the 90th and 1-13th Regiments, formed four deep. The guns and Gatlings were distributed at the corners, and on the other faces to flanks and rear, which were held by the 80th, 58th, 21st, and 94th Regiments. As the Cavalry came upon the Zulu skirmishers, fire was opened upon them, which they returned, and then gradually retired, ultimately sheltering within the hollow square, where were also the Generals and their Staffs, Royal Engineers, Native Contingent, carts, ammunition waggons, and some reserve companies of Infantry. The whole force of the enemy, numbering at least 15,000 men, rapidly came into sight, in a diminishing circle, environing the position, deploying in loose skirmishing order, firing and advancing alternately with great rapidity. This heavy converging fire would have been a trying ordeal, and caused great loss to the troops, had the enemy been skilled in the use of their rifles; but even as it was, it was warm enough, and the only matter for surprise is that the casualties

Charge of the Seventeenth Lancers at Ulundi.

were comparatively so few. So the dark masses, environing the British troops, quickly closed up around them, until the distance was diminished to two or three hundred yards. But here they were checked by the heavy, regular, and well-sustained fire from the various regiments, which swept the plateau, and gradually brought the Zulus to a stand, checked by the withering effects of that hail of bullets, which did such murderous execution as all their gallant efforts could not withstand. The boldest and the bravest struggled on, to within 100 yards, but vainly, and they could never come to anything like close quarters. This was an expiring effort, and at length the Zulu host wavered, broke, and fled.

At this decisive moment the order issued to cease firing, and the Cavalry to mount and gallop in pursuit. The Lancers were specially distinguished in the execution done by them among the fugitive Zulus, who, however, made in many cases a desperate though unavailing defence; numbers of them succumbed to the deadly lance, the sabre and the revolver of the troopers and officers, one of the latter unfortunately being killed in the pursuit.

The engagement, though sharp and decisive, was only short, as its duration did not exceed three-quarters of an hour. The flight of the enemy was very rapid, and they were seen retreating in large bodies and numbers almost undiminished, over the hills to the eastward, beyond possibility of farther pursuit. Some 500 or 600 dead bodies were left lying on the field of battle, the greater proportion within 400 or 600 yards, mowed down by the rifle-fire and Gatlings, while outside of that range the shrapnel-fire from the guns had done considerable execution. The British forces engaged comprised a grand total of 5,165 men and 14 guns; namely Wood's Column, 2,192 Europeans, 573 natives, 2 Gatlings and 4 guns; and Newdigate's Division of 1,870 Europeans, 530 natives, and 8 guns. The enemy must have exceeded 20,000 Zulus, of whom at least 5,000 were in reserve, and never came into action but retreated without having fired a shot. Besides these there were, as previously mentioned, 840 Europeans and 240 natives left in garrison at the laager. Our casualties represented a gross total of 108, and 71 horses killed; there being two officers, 18 noncommissioned officers and men, and 8 natives, or in all 18 killed; and 19 officers, 59 non-commissioned officers and men and 7 natives, or in all 85 wounded.

From a subsequent despatch, sent to the Military Secretary by General Wood, it appears that he learnt, by examination of four prisoners who were captured, that the Zulu Regiments engaged in the fight were the Tulwana, the Ndhlondhlo, the Indowyengwe and the Ngobamakosi, of the Undine Corps; the Nokenke Regiment, of the Unixopo Corps, and the Unddududu Regiment, which lived in the Umlambongwenya Kraal, and not in the Nodwengo Kraal, as stated in the Zulu "Army List"; the Umcityu Regiment, of the Umkendampenvu Corps; the Umxape, the Ndloke, and the Amakwenkwe

Regiments, of the Quikykosi Corps; the Ngumgeni Regiment, of the Bulawayo Corps; the Uduhuza Regiment, of the same-named Corps; and the Isangu Regiment, of the Nodwengo Corps. The Uve Regiment worked with the Ngobamakosi. General Wood added that the Zulu attack was conducted in a hurried, disorderly manner, contrasting strongly with the methodical system pursued at Kambula. The Corps became mixed up before coming under fire; but the greater numbers were on the right flank and rear, though more regiments were said to be attacking the left flank. The attack on our front was made by the Ndloke and Amakwenkwe; on the right flank by the Tulwana, the Indowyengwe, and the Nodwengo; on the left flank by the Nolondhlo, the Nokenke, the Uduhuza, the Unddududu, the Ngumgeni, and the Unixopo; and on the rear by the Umdtyu, the Ngobamakosi, and the Uve. On the 2nd of July, at a meeting attended by the chiefs Nyamane, Usirayo, Umavumgingivulu, Cefuga, son of Maquondo, Palane (the second in command of the Ngobamakosi), and Untuza, brother of Seketwayo, it was resolved to send to Lord Chelmsford the Royal Coronation White Cattle, but when they were five miles from our camp, the Umcityu prevented their being given to us, being resolved to fight. There is no doubt that Cetywayo had an interview with Nyamane, at the Umbambongwenga Kraal, on the evening of the 3rd, and that both left it early on the morning of the battle. Umangwina and Dabulamanzi were seen near the Nodwengo Kraal, on the 4th, and General Wood saw a mounted chief, since known to have been Usilutu, leading the Ndloke to within 500 yards of the left bank of the Ulundi River, but he then turned back. Tyingwayo and Upogoti, who were second and third in command in the Quixzi Kraal to Usilepu, did not come prominently to the front. Upogoti was seen near the river, but Tyingwayo did not cross the Ulundi River. General Wood attributes to this bad conduct on the part of the chiefs the

The burning of the kraal at Ulundi

want of resolution shown by the Zulu Army.

It is beyond a doubt that, from whatever cause arising, but chiefly from their previous experience during the latter part of the campaign, the military spirit and ardour of the Zulus had materially deteriorated, even before the battle of Ulundi; and this victory, though not in itself disastrous to them in point of actual loss, put the finishing touches to their recognition of defeat, and sense of the supremacy of the British Army. For although the force that retreated from Ulundi was strong in numbers, yet they speedily dispersed; and practically there was no more fighting subsequently. The military power of the Zulus was found to be completely broken and crushed. There was not even an attempt made to rally for the defence of the King's kraal. So soon as the pursuit of the fugitives by the Cavalry had terminated successfully—and after a few parting shots from Colonel Harness's nine-pounders at the flying mass of Zulus crossing a mountain spur some two miles away, among whom the shrapnel created some confusion and evident loss— Colonel Buller was ordered to advance on Ulundi, and set fire to the King's kraal. There was considerable emulation among the dashing British

Cavalry officers, for the honour of first arrival at the long-desired goal; and the competition in the race between Lord Beresford and Captain Baker resulted in the former reaching Cetywayo's residence first, though the latter, hitting upon the entrance, was actually the first in. Ulundi itself was found to cover an area more than 600 yards in diameter, and formed by half a dozen concentric rows of huts. The Royal Residence of the King was described as being a sun-dried brick edifice, only one-story in height, plastered on the outside and papered over on the inside, and comprising three rooms, with one door, and glass windows. The building was quite empty and bare, as all the furniture had been cleared out. The whole place was speedily in a blaze; so that, although the troops themselves—after a halt of an hour on the site of the engagement, to rest and repair damages—were ordered forwards, yet they had not advanced very far before the smoke and flames from the fiery circle announced the actual destruction and downfall of Ulundi; and as no object of any importance could be gained by a mere military promenade to the site, the army returned to the main laager, and subsequently retraced their steps to Entonganeni and Magnibonium.

The annexed sketch-plan of the ground and of the formation of the troops in hollow square at the battle of Ulundi was prepared by me from information received from officers present and from Mr. Melton Prior. In Appendix I will be found the official account of the battle, together with the returns of killed and wounded, and the statements of two of the prisoners.

CHAPTER XXIX

APART FROM the doings of the 1st and 2nd Divisions, there is little of moment to chronicle. During the last week of June, a Border-raid was made into Natal by a body of about 1,000 Zulus; and this was the only time at which there was anything like a realisation of the apprehensions of the Colonists, during the whole five months which elapsed after the disaster at Isandwhlana. It was in fact the only real raid that occurred, and singularly enough was delayed until the two Columns had nearly attained the object of their advance, but many miles in their rear. The invaders belonged to the frontier tribes of Domba and Homoya, and crossed the Tugela at daybreak on the morning of the 25th of June, under cover of a dense fog, at the Middle Drift and the Hot Springs. They were in two parties, and, acting under the King's orders, limited their raid strictly to the Tugela valley, where they burnt seventy-four kraals, captured about 1,000 head of cattle and goats, killed about twenty-seven persons and carried off some forty women and children captives. They were speedily discovered by the Border Guard and Police, who proved quite equal to the task of driving them back across the river, and retaking many of the captured cattle. The battalion of N.N.C. at Kranzkop only heard the news early on the following day, but their services had fortunately not been necessary.

Another interesting event was Colonel Black's third visit to Isandwhlana, this time for the purpose of burying the dead. On Friday, June 27th, 1879, Lieutenant-Colonel Black wired:

"Isandwhlana, 26th June, 1879.

"I have just completed burying the dead after four days' work. Some out-lying dead may remain, but all those on the field of battle are now interred, and the property found will be conveyed to the relations, but not much has been found. Men under my command worked most excellently; the foot men having had to march twenty-two miles each day, in addition to their work. The few remaining bodies are down in the Fugitives' Drift track, and will be interred in a day or two. I will furnish a detailed report next Monday of the whole operations."

And the following extract describing the scene, from a private letter, will be of interest:

"On Thursday last I was at Isandwhlana in charge of a party of men. I had not time to follow down the whole of the fugitives' track; but that it is very rough and bad I could see, and people who go down it say it is a wonder that any one ever escaped that way; there are no end of dead bodies scattered along it. I was in the camp about two and a half hours and saw all I cared to see; it is not a cheerful place to be in, but there is a peculiar fascination about it. Looking for, and identifying the bodies is very interesting; the soldiers are very easily recognised by their dress. Most of the white men's bodies in camp are buried now, but in a most superficial way, and the first heavy rain will expose them again. I speak of what I saw. Military only, and military doing it— I daresay the volunteers and police were done very differently. There are no skeletons, every body has the skin drawn tightly over the bones. The amount of valuable property destroyed is painful; there are over fifty waggons lying scattered all over the place, some in most extraordinary positions where the oxen had run away with them, and a most wonderful amount of miscellaneous property, papers and books no end—this too after the place has been visited over and over again by parties of men whose looting propensities are proverbial. Hundreds of tins of preserved meats, milk, jam, &c., perfectly uninjured, are kicking about the place, and hundreds of others just pierced by assegais. Brushes and boots are a feature. It really is astonishing the amount of things it is thought necessary for a British army to drag about with them. It has never been noticed I believe, what a suitable monument the Isandwhlana hill is for the 24th Regiment. It is very much in the form of the Egyptian Sphinx, which is their badge!"

Lieutenant Royston, commanding the Natal Carbineers, writing from Landmann's Drift, on the 22nd June, 1879, gives the following interesting details as to the finding of those members of the corps who were killed on the 22nd January:—

"We arrived at the camp about nine o'clock, and commenced at once to bury the dead just where they lay. We buried Lieutenant Scott, Troopers Davis, Borain, Lumley, Hawkins,. Dickenson, Tarboton, and Blaikie. These were lying near together between the road and the 1-24th camp. About four-hundred yards higher up were Hoodie and F. Jackson close together. Swift was lying on the neck under the Kopjie. The dead are lying very thick about where Scott and the others were found, 24th men and Mounted Police, over one hundred I should think. We searched the whole camp to find some trace of poor London, Bullock, and the others, but without success. I made inquiries among the 24th men, but they had come across none of our men except those we knew of. I searched all about where the waggons had stood and where London and Bollock were last seen, but could not find any trace. After we had buried all in camp, I extended the men in skirmishing order, and thoroughly searched the country along the line of retreat to the Nanginyama Spruit. We found poor Macleroy's remains about a mile from the neck and buried him there. I took the watch and other things from his pocket. There is still another good day's work to do. Most of the bodies in the camp are buried, but there are quite as many between the neck and the spruit. I don't give up hope yet of finding the bodies of our other poor fellows."

The whole history of that sad day and its memory is aptly brought to a close by the able report from Colonel W. Black, who was not only in command of the burial party, but had also been present with us on the night of the 22nd January, and was one of the first to visit the scene afterwards:—

"Rorke's Drift, 28th June, 1879.

"The force under my command—thirty Song's Dragoon Guards (mounted), fifty on foot, 140 2-24th Regiment, 360 natives, and fifty Native Horse, were working on the 20th, 23rd, and 26th inst., and have completed the burial of the remains of those who fell at the battle of Isandwhlana. Major Dartnell, with some Natal Mounted Police, and representatives from the Natal Carbineers, Buffalo Border Guard, and other volunteers, co-operated with me on the first day, and looked after the burial of their own comrades. As I reported in March last, the bodies of the slain lay thickest on the 1-24th camp; a determined stand had evidently been made behind the officers' tents; and here an eye-witness told me that while he was escaping from the camp he saw a compact body of the 24th men fighting, surrounded by Zulus; seventy dead lay here. Lower down the hill in the same camp another clump of about sixty lay together, among them Captain Wardell, Lieutenant Dyer, and a captain and subaltern of the 24th unrecognisable. Near at hand were found the bodies of Colonel Durnford, Lieutenant Scott, and other Carbineers, and men of the Natal Mounted Police, showing that here also our men had gathered and fought in an organised body. This was evidently a centre of resistance, as the bodies of men of all arms were found converging as it were to the spot, but stricken down ere they could join the ranks of their comrades. About sixty bodies lay on the rugged slope, under the southern precipice of Isandwhlana, among them those of Captain Young-husband, and two other officers, unrecognisable; it looked as if these had held the crags, and fought together as long as ammunition lasted. The proof of hand to hand fighting was frequent; three soldiers were lying by as many dead Zulus, Zulu and white man confronting each other, as living they had stood. A 24th man was found here, face downward, with a Zulu knife up to the haft in his back, evidently killed while defending himself from a front attack; an assegai bent double lay by him, and another in like state near by. It is bootless, however, to multiply such instances now. For example, lower down the field an N.M. policeman and a Zulu, the Englishman uppermost, lay still locked in each other's embrace; in another place a Zulu skull was found pierced by a bayonet, while his assegai lay rusting in the white man's breast. Up among the rocks a Zulu chief, covered by his shield, lay swathed in four distinct wrappings of canvas, and as many other Zulu bodies were here. I gather that this was the last scene of resistance, and that, therefore, the Zulus had less time for carrying away their dead, which they have so completely done from the other parts of the field. A soldier of the 24th was found close under the precipice, head downward, with shattered skull, showing that he had fallen or been hurled from the top; hereabouts, too, was an artillery tent mallet by the side of a soldier, who had vainly matched this feeble club against the assegai. Many dead lay on the Buffalo side of the neck, and I think it will not be out of place if I describe how the line of retreat led here. When our two lines of infantry, one facing to the left of the camp, in the position naturally taken up after retiring before the chest or main body of the Zulu army, as it swarmed over the Ugulu hill, the other facing more towards the front and parallel to the Donga, making head with the Mounted Volunteers against the Zulu left wing—when these two separate lines of skirmishers, outflanked on both sides, ammunition well nigh expended, retired almost at the same time to rally in the camp, form square around the ammunition waggons, and there refill their pouches, some of those men present tell me that the attention of all being fixed on their own front, none had realised how it fared behind them—once they turned round towards the tents, they saw that all was lost, the camp was full of Zulus, sweeping round the flanks of isolated lines, following through the gap between them made by the retreating Natal natives. The Zulus were already masters of the place of refuge, while those who had made the front attack now stormed behind the retreating lines. The ordered battle was over, all that disciplined men can do had been done—the lines melted into groups, into files, coherence ceased, friend and foe mingled in one mass, a surging stabbing crowd—their very numbers prevented the Zulus from making an immediate end. The horsemen who escaped, the footmen who straggled through the tents, the very guns moved at a walk wherever a gap opened in the mass, and slowly won their way towards the neck. Once here, once on the road, the hope of escape arose only to be quenched at the next glance, for circling round the Isandwhlana the right horn of the Zulu horde barred the way to Rorke's Drift; the only gap in the ring of steel was the rough ground to the south between the road and the kop that faces the fatal hill. Here, then, of necessity and not of choice, the broken ranks pushed on; Zulus on the kop fired down. Zulus in their midst and Zulus on each flank pressed on with equal pace. The tracks became rough indeed, scored by dongas, strewn with rocks, seamed with water courses, here dry and stony, with steep sides, there wet and boggy. The horsemen moved on at foot pace, and only escaped because the horse could keep up the exertion longer than the panting foot soldiers. Here to us was the saddest sight, the camp left, the face set toward the Buffalo, all might give hope for life; but the record of death shows heavily here, and not ignobly is it written. Here and there around a waggon, here and there around a tree, a group had formed, and stood at bay—shoulder to shoulder they fired their last cartridge, shoulder to shoulder they plied the steel, side by side their bones are lying, and tell the tale; but other evidence is forthcoming, and I have heard from those who saw and live, how dearly our countrymen sold their lives, how fiercely fighting they fell. 800 yards from the road the guns, long ere this without gunners—they died in the camp—came upon ground that no wheels could pass, and the horses which, on my first visit, I saw hanging in their harness over a ravine, now mingle theirs with the drivers' bones.

From here the bodies are even more and more apart until, about two miles from the camp, the last one lies and marks the limit reached by white men on foot. The fatal trail begins again near the river bank, where Stewart, Smith, and others rest a river's breath from Natal; across the river it runs until the graves of Melville and Coghill pearly mark its end.

Of the greater part of those buried, all that can be known is their regiment, for weather and the operations of nature have left but little that is recognisable; where clothes remained, due search was made, but in most cases the pockets had been cut out, and but little property was found by us; that recovered has been sent to the relatives of the slain.

I cannot close my report without calling attention to the hard work so cheerily undergone by the fifty dismounted King's Dragoon Guards, and 140 men of the 2-24th, who each day trudged twenty-two miles to and fro, besides their labour on the widespread field. The natives were principally employed as outposts on the hills, lest peradventure another impi might follow the track of its forerunner across the Ngutu range, or appear on our right from the tunnelled hills between us and the Qudeni.

I need not say that no cross or stone marks the graves of the fallen, above them the Lich Kop, the majestic monument of Isandwhlana holds guard, and for ever tells that 800 sons of England lie beneath."

The third and last event of any importance (which I omitted naming in my account of the march to Ulundi) was the sad death of Lieutenant Scott Douglas, of the Scots Fusiliers. It appears that, being signalling officer with General Newdigate's Column, he rode back to Fort Evelyn, a few days before the battle of Ulundi, with a message which, owing to the want of sunshine, could not be sent by the heliograph. He reached Fort Evelyn safely, and, against the remonstrances of the officer in command, started on his ride back at three o'clock in the afternoon, having only one man with him. Corporal Cotter, 17th Lancers, his companion. This was on the 30th June, and he was never afterwards seen alive. Their bodies were found subsequently not far off Koomanga Hill, close by the cross road from Fort Evelyn to Kwamagwasa, having clearly lost their way in the fog. To this lamentable affair the best commentary will be the letter sent by General Wood to the D.A.G., dated from Kwamagwasa Camp on the 13th instant, as follows:—"I have the honour to report that Commandant White, of Wood's Natives (Irregulars), informed me this morning that one of his subalterns had found the body of a corporal of the 17th Lancers a short distance outside the camp. I therefore proceeded with a few of his natives and my own personal escort, to a ravine about one and a half miles E.N.E. of the Mission Station of Kwamagwasa, and near a path leading to Ulundi. I found the body of Corporal William Cotter, 17th Lancers, as pointed out by a private of Wood's Irregulars, and about a hundred yards on the Kwamagwasa side of it the body of Lieutenant Scott Douglas. Both soldiers had been killed by assegai wounds, I imagine four or five days ago. Neither body had been mutilated. There was no property on the body of Corporal Cotter, except a note-book and a missal. Lieutenant Scott Douglas had been removed. In the trowsers pocket was a small purse containing £10 10s., which had evidently been overlooked. I knew Lieutenant Douglas, and his name is on his linen. I sent back to camp for entrenching tools and a clergyman, when the Revs. Coar and Baudrey attended, and buried the bodies in the presence of the Lieutenant-General Commanding."

CHAPTER XXX

THE CONCLUDING portion of my narrative may perhaps best be initiated by resuming the thread at the point of the arrival of His Excellency Lieutenant-General Sir Garnet Wolseley, G.C.M.G, K.C.B., High Commissioner and Commander-in-Chief in British South Africa. The account of his subsequent movements will be found to cover every event of importance, culminating in the capture of Cetywayo, and the pacification and resettlement of Zululand, with the successful prosecution of the supplementary campaign against Secocoeni.

On his landing at the Cape, June 23rd, His Excellency was accompanied by the following officers:—Mr. St. Leger Herbert, Secretary, Lieutenant-Colonel Baker Russell, C.B., 13th Hussars, Lieutenant-Colonel Brackenbury, R.A., Major Webber, R.E., Major the Hon. H. Wood, 12th Lancers, Captains Bushman, 9th Lancers, Yeatman Biggs, H.A., Paterson, 16th Regiment, Maurice, R.A., Braithwaite, 71st Regiment, Doyle, 2nd Dragoon Guards, Lieutenant Creagh, R.A., Dr. W. Howard Russell, Brevet-Colonel Pomeroy Colley (2nd Queen's Royals), C.B., C.M.G., Chief of the Staff, Brevet-Major H. McCalmont, 7th Hussars, Captain Lord Gifford, V.C., 57th Regiment, Lieutenant Braithwaite, 71st Regiment, and Lieutenant Creagh, R.A., Aides-de-Camp.

Leaving Capetown by the C.R.M.S. Dunkeld on the 24th, Sir Garnet landed at Durban on the 27th, and proceeded at once to Pieter Maritzburg, being received at both towns by the Civil and Military Authorities with all due honours and ceremonials, addresses, &c., &c., qua nunc prascribere longum est. Immediately after his arrival at the capital on Saturday afternoon, His Excellency was sworn in as Governor of Natal,

Sir Garnet Wolseley's camp at Ulundi: Zulus coming in to give up their arms.

in presence of the Executive and Legislative Councils, and the principal Civil and Military Officials. His stay was limited to three days only, and in addition to the necessary conferences with General Clifford, Inspector-General of the Base and Lines of Communication, and with Commissary-General Strickland, the most important business transacted was that of an interview with a number of the Natal Native Chiefs, as pre-arranged.

Sir Garnet's plans as to our sable allies, and the manner in which he would seek to overcome the enormous difficulties of transport for the supplies and munitions of war to the troops in Zululand, were evidently matured before his arrival. In pursuance of instructions sent forward by telegraph from the Cape, the native chiefs had been requested to meet His Excellency on the 30th of June. The number who attended was about 70, and their retinues augmented the gathering to about 250. The Colonial Secretary, Colonel Mitchell, Mr. J. Shepstone, the Honorary Secretary for Native Affairs, Colonel Brackenbury, Mr. Bulwer (Sir Henry Bulwer's nephew), and Sir Garnet's Private Secretary, were present at the conference, the object of which was explained by His Excellency to obtain the co-operation of the chiefs, by their sending a large number of their young men (armed with assegais) to carry the provisions under their own indunas, being paid and fed for the service; whereby, as Sir Garnet stated, the war would be terminated in six or eight weeks. This arrangement was subsequently carried out.

Sir Garnet Wolseley's commissions as Commander-in-Chief, Governor of Natal, and High Commissioner in South-East Africa, together with the Proclamation of Sir H. Bulwer's retention of the Governorship of the Colony, was duly made public in the Government Gazette, and they will be found in Appendix E.

After sending telegrams to Lord Chelmsford and the other generals. Sir Garnet Wolseley returned to Durban on the 1st of July with his Staff, and proceeded in H.M.S. Shah to Port Durnford, with the intention of landing there. But, as already mentioned, the attempt was a failure; and the Shah brought her distinguished passenger back to Durban, whence he proceeded vid Fort Pearson to the camp at Port Durnford, where he finally arrived on the 7th of July. Immediately on Sir Garnet's arrival at Head-quarters of the 1st Division, he devoted his attention to the reorganisation and reduction of the British Forces; and the orders issued gave abundant evidence that the one and chief aim of his specific instructions from the Home Government was to cut down the expenditure as speedily and as largely as possible. He had evidently also taken a bold and sanguine view of the situation, based upon the conception that all material resistance would be found to have ceased, since the victory at Ulundi had practically terminated the campaign; and farther, that some of the native populations, such as the Swazies and Amatongas, being now assured of the supremacy of the British over the long-dreaded Zulus, would now aid in any farther operations which might become necessary for the capture of Cetywayo, and the pacific settlement of the country. There can be no doubt that the action of the Home Government in superseding the Civil and Military Authorities in Natal at a critical period excited no little comment and even adverse criticism. And the same remark holds good of the unaccountable inaction and subsequent retreat of the troops after Ulundi. For it afterwards appeared that, as the Zulu hosts had dispersed, there was no thought of farther fighting, and Cetywayo was virtually deserted. Had he been followed up at once and hard pushed, he would in all probability have been made a prisoner in a day or two at the most. Again, it is to be noted that among the Local Authorities and many Colonists of judgment and experience, the opinion prevailed that Sir Garnet's estimate of the future was much too sanguine, and that it was a hazardous venture to cut down the strength of the expedition by sending so many troops back to Natal on their way home. However, it is equally clear that the result fully justified the Commander-in-Chief's action in all respects, and showed that his military genius and general insight had instinctively but effectively grasped the entire features of the situation, the necessities of the proximate future and the drastic measures of reduction and retrenchment, which might safely be put into immediate execution.

It may be noted that large drafts for various regiments had been arriving successively on board the Euphrates, Egypt, and Queen Margaret. The City of Venice, sent up from Durban to Port Durnford to bring back Sir Garnet, also brought back the Naval Brigade of the Shah, who went on to Capetown on the 25th July. Most noteworthy, however, among the reinforcements, whose services were no longer considered requisite, may be named the Royal Marines in the Jumna. The briefest mention will suffice to recall the dissatisfaction expressed at home at the fact of this gallant corps having been passed over in the original selection of reinforcements; the interest and excitement subsequently aroused by their tardy despatch, and the hopes and anticipations founded on their seasoned efficiency. As it turned out, the corps were sent back to England, without being called upon to do duty in South Africa.

As regards the inaction after Ulundi, and the recall of the united forces under Newdigate and Wood, there can be little doubt that the course of events was materially affected by Sir Garnet Wolseley's appearance on the scene at this critical juncture, and his special powers. Lord Chelmsford—while divested of full command, and having probably in contemplation or sent in his resignation—was, nevertheless, so situated that he had no alternative but to advance and fight. Before bringing matters to a definite issue with the enemy, and destroying Ulundi, no alternative of withdrawal was open to him. That victory gained, the alternative became imposed upon him, as he was necessarily debarred from independent action. In all these matters, suffice it to say, that few persons would be competent to form a right opinion on true knowledge of facts; and therefore any criticism, decidedly adverse to the course of action pursued by those in authority and having responsibility, must be received under considerable reserves, if not rejected prima facte as crude and ill-founded.

It would be impossible here to follow out in detail the various arrangements ordered and carried into execution. A brief summary of their results and general effects must suffice; and for detail I must refer my readers to the Appendix L, where will be found the general orders for the redistribution of the troops and Staff of the British Forces in South Africa, issued on Sir Garnet's second arrival at the capital at the end of July.

During the interval some minor occurrences should not be omitted from notice. An important meeting took place at Mangweni, in the coast-district, between Sir Garnet Wolseley and an assemblage of the local chiefs making their submission, with a view to the ultimate settlement and re-arrangement of Zululand on the plan devised by the General Commanding-in-Chief. Among the more important chiefs, whose surrender took place about this time, may be mentioned Dabulamanzi, one of the principal Zulu commanders, Umlandela, Sohlkeli, Segweligwele, Sindquella, Somapo, and Umquli the King's head manufacturer of powder, gunlocks, &c. The transport-arrangements, by means of a corps of about 2,500 Natal natives, were completed in due course, as a preliminary measure in view of prospective movements.

The Flying Column, under General Wood, proceeded via Kwamagwasa to St. Paul's, accompanied by Lord Chelmsford himself. And here in the Umlatoosi valley, they were met by Sir Garnet Wolseley and his Staff, and an inspection of the troops took place. By a General Order, under date 16th July, 1879, Lord Chelmsford and his forces were complimented by the Commander-in-Chief upon their brilliant success at the battle of Ulundi, and on their admirable behaviour and gallant services. The inspection of the troops was made the occasion of a gratifying ceremony, namely the investiture, by Sir Garnet himself, of Major Chard, R.E., with the Victoria Cross for his gallant conduct at the defence of Rorke's Drift on the 22nd and 23rd of January. Subsequently, another General Order was issued, announcing the departure for England of General Wood and Colonel Buller, and paying to those meritorious officers a well-merited tribute of recognition for the services rendered during the war by their military ability and untiring energy.

Lieutenant-General Lord Chelmsford, having resigned his command, was also numbered, together with Major-Generals Crealock and Newdigate, among the distinguished officers whose departure for home was announced. At all points of their journey, within the colony,—at Fort Pearson, Pieter Maritzburg, and Durban—their progress was marked by public receptions of the most complimentary and enthusiastic character, and public dinners, addresses, and other ceremonials, bore ample testimony to the general appreciation of their ability and success. Cape Colony and Capetown itself were in no way backward in similar demonstrations of public approval and respect. The details of these triumphant receptions on their homeward route present many points of interest; but their reproduction here would be undesirable. Nevertheless, and even at the risk of being deemed monotonous, I cannot refrain from quoting some passages from the reply delivered by Lord Chelmsford to the address of the Colonists on his arrival at the Cape; because it will suffice to perpetuate his Lordship's vindication of himself and his plans.

"I thank you most sincerely for the honour you have conferred upon me, and for the flattering terms in which you have alluded to services which, under God's Providence, I have been able to render to South Africa. I shall ever look back with pride to the manner in which these services have been recognised by the Cape Colony. I feel deeply grateful to those lately serving under my command, who, by their loyal assistance and gallant conduct, first won for me the highest distinction the colony was able to bestow, and have now obtained for me this additional mark of its favour and esteem. Possessing, as I now do, such substantial proofs of your confidence and regard, I have been content to pass by, without comment, the serious misrepresentations regarding my conduct of the war which have appeared from time to time in the public press. So important a public question is, however, mixed up with the personal one, that I feel compelled to take the earliest opportunity of expressing my opinions. Gentlemen, if party feelings and political bias are to be allowed in the future to colour the writings, and warp the judgment of newspaper correspondents accompanying our armies when in the field; and if, whilst active operations are actually going on, persistent attempts to lower the General in the estimation of those he is commanding are to be considered as not exceeding the license granted to the press; I foresee that the gravest consequences to our arms must ensue, and I fear that the proper conduct of a campaign will become almost impossible. Gentlemen, I have been publicly accused of hesitation and vacillation, and it has also been stated that I had completely lost the confidence of all but my personal Staff. As regards the last charge, I am proud to feel justified in meeting it with distinct denial, and I am confident that it never had the slightest foundation. With regard to the charge of hesitation and vacillation, I can only assure you that I made up my mind at a very early date that I would endeavour to reach Ulundi by the route which I eventually took, and that I have never swerved from that determination. Before advancing to the relief of Etshowi, I left instructions as to the distribution of reinforcements which were about to arrive, and that distribution was not altered.

"The soundness of my plan of campaign is, of course, fairly open to criticism, but I have no hesitation in saying that, had I the work to do over again, I should make no change in my arrangements. My demands for supplies and transport on the northern line of advance were such as to tax severely the energies and resources of the commissariat. Those demands, however, were met to the fullest extent, and I was thus enabled to carry out my plans to a successful issue. Charges of extravagance have been brought against the commissariat, and of extortion against the inhabitants of Natal, with regard to the transport difficulty. When every day's delay, however, was a matter of serious moment, it would not have been wise to haggle too closely about prices; and I believe that, on inquiry, it will be found that the laws of political economy relating to supply and demand furnish a satisfactory defence to the sweeping accusation brought against the Natal Colonists. In every community men, no doubt, will be found who are ready to sacrifice everything to their greed for gain, but it would be unfair to condemn the many for the fault of the few. I am also anxious to remove some slight misapprehensions which appear to exist regarding my movements before and after the battle of Ulundi. I have seen it stated that I had always reckoned upon receiving direct assistance from the coast-Column, and that the advance on Ulundi was consequently a desperate undertaking, made against the express orders of my gallant friend and successor, Sir Garnet Wolseley. The difficulties of our advance on Ulundi by the coast-roads had been brought to my notice soon after my arrival in Natal by those who knew them well. I, therefore, never calculated that the upper Column would receive more than indirect support from the troops on that line, and I felt quite satisfied that the former would be strong enough to carry out the task which lay before it. I need scarcely tell you that I received no orders forbidding me to advance after the crushing defeat inflicted upon the Zulus at Ulundi, and their subsequent complete dispersion. There would have been no advantage gained by endeavouring to penetrate the difficult country lying to the north of the King's kraal, even had the state of the supplies permitted it. Whilst, therefore, one portion of the force retraced its steps towards the Blood River, escorting the sick and wounded, and taking with it all the empty waggons, the other moved vid, Kwamagwasa to St. Paul's, and thus completed the chain of strongly entrenched posts which now extend from east to west across the centre of Zululand at intervals of about twenty miles. The effect of this move was shown in the submission of several important chiefs, whose kraals lie within striking distance of that line. I must apologise to you for having detained you with these lengthy explanations, but I was anxious to remove any misconception that may possibly have existed in your minds regarding the present military situation in Zululand. I can fully endorse what you have said regarding the individual heroism which has been so conspicuous during the Zulu War, and I feel sure that many brave and noble acts have been passed unnoticed, simply because their performance had come to be looked upon as a matter of course, in consequence of their frequency. One of the finest episodes during this eventful war was the reconnoissance made by the mounted force of the Column under Lieutenant-Colonel Buller on the day preceding the battle of Ulundi. On that day dash and daring, steadiness and coolness, were all conspicuous—conspicuous at the proper moment; and it will be gratifying to you to know that, with the exception of one squadron of mounted British Infantry, the force in question was entirely colonial, and two-thirds of it was from the Cape Colony. South Africa may well feel proud of the behaviour of her sons on that occasion. In conclusion, I thank you most heartily for the good wishes so kindly expressed in the concluding paragraph of your address. I shall watch with anxiety the progress of events in South Africa. I trust most sincerely that the blessings of peace may shortly be restored to it in every part, and that the time may soon arrive when its separate colonies will be welded into one powerful confederated whole."

Thus fitly terminated Lord Chelmsford's connection with British South Africa, extending over a period of two years, and the results must be left to speak for themselves.

CHAPTER XXXI

THE 12TH August was the day upon which Sir Garnet Wolseley appointed to be at Ulundi, whither he had previously summoned the Zulu chiefs to meet him. The interval which elapsed was devoted to all the arrangements involved in the redaction and redistribution of the British Forces in the field, and in the concentration of the troops designated for farther active service, the forwarding of the convoys with all necessary stores, and the other essential preparations. Having myself seen the commencement of the campaign, and been present at various points throughout its progress, though having been disappointed in not being able to assist at the battle of Ulundi, I determined to be "in at the death," and therefore made my arrangements to accompany the General to the front, for the concluding episodes of the war.

Sir Garnet Wolseley left Pieter Maritzburg on the 30th of July with his Staff, and a mounted escort under Captain Lord Gifford, V.C., 57th Regiment, who had charge of all the arrangements for encampment, &c., at the various halting-places by the way—Grey Town, Mooi River, Helpmakaar, Rorke's Drift, Isandwhlana, Forts Marshall and Evelyn, Entonganeni, Magnibonium, and the rest, names now become historical. At Rorke's Drift a parade was ordered of the two companies of the 2-24th, under Colonel Degacher and Lieutenant-Colonel Black, when Sir Garnet decorated Private Hook with the Victoria Cross, which had been awarded him for his conduct at the defence of Rorke's Drift. This ceremony was originally intended to include similar presentations of honour to Major Bromhead and Private Williams (at that time stationed at Dundee), but they were not present on this occasion. Sir Garnet also visited the buildings which were the scene of that brilliant and successful defence, and subsequently also went down the Buffalo River to Fugitives' Drift, and the graves of Melville and Coghill.

I pass over the details of Sir Garnet Wolseley's progress, terminating in his arrival at Ulundi on the appointed day, where he was joined by Bishop Schroeder, who had ridden over from the Tugela to meet him, and by the Hon. J. Shepstone, the General's interpreter and right-hand man. The object which His Excellency had in view was now attained; namely, the formation of an advanced camp at Ulundi, in direct communication with all our fortified posts along both roads, that inland to Landmann's Drift, by which we had just come, and the coast-road vid Kwamagwasa and St. Paul's. This station would be a central point, whence Clarke's Brigade might make raids in all directions in pursuit of the King; while Baker-Russell's Flying Column, starting from Fort Cambridge—a new position just established on the White Umvoloosi at the crossing of the road from the Blood River to Ulundi—should work round to the west and north, so as to intercept Cetywayo if he should attempt to escape in that direction. Still farther away McLeod was gathering his Swazies, and Oham the men of his tribes, with a similar object. Thus, with a good central position, well garrisoned and provisioned, and directly supported from the lines and base of operations, the capture or extermination of Cetywayo and the chiefs remaining with him, such as Sirayo and Matshana, would be only a question of time—no matter whether they chose to fight us on the Black Umvoloosi, or decided to seek safety in continued flight.

The approach to and arrival at Ulundi was naturally attended with many interesting circumstances and associations. Among them may be noted the visits to the sites of the preliminary skirmish and the decisive battle itself, the inspection of the ruins of the King's kraal, and of the other large military kraals in the immediate vicinity which had been destroyed by our victorious troops. These comprised Nodwengo, Bonambi, Bulawayo,

Ukandampanion, Enokweni, Undi, Indasakompi, Likazi, and Umpambongwena, and were all found deserted, and bearing no signs or traces of recent visitations by the enemy, except on the immediate field of battle. Here very few skeletons were found, and still fewer weapons, arms, or dresses; probable indications that the Zulus must have buried many of their dead and taken away their relics. Lord Gifford commanded the patrol (on the 9th), which made a thorough search over all the ground, in company with John Dunn and all the mounted men in camp; and not more than 800 bodies were found in all.

Sir Garnet made a detour, in company with his Staff, myself, and a few others, attended by a small escort, for the purpose of visiting the ruins of Nodwengo, which was really the principal kraal, and contained at one end, the farthest from the entrance, the King's residence, with the huts of his wives and servants, and a small inner enclosure or kraal for the royal cattle. We found that parts of the exterior palisade were still remaining, and showed skilful construction and capital workmanship. It appeared to be over 650 yards in extreme diameter, and even larger than the kraal at Ulundi. In fact. Bishop Schroeder—who, from his long residence of thirty-four years among the Zulus, was evidently familiar with the locality— assured Sir Garnet that Nodwengo was of older standing and higher rank than Ulundi as a royal residence; and he strongly recommended that it should be selected for the encampment, and for the reception of the chiefs. His Excellency, however, was resolved to make no change in his projected plans.

Ulundi, as may be supposed, was thoroughly explored for objects of interest and value; but nothing of great importance was found. For one thing Lieutenant Milne's uniform case, taken from Isandwhlana, was discovered: and I and Captain Julien (commanding mule train) succeeded literally in unearthing two portraits of Her Majesty the Queen and H.R.H. the Prince of Wales, presented to Cetywayo on his coronation, and which had been buried near his mansion. This treasure-trove was at once conveyed in triumph to Sir Garnet. On Monday the 10th of August, however, a much more important trouvaille was recovered by Major Barrow with a mounted patrol, accompanied by Major McCalmont, A.D.G., and other officers, who had been sent off to Amanzekanze, where Cetywayo had two military kraals and a newly-built magazine. Close by their destination they came across some shells and other articles of artillery equipment and use; and a careful search was duly rewarded by the discovery of the two 7-pounder guns of Major Harness's battery, captured at Isandwhlana. This was a prize indeed, and the guns were quickly mounted on their carriages and brought back into camp, a distance of 6 miles, over a rough country. They were placed in triumph on either side of the flagstaff, just in front of the General's tent at Head-quarters camp, with the Union Jack once more floating over them, greatly to the gratification and admiration of the entire force. One gun was found, on examination, to have been loaded with an empty shell rammed down on a small charge of powder. But the Zulus had evidently had no conception of any due proportion between the powder-charge and the projectile; for on being fired, the shell dropped quietly about five yards from the muzzle of the gun.

At noon on the 12th General Wolseley, with Colonel Brackenbury, John Dunn, an escort of artillery, two empty ammunition carts, and a spare span of led mules, started off for a cave some ten miles away, where an ambulance waggon, removed from Isandwhlana, and large quantities of powder were said to be concealed. The road was so rough that the carts were sent back; but the object of the expedition was obtained by the blowing up of the powder, upwards of 100 barrels, chiefly of Portuguese and English manufacture.

During these few days, John Dunn had been very busy negotiating with Zulu chiefs for their surrender, and on Wednesday, the 13th of August, all these pourparlers culminated in the advent of a large number of celebrated chiefs, bringing in their own and the King's cattle in a considerable herd. The Zulu Prime Minister, Umnyamana, with his bosom friend Tshingwayo, the celebrated general, Lumbu and other principal chiefs, formed the party, which consisted of over 107, besides the cattle-tenders. They were received at the Head-quarters camp by the Hon. John Shepstone, General Colley, Colonel Brackenbury, and John Dunn. Five of the principal chiefs and two brothers of the King, Umghlana and Sukani, remained at the camp with John Dunn after the conference, as hostages, for the due delivery of the rest of their cattle, together with their guns and assegais, which had been left behind. The Prime Minister was a tall thin man, apparently about sixty-five years old, with an intelligent face, and a slight peaked beard, and a small whisker and moustache, just turning grey. Tshingwayo is short and fat, and much greyer, having also a very sharp and intelligent look, and greater volubility of speech than Unmyamana. The two have always been and still are almost brothers. Cetywayo's two brothers were both fine men; Sukani, the elder, being fully six feet high and stout in proportion, while the younger was decidedly the handsomest and best-built Zulu present at the conclave, apparently about thirty years old. No information was obtained, nor even sought for, from them in reference to Cetywayo, his whereabouts and intentions.

From this date until the end of the month there is little to chronicle, beyond the continuous surrender of the Zulus and their chiefs, in parties more or less numerous; and the despatch of scouting parties and patrols in search and pursuit of Cetywayo, who was ultimately captured on Thursday the 28th.

CHAPTER XXXII

This exciting King-chase was inaugurated on Wednesday, the 18th August, when all the regular and irregular cavalry in camp —with the exception of part of a squadron K.D.G. under Major Marter—were sent away under Major Barrow and Lord Gifford on a three days' expedition. A German trader named Vynne, the same that was with Cetywayo and sent messages to Lord Chelmsford prior to the battle of Ulundi, gave information of the place where Cetywayo was said to be concealed with only seven followers. It is somewhat curious to remark that although the ultimate capture of the Zulu monarch was substantially due to the untiring energy with which a most persistent pursuit was maintained by the party under Major Barrow, and in the end more particularly under Lord Gifford: yet the honour of the actual capture, by a freak of fortune, fell to the officer who was left behind, Major Marter.

Major Barrow and his detachment speedily came across Cetywayo's track, and following it hotly, and "trekking" night and day, headed the flying King and his party, which comprised a few of his wives, girls, servants, cattle and about ten followers, and compelled them to turn back towards the Black Umvoloosi river. The fugitives were closely pressed, and it was expected that they would probably re-cross beyond the junction of the two Umvoloosi rivers, and try to work their way to some large forest inland, or down to the seaboard. Upon this news reaching the camp on Friday, the 15th, Captain Stewart, 3rd Dragoon Guards, organised a volunteer party of officers, which I accompanied, seventeen in number, to try and intercept the King's retreat. Almost every officer who had a horse, or who could "beg, borrow, or steal" a mount, was eager to join the expedition, which started with about four days' food, and only blankets, waterproof sheets, and arms—prepared, if need be, as our leader said, to follow Cetywayo, if we came upon his track, even to the sea, until we ran him down. In this, however, we were disappointed; for on our second day out, we fell in with Major Barrow and the bulk of his men, returning to camp, having been thrown off the scent. Men and horses were almost worn out with travelling, often through the night, on short commons. A detachment had been left at the Umona river, under Captain Willan; and Lord Gifford, acting on some native information, had gone off, with only eight mounted men, on what was supposed to be the King's track. Shortly afterwards we received messages from him, saying that he fancied he was on the scent, and that the King was mounted, and making for the Engoa, or Inkankhla forest, whither men and provisions were to be sent on to his pursuers. Believing that Stewart's excursion to the north-east would be fruitless, I volunteered to return to camp, as bearer of the despatches to Sir Garnet, and got back on Sunday evening the 18th. Major Barrow returned on the following day, and from his account it appeared that he was at first so close upon the trail of Cetywayo, that nothing could have prevented the desired capture except the misleading information given by the natives. However, all traces of the King were now so effectually concealed that for nearly a fortnight, during which the search and pursuit were kept up by numerous patrolling and scouting parties, not one of them got fairly on the track.

Meanwhile, at Ulundi, the Zulus came in daily from all parts in large numbers to make submission, and many hundreds of guns and assegais were given up. One of the Indunas who came in gave an account of an incident of the slaughter at Isandwhlana, at which he was present. This Zulu chief said that when they were surrounding the troops at the camp, on the neck of the plain, two officers with pieces of glass in their eye came forward

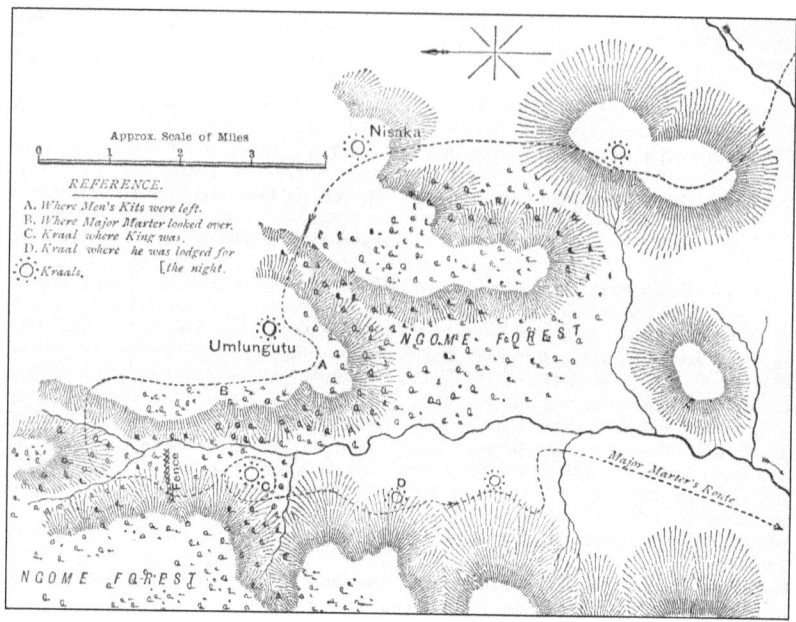

Plan of the ground where Cetewayo was captured.

shooting at him with their revolvers. One fell dead from a gun shot, and the other kept firing his revolver at the induna, a ballet grazing the right side of his neck, another grazing the left side, and another entering his leg. The induna then flung an assegai, which entered the officer's breast. The officer, with a supreme effort, almost succeeded in pulling out the weapon (here the Zulu writhed his body in pantomime of the movements of the officer), but the induna fell on him and instantaneously finished his dreadful work with another assegai. This minute account of the deaths of two officers, there can be little doubt, relates to Lieuts. Austin and Pope, of the 2-24th, who were the only two officers of that regiment who constantly wore eye-glasses. A patrol party under Capt. Maclean, N.N.G., about two miles beyond the Ulundi kraal, discovered the dead body of poor Drummond, who was returned as missing after the battle of Ulundi. The body was much mutilated, but easily recognisable, and was at once buried close by the spot where it was found.

In reference to his sad fate, all that is known is contained in the following extract from a despatch of General Wood's to the Military Secretary, under date 18th July, 1879, as follows:—

"Usibanjabeyana, son of Ududu, of the Umbonambi regiment, one of the men sent by Gansi (Kaboose), informed me yesterday that he was on the ridge between the Udabakambi and Nodwengo kraals, on the morning of the 4th inst., and, when the shells burst, ran away towards Ulundi. He there saw a European ride out in front of our troops towards Ulundi, and, while running, he watched him turn towards the river, baring the Undi kraal on the left. Usibanjabeyana, when running away from our troops, passed a dead European, who, he is confident, was the same man. The body was quite naked, no beard, small moustache, age about 35."

On Sunday, the 24th of August, Sir Garnet Wolseley had another interview with the chiefs, at which he expressed himself as much dissatisfied with the way in which things were going on. This extra pressure produced some effect; inasmuch as, within a few days, a party came in and gave up Sirayo's son, one of those whose surrender was specially demanded by the Natal Government in Sir Bartle Frere's Ultimatum. Sir Garnet at the same time, urged upon the assembled chiefs the necessity of their making a more complete and rapid surrender of arms and cattle, and especially that they should render assistance in the capture of Cetywayo, since he was dethroned and a fugitive. Otherwise, he informed them, he should have to take steps to enforce compliance with his commands, which would, of course, fall heavily upon them. Meshlakwasulu (Eye of the Zulus) was the sole survivor of the leaders in the border raid (when the captured women were murdered), which was one of the proximate causes of the war; Sirayo's other son, and Umbeline, having both been killed during the campaign. It may be interesting to note that he was sent, under arrest, to Pieter Maritzburg to be tried for murder; but by some inexplicable miscarriage of justice he was discharged, and escaped the punishment due to his crime.

Among the unsuccessful expeditions sent out in search of the King, and to intercept his flight, during this period, perhaps the most noteworthy was that of a large party of officers, men of the R.A. and R.E., and a company of the N.N.G. under Commandant Nettleton, the whole under Captain Yeatman Bigges, R.A., which started from Port Durnford on Sunday, 17th of August, and was fifteen days out, traversing a large extent of wild country seldom, if ever, previously visited. They went eastward along the coast to St. Lucia Bay, and thence inland by the Amanzekanze district, across the fork of the Umvoloosi rivers. White and Black, and arrived at the camp at Ulundi, on Friday the 29th, the very day that the news of Cetywayo's capture was received. They had throughout been well received and peaceably treated; which testifies to the complete pacification of Zululand and subversion of their military power, as the result of the war.

It was also on the same Friday evening that Captain Lord Gifford, V.C., 57th Regt., returned to camp, with Lieutenant Creagh, R.A., Captains Hay and Nourse, and their party, after having been seventeen days in chase of the King, under difficulties almost unexampled. The utmost credit must be given to Lord Gifford and his party for the perseverance, pluck, and resolution displayed by them in this long and splendid pursuit, which mainly contributed to the final success, of which they were accidentally deprived. This may be said without in any way detracting from the merits of the actual captor of the King, Major Marter, K.D.G., who effected the capture on Thursday, the 28th of August, at a kraal near the centre of the Ngomi Forest, and arrived in camp on the Sunday following with his important prisoner, whom he had the satisfaction of delivering over to Sir Garnet Wolseley for safe custody. With this auspicious event the practical termination of the campaign was happily attained.

From Lord Gifford, Major Marter, and the others present, I obtained, and noted in my diary, the full particulars of their labours, which will be found interesting and worthy of reproduction here. Following the strict chronological sequence of events, Lord Gifford's narrative takes natural precedence—commencing from the starting-point on Wednesday the 18th August:—

"The force reached the Black Umvoloosi at 2 p.m., having ridden all night, crossed it at a fair drift, and went out to a place called Dutchman's Kraal, where the King was then sup-posed to be. Upon their arrival they found that the King had been there, but left two days previously, in consequence of messages sent to him by Dabulamanzi threatening his life, and stating that, unless he (the King) did all that was required, he would be sent across the water. This frightened the King from coming in, as it is looked upon as a great degradation to go on the sea in a boat. Nothing daunted, they set to work to find the direction taken by Cetywayo in his flight, and in so doing, Gifford came upon the trail of three horses, which led up a hill to some bush. He got near enough to see the men riding them, but could not catch them, as it was getting dark. That evening they slept at Imbobo's kraal dose by, and early next morning, Thursday, they got a guide and made straight for the kraal of Cabanini, who was a great friend of Imbobo's. This kraal was under the Lebombo, and they found there some oxen of the King, which he had been driving with him, but was forced to leave behind. Major Barrow remained there, but Gifford went down into the valley below, where there were two kraals. Going down to them, he saw a mounted man leave the kraals, about two miles before him, and he then started to give chase, and ran him to a mile of the Umvoloosi, when the man left his horse, which Gifford captured, and took to the bush. In returning, he captured a servant of the King's, and got some information out of him. Captain Hay, who had also gone out, but in another direction, captured two more servants and their horses, but let the men go. On Friday morning they made the servants take them to where the King had slept the previous evening in the Morna Bush, which borders the Black Umvoloosi, and runs almost in a due northerly direction for miles. Gifford then took up the track of the King from that point, and succeeded in tracing it through the bush to near the river again, when Major Barrow decided to move back into the main road, as he thought his track was a false one. They then re-crossed the river, and went to Fuani's kraal, Barrow, with most of his men, staying at the river. At this kraal Gifford obtained news that the King's servants had passed through that way, and that the King himself was somewhere about the hills. So he sent word to Major Barrow, and left at once on the new trail, travelled all the night, and carried it on to Scharmaan's kraal on Saturday afternoon, having ridden all that night. Here they got a goat, some mealies, and beer, for they were almost starving, having quite run out of food, and after sleeping the night there, they left on Sunday morning at daylight for the south, leaving two notes for Major Barrow and Sir Garnet. Barrow and our party, under Captain Stewart, having met that morning, reached the same place about 10 a.m., and, resting there, decided to send Jantje's Native Horse, under Captain Hay, after Gifford, with what provisions they could spare, and all the rest returned to Ulundi. Gifford had taken eight mounted infantry men and two natives with him. He followed on the trail thirty-five miles that day, to a place close to Umgitywa's kraal, in Umkozana's district, towards the Uvulu River. From there they went up on to the hills that night, and reached a pass where people coming out of the valley and going south must come through. Next day they went on to another

Peace messengers from Cetewayo.

pass towards the Entonganeni range, and on the road captured some of the King's women, and later on a servant and ten more women. In this they were aided by Captain Hay, who had just arrived with the natives. The prisoners all expressed great astonishment, and said they expected the King had been caught near the Black Umvoloosi, as the white men had been so close on them as to necessitate their scattering. They had fled from there to rejoin their people, and did not know in the least where the King was. Hearing this from several, and finding it was corroborated by the fact of their never having got the least trace of Cetywayo on that side of the river, they decided to turn back; and next morning, after letting all the prisoners go except two, they did so, and reached the White Umvoloosi at noon, and went on to within a few miles of Furnian's kraal that night. Next day, Wednesday the 20th, Lieutenant Creagh, R.A., A.D.C., joined the party, having left camp with provisions for them all on pack mules. This proved a very welcome addition to the force in several ways. They trekked to the Black Umvoloosi, and again picked up the trail, which went to the Umgeni Bush; but having got a clue, Gifford proceeded straight to the kraal of Cabanini, as he had reason to believe that the King had passed through it lately. He there heard that a party of officers had recently gone past. The chief was not visible, having bolted, fearing punishment for having previously put them off the trail; but Gifford went in before them and helped himself. They found the King's water-bottle and some rugs, so they naturally imagined they were at last on the right track. Finding that their previous policy of letting the natives alone did not pay, they decided to take prisoners at each kraal, capture the cattle, and keep harassing them in every way until they got the King; and in pursuance of this scheme took one of Cabanini's lot, and made him guide them. It was also found out that some of the girls from this and a neighbouring kraal had taken beer and meat out one evening and returned the next. This aroused their suspicions, and in the morning they made the man lead them off to a place where they learned the King might be. The guide took them into a kloof to search, where they had to dismount, and even then found it most difficult. They found a hut ready prepared as a hiding-place, but no one was there. Next day, Friday, Gifford took out a small party only, and made excursion round to the north, and on his return was joined by Major Barrow and a few men; and the following morning he went to the Umgeni bush with his own men and some of John Dunn's scouts. They captured several people en route, including a witch doctor; and heard later on that an ox had been killed for the King at a kraal ten days ago; on arriving there, however, the people protested that the ox had died from lung-sickness, and that they knew nothing about the King. They searched through some very thick bush, but found no trail, so they returned to Cabanini's. They rested all the next day, Sunday, only riding very short distances to get information. On Monday the 25th, Gifford, Hay, and Nourse, with their parties, started off at 8 a.m. in the direction of the Lebombo

Mountains, visible from there, and rode close to them that day. While coming along they took nearly 200 guns in different kraals, and broke them up. They also got many cattle, and took several prisoners. They searched about well, and making sure that the King was not in that direction, cut across the country, and went to the kraal where the King had slept the first night after they crossed the river. All Monday nothing was done except to herd the cattle, and drive in others from the distance, in doing which they were fired at. At daylight on Tuesday they saddled-up, leaving Barrow and his party with the cattle; and, getting on the trail, they followed it up, and arrived within two miles of the drift at the Black Umvoloosi, where they heard that Colonel Clarke and the 60th Rifles were encamped. So Gifford sent for two more days' rations, saddled-up at 10 p.m., and travelling through that night in some of the most difficult country they had yet been in, reached a kraal at daylight, which belonged to Umyamana, where they heard that the King was only six miles off. They had previously got another message to the same effect, and now thought it was all right. Up to this time they had taken six horses from Cetywayo, the three last being only taken four days previously. The King was now walking, being unable to ride any more. That evening they slept at the kraal, and next day sent out scouts to find out where this place was, and how it was situated. Very soon some of them returned and said that it was in a small valley surrounded by high mountains on three sides, and approachable only at night from the fourth, as it was over perfectly open ground, upon which they saw the King's spies. Upon this, as Lord Gifford had only a small force with him, he sent off a note to Captain Maurice who was supposed to be near, and a messenger to the King's Dragoon Guards, who he learnt had gone to the north, that the King was close by; and asking for assistance. They then held a council of war, and decided to wait till night to surround it, and in the meantime sent out some of their natives to keep a good watch all day, to see that the King did not leave. The day passed, and at 5 p.m. they were off-saddling when a Zulu rushed in and said a party of mounted men and natives had surrounded the kraal that afternoon and captured all the inhabitants, including the King. This caused, as may be supposed, a good deal of surprise and regret, but it was mingled with satisfaction at knowing, that if Cetywayo was caught, it was only through their many days' hard work on the trail, and their constantly following him up. They rode on towards the kraal to verify the news, and about half-way met a party of Dragoons with baggage, who said that Major Marter was returning with the prisoners round an easy way to the right, and would not reach the kraal of Umyamana that night, as the King travelled so very slowly; so they all returned, and next morning, about ten, Marter arrived with his dejected but distinguished captive. He told Gifford how the whole thing had occurred, and said he should be at least two days getting in, unless a cart was sent to help to get the King on."

A cart having been obtained from Colonel Clarke's detachment, as well as an additional escort, the whole party reached the camp at Ulundi, on Sunday 31st August. Cetywayo was naturally much fatigued and worn, but nevertheless maintained a very erect and dignified aspect and gait. He appeared to be a fine, tall, stout man, about forty-five years old, with fairly good features, a high forehead and intelligent face; he had well-shaped hands and feet, and long nails, on which he seemed to pride himself; and altogether, he is certainly the finest and best looking native that I have ever seen. Sir Garnet Wolseley was present at his arrival and subsequent departure, and the Hon. J. Shepstone, with an interpreter, had an interview with His Majesty; but there was nothing in the shape of official proceedings of any kind. Orders were issued, and arrangements made for the preparation of an ambulance and mule team with adequate escort, for the King's immediate conveyance to the coast, and thence by sea, to be delivered up as speedily as possible to the custody of the civil authorities. So promptly was all this done that the first stage of the journey, to Entonganeni, was commenced that very evening.

The particulars which I obtained from Major Marter relative to the actual capture are as follows:—

On the night of the 26th August news from the Chief of the Staff at Ulundi was received by Brigadier Clarke in his bivouac on the Black Umvoloosi, that it was believed the King was heading towards the Ngome Forest, and accordingly Major Marter was despatched on the morning of the 27th in command of one Squadron K.D.G., a Company of Natal Native Contingent, and an officer and ten men, mounted infantry, and Lonsdale's Horse, with a view of endeavouring to get on the trail and capturing the King, if possible. Having marched about twenty-four miles on the 27th, the column halted for the night on the summit of the Inenge Mountain, and by 10 a.m. on the 28Ui had descended and crossed the Ibuluwane River, when a native came down the hill in front and began to talk on indifferent subjects, not appearing to wish to enter on the matter of the King. After some time he remarked, in a very casual manner, "I have heard the wind blow from this side to-day," pointing towards the Ngome Forest, "but you should take that road," showing a track leading upwards and skirting along the side of the range, "until yon come to Uisaka's kraal." About half an hour afterwards a note addressed to Captain Maurice, R.A., was brought to Major Marter by another native, which he read, knowing that Maurice was out on the same service, in another direction, and thinking it might contain information concerning the King. It was from Lord Gifford, and informed the Major that he (Gifford) was on the track again, and hoped for speedy capture. But Major Marter says he was unable then to gather from it any direct or distinct information as to the whereabouts of either the King or Lord Gifford himself, and therefore sent the man off in the direction in which he believed Captain Maurice to be. Taking the road Usilelo had pointed out, the party found Uisaka's kraal about three parts of the way up the mountain. This man also talked for some time on general subjects, when at last, fearing to allude to the King too plainly, Major Marter said, "I suppose you know why we are in your country; I want guides." Upon which he replied, "You had better go to my brother, Umhlungulu, whose kraal is on the top of the mountain," and he called two men as guides. On reaching the brother's kraal, which is quite on the summit of the range, the guides made a sign to the party to halt, where tall forest trees on their left hid the men and horses from being seen from below; and when they had dismounted, they called Major Marter to the edge of the precipice, where the trees opened out a little, crawling along on hands and knees. Stopping there themselves, they told the Major to go on to a bush a little farther round the edge, and to look down. This he did, working himself along through the grass on his side, so as not to be seen from below, and then looking through the bush, saw a kraal in an open space 2,000 feet or more below, at the bottom of a basin, three sides of which were precipitous and clothed with dense forest. It seemed to him that it would be perfectly useless to approach the kraal from the open side, in view of surprising the King, as he would certainly have some one on the look-out in that direction, and with warning of a clear minute he could have reached the nearest point of the forest, and Major Marter, therefore, decided to venture the attempt down the sides of the mountain under cover of the forest, feeling that if he killed half his horses in the descent, but captured the King, the prize would be cheaply bought. The Native Infantry were led down the precipitous side of the mountain to the lower fringe of the forest, where they remained concealed until they saw the cavalry debouch from the foot of the forest in the opposite direction, when they rushed from their hiding-place towards the eastern, or open side, of the kraal, cutting off retreat by that line, at the same time extending round it to the right and left, in co-operation with the advancing cavalry. All instructions were given, and the Dragoons started as quickly as possible, feeling that every second was of value, lest the King should get wind of troops being in the neighbourhood. Being sheltered by trees, they were enabled to mount once or twice before reaching the point from which the guides said it would be least difficult for them to descend. The party left the upper edge at 1.45 p.m., scrambling over rocks and watercourses, sometimes floundering in bogs on the ledges, in one of which Major Marter nearly lost his own horse; and, hampered everywhere by the forest of gigantic creepers hanging in festoons from the trees, they made their way down, meaning to go, and little recking how they got there, as long as they could capture the King, reaching the foot at three minutes before three o'clock, two horses having fallen to rise no more, and a man's elbow having been dislocated in this part of the run. Here fortune favoured them; for on the lower edge of the forest was a little dell, hidden in which the party could mount unobserved. This was a great saving; and waiting till all were out and on their horses, a low word was given, "Gallop, march," and gallop they did; and with spurs well in, crashed over the boulders, through the high grass and gullies—for, although clear of wood, the ground was very broken and rugged. To the Major's intense delight, on coming in full view of the kraal, he saw the natives of the Contingent had already reached, and were also enduring it from the other side. The troops, acting in strict accordance with their orders, a large circle was at once formed, and all possibility of escape cut off. Seeing that all men of the kraal were armed with guns as well as assegais, Major Marter made

Major Marter and his men guarding Cetewayo in the native kraal.

his interpreter, Mr. Oftebro, who had closely followed him in the most praiseworthy manner, call out that if resistance was offered, he would shoot down every one in it and burn the huts. After giving them a little time to digest this, the Major dismounted, and, with a few men at his back, entered the enclosure, which was strongly stockaded, the double entrance being narrow and laced across from within about four feet of the ground, so that one had to duck one's head to get in. The Chief Umkosana met Major Marter, who demanded where the King was. After some delay, seeing that the case was hopeless, he showed him a hut on the other side of the circle. Major Marter called on the King to come out, which he declined to do, insisting that he should go in to him. Being unable to turn him from this, and at the same time determined that he should come out and surrender himself, Major Marter said he was very sorry, but having no more time to waste, he was about having a match applied to the hut, when the King asked the rank of the officer to whom he must yield, and stipulated that he should not kill him. Major Marter said he represented the High Commissioner (Governor), and had been sent specially by him to bring him to him, and that he would not kill him if he came quietly. At last he came out, and throwing his mantle over his shoulder, stood looking at his captor, erect, and quite " the King." The first words he said were, " You would not have taken me, but I never thought troops could come down the mountain through the forest." Besides the Chief Umkosana, there were with him seven men and a lad, five women and a girl of his personal attendants, and two men belonging to the kraal, one too old and infirm to travel; but all the rest were put under charge and brought away. There were about twenty guns in the kraal, four being Martini-Henry rifles, marked "24th Regiment," much ammunition, some old 24th belts, &c., and many assegais, one of which, a beautiful barbed-headed one, which John Dunn said he had often seen "quiver in the King's hand," was sent by Sir Garnet Wolseley to Her Majesty the Queen. Cetywayo offered much passive resistance on the road to Ulundi, taking advantage of every pretext for delay, and endeavouring to insist upon sending some of his attendants to distant kraals for beer, snuff, &c., no doubt contemplating setting on foot an attempt at rescue. On the evening of the 20th, when the party were making their way in single file through thick bush and clambering over rocks after dark, three men and a woman of the attendants—all of whom had been attenuating the line as much as possible, pretending to be knocked up—sprang like wild animals into the thicket, attempting to escape. Positive orders had been given to our men to shoot any one who attempted to escape or rescue, and two men of the runaways were accordingly shot; the other (the King's snuff-box carrier) and the woman escaping. This summary action had a very good effect on Cetywayo, who became much more amenable afterwards.

It will be most convenient here to depart from the strict sequence of events in mere order of date, and briefly to notice the dispositions made for the disposal of Cetywayo, by his conveyance to Port Durnford and the Cape. The following confidential correspondence in relation thereto was subsequently published, and testifies to the clearness with which Sir Garnet Wolseley formed his purpose, and the steadiness with which it was carried into execution:—

Copy of His Excellency the Governor's Minute to Ministers, dated September 1st, 1879, respecting the disposal of Cetywayo:—

[Minute, No. 590.]

"I have received a confidential communication from Sir Garnet Wolseley asking this Government to provide for the custody of the late Zulu King as a state prisoner. I shall be glad if Ministers will favour me with their advice on the subject, and let me know whether I may authorise Sir Garnet to send him down to Table Bay, and when. He will embark immediately at Port Durnford, and remain there on board ship until Sir Garnet hears from me. Shall therefore be obliged by an early reply.

(Signed) " H. E. B. Frere, Governor."

September 1st, 1879.

***

[Minute.]
Colonial Secretary's Office,
September 2nd, 1879.

1. Ministers have given their most careful consideration to His Excellency's Minute No. 590 of the 1st instant.

2. The detention of the Zulu Cetywayo in custody, as a prisoner of war, being in their opinion indispensable with a view to the maintenance of peace in South Africa, Ministers desire to express their readiness to co-operate with Her Majesty's Government in securing that object by providing a suitable place of detention for Cetywayo pending the pleasure of Her Majesty as to his future disposal.

8. Ministers, however, point out the urgent necessity for a legal

warrant from Her Majesty's High Commissioner in Zululand for Cetywayo's removal to this Colony for due custody, and further for a legal warrant under the hand of Her Majesty's representative in this Colony, authorising his detention as a prisoner of war within this portion of Her Majesty's dominion.

(Signed) J. Gordon Sprigg.

Cetywayo embarked on the 4th September at Port Durnford, on board the hired transport s.s. Natal, which had been prepared for his coming, and left that day for Capetown; H.M.S. Forester escorting the Natal. Both vessels arrived at Simon's Bay on the 9th, after a slow voyage. On his arrival at Gape-town, Cetywayo was at once consigned to the quarters provided for him at the Castle, where he has remained ever since.

Of the many interesting details of the King's journey, and the frequent conversations with him upon the subject of the various incidents and engagements of the campaign, it would be impossible here to give a consecutive narrative: but it may be interesting to give a brief statement of some of the information obtained, as supplementing and completing the particulars which I have previously given.

As to the death of the Prince Imperial, Cetywayo asserted that the first intelligence he had of the unfortunate event was conveyed by Lord Chelmsford's demand for the return of the sword of his Imperial Highness. The King at once sent to the district in which the Prince had been killed, and the sword was sent to him. Cetywayo declared that he never knew how the Prince came by his death, and his impression was that at the outside there were not more than ten Zulus in the donga. With reference to Isandwhlana, it is difficult, to get an accurate idea of the number of Zulus who fought at Isandwhlana, because the Zulu has no idea of numbers. When they speak of the strength of an army they say there were so many companies, and inasmuch as the Zulu companies range from eighty to two hundred, it is impossible thus to get the exact figures. The conclusion I have arrived at, after hearing many stories, from the King's downwards, is that there were at least 25,000 Zulus under Mavumengwana and Dabulamanzi at Isandwhlana. The fight taking place on the day that it did was an accident. For, to use a Kafir metaphor, the moon was dead. The following day would have seen a new moon, and it is a Kafir's superstition never to do any work or business on the day before a new moon—the day is always kept as a holiday. The main body of the army arrived at the range—the Ngnutu— overlooking the valley of Isandwhlana on the night of the 21st January, and the stragglers only came up on the morning of the battle. So when we pitched our camp in this valley on the 19th there were no Zulus in the neighbourhood. On the morning of the 22nd the Zulu army was about five miles from the camp, and it was disturbed by the mounted Basutos who were sent out by Colonel Durnford to draw them on. The Zulu army was sitting in an immense half circle retaining its battle array, when the left horn was fired on by the Basutos, the result being that the Zulus rushed to the fight without any order whatever. The two horns were composed of four regiments of unmarried men, the chest of the army being older men. The two horns rushed away to the attack, hut the married regiments moved steadily up to the right until they outflanked the British position, when they doubled down to the left, and then the English were completely surrounded. The Zulus say the battle lasted for a little while— certainly not an hour. They did not lose heavily until the last when they got into close quarters, and they tell with admiration of how sometimes four or five soldiers would get back to back and hold their numerous enemies at bay for ever so long. One square of about sixty men defied the repeated attacks of one horn of the army, and so courageous did it become that the men beckoned the Zulus to come on. At last by overpowering numbers, or by the exhaustion of ammunition, and through repeated charges the little square was destroyed. The Zulus say that was the only square they fought that day. Cetywayo estimates his Isandwhlana losses at 1,000. It was reported to him that the whole Column had been destroyed, and he reckoned that the column was 4,000 strong. His victory at Isandwhlana, and his defeat by Colonel Pearson's Column, were almost reported to him simultaneously. He said, however, "We have done very well. There is one column we shall never hear of again." His fighting force he still reckoned at close on 60,000, so he decided on investing the column at Etshowi, and hoped by destroying Wood's Column to lay the Transvaal at his feet. Isandwhlana gave him great hope of saving his kingdom, and he only lamented that he had not in his kraals some of the officers who died at Isandwhlana. I mention this to show what the effect of Isandwhlana was upon his mind. The arrangements for the attack upon the camp at Kambula were made with the greatest care, and the King never dreamt of failure. The result of that fight settled in the King's mind what the end of the war would be, and when he heard of the arrival of reinforcements he was in earnest in his desire for peace. But his warriors, less sagacious than himself, would not confess that they were beaten, and the young bloods were eager to destroy the small force with which Lord Chelmsford advanced upon Ulundi. And thus it is that the Zulus cannot understand why Cetywayo has been taken captive. Dabulamanzi may be taken to represent the Zulu nation in his question as he saw the King carried into captivity: "What has he done that he should be punished; it is not he that has been beaten but his soldiers."

The General's despatch, announcing Cetywayo's capture and the close of the war, will be found in Appendix M.

CHAPTER XXXIII

AT ULUNDI, on Monday Sept. 1st, 1879, the day after the departure of Cetywayo under escort for his destination, a mass meeting of the Zulu chiefs was held to receive an address from Sir Garnet Wolseley, announcing the definitive arrangements for the re-settlement of Zululand. More than 300 chiefs and indunas were assembled together at this important gathering, which comprised, besides many whom I did not know, nearly all those who had been present at former meetings, including the ex-Minister Umyamana, Tshingwayo, Scheluza (a brother of Panda's former Prime Minister), Usibebo, Umalagwala, Umgitywa, Oaozi, Umkojana, and Somkeli; in fact most or all of the chiefs (except Oham) nominated for the different districts, 13 in number. In attendance on the General were General Colley, Colonel Brackenbury and the rest of the staff, the Hon. J. Shepstone, Mr. St. Leger Herbert, John Dunn, with all the officers present in camp.

Sir Garnet's address occupied about three-quarters of an hour in the delivery, being interpreted by the Hon. J. Shepstone. He reminded the chiefs that six years previously on that very day (by a curious coincidence) Cetywayo, their late King, had been crowned in that valley by the representative of Her Most Gracious Majesty the Queen. Upon that occasion he had made vows and given pledges which he had never fulfilled. His captivity and deposition from the Sovereignty should be a warning to them to observe strictly all the conditions on which alone they would be appointed as chiefs of their several districts. After explaining in detail those stipulations, Sir Garnet concluded by informing them that there would be a Boundary Commission of officers to regulate their respective districts; and that a British Resident in

Zululand would also be appointed, who would be the eyes and ears of the people, would see that the country was governed by them in the spirit of liberty, equality, and justice, and report to the British Government any infraction on their part of those principles or of the conditions of their appointment.

The names of the chiefs appointed were then read out, and the location and extent of their districts were described to them.

(1.) The 1st district was assigned to the now well-known John Dunn, comprising the territory between the Umlalosi and the Tugela rivers, and from the Iquidini Forest to the sea.

(2.) Umkojana. —This district will lie between Oham's and Usibebo's, and will enable the lmchwambo tribe to regain the portion they held before.

(8.) Usibebo. —This district is in the north-west.

(4.) Somkeli retains his territory on the map.

(5.) Umgitywa's lies almost in the centre.

(6.) Umyamana. —Between the two Umvoloosis.

(7.) Gaozi. —Also in the centre; and

(8.) Oham, in the north-east corner.

Five other districts remained unfixed, including those of Seketwayo, Tshingwayo, and Sirayo, the latter to be superseded by a Basuto chief.

The chiefs present then signed the following terms and conditions of tenure, summarised here for convenience:—

"I recognise the victory of British arms over the Zulu nation, and the full right and title of Her Majesty Queen Victoria, Queen of England and Empress of India, to deal as she may think fit with the Zulu chiefs and the people, and with the Zulu country, and I agree and hereby signify my agreement to accept from General Sir Garnet Joseph Wolseley, G.G.M.G., K.C.B., as the Representative of Her Majesty Queen Victoria, the chieftainship of a territory of Zululand, to be known hereafter as , subject to the following terms, conditions, and limitations:—

Terms, conditions, and limitations laid down by General Sir Garnet Joseph Wolseley, G.C.M.G., K.C.B., and assented to by me——as the terms, conditions, and limitations, subject to which I agree to accept the Chieftainship of the aforesaid territory.

1. To observe and respect whatever boundaries shall be assigned to his territory by the British Government, through the Resident of the Division in which his territory is situated.

2. Not to permit the existence of the Zulu military system, or the existence of any military system, or organisation whatsoever within his territory, and to proclaim and make it a rule that all men shall be allowed to marry when they choose and as they choose, according to the good and ancient customs of his people, known and followed in the days preceding the establishment by Chaka of the military system, and to allow and encourage all men living within his territory to go and come freely for peaceful purposes, and to work in Natal, or the Transvaal, or elsewhere, for themselves or for hire.

3. Not to import, or allow to be imported, into his territory by any person, for any object whatsoever, firearms or other goods of any description, and ammunition, from any part of inland or sea coast, and to confiscate all such goods or arms, &c., as come in, fining the owners, or possessors of them, with heavy fine, or such other punishment as may be allowed.

4. Not to allow life to be taken on any pretence, without trial, before the Council of Chief Men, allowing fair and impartial defence and examination of witnesses in the chiefs' presence, and further not to permit of witchcraft, witch doctors, or " smelling out."

6. To surrender all fugitives demanded by British Government flying from the laws, and to prevent them coming into Zululand, and, if in, to exert himself and his people to catch them.

6. Not to make war on any other chief without the sanction

of the British Government, and any unsettled dispute must be settled by arbitration of the British Government, through the Resident of District.

7. The succession to the Chieftainship to be decided by ancient laws and customs, and nomination of successors to be submitted for approval of Government.

8. Not to sell or alienate land.

9. To permit all people now in the district to remain upon recognition of his power, and any wishing to leave are to be allowed to do so.

10. In all cases of dispute in which British subjects are concerned, to appeal and abide by decision of British Resident, and, in other cases, not to punish until approved of by Resident.

11. In all cases not included in the above, or in any doubt or uncertainty, to govern and decide in accordance with ancient laws.

These terms, conditions, and limitations, I engage and I hereby solemnly pledge my faith to abide by and respect, in letter, and in spirit, without qualification or reserve.

Signed at Ulundi on this first day of September, 1879.

Chief ——————   + his mark.
Induna ——————   x his mark.
Induna ——————   X his mark.

Garnet Joseph Wolseley, General Commanding Her Majesty's Forces in South Africa, and High Commissioner for South-Eastern Africa.

Signed also by John Shepstone as witness of the correct interpretation by him, and thorough knowledge of the contents of the document which the Chief had signed.

CHAPTER XXXIV

AFTER THE capture and removal of Cetywayo, and the completion of the arrangements with the chiefs, chronicled in the last preceding chapters, nothing remained but to close the campaign by the necessary dispositions for breaking up the Divisions and Flying Columns, and for the return of the troops. To describe in detail these important and essential operations would absorb too much space. Our movements at Ulundi were somewhat precipitated, and our farther stay there shortened, by telegrams to Sir Garnet from Utrecht, conveying the intelligence that apprehensions were entertained of disturbances on the part of the Boers at Wesselstrom, on the 10th September, when some of them were summoned before the Local Court for non-payment of taxes to the British Government of the Transvaal; and threats of active resistance had been made publicly, in case of any conviction and forcible attempt to compel the defaulters to pay.

The General, therefore, held a general inspection of all the troops at Ulundi on Tuesday the 2nd September, prior to breaking up the camp. Colonel Clarke's Column then commenced its journey to Natal; and the 80th Regiment, with two guns R.A., started for Utrecht via the fortified station at Conference Hill, followed by Sir Garnet himself, with the Headquarters and Staff. The line of march was by the direct route to General Wood's old camp on the Blood River, and being previously untraveiled by any of our troops, the difficulties of transport and "trekking" with the waggons—of which several came to unutterable grief by the way—were quite equal to any that had become memorable in our previous experience.

Our journey was commenced by moonlight on the following

(Wednesday) evening, and following the Usishwiti Valley, we passed the ruins of the old Norwegian Mission Station at Amhlabitini. Crossing the northern end of the Intendeka Range, we went almost due north-west, across the Mahbehlane Hills, passing the large kraal of Undahaksombe about midnight. The labour of getting the overloaded and under-teamed waggons across some of the spruits was very heavy, requiring the constant aid of fatigue parties of the cavalry and doubling the teams. Our rate of progress was slow, as we had only got over ten miles in seven hours. Passing on the left the enormous mass of rocks forming the Inshlazatsye or Greenstone Mountains, we crossed the Umlslau River and skirted the south side of the remarkable peak called Ishilalo Si-ka Manyozi, which means "The King's Seat." The country afterwards improved, and we encamped by the ruins of the old German Mission House at the sources of the Umlslau, about twenty-five miles from Ulundi. Thence our next point was Fort George, in the vicinity of the Intabankulu Range and Ingobe's kraal. This fort was built by Baker Russell's Column on a rise, close to another German Mission Station, with the river Enhlongana flowing close by and the Unyati Mountains running away to the north-east. Here we found a little garrison of two Companies of the 2-24th, under Major Bromhead, with some of Raaff's Rangers and a company of Bengough's Battalion N.N.C. Quitting Fort George on Saturday the 6th, our road led over the White Umvoloosi and past Fort Cambridge (held by a small mixed detachment); and after camping one night by the way, Conference HiU was reached on Sunday the 7th September.

Sir Garnet had a conference with Seketwayo on the journey; and during his stay of three days, Mr. Rudolph, Landdrost of Utrecht, Captain Moore 4th Regiment, staff officer to Colonel Baker Russell, and Oham, the Zulu chief, came over from Utrecht to see him, and settle the business of the latter's appointment to his district. Leaving the camp on Wednesday, September 10th, Sir Garnet and our party arrived at Utrecht on the following day, en route for Pretoria, via Wesselstrom, whither a detachment of three officers and 100 men of the K.D.O. had been despatched on Tuesday night in anticipation of disturbances. I may here note that, in pursuance of orders previously issued, all the various forts and stations were to be deserted, and arrangements made for the removal of the stores and the return of the several garrisons by various routes to Natal, as the commencement of their journey homewards, or to other destinations as designated, so as to complete the speedy evacuation of Zululand. The country may be said to have become thoroughly pacificated. The Zulus had mostly returned home and settled down to their ordinary avocations; on our road from Ulundi to the Blood River we had passed many kraals, and all the natives met with were perfectly peaceful and friendly in their disposition and manifestations.

The General was duly welcomed at Utrecht by the civil and military authorities; and also took advantage of the occasion to complete the award of V.C. decorations for the defence at Rorke's Drift, by investing Brevet-Major Bromhead, and Private Jones with their well-merited rewards of bravery. The ceremonial took place on Thursday, 11th September, at a general parade of all the troops in garrison, the 2-24th Regiment, Dragoons, and Royal Artillery.

Among the General's closing duties, in connection with the ultimate settlement of Zululand, was the appointment of the Boundary Commission, consisting of Lieutenant-Colonel the Hon. G. Villiers (president). Captain Moore, 4th Regiment, Captain Alleyne, R.A., and Mr. Wheelwright, Magistrate of Grey Town. Their work commenced immediately on the arrival of Hlubi, the Basuto Chief newly appointed over Sirayo's district, and occupied the greater part of two months.

Mr. Wheelwright had received and declined the offer of the appointment as first British Resident in Zululand; in regard to which, I thought at the time, there might be some difficulty in finding a fit and suitable person, willing to take it, owing to the terms proposed. It seemed to me also that it would have been expedient to make the Zulu chiefs and nation feel that their power was really held by favour of the Queen and under British protection, by making each district pay a levy or impost of, say £100 a year—a mere bagatelle, amounting to, perhaps, an ox from each large kraal—the amount to be appropriated to the salary and expenses of maintaining the Residency. However, this is foreign to my subject, to which I return.

My personal reminiscences of events close at this point, as I was unfortunately prevented from continuing the journey with Sir Garnet Wolseley to Pretoria, and witnessing the outcome of the disputes with the Boers, and with Secocoeni. Partly on account of my health giving way, and partly owing to telegrams requiring my return to Pieter Maritzburg, I had to forego my previous intentions, and accordingly paid my parting respects to the General, and took leave of all friends among the officers of his Staff and the other troops. My journey was, however, most disagreeably interrupted at Newcastle, as on the day after my arrival there, my health broke down entirely, and I was laid up a prisoner in my bed and room for more than a fortnight, by a severe attack of inflammation of the liver. On my partial recovery—due to the kind care and attention of Messrs. Skeen, of the Medical Staff, and Boss (surgeon and chief commissioner of the Stafford House Committee)—I was but just enabled to complete my journey to the capital, and managed to struggle through until I reached home. I congratulated myself, however, on one thing, namely that I had previously been enabled to undergo all the fatigues and privations of the campaign without suffering in health; and that I had not fallen ill under much more unfavourable conditions which might not have had so favourable a result. As it was, my illness came on just after the real work had been done and the object of the war attained. My convalescence was tedious in the extreme and prolonged by several relapses, whereby not only was my general health impaired, but—a subject of even greater regret—my labours in the preparation of this book for press were materially postponed and continually impeded. That, however, has been entirely unavoidable, but I need not trouble my readers with any more personal details.

The last British soldier—for this war at least—may be said to have marched out of Zululand with the Column of Brigadier Clark (Lieutenant-Colonel of the 57th Regiment), on their return from Ulundi. Their journey occupied an entire month, the route selected lying in part over a track hitherto untrodden by soldiers, through a wild and rugged district, entirely innocent of waggon roads. Passing through the former encampments at Entonganini and Kwamagwasa, they arrived at St. Paul's on the 6th of September, where the first disruption of the Column took place, part proceeding to Fort Pearson on the Lower Tugela; but the principal portion going by the Middle Drift, and Fort Buckingham, Kranzkop, and Potspruit, to Fort Napier at Pieter Maritzburg, where the force was finally dissolved. Brigadier Clark subsequently accepted the post of Colonial Commandant of the South African Forces.

Comparatively little has been said of the doings of Baker Russell's flying column, which operated mainly on the northern and north-western frontier of Zululand, in combination with Colonel Villiers's force, and Captain McLeod's 800 Swazis, as well as Oham's Natives. They were successful, though not entirely by conflicts with the enemy and bloodshed, in reducing to submission the Mahlatusi, Makulusini, and other tribes and chiefs in north-western Zululand. The scene of the memorable conflict on the Zlobani Mountain was visited, and the body of Piet Uys recovered by his son, while the other dead bodies were properly interred. When ultimately broken up, Lieutenant-Colonel Baker Russell himself took the 94th Regiment, the Mounted Infantry, Ferreira's and Raaff's Horse, to aid in the reduction of Secocoeni, with which movement all actual fighting was terminated. Here he took command of the expedition, organised at Middleburg, under the personal direction of Sir Garnet; and had in addition to the above-named troops, the 21st Fusiliers, a squadron of the E.D.G., and two guns, Transvaal Artillery. Fort Weber, eighteen miles from Secocoeni's stronghold, was made the base of supplies, the first moves having been made by the General and troops from Utrecht on Friday and Saturday, October 17th and 18th; and the camp at Fort Weber was reached by the end of the month. Here considerable delay occurred, in connection with supplies, convoys and the general organisation of the operations, before any forward movement could be made, for which all was not in readiness until the 20th of November. The actual fighting commenced on the 23rd of November, with the successful assault on Umkwana's town, one of the enemy's advanced posts. This was speedily followed by the capture of successive positions, the Water Koppie, Secocoeni's town, and finally of the Fighting Koppie, which was his citadel and stronghold; the crowning assault took place on the 28th, and was completely successful, excepting only that Secocoeni himself managed to escape and find shelter and safety, for a brief period, in a cave at some little distance. These occurrences were successively notified by the annexed official telegrams:—

"Head Quarters, Port Albert Edward, Mapahlela's Drift, Oliphant's River,

24th November, 1879.

"Yesterday Ferreira's Horse, and Rustenburg and Zoutspansberg native contingent stormed and took Umkwana's town, losing about four killed and ten wounded. Natives behaved well; women and children brought safely into our camp. Advance guard will to-night seize Water Koppie, near Secocoeni's town; at the same time Lydenburg column, advancing from Fort Burgers, will seize a position equally near on that side. Each Column will concentrate on its advanced post on night of 26th; simultaneous attack should take place on night of 27th. Force on this side available for assault, about 1,800 Europeans, 2,000 Natives; on Lydenburg side, 400 Europeans and 6,000 Natives. Heat oppressive, but health of troops good."

"26th November 1879.

"Advanced guard—300 Horse, 150 Engineers and Infantry carried on mule waggons, and 250 Infantry on foot—marched through the night, and at daybreak to-day seized and fortified good position beyond Water Koppie, within three miles of Secocoeni's Town, establishing a post called Fort Alexandra. Ample supply of water. Mounted troops return to-night, and will escort remainder of force, with ten days' supplies, to-morrow to Fort Alexandra."

"November 26, 1879.

"Simultaneously, with the seizure of Water Koppie and establishment of Fort Alexandra by Major Carrington on the morning of the 25th, the Lydenburg column, under Major Bushman, seized the hill Marakaneny, and established a post called Fort George, five miles from the base over Secocoeni Town, and within three miles of Fort Alexandra. Patrols from the two Columns met halfway between their respective posts. Captain Stewart, staff officer to Colonel Baker Russell, visited Fort George from Fort Alexandra. Two hundred mounted troops have returned to Seven Mile Post. The main body moves tonight to Fort Alexandra with ten days' supplies. Hope to attack with both Columns at daybreak on the 28th. My headquarters march to Alexandra to-night."

Colonel Harrison, Commanding, Pretoria, To General Clifford.

"The following message, which left Secocoeni's Town at 3.45 p.m., 28th November, and reached Pretoria by mounted orderly at 10 a.m., December 1, is forwarded for your information:— Baker Russell's Column encamped before this place yesterday, as previously planned. Arrangements made for simultaneous attack this morning from both sides of mountain. At daybreak the attack commenced. Ferreira led the right attack, and took Secocoeni's own kraal from the heights to the south. Colonel Murray commanded central attack with detachment of R.E., 21st Fusiliers, 94th Regt., detachment of 80th Regt., four guns Transvaal Artillery, and Rustenburg Contingent. This attack was chiefly directed on the Fighting Koppie. Major Carrington led the left attack, with Mounted Infantry, Border Horse, Transvaal Mounted Rifles, and Zoutspansberg Native Contingent. He captured the Lower Town, and cleared the hills above, sweeping round to Secocoeni's own kraal. About seven o'clock the Swazies appeared on the hills above, having fought their way up from the eastward. The town and most of the caves having been cleared and burnt, at ten o'clock the Fighting Koppie was stormed. All the corps took part in the assault, which was completely successful. Fighting Koppie and town are now in our hands. Enemy's loss heavy. Officers killed on our side are:—Captain Macaulay, late 12th Lancers, commanding Transvaal Mounted Rifles; and Capt. Lawrell, 4th Hussars, Orderly Officer to Colonel B. Russell. Officers wounded are:— Captain Maurice, R.A., acting as Staff Officer to Major Carrington, slightly; Captain Beeton, Rustenburg Native Contingent, severely; Lieut. O'Grady, 4th Regt., commanding Mounted Infantry, severely; Lieutenant Dewar, E.D.G., attached to Mounted Infantry, severely. Loss in non-commissioned officers and men is not correctly ascertained, but is not very heavy. Troops halt here to-day."

"Head Quarters, Secocoeni's Town, Transvaal, Dec 1.

"The fighting Koppie has been surrounded by our troops ever since the action of the 28th. More than 500 natives have come out from its caves and surrendered. These prisoners are now living in our camp. Some few have escaped; others have been killed in trying to escape. A few hours more must end all necessity for farther watching, as the Koppie is without water. A strong picket was established on the night of the 29th at the water above Secocoeni's kraal. The same night all the caves in the mountain over the kraal were abandoned, and Secocoeni himself effected his escape. At daybreak of the 80th a strong post of infantry was established on a plateau at the top of the mountain over the kraal, and Ferreira, with his mounted corps, succeeded in surrounding a cave in which Secocoeni now is, about twelve miles from this place, in the mountains. Ferreira has been reinforced by the Lydenburg Mounted Rifles, Eckersley's Native Contingent, and 40 British Infantry. I therefore consider it most probable that we shall capture Secocoeni within the next few days. All neighbouring kraals have been cleared out, and the northern half of the mountains is now free from the enemy. Our post on the mountain is supplied by pack animals. I regret to have to announce that the name of Mr. Campbell, attached to the Swazies, who was shot dead at a cave when leading his men, was omitted from my previous list of officers killed, and the name of Captain Willoughby, 2-21st Regt., from the list of wounded; the latter was slightly wounded."

Considering the rugged and rocky nature of the ground, and the enormous strength of this natural position, the successful assault of Secocoeni's mountain stronghold must be ranked with the most gallant achievements of British troops in this war, or perhaps in any other. A close and continuous fire was maintained, from a range of less than 800 yards of the principal position, for seven hours. The 21st and 94th Regts., under

Major Hazelrigg and Colonel Murray, led by Colonel Baker Russell in person, then stormed the heights at the point of the bayonet. Valuable aid was rendered by the mounted men, under Lieutenant O'Grady, 94th Regt., and Ferreira's Horse, who displayed great gallantry; and scarcely less efficient was the onslaught of our native allies, the Swazies, under Major Bushman. Although futile, farther resistance was maintained in an isolated manner for several days. But on the 2nd December Secocoeni finally surrendered to Ferreira, who brought him to the General, at the camp; whence the chief was sent as a prisoner to Pretoria, and lodged in gaol on the 9th December. His subjugation and capture removed the last of the native hindrances to the tranquillisation of the district, and brought active operations to an honourable, successful, and satisfactory close.

At Pretoria, on the 10th December, Sir Garnet Wolseley held a grand review and sham fight by the troops, 8,000 in number, and at the same time decorated a gallant officer, Commandant D'Arcy, with the Victoria Cross. The only remaining symptoms of a disquieting character were those of the attitude assumed by the Boers in the Transvaal, a subject entirely separate from the Zulu Campaign.

CHAPTER XXXV

THE CAMPAIGN in Zululand, although successfully finished, was certainly one of the slowest, most unfortunate and expensive of the many little wars that England has undertaken of late years. However, the campaign speaks for itself; but I think it is only fair to Lord Chelmsford to reproduce a memorandum addressed by him to Governor and High Commissioner Sir Bartle Frere, and dated just a week before the disaster at Isandwhlana, sketching out his plan of the campaign. This, taken with the justification of his policy given at Capetown in reply to an address, will, at any rate, secure to him the satisfaction of showing that he, throughout, acted with perfect bona fides and consistency. The memorandum runs as follows:—

"Head-Quarters Camp, Zululand, near Rorke's Drift, January 16, 1879.

"The reports which I receive from officers commanding the several Columns now operating against Cetywayo show clearly that at this season of the year a rapid advance into the heart of Zululand is absolutely impossible. The present state of the roads in Natal will be sufficient to bring home to the mind of every one what difficulties must stand in the way of those who are endeavouring to move forward into the enemy's country, over tracts which have never been traversed, except by a few traders' waggons. No. 8 Column at Rorke's Drift cannot possibly move forward even eight miles, until two swamps, into which our waggons sank up to the body, have been ma4e passable. This work will occupy us for at least four days, and we shall find similar obstacles in front of as, in every march we are anxious to make. Accepting the situation, therefore, it remains for me to determine what modification of the plan of campaign at first laid down will be necessary.

I consider that my original idea of driving, as far as possible, all the Zulus forward towards the north-east part of their country, is still thoroughly sound. Without, therefore, attempting to push forward faster than our means will admit of, I propose with Nos. 1, 2 and 8 Columns to thoroughly clear or subjugate the country between the Buffalo and Tugela Rivers and the Umhlatoosi River, by means of expeditions made by those Columns from certain fixed positions. No. 1 Column will, as already instructed, occupy Etshowi. Instead, however, of crossing the Umhlatoosi River to Mr. Samuelson's mission station (St. Paul's), it will move a portion of its force to Entumeni, and occupy that position as well as Etshowi. Having established itself firmly in those two positions, the main object of this Column will be to clear the Inkandhla bush and forest, or to induce the chiefs and headmen of the tribes residing or specially stationed in that part of the country to render their submission. No. 8 Column will first advance to a position near the Isandwhlana hill, and from there, assisted by a portion of No. 2 Column, will clear the Equideni forest, or induce the chiefs, &c., to submit. This work completed, the portion of No. 2 Column, under Lieutenant-Colonel Durnford, will move towards the mission station near the Empandleni hill, while No. 3 Column advances to a fresh position near the Isipezi hill, detaching, if necessary, part of its force to support No. 2 Column. These combined movements will, I hope, have the effect of removing any dangerously large body from the Natal border. Colonel Wood, commanding No. 4 Column, has been informed of these intended movements, and has been instructed to act independently about the head waters of the White Umvoloosi River. When Seketwayo has either surrendered or been defeated, which can only take a few more days to decide. Colonel Wood will take up a position covering Utrecht and the adjacent Transvaal border, wherever he considers his force can be most usefully employed. He will not attempt to advance towards the Inhlazate mountain until an advance by the other three columns across the Umhlatosi River has become possible.

By these movements I hope to be able to clear that portion of Zululand which is situated south of the Umhlatosi River, and behind a straight line drawn from the head waters of that river to the head waters of the White Umvoloosi River. Should the Swazies come down to the Pongolo River, that part of Zululand which is behind a straight line drawn from the head waters of the Umvoloosi River to the junction of the Bevan and Pongola Rivers, will also no doubt be abandoned, and possibly as far as the Lebombo mountains. I trust that this plan of campaign will meet with the approval of the High Commissioner. From a military point of view, I am convinced that it is the only practicable one at this time of year, and, if successfully carried out, is capable of producing very satisfactory results. I am equally confident that, politically, it will also have good results.

We shall occupy a large extent of Zululand, and shall threaten the portion which remains to the King. We shall completely cover the Natal Border, and shall to a considerable extent do the same for the Transvaal. We shall oblige Cetywayo to keep his army mobilised, and it is certain that his troops will have difficulty in finding sufficient food. If kept inactive, they will become dangerous to himself; if ordered to attack us, they will be playing our game.

In every way, therefore, so far as my judgment guides me, the modifications of my original plan will be advantageous to us, and disadvantageous to our enemy.

(Signed) Chelmsford,

Lieutenant-General. Governor Sir Bartle Frere, G.C.B., G.C.S.I., &c."

The respective labours of Colonels Wood and Pearson, and

afterwards of Generals Newdigate, Marshall, Clifford, and Crealock, must be judged by results, and in so doing the palm must clearly be given to General Wood; for without his Flying Column, a much longer time must have elapsed before the end could have come, and in the meantime the Transvaal would have suffered largely. Among the many brave soldiers who died with Wood's Column, the name of Piet Uys certainly ranks high as that of a thorough patriot who sank all party feeling for the general good, and in so doing found a noble and never-to-be-forgotten death.

Piet Uys came from a family whose names are celebrated in connection with the earliest Kafir wars. He was born at Brakfontein, near the mouth of the Kromme River. The family left this neighbourhood for Natal in 1837, and in 1838 Piet Uys's father and brother were killed whilst fighting against Dingaan. There were few men in the field against the Zulus whose death will be more deeply deplored than that of the gallant Dutch leader, Piet Uys.

Another much valued and useful life also ebbed away its last blood on the same spot as that whereon Piet Uys had fallen; I allude to my friend Otto von Steitencron. This gallant officer, killed at the Zlobani Mountain on March 28th, is the same so often and honourably mentioned in connection with the first Secocoeni War. He bad formerly been a lieutenant in the Austrian cavalry, and arrived in Africa early in 1876. He joined Aylward's Company, Von Schlickmann's L.V.C., on the 3rd September, 1876, and was present at the fatal affair of the 18th November at Mahera's kloof, and served with the company till its disbandment in June, 1877. In November of the same year he took service in the Capo Colony, and was honourably mentioned in two engagements. He then joined the Frontier Light Horse, and, coming with them to Natal, remained with the corps until the end. By the fall of the Baron Otto von Steitencron, that

Commandant Piet Uys, of the Transvaal Mounted Volunteers.

corps lost one of its bravest and most experienced and popular officers. I might go on citing case after case like the above, all equally deserving, but not, perhaps, better known; and I must therefore be satisfied with these two short notices of men whom I was proud to call my friends, and who were both noble examples of men fighting in a just and patriotic cause.

It would occupy more space than I have at my disposal to name in detail the admirable work of the other generals; but I cannot in common fairness pass over the names of General Clifford and Commissary-General Strickland, without adding my small meed of praise for their self-sacrificing labours. The work done so steadily, perseveringly, and thoroughly by the Commissary-General, met with the highest approbation from all; and that done by General Clifford, in command of the Lines of Communication and Base of Operations, aided so ably by Major Butler, C.B., at Durban, will never be really known out of the colony, being of that quiet and monotonous description usually denominated " routine."

Before bringing to a close these few valedictory words, I feel that I can, without seeming invidious, or slighting the claims to prominence of numbers of other officers, allude to the services rendered by Major Barrow. The estimation in which he was held by those under his command, was clearly shown by the address presented to him previous to his departure from Durban in October, as follows:—

"Durban, Natal, October 6th, 1879.

"To Major Barrow, late commanding Mounted Volunteers, No. 1 Column, Zululand,

"Sir,—Hearing that you are shortly to leave Natal, at the termination of your prolonged, arduous, and distinguished services among us, those of the local volunteers who became aware of it expressed a wish to have conveyed to you, however hurriedly and imperfectly, their regret at your sudden departure, and their warmest and best wishes for your safe voyage, and your future advancement in your profession.

"Arriving, as you have done, unexpectedly at our port, and your stay in Durban being so short, it prevents us from, at this time, carrying out our intention of waiting upon you by a representative committee, and personally conveying to you a more substantial evidence of our admiration for, and high appreciation of, your many excellent qualities as a soldier and a commanding officer, and of expressing, on behalf of the Natal Volunteers who served under you in the recent campaign, the esteem in which you were held by all ranks of the service.

"We intend still carrying out part of our original programme by sending after you, for your acceptance, a trifling souvenir of your share in the campaign, and of those who served under you in Zululand. We shall, you may be sure, follow with the greatest interest your future career in your profession; and, wishing you every prosperity,

"We remain. Sir, very faithfully yours,

"(Signed by the Officers of different Mounted Volunteer Corps)."

To which the Major forwarded the following written reply from Capetown:—

"To Captain Shepstone, D.M. Rifles, Captain Arbuthnot, A.M. Rifles, Captain Saner, V.M. Rifles, Captain Norton, Natal Hussars, Captain Stainbank, I.M. Rifles, Captain Addison, S.M. Rifles.

"Sirs,—I am very grateful for the kind wishes expressed in your address on my leaving Natal, and I hope that you will express to all the officers, non-commissioned officers, and troopers of your respective corps my sincere thanks for the same.

"I have no hesitation in saying that I never wish to have under my command a force better mounted, organised, equipped, or better adapted for the work in front of them than the corps of Natal Volunteers which were under my command during the commencement of the Zulu campaign. It has been a continual source of regret to me, that by the circumstances of the campaign I was unavoidably deprived of their services in Zululand, within a month after the commencement of active operations.

"The good service performed by all the corps during that month, and the invaluable service rendered by the Natal Guides throughout the campaign, assure me of the value of the force which I had the honour to command.

"I shall always preserve with pride the souvenir that you propose sending to England, and shall ever have pleasant reminiscences of my connection with the Natal Volonteers.

"Wishing yon, one and all, every success in the future,

"I remain, Sirs, very faithfully yours,

"P. H. Barrow, Captain, 19th Hussars."

Again, as many have said that it was a colonial war, in which the colonists did nothing to help, I may be permitted to point out what Natal actually did.

From the return presented to the Legislative Council last month of the colonial forces (European and Native) raised under the authority of the Natal Government for the Zulu campaign, as published in last Gazette, it would appear that the help in men afforded by Natal was numerically larger than that provided by the mother country. In addition to the reserve, composed of 360 Europeans and 2,500 natives, the summary of the Natal forces called out was as follows:—Natal Mounted Police, 130; Volunteers, 582; European Leaders of Levies, &c., 86; Natives, 20,087; total, 21,456.

I have been unable to get at the loss of officers and men among the colonial forces, but that of the regular forces since the commencement of the Zulu war has reached a total of fifty, no less than thirty-six of whom have fallen in action, the remaining fourteen succumbing to fever, dysentery, and exposure during the campaign. This calculation is exclusive of the officers of the colonial forces, and native contingents, who also lost their lives. The death-roll of officers killed in action comprises one colonel, two brevet lieutenant-colonels, nine captains, nineteen subalterns, one surgeon-major, one staff-paymaster, two quartermasters, and one officer of the Army Hospital Corps. The thirteen officers who have died in South Africa since the commencement of hostilities comprise four captains, five subalterns, two officers of the Commissariat and Ordnance Departments, one officer of the Army Hospital Corps, and an officer of the Naval Brigade.

And now, in veritable conclusion, I take the opportunity of placing before my readers a few facts of interest as bearing upon the assertion that we went to war with Cetywayo needlessly. The first link in the chain of evidence that I wish to bring forward is an Inclosure to Minute No. 156, dated 1876, and is the—

Reply of Cetywayo, King of the Zulus, to a message from His Excellency the Lieutenant-Governor of Natal, conveyed by

Umujile and Umhlana.

"You will convey my thanks to His Excellency the Lieutenant-Governor of Natal for the kind words he has sent me by you. I am not aware that I have ever done anything which would be thought wrong by, or contrary to the wishes of, the Natal Government. The English nation is a just and peace-loving one, and I look upon the English people as my fathers. I shall not do anything outside their Government. I cannot understand, though now I am a King, that from the time the Zulus became a nation it has been the custom or law to wash spears after the death of a King, and I have not washed mine." Cetewayo could not see us until a fortnight after our arrival, but showed us great kindness, giving us a beast to kill, and presenting us with three head of cattle each. We heard that the King was causing some of the Zulus to be killed on account of disobeying his orders respecting the marriage of girls, and we saw large numbers of cattle which had been taken as fines; otherwise the land was quiet.

Taken before me,

(Signed), Fred. B. Finney.

Interpreter to the Natal Government.

In the following month (2nd November) Cetywayo indignantly denies that he had ever made the promises imputed to him, and asserts his independence.

The King said in reply:

"Did I ever tell Mr. Shepstone I would not kill? Did he tell the white people I made such an arrangement? Because if he did he has deceived them. I do kill; but do not consider that I have done anything yet in the way of killing. Why do the white people start at nothing? I have not yet began; I have yet to kill; it is the eastern of our nation, and I shall not depart from it. Why does the Governor of Natal speak to me about my laws? Do I go to Natal and dictate to him about his laws? I shall not agree to any laws or rules from Natal, and by so doing throw the large kraal which I govern into the water. My people will not listen unless they are killed! and while wishing to be friends with the English I do not agree to give my people over to be governed bylaws sent to me by them. Have I not asked the English to allow me to wash my spears since the death of my father 'Umpandi' and they have kept playing with me all this time treating me like a child? Go back and tell the English that I shall now act on my own account; and if they wish me to agree to their laws I shall leave and become a wanderer; but before I go it will be seen, as I shall not go without having acted. Go back and tell the white men this, and let them hear it well. The Governor of Natal and I are equal; he is Governor of Natal, and I am Governor here."

This certainly does not seem to indicate peaceful intentions, or afford ground for any hope of the fulfilment of the numerous promises made at his coronation.

Again, below I give a copy of an interesting memorandum from Mr. Rudolph (Landdrost of Utrecht) of his interview with Cetywayo in company with Sir T. Shepstone at the end of 1877, as given in recent Blue Books, which is link No. 2. Cetywayo addressed Sir Theophilus as "Somtseu," never saying "Inkos," and suddenly broke up the meeting by striking his assegai defiantly on his shield, and departing without saying farewell. Next day, Mr. Rudolph and Mr. Henrique Shepstone came to Cetywayo, and the interview is thus described:—

We advanced towards the King, who was sitting on a native chair, with Zulus holding shields (not an umbrella) over him to keep off the san. The King would use nothing European that day. It was very hot. When we came near, I saw that there were no seats. Shepstone stood still, but I moved to where I saw Manyana, and asked him for a seat. "Did you give us seats at Conference Hill?" said he with a sneering smile. "What are you walking about for?" asked the King when I returned to where the chair was. "I walk, oh son of Umpanda! for as you know it is against the rules of your people to remain standing before you, yet you send us not seats." "Look," said the King, "this Chela (my name among the Zulus), he is a man; he moves about; but this son of Somtseu, what is he? he stands still." He then ordered mats to be placed on one side, and not in a place of honour. Before the King allowed us to speak, he asked why we had not slept at the royal kraal. "How have I always treated you?" said he; "have I not always treated you well, Chela, when you have come to see me? Why then did you not sleep at my kraal? "I said that as horse sickness was very prevalent, and the grass round the royal kraal not good, we thought it more prudent to keep at the missionaries'. On this the King ordered some one to bring him a handful of certain poisonous grass. "Here, feed your horses on this; it will not harm them," said he. This was to show he did not believe the excuse. He was difficult to deal with that day. When Shepstone began speaking, he addressed the King as Cetywayo. The King stopped him. "Are you the son of only an induna to speak to me like that?" So Henrique Shepstone said he was in error, and proceeded. Then I spoke. I called him "Cetywayo" first; then "King of the Zulus," or "Son of Umpanda," and then again "Cetywayo." He then put out his band towards me. "You heard," he said, "the word I spoke to that son there of Somtseu. I meant it also for you, yet you have since called me' Cetywayo.'" I said, "You must forgive me, oh son of Umpanda; but I, I have known you well, and have so often so called you that my tongue slipped." Our talk did no good. When we departed, the King pointed out a small beast to us: "There, you may take that beast; go eat it with the missionaries." And lastly, the following letter from a highly influential and trustworthy source brings forward all the other points that are noteworthy in this connection, in support of what may be called the Colonists' views and opinions thereon:

Prince Dabulamanzi KaMpande, Cetywayo's half-brother.

"I think you will find some facts which show very clearly that Cetywayo, or at least some of his chiefs and people, have for some time past been preparing for a struggle with the whites, and have tried to provoke a war with them. As a resident of many years in Zululand, I have had some experience and means of observation. The year before the Commission sat at Rorke's Drift, the Chief Usirayo built his head kraal at Usogexe, and a strong stone wall with loop holes round it; and his people often told me that they hoped to use them against the white men. They often talked about war; and I more than once remonstrated with Usirayo and his people, telling them that they should take care not to bring about a war with abelungu (the white men), as it would be worse for themselves, but in vain, as they felt confident in their guns and their numbers. Cetywayo once sent an ox hide to Sir T. Shepstone, and said, if he could count the hairs on it, he would perhaps be able to form an idea of the number of the Zulu warriors; but I do not think the hide reached its destination. When the Commission was sitting at Rorke's Drift, Usirayo threatened to destroy the men and tents, if they came across the Buffalo to inspect the border line near Usirayo's head kraal, where you still see the stone heaps left since the beacons. I warned the Commission through a missionary, and the late Colonel Durnford noted it. The Zulus have bought thousands of guns, for the purpose of using them against the whites; have bought most of their ammunition with the same intention, having engaged people from Basutoland to teach them to make powder; and they have had a good deal of training in shooting. When Umbeline committed his first massacre at Umpongolo—I think in 1877— he went to the King, who adorned him with the usual sign of an iqawe (a plucky and brave fellow); so it seems to be little use in saying the King did not agree with the rascal in his doings, as somebody seems to mean. Why did the King allow Usirayo and his people to steal horses, cattle, and sheep, from the Boers, year after year without punishing them? Why did he not at once punish Usirayo, and his men, for crossing the border with arms last winter, and dragging away the poor women, who had fled for their lives? Why did he not care for the promises made at the coronation? He wished for war, and he has got it; and that which brought him to that madness is chiefly this: First, that he despised the gospel, of which he knows a good deal; and would not allow his people to become Christians. Secondly, because the Christian Government would not allow him to make war with other tribes, as his forefathers had done. And thirdly, his strong belief that he should succeed in exterminating the whites, because he thought them only a handful, and his own soldiers as plentiful as grass— which phrase he often uses with regard to them in conversation. Could he but get rid of the whites, he would soon subdue the black tribes—that has been his hope. And now we must be thankful to God, who sent such a man as Sir Bartle Frere to save the colonists from such a blow as Cetywayo intended to have aimed at them."

This completes my chronicle of the active operations of the

war in Zululand, and the doings in connection therewith. I can vouch for the accuracy of those accounts of events which I myself did not witness personally. Altogether—I say it with some little pride—I do not think any one has been situated so favourably as I have been throughout the whole war for giving a complete and accurate, though necessarily somewhat discursive, history of the whole of the events which happened in South Africa from November 1878 to December 1879, and if the verdict of the public endorses this opinion, even to ever so slight an extent, it will well repay the time and trouble devoted by the author to this work.

APPENDICES

APPENDIX A.

List of Officers and Men Killed in Action at the Camp, Isandhlwana Hill, Zululand, on the 22nd January, 1879.

- "N" Battery, 5th Brigade, R.A.—Captain and Brevet-Major Stuart Smith, Brevet-Major Russell, R.A., Rocket Battery, and sixty-one Non-Commissioned Officers and Privates.
- Royal Engineers.—Lieutenant-Colonel Durnford, Lieutenant McDowell, Captain G. Shepstone, Political Assistant to Colonel Durnford, and four Non-Commissioned Officers and Privates.
- 1st Battalion 24th Regiment.—Major and Lieutenant-Colonel H. B. Pulleine, Captain William Detacher, Captain W. E. Mostyn, Captain G. V. Wardell, Captain R. Younghusband, Lieutenant and Adjutant T. Melville, Lieutenants F. P. Porteous, C. W. Cavaye, E. D. Anstey, N. J. A. Coghill, J. P. Daly, G. F. J. Hodson, C. J. Atkinson, 2nd Lieutenant E. H. Dyson, Paymaster F. F. White, Quarter-Master J. Pullen, and 411 Non-Commissioned Officers and Privates.
- 2nd Battalion 24th Regiment. —Lieutenants C. D. A. Pope, F. Austen, H. J. Dyer, Sub-Lieutenant T. L. G. Griffiths, Quartermaster E. Bloomfield, Bandmaster H. Ballard, and 168 Non-Commissioned Officers and Privates.
- Army Service Corps. —1 Corporal and 2 Privates.
- Army Hospital Corps. —Lieutenant of Orderlies Hall, and ten Non-Commissioned Officers and Privates.
- Army Medical Department. —Surgeon-Major Shepherd, and a Boy.
- Mounted Infantry. —Eleven Non-Commissioned Officers

and Privates, and two Civil Servants.
- Natal Mounted Police. —Twenty-six Non-Commissioned Officers and Privates.
- Natal Carbineers. —Lieutenant P. J. D. Scott, Quartermaster W. London, and twenty Non-Commissioned Officers and Privates.
- Newcastle Mounted Rifles. —Captain Bradstreet, Quartermaster Hitchcock, and five Non-Commissioned Officers and Privates.
- Buffalo Border Guard. —Three Privates.
- 1st Battalion, 3rd Regiment, N.N.C. —Captains Robert Krohn, James Lonsdale, Lieutenants Samuel Avery, Frank Holcraft, Charles Jameson, Acting-Surgeon Frank Ball, Quartermaster John McCormick, Interpreter Samuel Grant, and twenty-nine Non-Commissioned Officers and Privates.
- 2nd Battalion, 3rd Regiment, N.KC. —Captains Edward Erskine, A. T. Barry, O. E. Murray, Lieutenants It. A. Pritchard, L. D. Young, Arthur Gibson,—Standish, H. O. Rivers, Quartermaster A. Chambers, and twenty-eight Non-Commissioned Officers and Privates.

APPENDIX B.

OFFICIAL REPORT OF THE DEFENCE OF RORKE'S DRIFT.

Rorke's Drift, January 25th 1879.

Sir,—I have the honour to report that on the 22nd instant I -was left in command at Rorke's Drift by Major Spalding, who went to Helpmakaar to hurry on the company of the 24th Regiment ordered to protect the ponts.

About 3.15 p.m. on that day I was at the ponts, when two men came riding from Zululand at a gallop, and shouted to be taken across the river. I was informed by one of them, Lieutenant Adendorff, of Lonsdale's Regiment, who remained to assist in the defence, of the disaster at Isandwhlana Camp, and that the Zulus were advancing on Rorke's Drift. The other, a Carbineer, rode off to take the news to Helpmakaar.

Almost immediately I received a message from Lieutenant Bromhead, commanding the company 24th Regiment at the camp, near the Commissariat Stores, asking me to come up at once.

I gave the order to inspan, strike tents, put all stores, &c., into the waggon, and at once rode up to the Commissariat Store, and found that a note had been received from the third Column to state that the enemy were advancing in force against our post, which we were to strengthen and hold at all costs.

Lieutenant Bromhead was most actively engaged in loopholing and barricading the store building and hospital, and connecting the defence of the two buildings by walls of mealie bags and two waggons that were on the ground.

1 held a hurried conversation with him and with Mr. Dalton, of the Commissariat (who was actively superintending the work of defence, and whom I cannot sufficiently thank for his most valuable services), entirely approving of the arrangements made. I went round the position, and then rode down to the ponts and brought up the guard of the sergeant and six men, waggon, &c.

I desire here to mention the officer of the pont man (Daniells) and Sergeant Milne, 3rd Buffs, to moor the ponts in the middle of the stream, and defend them from their decks with a few men.

We arrived at the post about 3.30 p.m. Shortly after an officer of Durnford's Horse arrived, and asked for orders. I requested him to send a detachment to observe the drifts and ponts, to throw out outposts in the direction of the enemy, and check his advance as much as possible, falling back upon the post when forced to retire, and assisting in its defence.

I requested Lieutenant Bromhead to post his men, and having seen his and every man at his post, the work once more went on.

About 4.20 p.m. the sound of firing was heard behind the hill to our south. The officer of Durnford's returned, reporting the enemy close upon us, and that his men would not obey his orders, but were going off to Helpmakaar, and I saw them, apparently about 100 in number, going off in that direction.

About the same time Captain Stephenson's detachment of Natal Native Contingent left us, as did that officer himself.

I saw that our line of defence was too extended for the small number of men now left us, and at once commenced a retrenchment of biscuit boxes.

We had not completed a wall two boxes high, when, about 4.30 p.m., 500 or 600 of the enemy came in sight around the hill to our south, and advanced at a run against our south wall. They were met by a well sustained fire, but, notwithstanding their heavy loss, continued the advance to within fifty yards of the wall, when they met with such a heavy fire from the wall, and cross fire from the store, that they were checked, but, taking advantage of the cover afforded by the cook-house, ovens, &c., kept up a heavy fire. The greater number, however, without stopping, moved to the left around the hospital, and make a rush at our N.W. wall of mealie bags, but, after a short but desperate struggle, were driven back with heavy loss into the bush around the work.

The main body of the enemy were close behind, and had lined the ledge of rock and caves overlooking us, about 400 yards to our south, from where they kept up a constant fire, and, advancing somewhat more to their left than the first attack, occupied the gardens, hollow road, and bush in great force.

Taking advantage of the bush, which we had not time to cut down, the enemy were able to advance under cover close to our wall, and in this part soon held one side of the wall, while we held the other. A series of desperate assaults were made, extending from the hospital along the wall as far as the bush reached, but each was most splendidly met and repulsed by our men with the bayonet. Corporal Schiess, N.N.C., greatly distinguished himself by his conspicuous gallantry.

The fire from the rocks behind us, though badly directed, took us completely in reverse, and was so heavy that we suffered very severely, and about 6 p.m. were forced to retire behind the retrenchment of biscuit boxes.

All this time the enemy had been attempting to force the hospital, and shortly after set fire to its roof.

The garrison of the hospital defended it room by room, bringing out all the sick who could be moved before they retired, Privates Williams, Hook, R. Jones, and W. Jones, 24th Regiment, being the last men to leave, holding the doorway with the bayonet, their own ammunition being expended.

From the want of interior communication and the burning of the house, it was impossible to save all. With most heartfelt sorrow I regret we could not save these poor fellows from their terrible fate.

Seeing the hospital burning, and the desperate attempts of the enemy to fire the roof of the stores, we converted two mealie bag heaps into a sort of redoubt, which gave a second line of fire all round; Assistant-Commissary Dunne working hard at this, though much exposed, and rendering valuable assistance.

As darkness came on we were completely surrounded, and after several attempts had been gallantly repulsed were eventually forced to retire to the middle and then inner wall of the kraal on our east. The position we then had we retained throughout.

A desultory fire was kept up all night, and several assaults were attempted and repulsed, the vigour of the attack continuing until after midnight; our men firing with the greatest coolness did not waste a single shot, the light afforded by the burning hospital being of great help to us.

About 4 a.m. on the 23rd inst. the firing ceased, and at daybreak the enemy were out of sight over the hill to the south-west.

We patrolled the grounds, collecting the arms of the dead Zulus, and strengthened our defences as much as possible.

We were removing the thatch from the roofs of the stores, when about 7 a.m. a large body of the enemy appeared on the hills to the south-west. I sent a friendly Kafir, who had come in shortly before, with a note to the officer commanding at Helpmakaar, asking for help.

About 8 a.m. the Third Column appeared in sight; the enemy, who had been gradually advancing, falling back as they approached. I consider the enemy who attacked us to have numbered about 3,000 (three thousand). We killed about 350 (three-hundred and fifty.)

Of the steadiness and gallant behaviour of the whole garrison I cannot speak too highly. I wish especially to bring to your notice the conduct of Lieutenant Bromhead, 2-24th Regiment, and the splendid behaviour of his company B 2-24th.

Surgeon Reynolds, A.M.D., in his constant attention to the wounded, under fire, where they fell.

Acting Commissariat Officer Dalton, to whose energy much of our defences were due, and who was severely wounded while gallantly assisting in the defences.

Assistant-Commissary Dunne, Acting Storekeeper Byrne (killed), Colour-Sergeant Bourne, 2.24th, Sergeant Williams, (wounded dangerously), Sergeant Windridge, 2-24th, Corporal Schiess, 2-3rd Natal Native Contingent (wounded), Private 1395, Williams, 2-24th, 693, Jones, McMahon, A.H.C., 716, R. Jones, 2-24th, H. Hook, Roy, 1-24th.

The following return shows the number present at Rorke's Drift, 22nd January, 1879:

	Officers	N.C.O. & Men	Sick		Total
			Officers	N.C.O. & Men	
Staff		1			1
Royal Artillery		1		3	4
Royal Engineers	1	1			2
3rd Buffs		1			1
1-24th Regiment		6		5	11
2-24th Regiment, B Company and 17 casuals sick	1	81		17	99
90th Light Infantry				1	1
Commissariat and Transport Department	3	1			4
A.M.D.	1	3			4
Chaplain	1				1
Natal Mounted Police				3	3
Native Contigent	1			6	7
Ferryman		1			1
Total	8	96	0	35	139

The following is the list of the killed:—

Sergeant Maxfield, 2-24th, Privates Scanlon, Hayden, Adams, Cole, Fagan, Chick, 1398, Williams, 2-24th, Nicholls, 1-24th, Horrigan, Jenkins, Mr. Byrne, Commissariat Department, Trooper Hunter, N.M.P., Anderson, N.N.C., one Private Native, N.N.C. Total fifteen.

Twelve wounded, of whom two have since died—viz., Sergeant Williams, 2-24th Regiment, and Private Beckett, 1-24th Regiment, making a total killed of seventeen.

I have the honour to be,

Your obedient servant,

(Signed) Jno. R. M. Chard, Lieutenant R.E.

To Colonel Glyn, C.B., Commanding 3rd Column. Rorke's Drift, 3rd February, 1879.

APPENDIX C.

From Colonel Pearson, Commanding No. 1 Column, to the Military Secretary to His Excellency the High Commissioner.

Etshowi, Zululand, 23rd January 1879.

Sir,—I have the honour to report my arrival here at 10 a.m. this day, with the Column under my command, and, I am happy to state, without a casualty of any kind—except, of course, those which occurred in the engagement of yesterday, of which I have already duly informed you by telegram, despatched yesterday evening.

Yesterday morning, the mounted troops which preceded the Column, under Major Barrow, had crossed the Inyezani River— which is about four miles from our camping ground of the previous night,—when I received a note from him to say that he had selected a fairly open space for a halting-place, which he had carefully videtted. I at once rode forward to reconnoitre, and found the ground covered with more bush than seemed desirable for an outspan; but as there was no water between the Inyezani and the places where we bivouacked last night— four miles farther on, and with several steep hills to climb,—I decided upon outspanning for a couple of hours to feed and rest the oxen, and to enable the men to breakfast.

It was then just eight o'clock, and I was in the act of giving directions about the piquets and scouts required for our protection, and the waggons had already begun to park, when the leading company of the Native Contingent, who were scouting in front—personally directed by Captain Hart, Staff officer to the officer commanding that regiment,—discovered the enemy advancing rapidly over the ridges in our front, and making for the clumps of bush around us.

The Zulus at once opened a heavy fire upon the men of the

company who had shown themselves in the open, and they lost one officer, four non-commissioned officers, and three men killed, almost immediately after the firing began.

Unfortunately, owing to scarcely any of the officers or noncommissioned officers of the Native Contingent being able to speak Kafir, and some not even English (there are several foreigners among them), it has been found most difficult to communicate orders, and it is to be feared that these men who lost their lives by gallantly holding their ground, did so under the impression that it was the duty of the contingent to fight in the first line, instead of scouting only, and, after an engagement, to pursue.

I must add, however, that every exertion has been made by Major Graves, Commandant Nettleton, and Captain Hart, to explain to both the officers and men the duties expected of them. These officers, indeed, have been indefatigable in their exertions.

As soon as the firing commenced, I directed the Naval Brigade, under Commander Campbell, Lieutenant Lloyd's division of guns, and Captain Jackson's and Lieutenant Martin's companies of "The Buffs," to take up a position on a knoll close by the road (and under which they were halted), and from whence the whole of the Zulu advances could be seen and dealt with.

Meanwhile the wagons continued to park, and as soon as the length of the Column had thereby sufficiently decreased, I directed the two companies of the Buffs, which were guarding the waggons about half way down the Column, to clear the enemy out of the bush, which had been already shelled and fired into with rockets and musketry by the troops on the knoll above mentioned. These Companies, led by Captains Harrison and Wyld, and guided by Captain Macgregor, D.A.Q.M.G., whom I sent back for this purpose, moved out in excellent order, and quickly getting into skirmishing order, brought their right shoulders gradually forward, and drove the Zulus before them back into the open, which again exposed them to the rockets, shells, and musketry from the knoll.

This movement released the main body of the Mounted Infantry and Volunteers, who, with the company Royal Engineers, had remained near the Inyezani, to protect that portion of the convoy of waggons. The Royal Engineers happened to be working at the drift when the engagement began.

When thus released, both the Engineers and mounted troops, under Captain Wynne and Major Barrow respectively, moved forward with the infantry skirmishers on the left of the latter, the whole being supported by a half-company of "The Buffs" and a half-company of the 99th Regiment, sent out by Lieutenant-Colonel Welman, 99th Regiment, who, with the rear of the column, was now coming up.

About this time the enemy was observed by Commander Campbell to be trying to outflank our left, and he offered to go with a portion of the Naval Brigade to drive away a body of Zulus who had got possession of a kraal about 400 yards from the knoll, and which was helping their turning movement. The Naval Brigade was supported by a party of the officers and non-commissioned officers of the Native Contingent, under Captain Hart, who were posted on high ground on the left of the Etshowi Road, and who checked the Zulus from making any farther attempt on our left.

Shortly afterwards, when the kraal was evacuated. Commander Campbell suggested that the enemy should be driven off still farther, to which I at once assented, and I desired Colonel Parnell to take Captain Forster's Company, "The Buffs," which up to this time had remained at the foot of the knoll, and assist the Naval Brigade to attack some heights beyond the kraal, upon which a considerable body of Zulus were still posted.

The action was completely successful, and the Zulus now fled in all directions, both from our front and left, and before the skirmishers on the right.

I now ordered the Column to be reformed, and at noon we resumed our march, and bivouacked for the night on the ground described in the first part of my letter.

The last shot was fired about half-past nine a.m.

I enclose a list of the killed and wounded, and, in addition, I beg to state that both Colonel Parnell and myself had our horses shot under us.

The loss of the enemy I can, of course, only approximately give. By all accounts, however—and I have taken every pains to verify and confirm the statements made,—upwards of 300 Zulus were killed. The wounded, if there were any, were either carried off or hid in the bush, as only two were found. The dead were lying about in heaps of seven and eight, and in one place ten dead bodies were found close together. At another, thirty-five were counted within a very small space.

As far as I can ascertain, the numbers opposed to us were about 4,000, composed of the Umxapu, Umdhlanefu, and the Ingulubi regiments, and some 650 men of the district.

I had already been warned through Mr. Fynney, border agent, and other sources, that I might expect to be attacked at any moment after crossing the Umsindusi River, but the number of Zulus stated to be in the neighbourhood was estimated at about 8,000.

All the commanding officers speak highly of the behaviour of their men during the engagement, and of the coolness of the officers and the pains taken by them to control the expenditure of ammunition. This I can personally vouch for as regards the troops on the knoll, as I was present with them the whole time. The practice made by Lieutenant Lloyd's guns, and by the rockets of the Naval Brigade, directed by Mr. Cotter, boatswain of H.M.S. Active, was excellent, and no doubt contributed materially to the success of the day.

Major Barrow particularly wishes me to mention the steadiness and good conduct under fire of the Natal Mounted Volunteer Corps. Those engaged were the Victoria and Stanger Mounted Rifles, and the Natal Hussars.

Of the commanding officers themselves I have already spoken.

From the officers of my Staff, Colonel Walker, C.B., Captain MacGregor, and Lieutenant Knight, "The Buffs"—my orderly officer,—I have received every assistance—not only during yesterday's engagement, but ever since they joined me.

I cannot speak too highly of the energy and attention to their duties of Staff Surgeon Norburg, R.N., my senior medical officer, and his assistants. The Field Hospital was established in a convenient place almost immediately after the firing began, and the wounded received every attention.

Lastly, I wish to report the good example shown to the Native Pioneers by Captain Beddoes and Lieutenant Porrington, who, throughout our march, under the direction of Lieutenant Main, R.E., repaired our road in front, and during the engagement remained on the knoll fighting rifle in hand.

I must apologise for the great length of this letter; but as the present is the first campaign of British troops against the Zulus, and as the Natal natives were being tested as soldiers for the first time, I have purposely gone into details. Should we again be engaged with the enemy, there will, of course, be no farther necessity for describing everything so minutely.

To-morrow morning I propose sending two companies of the Buffs, two companies of the Native Contingent, and a small number of mounted men, to reinforce Lieutenant-Colonel Ely, 99th Regiment, who, with three companies of his regiment, left behind for the purpose, is now on his way to Etshowi, with a convoy of sixty Commissariat waggons.

I have written to request Colonel Ely not to advance beyond the Umsindusi till reinforced.

On Saturday Major Coates starts for the Tugela with fifty empty waggons, escorted by four companies infantry, two native companies, and a few troopers to bring up more stores.

I enclose a couple of sketches of the ground on which the engagement took place, made by Captain MacGregor and Lieutenant Knight from memory.

I have the honour to be. Sir, Your most obedient servant,

C. K. PEARSON, Colonel.

The following is the List of Killed and Wounded in the Action of Inyezane on the 22nd January.

Regiment	Regimental No.	Rank and Name	Killed	Wounded Dangerously	Severely	Slightly	Nature of Wound	By what inflicted	Remarks
2-3	1266	Private John Bough	Killed						
"	766	Private James Kelleher	"						
1-2 NNC		Lieut J.L. Raines	"						
"		Lieut Gustav Plattner	"						
"		Sergt Emil Unger	"						
"		Corpl Wilhelm Sieper	"						
"		Corpl Edward Miller	"						
"		Corpl. Carl Goeach	"						
2-3	1100	Private Peter Dunn	"	"			abdmn	Gun shot	Since dead
"	865	Private John Cordell		"			head	"	
"	1244	Private F. Smith			"			"	
"	716	Private F. Clifford			"		left arm	"	
"	548	Private Henry Walker			"			"	
1st Sqd., Mntd Inftr., 90 Reg. 2-24	1554	Q.M.S. Kelly			"		left arm	"	
	1290	Private W. Devenport	"					"	
Naval Brigade		A.B. H. Gosling			"			"	
"		O.S. G. Berryman			"			"	
"		O.S. George Doran	"					"	
"		A.B. T. Butler				"		"	
"		O.S. E. White				"		"	
"		O.S. Krooman (Jack Ropeyarn)				"		"	
"		O.S. Ducklewis				"		"	
1-2 NNC		Lieut H. Webb			"			"	
"		Sergt O. Heydenburg		"			knee	"	leg ampt
Natives			4						

APPENDIX D.

Return of Killed and Missing of 80th Regiment at Intombi River, 12th March, 1879.

In the following list the killed and missing are distinguished by "k" and "m."

Captain D. B. Moriarty, Company E, k; 459, Colour-Sergeant Henry Frederick, Company A, m; 544, Lance-Sergeant Ernest Johnson, Company E, k; 1726, George Sansam, Company C, k; 733, Corporal John McCoy, Company F, k; 1647, Drummer John Leather, Company A, m; Privates of the following Companies: 585, John Anthony, Company A, k; 203, Arthur Banks, Company A, k; 943, John Banner, Company A, m; 745, George Broughton, Company A, k; 488, Henry Brownson, Company A, k; 1797, James Christie, Company A, k; 1042, Alfred Day, Company A, k; 753, John Dodd, Company A, m; 260, Henry Dutton, Company A, k; 1028, William Farrell, Company A, m; 176, William Flyfield, Company A, m; 1465, William Pox, Company A, k; 1925, John Fourneaux, Company A, m; 500, Edward Gittings, Company A, k; 1696, Joseph Green, Company, A, k; 526, George Hadley, Company A, m; 227, George Haines, Company A, k; 999, Eli Hawkes, Company A, m; 783, Thomas Healey, Company A, m; 709, Thomas Hodges, Company A, k; 902, John Ingram, Company A, k; 1865, John Luffarty, Company A, k; 1931, Henry Lodge, Company A, m; 1976, George Mitchel, Company A, k; 2048, Robert Moore, Company A, k; 1032, William Moran, Company A, k; 1926, Henry Night, Company A, k; 1770, Joseph Silcock. Company A, m; 510, Henry Smith, Company A, m; 587, Joseph Tibbett, Company A, k; 716, Joseph Weaver, Company A, k; 48, James Brown, Company C, k; 222, William Findley, Company C, k; 2008, Julien Hart, Company C, m; 1919, Henry Jacobs, Company C, k; 999, Ralph Leese, Company C, k; 2063, Arthur

Middow, Company C, k; 2085, Charles Pritchard, Company C, m; 2070, Henry Ruffle, Company C, k; 546, Jonah Adey, Company E, k; 1290, John Chadwick, Company E, k; 1163, Arthur Pummell, Company E, m; 1291, Richard Tomlinson, Company E, m; 1705, George Tucker, Company E, m; 104, Thomas Tucker, Company E, k; John Robinson, Company E, k; 370, James Vernon, Company E, k; 1605, Herbert Woodward, Company E, m; 1021, Henry Hill, Company B, k; 1499, John Hughes, Company B, k; 1378, Bernard McSherry, Company B, k; 220, William Phipps, Company B, k; 615, Michael Sheridan, Company B, m; 520, Henry Meadows, Company F, k. Civil Surgeon Cobbin and a waggon conductor are also missing.

C. TUCKER, *Major 80th Regiment, Commanding Troops.*

APPENDIX E.

Return of Killed and Wounded in the Action at Gingihlovo.

- *Killed.* —Colonel Northey, 3-60th Rifles; Lieutenant Johnson, 99th; Privates J. Smith and Lawrence, 99th; Private Marshall, 91st; Private Pratt, 60th; and three natives.
- *Dangerously Wounded.* —Ship-Surgeon Longfield, Royal Navy; Private Flannery, 2-3rd Buffs; Private T. Perkins, 57th; Privates W. Poplett and M. Xshiff, 60th; Sergeant McIntyre, Privates Byran, Malley, and Hanlons, 91st; Privates J. Drew and P. Armstrong, 99th; J. Hinchley (boy), Boadicea, R.N., Actg.-Bomb. Parfit, Boadicea, R.M.A.
- *Severely Wounded.* —Privates H. Richards, Sutton, and Gillespie, 91st; Private A. Hartley, M.I., 90th; J. Burd and J. Bulger, A.B. Seamen, Shah, R.N.; eight Natives, Nettleton's Contingent.
- *Slightly Wounded.* —Colonel Crealock, Staff; Captain Barrow, 19th Hussars; Captain Hinxman, 57th; Privates Deacon

and Harris, 67th; Colour-Sergeant E. Dallard, Privates F. Aylett, and E. France, 60th; Private Standge, 91st; Privates J. Blackwell and G. Baker, 99th; Private P. Bryan, M.I., 88th; P. Condy, Captain's Mate, Boadicea, R.N.; Petty Officer Porteous, Tenedos, R.N.

APPENDIX F.

The following is a List of those who Died at Etshowi during their Isolation in Zululand, with the Causes of their Death:—

2-3rd Regiment, Private F. Dunn, January 23rd, wounds in action; N.N.C., Sergeant Heydenberg, January 26th, ditto; 2-3rd Regiment, Private A. Kingston, February 1st, continued fever; Naval Brigade, Shoemaker J. Moore, February 11th, dysentery; 2-3rd Regiment, Private W. McLeod, February 13th, ditto; 2.3rd Regiment, Private E. Oakley, February 15th, chronic diarrhoea; 2-3rd Regiment, Lance-Corporal T. Taylor, February 21st, dysentery; 99th Regiment, Private J. Shields, February 21st, ditto; 99th Regiment, Private W. Knee, February 21st, suicide; 99th Regiment, Private J. Paul, March 4th, sunstroke; 2-3rd Regiment, Drummer A. Mortimer, March 6th, dysentery; Naval Brigade, L.-Seaman J. Radford, March 8th, continued fever; A.H.C., Private W. Barber, March 8th, ditto; 2-3rd Regiment, Private J. Stack, March 9th, intestinal obstruction; 2-3rd Regiment, Captain J. Williams, March 12th, continued fever; 99th Regiment, Private W. Tubb, March 16th, sunstroke; 99th Regiment, Private W. Kent, March 16th, killed on outpost duty; Naval Brigade, Midshipman L. Coker, March 16th, dysentery; Naval Brigade, Marine W. Stagg, March 16th, pneumonia; 99th Regiment, Private T. Venn, March 17th, enteric fever; 99thRegiment, Private C. Coombes, March 21st, ditto; 99th Regiment, Private P. Roden, March 26th, ditto; 2-3rd Regiment, Private A. Tarrant, March 27th, bronchitis; 99th Regiment, Lieutenant A. Davidson, March 27th, enteric fever; 99th Regiment, Private B. Lewis, March 28th, enteric fever; 2-3rd Regiment, Lieutenant Evelyn, March 31st, enteric fever; Naval Brigade, A.B., A. Smith, April 2nd, continued fever; 2.3rd Regiment, Private Monk, April 4th, enteric fever.

APPENDIX G.

Return of Killed and Wounded at Zlobani Mountain.
KILLED.

- *Frontier Light Horse.* —Captain Barton, Coldstream Guards, Sheffield; Corporal George Dodwell, Bedfordshire; Troopers Alfred James Burton, London; K. Dobson, England; W. Gordon, Port Elizabeth; J. Hesseldine, Cheshire; J. Kirwien, late of Port Elizabeth; W. D. Rogan, Liverpool; G. Seymour, England; J. May, London; P. W. Caffin, England; Archibald L. Stewart, Australia; Lieutenants Von Stietencron, Austrian; Williams, England; Corporal H. Plante, Grahamstown; Lance-Corporal H. Bunch, man, Kingwilliamstown; Troopers T. Halliday, England; G. Horn, German; Henry Hillwig, German; James Grills, Port Elizabeth; Lindsay Shearer, ——; Julius Gebser, German; William Tirrill, Ladysmith; A. Shermer, Kingwilliamstown; J. Livingstone, London; D. A. Robson, Herefordshire; Charles Lynden, Natal; M. Pendergast, England; E. Higgins, Grahamstown; total, three officers and twenty-six men.
- *Burgher Force.* —Mr. Piet Uys.
- *Transvaal Burghers.* —Lieutenant T. R. Hamilton, England; Thomas Brophy, Cape Colony; J. F. Cummings, Cape Colony; T. Berley, England; W. H. Martin, England; Charles Stanley,

England; J. Beukes, Cape Colony; total one officer and six men.
- *Border Horse.* —Colonel Weatherley, England; Adjutant Lys, England; Lieutenant Poole, England; Sub-Lieutenants Weatherley, England; Parminter, Statgarelt; Regimental Sergeant-Major Brown, England; Sergeant-Major Fisher, England; Quarter-Master Sergeant Russell, England; Orderly-Sergeant Brissenden, England; Sergeant Stewart, Scotland; Corporals Porter, England; Ford, England; Blackmore, England; Coetzee, Cape Colony; Paymaster-Sergeant Johnson, England; Farrier-Major Friere, Ireland; Troopers Wynan, Holland; Shepherd, England; Mann, England; Trumpet-Major Meredith, England; Troopers Underwood, England; Reed, England; Evans, Ireland; Craig, Ireland; Jefferys, Cape Colony; Brooks, Cape Colony; Bart, Germany; Bourdoin, France; Mulot, France; Jacob Muller, Germany; Milma, France; Muller, Germany; F. G. Westhuisen, Cape Colony; Hartman, Cape Colony; Cameron, Scotland; Grandenr, France; B. J. Crany, Cape Colony; Martin, Scotland; Thompson, England; King, England; Darcy, Scotland; Farquarson, Scotland; Lance-Corporal Burnhard, Germany; Trumpeter Riley, Ireland; Trooper Williams, Cape Colony; total, five officers and forty men.
- *Baker's Horse.* —Troopers W. Walters, Port Elizabeth; Ward, Port Elizabeth; W. Dunbar, late of Port Elizabeth; J. Campbell, Port Elizabeth; J. Robinson, late of Port Elizabeth; J. Darwin, Sheffield; M. Christian, Norway; R. Davis, Plymouth; total, eight men.
- *Political Agent.* —Mr. Lloyd.
- *Staff.* —Captain the Hon. R. Campbell.

WOUNDED.

Note. — a denotes "dangerously wounded," h "severely wounded," and c "slightly wounded."

- *2-3rd Mounted Infantry.* —Private H. Weller, b, gunshot wound of upper arm.
- *Frontier Light Horse* —Corporal W. Brusseau, b, gunshot wound of hand; Trooper A. Rosser, c, assegai wound of back.
- *Transvaal Rangers.* —Trooper A. Tourkien, b, assegai wound of forearm; Trooper G. Vegeneiff, b, ganshot wound of upper arm.
- *Baker's Horse.* —Trooper W. Hutchins, b, gunshot wound of groin.
- *Weathrrlet's Horse.* —Trooper H. Hammond, b, gunshot wound calf of leg.

* * *

Engagement at Kambula.
RETURN OF KILLED.
- *2-3rd Mounted Infantry.* —Private C. Moore.
- *1-13th Regiment.* —Privates J. Duncan, J. Hayes, J. Collins, S. Montgomery, H. Arthur.
- *90th Regiment.* —Colour-Sergeant T. H. McAllen, Privates R. Murphy, J. Richardson, J. McLean, J. Fairclough, W. Peace, W. Spence.
- *Frontier Light Horse.* —Sergeant J. Tibbits, Trooper C. Merk.
- *Contractor's Agent.* —Mr. J. Ferreira, civilian.

RETURN OF WOUNDED.
- *Royal Artillery.* —Lieutenant Nicholson, a (since dead), Gunner McCann, a.
- *80th Regiment.* —Sergeant Broom, b.
- *1-13th Regiment.*—Captain Cox, ft. Captain Persse, c, Sergeant Tucker, b, Sergeant Woods, b, Bugler Clery, c. Privates Mooney, b, Foster, a, Blakemann, a, Kearney, b, Hayball, a, Davis, b, Medlem, b, Nutt, a, McNultz, a. Parsons, b, Karkness, c, Bellancy, c, Grosvenor, a, Redpath, a, Roberts, c, Stevens, c.

- *90th Regiment.* —Major Hackett, a. Lieutenant Smith, b, Lieutenant Bright, a (since dead), Sergeant Allen, b. Corporal Delaney, b, Corporal Grey, c. Privates Daly, a. Peacock, c, Ferguson, b, Chapman, a (since dead), Butler, b, Mullins, b Jones, b, Pearson, a, Connors, a, Meally, b, Shears, c, Meller, c. Branch, b, Forbes, c, Morris, c. Mead, ft. Smith, c, Rispin, c, Morgan, c, Shear, c, Bryan, a (since dead), Gilbert, a (since dead), Ryan, a (since dead).
- *Mounted Infantry.* —Private Anderson (4th Regiment), c. Private Beswick (ditto), b, Corporal Thompson (80th), b, Captain Gardener (14th Hussars), b.
- *Frontier Light Horse.* —Trooper Peterson, a, Trooper Stopforth, b.
- *Transvaal Rangers.*—Lieutenant White, a, Trooper Sulmontein, b
- *Baker's Horse.* —Trooper Crichton, c.
- *Kaffradian Rifles.* —Trooper Hansen, a.
- *Dutch Burghers.* —Trooper Cammering, b.
- *Mounted Basutos.* —Seeke, b.
- *Native Mule Drivers.* —One a (since dead), and two ft.

APPENDIX H.

PROCEEDINGS OF THE COURT-MARTIAL ON LIEUTENANT CAREY.

The officer, Lieutenant J. B. Carey, 98th Regiment, was tried on a charge of misbehaviour before the enemy, for having on June 1, 1879, when in command of an escort on the Prince Imperial, who was engaged in a reconnaissance, galloped away when surprised by the Zulus, without attempting to defend the Prince or to rally the escort. The Court was composed of Colonel Glynn, C.B., President, Lieutenant-Colonel Whitehead, 68th

Regiment, Colonel Harness, R.A., Captain Courtney, R.E., and Captain Bouverie, 17th Lancers. Major Anstruther, 94th Regiment, was officiating Judge Advocate, and Captain Brander, of the 2-24th, the prosecutor. Captain Brander said he proposed to bring evidence in support of the charge against the prisoner, which would fully explain the whole occurrence connected with the death of the Prince, from the moment of the arrival at the kraal on the banks of the Ityotyozi River on the 1st June. He would first submit a plan of the kraal and the adjacent dongas, adducing evidence of their correctness, and showing also the position of the bodies when discovered the next morning. He would next call the survivors of the escort, who would give a full account of the nature of the ground, and the precautions taken before, and subsequently, by the prisoner. He would then call the Assistant Quartermaster-General, to prove that Carey was in command of the party, and lastly produce evidence of the cause of death.

Captain A. W. Morris, of the 58th Regiment, was then called, and produced a sketch about a foot square, showing the relative positions of the kraal and dongas, or rather donga with several branches. He spoke as to its correctness, as he had been ordered, with Lieutenant Nuttall, of the 58th, to make the sketch, except as regarded the position of the bodies, which had been removed, but the places from which they had been taken had been shown to him by Captain Molyneux, Aide-de-Camp. In cross-examination, the prisoner elicited that the sketch, which was a copy of an original taken for the Court of Inquiry, which had at once assembled by command of Lord Chelmsford, had the north and south points improperly marked, that marked "N" being south, and vice versa. Lieutenant Nuttall, 68th, gave confirmatory evidence.

Captain Molyneux, Aide-de-Camp to Lord Chelmsford, said he was directed by his Lordship to accompany General Marshall and the party who went in search of the body of the 'Prince Imperial. He could identify the spot "A" on the plan as being that where the body of the Prince was found, but not the other points, as he had only casually noticed the bodies of the two troopers, and then had gone to where the body of the Prince lay, and his duty being to take care of that, he had remained by it; and had, on the 4th, pointed out to Captain Morris what, to the best of his belief, was the position of the other two. Cross-examined by the prisoner, he said the Prince was attached to the personal Staff of Lord Chelmsford without having any particular grade assigned him. He was not aide-de-camp. He did anything he was told, and at times performed duties under the Assistant Quartermaster-General, but he was not considered as an officer handed over entirely to that department. Beyond what he had stated, he had no idea what position the Prince held. He had never been gazetted to any particular position.

Corporal Grubb, of Bettington's Natal Horse, was next called. He said—I was one of the escort on the 1st of June. When we arrived at the kraal the Prince gave the word to off-saddle and let our horses out. The native guide, I, and Le Tock cooked some coffee. I then went away for a few minutes to the back of one of the huts, and when I came back I heard the Prince say, "At four o'clock we will go." The native guide then came in and reported that he had seen a Zulu come over the hill. We got the order then directly to stand to our horses. I caught mine and saddled. The Prince then gave the commands, "Prepare to mount," and "Mount." He mounted along with us, and I took the time from him. I had not time to get my right foot into the stirrup before a volley was fired into us. I had my head over on the right side trying to get my stirrup. I turned my eyes, and saw Lieutenant Carey put spurs to his horse. I think all did the same. I know I did. As we were galloping between the kraal and the donga, I heard a bullet come "whiz" up, and it struck something,

I cannot say what; but I saw Trooper Abel throw up his arms and fall back. He was riding not more than half a horse's length ahead of me. Trooper Rogers, when I last saw him, was running round the kraal, with his head stooped down, and presenting his carbine at one of the Zulus, who was about fifteen yards off. After Trooper Abel fell, I galloped a few horses' lengths, when Trooper Le Took passed me. He said, "Stick firm to your horse, boy, and put in the spurs; the Prince is down." I glanced round, and saw the Prince hanging to something, but below his horse, the stirrup-leather, or the wallet; and the horse seemed to trample on him. I steadied my horse and unslung my carbine to have a shot at them, when my horse jumped into the donga, and threw me on to his neck. I was obliged to let my carbine drop to cling to the horse. With some difficulty I got back to the saddle, and when I had gone on about six horses' lengths, I saw the Prince's horse alongside of me. I tried to catch him, but I could not, so I drove it before me, and as I cantered along, it followed. I was away rather down to the right, and on turning my head round saw Lieutenant Carey, Le Tock, and Cochrane a hundred yards away on my left front. I beckoned them to stop, and after a short time I drew up with them. It was then said that some one would have to ride the Prince's horse, and I told Lieutenant Carey that my horse was fagged and I would ride him. Then we all rode on together till we met General Wood and Colonel Buller. Lieutenant Carey reported to them the death of the Prince, and they went to the brow of the hill, and I heard Colonel Buller say that he saw six Zulus leading away four horses. After staying there a little while we all rode together towards General Wood's camp for three or four miles, when we turned off to the left and got to our own camp about seven or half-past seven. Lieutenant Carey reported the circumstance to Lord Chelmsford. We all went together, and I gave up the Prince's horse to his groom. I saw fresh marks of Kafirs at the kraal, for there were heaps of the peel of infi (Kafir sugar-cane) which they had been eating. I do not think the precautions taken for safety were sufficient. Lieutenant Carey led the party at the moment of flight. I saw Rogers trying to get away or to have a shot at the enemy, but I am not sure which, for I passed him in a moment. He was not mounted, for he had been looking for a spare horse which was missing. I did not see the Prince after he had been apparently trampled on by his horse. No orders were given as to rallying or firing on the enemy.

In cross-examination by the prisoner, the witness said there had been differences of opinion between the Prince and Lieutenant Carey as to off-saddling, long before going to the kraal. While still on the hill leading from the camp overlooking the kraal, the Prince gave the word to off-saddle, and then altered his mind and ordered the girths to be slackened for fifteen minutes. The Prince said, "It is hardly worth while to off-saddle for a quarter of an hour; we will go down to the huts by the river, where the men can get wood and water and cook something." There were six troopers, the native guide, Lieutenant Carey, and the Prince in the party, but I do not know who was in command. There were not many words of command given during the day, but the Prince gave the word of command, "Stand to your horses." I was told by my sergeant-major I was going to escort the Prince, not the Prince and Lieutenant Carey. I cannot describe the relative positions of myself, the Prince, and Lieutenant Carey, except that they were to the left and right of me; and as to the escort, they were all over the place. The Prince was three or four yards from me. I was not facing the line of retreat, and the grass was so long that I do not know what I was facing. After the volley I glanced round and saw the Zulus were within ten or twelve yards, and were advancing. I should think they were from forty to fifty in number at a rough guess. I was not quite in command of my horse, for I could not turn him when I wanted, having no curb. I did not notice the prisoner's horse was fagged, but he was sweating. I saw the Prince was riding a very good horse—much better than any one else. I do not recollect reporting seeing the infi peels. Rogers had caught his own horse, and was endeavouring to catch a spare one when I saw him last. When I got out of the kraal a little way I saw Zulus on our left, trying to surround us. I was six to eight yards from the Prince when I saw him clinging to his horse; it was not far from the donga. It was more than five minutes after that before I mentioned to any one that the Prince was down. The native guide did not seem to show any alarm when he reported a Zulu coming over the hill; he took it very quietly. I cannot answer for the others, but certainly I was taken by surprise at the attack. Every one seemed to gallop away from the kraal at the same time. I did not notice anything remarkable in your behaviour during the affair, except that you hardly seemed to believe the Prince's death when it was reported. I had not to pass the Prince in my flight. I was a little ahead of him. He was on my right. I galloped away because we all did. Lieutenant Carey, myself, and Le Tock left the kraal by the left side; the other two men by the right, but I do not know who went first. The Prince's horse was saddled, and there was no reason to prevent his mounting. I do not think we could do anything else than gallop away from the kraal. If we had remained and fired there, in my opinion, we should all have been killed. I am an old soldier of the Royal Artillery, and have seen sixteen years' service, and served in Beltini's Land and against Langabalalele. At the moment of the volley we had not time to look after each other. There was quick firing when we left the kraal, and I think if we had lost any time we should all have been killed. The Zulus were about forty to fifty in number, and were firing as we left I did not see Le Tock dismount from his horse. I did not see him till we got up the hill. If a man fell from his horse between the kraal and the donga he would have had no chance of escaping. No help could have been rendered by us to the Prince. I cannot say we all had an equal chance of escape as we left the kraal, for I do not know the position of the men left behind me. When I saw the Prince followed by Zulus they were ten or twelve yards behind; I was on the far side of the donga, about fifty or sixty yards off. Lieutenant Carey was then close alongside me. Nothing could have been done then to save the Prince's life; they were too close on him. I reported seeing this, but not till some time afterwards. I do not remember Lieutenant Carey asking me if there was any chance of saving his life by returning; I noticed nothing unusual in his conduct. I think I mentioned to him when I saw Zulus on our left, but there would have been no object then in getting us all together and firing on them. I do not know who was in command; no one gave any commands except the Prince to saddle-up and mount. I saw nothing of the native guide after the volley. We usually followed the Prince without word of command.

Trooper Robert Willis.—I was present on the 1st June at the attack on the Prince Imperial. I did not see him on foot after it began. We got no orders as to rallying or firing on the enemy. No attempt was made to help the Prince by any one. I was not surprised, for I do not think any rescue could have been made. If I had been in command of the party I should have got my men together to confront the enemy when clear of the donga. I think we could have rallied about 200 yards from the side of the donga and yet made good our escape. The escort was six troopers and a native, and there were two officers. I do not know who was in command, but I think it was the Prince. I am not certain.

Cross-examined by the prisoner.—The Prince and Lieutenant Carey were both engaged in sketching. I cannot say how we were standing, as I had two horses to look after; but we had got the word to mount, and were mounting, when the volley was poured in and the Zulus rushed out with a yell. I had got into the saddle, and to the best of my knowledge every one was mounted. I and a trooper left the kraal last, except the native, who was behind all. The Prince had left the kraal then. I saw two men fall from their horses before I got to the donga. The Prince's horse followed and passed me, but I only got a glance, as my foot was not in the stirrup, and I had enough to do to keep on. On crossing the donga I got firm in the saddle. On leaving I saw Trooper Rogers lying motionless against a hut, with his horse by him. I do not know whether he was shot or assegaied. It was not Rogers and the native that I saw fall from their horses. I thought that Rogers was shot. I did not see the place where Rogers's body was found. It must have been moved by the Zulus, who do not like dead bodies about a kraal. I believe he was dead when I left him. The two men I saw fall from their horses; whether they were properly mounted or not I cannot say. This was between the kraal and the donga; but I cannot fix the position. I know now the two men were the Prince and Trooper Abel. Neither of the men who fell had any chance of getting away, and nothing could have been done to save them, for the numbers of the Zulus were too great, and they were too close behind us. A man who lost his balance was done. We could do nothing but gallop from the kraal, for when they fired they were only three yards off. I had no command over my horse for 300 yards on the other side of the donga. We could not be rallied between the kraal and the donga. We were in two parties when over the donga, three in front, and Grubb and I behind. He mounted on the Prince's horse, and that delayed us. Corporal Grubb was not riding his own horse when he rejoined Lieutenant Carey. Grubb's horse was knocked up, and mine was very tired, when we got to the top of the hills. I noticed numbers of Zulus on our left in the mealies after crossing the donga. Though we could have rallied the men two hundred yards beyond the donga, we could have done no good then. I know no attempt was made to rescue the Prince, for all the men got out in front of me. From the number of shots fired at the attack, I think the Zulus with firearms must have been from forty to fifty. The firing was very rapid. The escort, by being rallied, could not, in my opinion, have defended the Prince. I was in charge of the escort till they joined Lieutenant Carey and the Prince, as I was the senior noncommissioned officer. I thought we were sent for the protection of the Prince and Lieutenant Carey. I was not told that any one in particular was to command the escort.

By the prosecutor.—I reported to Lieutenant Carey on joining. I was ordered to report to the Cavalry Staff Officer, and Lieutenant Long, of my regiment, gave me a paper, which I gave to Lien-tenant Carey; he returned it to me, and I gave it back to Captain Bettington.

Colonel Harrison, A.Q.M.G., said.—I gave prisoner no orders as to the command of the escort. The senior combatant officer would be in command of the whole party by the Queen's Regulations. Gave him no special orders as senior combatant officer, for I did not know who was the senior officer—Captain Bettington might have gone—not having seen the escort; but when Lieutenant Carey volunteered to go I said, to the best of my belief, "I am glad you are a volunteer, for you can now look after the Prince." If he had not gone, I should have directed some other officer of the Staff to go for that purpose.

Cross-examined by the prisoner.—I believe you volunteered to accompany the Prince to verify some work done previously. I might have said at first, "No, I want yon to stay behind and finish the map;" and yon may have pressed the point. If the Prince had been senior to yon he would naturally have been in command, unless there had been some officer senior to him in the escort. I cannot remember, without referring to my journal, whether yon have ever been alone with the Prince before on any duty. (On referring, Colonel Harrison said, "To the best of my belief, No.") The Prince had only been a few days on my Staff. The prisoner and the Prince were performing similar duties. It would depend upon the distance whether the prisoner would be justified in leaving the escort to verify any part of the road. He would not have been justified in leaving the escort altogether, because I had entrusted him with the charge of the Prince. I have already stated the words in which I gave the prisoner charge of the Prince. The prisoner and the Prince were doing different work on the same road, prisoner -verifying work already done, and the Prince making a more detailed report of the road for the march of the troops. The Prince had orders to choose a camp on the Ityotyozi River, which was on the road. If the prisoner had been alone the same escort would, under similar circumstances, have been detailed for him. When the Prince was put under my orders, I was instructed in the matter of escort to treat him, not as a Royal personage, but the same as any other officer, taking all due precautions. My written instructions to the Prince were lost with him.

Surgeon-Major Scott was next called. He said.—At the request of Lord Chelmsford, in company with Captain Molyneux, A.D.C., I went with the cavalry brigade to search for the body of the Prince Imperial. When approaching near to the kraal where I was told he and his party had off-saddled, I, in company with Captain Molyneux, went ahead of the line of scouts, and, guided by one of the troopers of the escort of the previous day, I went down into a field and saw the body of one of the troopers with two or three men looking on. Finding it was not that of the Prince, I went in a backward direction, my attention being called there by another crowd, and I found there another body, but not that of the Prince. After that my attention was drawn by a shout, which turned out to be from Captain Cochrane, of the Natal Native Cavalry. I went to where he was standing by the body of his Imperial Highness. To the best of my belief his body had not been moved before I got there—that is, the body had not been dragged after death. He died, in my opinion, where I found him. He was lying on his back with the left arm across, in a position of self-defence. I counted eighteen assegai wounds, all in front. It is true there were two wounds found on his back, but from their nature I am satisfied that they were the terminations of wounds inflicted in front. Any one of five of the wounds would have proved mortal. There were no bullet wounds. I believe the body was not moved for two reasons—first, because the body of the second trooper, which lay on the slope of a branch of the donga a little higher up, and I saw that he had been killed at some distance, and dragged into the donga. The other reason is that there were no abrasions on the body of the Prince indicating that he had been dragged. There was a patch of blood underneath the head and neck, caused, apparently, by a wound he received on the side of the neck, and also by a wound through the right eyeball. The body was stripped, except a fine gold chain round the neck, with a medallion and locket of his mother, which he wore next the skin. In the struggle they had got behind, and seem to have escaped the notice of the Zulus.

By the prisoner.—Captain Molyneux, who was with me, directed my attention to the signs of a struggle about the spot, and the Prince's spurs were twisted. He might have been carried after death before being undressed, but he could not have been dragged.

This closed the case for the prosecution. The prisoner announced that he intended to call a few witnesses, and pleaded that he had been punished already by suspension from Staff employment for the offence with which he was charged. This, however, the Court held to be no bar to subsequent trial by court-martial, the Queen's Regulations being precise on this point.

Colonel Harrison, R.E., A.Q.M.G., being called by the prisoner, said he had no fault to find with the prisoner, who had always done his duty while in the department to his entire satisfaction. He had seen, in orders on the 11th instant, that the prisoner had been removed from Staff employ. That was not done at his request or by his knowledge. He regarded the Prince as a civilian attached to the Staff. He was not aware that he had any status in the British army.

Captain Bettington, in command of Bettington's Horse, being asked his opinion of the character of the four survivors of the escort, said, as far as character went, two of them, Cochrane and Grubb, had only once been in the orderly room during six months' service, and then for a trivial offence. The other two had not been up at all. He had no reason for discrediting any of their statements; they were four of the most trustworthy men he had got.

Colonel Bellairs being called, said, the order removing Lieutenant Carey, dated 11th of June, was in consequence of the events of the 1st of June.

The Court then adjourned to give the prisoner time to prepare his defence.

Colonel W. Bellairs, D.A.G., was recalled, and said the events of the 1st of June, to which he had referred, were the circumstances of which the Court of Inquiry had taken cognisance, viz., the death of Prince Napoleon; and, in consequence of the opinion given by the Court, prisoner had been summarily removed from Staff employ, having previously been ordered to be tried by court-martial.

The prisoner said he hoped that statement would remove any bias the present Court might receive from such removal, supposing it to be from some other cause.

Prisoner asked that Colonel Bellairs might produce his report and rough sketch made on the night of June 1st, to which the

Court assented.

Witness said he could not specify any special circumstance of the 1st of June, for which the prisoner had been removed. He could only speak generally that the prisoner was removed by the Lieutenant-General on account of the report of the Court of Inquiry, he having power of selecting and removing at pleasure.

Captain Herbert Stuart, 5th D.G., Brigade Major Survey Brigade, was next called by the prisoner, and said that as senior officer of the prisoner's batch at the Staff College he had formed a very good opinion of him as a most conscientious, hardworking officer. Witness knew of three kraals in the neighbourhood of the spot where the Prince's body was found within a radius of three-quarters of a mile, and a number of others towards the Emshlanwan Hill within a radius of two or three miles. From the kraals on the west, if inhabited, the Zulus could have assembled around the party in a few minutes, and from one on the east side. From the other kraals in from half an hour to an hour.

By the Court.—The kraals were burnt after the Prince's death, with the exception of one to the west, which he believed was not burnt yet.

Trooper Cochrane was recalled, to bring before the Court that the escort were armed with carbines only, swords not being a part of the regular cavalry equipment.

At the next sitting of the Court the prisoner said he had then to address them in his defence against as serious a charge as any which could be brought against an officer, for the interpretation of misbehaviour before an enemy could only be cowardice. Before proceeding to the evidence he must ask the Court to dismiss from their minds any bias which they might have received from his having been dismissed from employment on the Staff. However deplorable might be the death of the Prince, and no one regretted it more than himself, for he would willingly have changed places with the Prince, yet he should assume if he was guilty he should have been equally guilty if, by his conduct, he had caused the death of the humblest soldier of the force. The escort was said to be under his charge, but such charge had never been put upon him, and he believed he was accompanying the Prince Imperial as a brother officer of junior rank, performing similar duties. At the same time he recognized that, whether senior or junior, it was his duty to do all in his power to rescue the Prince from his perilous position, and he hoped to show that he had done so. Proceeding then to review the evidence, he showed that the witnesses concurred in saying that after crossing the donga the survivors had pulled up to a walk; and that disposed of the charge of galloping away. It was true that they had galloped away from the immediate vicinity of the kraal, but that he contended was the only reasonable course open to them, and as to deserting the Prince he had seen him last with his left foot in the stirrup and his hands on the saddle, and the fair inference was that he had mounted with the rest on giving the word of command. At that instant the volley was fired, and the Zulus with a shout rushed out on them, frightening the horses. A hut was between him and the Prince Imperial, and they passed it on different sides, and that prevented him from seeing the Prince leave the kraal. The evidence showed that from forty to fifty Zulus attacked them, and that they came up in numbers on the left, and that fourteen were seen following the Prince in the donga, and the evidence of Captain Stuart proved that they were thick in the neighbourhood. With such proof of superior force about, and with the belief that the Prince was mounted, it was his duty, he conceived, for the sake of the rest of the party, seeing that they were under a heavy fire, with the enemy shouting and rushing upon them, to consider their safety; but the fact was that a rush took place, and in that rush he was carried away. That the Prince rode away with the rest he thought there could be little doubt, and once mounted, he was justified in considering the Prince had as good a chance of safety as any of them, considering the superior character of his horse. It was only the witness Grubb who said that he led the flight; every other witness said that all left together. His own impression was that two men rushed past him, and all left together. It might be said, why not rally at the kraal and charge the enemy? But was such a course possible when there were but six men with unloaded car-bines, no swords, and the horses bolting along across an unknown country. He contended it was not, and that there was no course open to them except to bolt from the kraal. He was next charged with not rallying the escort between the donga and the kraal. He had not done that because he had judged it at the time to be impossible; he had shouted at the time to every one to keep to the left, because he wished to direct them, knowing the country better than the men, to the best place for collecting. The charge was of so general a nature that the whole onus probandi was thrown upon him as regards the possibility and utility of doing so at all. He would, however, address himself to both points. With regard to the possibility of rallying between the kraal and the donga, they might reflect for a moment on the evidence of Le Took, who passing Grubb urged him to spur faster, as the Prince was down and Zulus upon them, while he himself was riding on his stomach in the saddle, and could only recover his seat when over the donga. Sergeant Willis's horse had bolted with him, and he could not have rallied on the kraal side of the donga. Grubb said he could do nothing but gallop till far beyond the donga, and all the witnesses concurred in saying that they considered any attempt to rally on the kraal side of the donga as utterly useless, and he at the time had to deal with the facts of long grass, an advancing enemy, frightened horses, and scattered men, and with the Prince not in sight, nor was he told of his fate until long after, so that he was under the impression he had got away, while all the while the Zulus were pursuing hotly on the left. They, however, soon walked their horses, and then he, as surviving officer, came to the conclusion of the rest of the party as to the impossibility of doing anything for the rescue of the Prince. With regard to the utility of rallying, all the witnesses agreed that nothing could have been done to save the Prince's life, and it then became his duty to take the steps necessary to save the rest of the escort. He had, therefore, shouted to the rest of the men to join him, and he asked the Court to consider the position he was in, with four men scattered and disorganized, out of reach of fire on the donga, Zulus seen everywhere and still rushing forward, and with nothing seen on the right but a riderless grey horse. Judging from the rapidity of fire, which all the witnesses confirmed, he saw no reason to doubt then that the Prince must have been shot off his horse. Considering, then, his duty with regard to the rest of the escort, he had called them to join him. When he had learnt the truth with regard to the Prince, the Zulus had already passed the spot where he had been last seen by the only witness who had seen him us. the donga, and he thought any one who was present could have come to no other conclusion than he and the witnesses had come to, viz., that nothing could be done then to save the Prince. He thought the Court would be of opinion that the evidence proved he had been calm and collected, and he hoped they would believe that he had acted under very difficult and perilous circumstances in the best way for the safety of the party. No one more deeply regretted than himself the loss of the Prince, but he honestly believed that no effort of his would have saved his Highness's life.

At the prisoner's wish the report he made on the night of the 1st June was put in and read. Its main points were that the escort ought to have had, in addition to the six white troopers of Bettington's Horse, six Basutos, who, however, had never joined; that the prisoner had differed with the Prince as to the place for off-saddling, he desiring to remain on the bridge, while the Prince insisted on going nearer the river; that he had suggested saddling-up at thirty-five minutes past three p.m., but the Prince said wait ten minutes longer, though in five minutes more he had given the order to stand to their horses. The report said that the prisoner heard the order given to mount, and at the same time saw the Prince's foot in the stirrup, and a number of black faces come rushing up behind the troopers, within twenty yards of them; and at the time of the volley he did not think any one was wounded, on account of previous experience of the bad shooting of the Zulus. It concluded by announcing the loss of the Prince, two white troopers, a native, and five horses missing.

For the prosecution, Captain Brander, in summing up, first dealt with the question of the command of the escort, asserting that there was no ground for the prisoner trying to evade that responsibility, seeing that Captain Molyneux's evidence showed the Prince to have no status in the British Army, and therefore no authority over any of Her Majesty's officers or men. Colonel Harrison, R.E., also showed that he had specially charged the prisoner with the duty of looking after the Prince, showing that the Prince had been committed to his special care, and that the charge was well founded. The prisoner himself had admitted that it was his duty to rescue the Prince, and he had gone on to say that he hoped to convince the Court he had done what he could; but he had utterly failed to do so, and for the very good reason that nothing had been done whatever. All had galloped away, and the evidence of Grubb went to show that the Prisoner had put spurs to his horse and was the first man to start after the volley. No orders had been given to rally or fire, though Le Took said that after getting seven hundred yards away they might have done so, and yet got away. Cochrane's evidence showed that no attempt had been made to help the Prince, and he expressed surprise that it was not done. The prisoner had no right to take credit for saving any of the escort, for it had been a clear case of each man for himself. It was shown by the evidence that the Prince had been seen in the donga, so that he had been able to run two hundred and fifty yards after the vanishing horsemen; and yet nothing had been done, and he had been left to his death by a party of men armed with breechloading rifles, who had not fired a shot in defence. Only Le Took, who had dismounted to get his rifle, and Rogers, who was seen taking aim at the kraal, had come well out of the affair. As to the possibility of rallying, the evidence of Sergeant Willis and of Le Took showed that it was quite possible to rally on the further side of donga, while it was there that Grubb had caught the Prince's horse. It was the prisoner's duty after passing the hut to see that the Prince was mounted or not, and that he was safe. He had not done so, and it was for the Court to decide whether the evidence did not establish the words of the charge—that the Prisoner had been guilty of misbehaviour before the enemy.

The Officiating Judge Advocate also summed up against the prisoner, enforcing the points referred to by the prosecutor, and the Court was then cleared to consider their sentence.

OFFICIAL DESPATCH FROM THE HORSE GUARDS ON THE COURT MARTIAL.

Horse Guards, War Office, August 16, 1879.

Sir,—The proceedings of the general court-martial assembled at Camp, Upoko River, Zululand, on the 12th June, 1879, for the trial of Lieut. J. B. Carey, 98th Regiment, on a charge of misbehaviour before the enemy, having been submitted to the Queen, Her Majesty has been advised that the charge is not sustained by the evidence, and has accordingly been graciously pleased not to confirm the proceedings, and to direct that the prisoner be relieved from all consequences of his trial. Captain Carey is released from arrest and will rejoin his regiment for duty.

The trial having been set aside, the Field Marshal Commanding-in-Chief offers no remark on the proceedings, but His Royal Highness has received Her Majesty's commands to make known his observations on the occurrences of the 1st June last, as they have come under his notice in official reports.

His Imperial Highness Prince Napoleon was, at his own request, permitted to proceed to South Africa, in order to witness the operations in Zululand. He was provided with private letters to Lord Chelmsford, describing his position, and stating that it had not been thought right, even if it had been possible, to comply with his earnest desire to be commissioned as an officer of the British Army. The Commander of the forces in South Africa made such arrangements as seemed to him desirable under the condition of the Prince's non-official position, and attached him at first to his own personal Staff, and afterwards, with a view to provide him with occupation, to the department of the Quartermaster-General.

The Prince was treated in all respects as if he had been a junior officer of the General Staff, with this exception, that Lord Chelmsford gave the most stringent instructions that His Imperial Highness was not to be permitted to proceed on any distant reconnoissance without his special permission, and that, when employed in surveying operations in close proximity to the camp, his party was always to be provided with a sufficient escort and to be accompanied by an officer.

His Royal Highness desires it to be known that he entirely approves of Lord Chelmsford's arrangements for the reception and occupation of the Prince; and that he considers the orders issued for his protection were marked with judgment and adapted to the occasion.

The reconnoissance which the Prince was allowed by Lieut.-Colonel Harrison, the Assistant Quartermaster-General, to make on the 1st June extended to a considerable distance from the camp. Lord Chelmsford's permission had not been sought or obtained; all the arrangements were made under Lieutenant-Colonel Harrison's orders; and the Lieutenant-General commanding had reason to believe that throughout the day the Prince was in the company of Lieutenant-Colonel Harrison, who was occupied in guiding a column in its change of camp.

Lieutenant-Colonel Harrison doubtless believed that in his arrangements for the expedition he had sufficiently complied with Lord Chelmsford's instructions to himself. In the opinion of the Field Marshal Commanding-in-Chief he was mistaken. His orders to Lieutenant Carey were not sufficiently explicit, and he failed to impress upon the Prince the duty of deferring to the military orders of the officer who accompanied him, and the necessity of guiding himself by his advice and experience.

If Lieutenant-Colonel Harrison had displayed more firmness and forethought in his instructions to Lieutenant Carey and to the Prince, His Royal Highness cannot but think that that train of events would have been averted, which resulted in bringing a handful of men, in the middle of the enemy's country, into a position so well calculated to invite surprise and to court disaster.

Lieutenant Carey from the first formed a wrong conception of his position. He was sent, not only to perform the duties of his staff office, but to provide that military experience which his younger companion had not yet acquired. If his instructions were defective his professional knowledge might have prompted him as to his duty.

He imagined, but without the slightest foundation for the mistake, that the Prince held a military rank superior to his own, and acting throughout on this strange misconception, he omitted to take for the safety of the party those measures of precaution which his experience had taught him to be essential.

At the moment of attack defence was impossible, and retreat imperative. What might have been done, and what ought to have been done when the moment of surprise had passed, can only be judged by an eye-witness; but His Royal Highness will say, and le feels that he speaks with the voice of the army, it will ever remain to him a source of regret that, whether or not an attempt at rescue was possible, the survivors of this fatal expedition withdrew from the scene of disaster without the full assurance that all efforts on their part were not abandoned until the fate of their comrades had been sealed.

I have the honour to be, Sir, your obedient servant,

C. H. Ellice, Adjutant-General.

To the General Officer Commanding in South Africa, Natal.

APPENDIX I.

Telegraphic Despatch by Lord Chelmsford, Received by the General Commanding, and Published by His Order for General Information.

"Cetywayo not having complied with my demands by noon yesterday, July 3rd, and having fired heavily on the troops at the water, I returned the 114 cattle he had sent me, and ordered a reconnoissance to be made by the mounted force, under Colonel Buller, this was effectually made, and caused the Zulu Army to advance and show itself. This morning a force under my command, consisting of the 2nd Division, under Major-General Newdigate, numbering 1,870 Europeans, 530 Natives, and 8 guns, and the Flying Column, under Brigadier-General Wood, numbering 2,192 Europeans and 573 Natives, four guns and two Gatlings crossed the Umvolosi River at b.15, and, marching in a hollow square, with the ammunition and intrenching tool-carts and bearer company in its centre, reached an excellent position betweeen Unodwengo and Ulundi about half-past eight a.m.

This had been observed by Colonel Buller the day before. Our fortified camp on the right bank of the Umvolosi River was left with a garrison of about 900 Europeans, 250 Natives, and one Gatling gun, under Colonel Bellairs. Soon after half-past seven the Zulu Army was seen leaving its bivouacs and advancing on every side. The engagement was shortly after commenced by the mounted men; by nine o'clock the attack was fully developed; at half-past nine o'clock the enemy wavered, the 17th Lancers, followed by the remainder of the mounted men, attacked them, and a general rout ensued. The prisoners state Cetywayo was personally commanding, and had made all the arrangements himself, and that he witnessed the fight from Qikazi kraal, and that twelve regiments took part in it, if so 20,000 men attacked us. It is impossible to estimate, with any correctness, the loss of the enemy, owing to the extent of country over which they attacked and retreated, but it could not have been less, I consider, than 1,000 killed. By noon Ulundi was in flames, and daring the day all military kraals of the Zulu Army, and in the valley of the Umvolosi destroyed. At 2 p.m. the return march to the camp of the Column commenced. The behaviour of the troops under my command was extremely satisfactory, their steadiness under a complete belt of fire was remarkable, the dash and enterprise of the mounted branches was all that could be wished, and the fire of the artillery very good. A portion of the Zulu forces approached our fortified camp, and at one time threatened to attack it. The Native Contingent forming a part of the garrison were sent out after the action, and assisted in the pursuit. As I have fully accomplished the object for which I advanced, I consider I shall now be best carrying out Sir Garnet Wolseley's instructions by moving at once to Entonganini, and thence towards Kwamagasa. I shall send back a portion of this force with empty waggons for supplies, which are now ready at Fort Marshall. I beg to forward a list of casualties.

KILLED.

- *Second Division.*—Captain Wyatt Edgell, and Farrier-Sergeant Taylor, 17th Lancers; Corporal Tomkinson, and Private Coates, 58th Regiment; Private Kent, 94th Regiment; Trooper Sifoma, Shepstone's Horse. (Flying Column).—Corporal Carter, R.A.; Bugler J. Bums, and Private W. Bridley, 13th Regiment; Private Floyd, 80th Regiment; Trooper Jonas, Natal Native Horse.

WOUNDED.

- *Second Division.*—Dangerously: Troopers E. Jones, and Charles Waite, 17th Lancers; Privates H. Calder, and W. Benner, 21st Regiment; Privates N. Fash, W. Stewart, and M. Moroney, 58th Regiment; Private Muzaaza, Shepstone's Horse. Severely: Major Winslow, Privates Dowdle, G. Brown, F. Fidler, and J. Daveney, 21st Regiment; Major Bond, Privates Collerell, H. Howie, and W. Severett, 58th Regiment; Lieutenant Jenkins, 17th Lancers; Lieutenant Phipps, 1-24th Regiment; Lieutenant Dudenrood, Sergeant Piper, 58th Regiment; Driver Breman, R.A.; Hospital-bearer Umbique. Slightly: Captain the Hon. Cotton, Lieutenant James, Scots Greys; Lieutenant A. B. Milne, R.N.; Trooper J. Keegan, 17th Lancers; Private Aly, 1-24th; Private M. Murhill, 94th Regiment; Lieutenant Jenkins, N. N. Contingent. (Flying Column).—Dangerously: Lieutenant Pardoe, Privates J. Davis, W. Shepstone, Bugler M. Cockling, 13th Regiment; Gunner J. Morton, R.A.; Privates P. Tully, and W. Hunt, 80th Regiment; Trooper Siagdo, Mounted Basatos. Severely: Gunner W. Morshead, R.A.; Sergeant R Wood, R.E.; Privates J. Bourne, H. Owens, C. Johnson, W. Hirt, and J. Owing, 13th Regiment; Sergeant O'Neil, Privates A. Beecroft, and M. Duffy, 80th Regiment; Private J. Flood, 90th Regiment; Trooper P. Segos, Baker's Horse; Captain Hurber, Lieutenant Cowdell, Wood's Irregulars; Trooper Salem, Mounted

Basutos. Slightly: Private P. Stokes, 13th Regiment,

The despatches conclude with the following returns:—

Return of casualties at Ulundi, Zululand, on July 4th, 1879:—

- *Killed:* 2 officers, 13 non-commissioned officers and men, 3 natives. Total 18. 71 horses killed, wounded, and missing. Wounded: 19 officers, 59 non-commissioned officers, and men, 7 natives. Total 85. Grand total: 21 officers, 72 non-commissioned officers and men, 10 natives. Total 103.

Return of Casualties amongst Officers at Ulundi, Zululand, on 4th July, 1879.

- *17th Lancers.* —Captain Wyatt-Edgell, killed.
- *Interpreter.* —Hon. W. Drummond, missing.
- *Staff.* —Lieutenant Milne, RN., A.D.C., slightly wounded; Lieutenant and Captain Hon. R. Cotton, slightly wounded; Lieutenant Barry Phipps, severely wounded.
- *Royal Artillery.* —Lieutenant Davidson, slightly wounded.
- *Staff.* —Lieutenant Liebenrood, severely wounded.
- *17th Lancers.* —Lieutenant - Colonel Drury-Lowe, slightly wounded; Lieutenant James, slightly wounded; Lieutenant Jenkins, dangerously wounded.
- *21st Foot.* —Major Winslow, severely wounded.
- *58th Foot.* —Major Bond, severely wounded.
- *94th Foot.* —Lieutenant Brooks, slightly wounded.
- *1st Battalion 13th Foot.* —Lieutenant Pardoe, dangerously wounded (died afterwards).
- *Natal Native Contingent.* —Lieutenant Lukin, slightly wounded; Lieutenant Moncrief, slightly wounded.
- *Wood's Irregulars.* —Commandant White, slightly wounded; Captain Horton, severely wounded; Lieutenant Cowdell, severely wounded.
- *Natal Native Pioneers.* —Lieutenant H. Hickley, slightly wounded; Lieutenant F. Andrews, slightly wounded.

- *Total.* —Killed 1; wounded, 19; missing, 1.

The following are copies of statements made by prisoners captured at Ulundi on July 4th:—

Statement made by Prisoner taken at Battle of Ulundi on 4th July, 1879.

To the left of Ulundi, coming past the old Mission Station, was the Umlambongwingi Regiment, now called the Impunza; to the right of them, and below Ulundi, was the Qikazi. Both these regiments attacked the front. On the right and rear face we attacked from behind Nodwengu, by the Ulundi, Ngobamakosi, Uve, and Umbonambi. These were led on by Dabulamanzi, in person, mounted on a bay horse, and attacked without any sign of order, not having had time to collect in regiments; and on the left the Nokenki and Nodwengo Regiments attacked, coming from Umpanda's grave. The Umcityu attacked the left rear of the square.

Statement of Undungdnyanga, Son of Umgenane, a Prisoner taken at the battle of Ulundi 4th Juy, 1879

The regiments engaged were Undi, Inhlonhlo (combined), Uhloko, Umxapu, Nodwengu, Umbone, Nokeake, Umcityu, Ngobamakosi, and Ingnlube (one company Dakuzas); these formed the attacking force. The Undabakamina and the Uhlambohle Regiments were with the King at Umlambongwenga, they were his body guard.

The King saw the battle from the kraal. The King said he wanted to make peace, and three days ago he sent 140 of his white cattle as a peace offering to the Great Chief heading the white army. These cattle were turned back at the White Umvolosi River at Nodwengu, by the Inbanodunga Regiment. This regiment refused to let them pass, and said they would not have peace; they preferred to fight and turned the cattle back. The King was then at Ulundi. Some of these cattle were killed the day before yesterday by the King's orders for the army to eat. The principal leaders of the army were Tyingwayo, Mnyamane,

Dabulamanzi, and Mundula (headman of Nodwengu). Sirayo and his son Mehklaka Zulu were also present. We had no idea that the white force was so strong in numbers till we saw it in the open. We were completely beaten off by the Artillery and bullets. The Zulu Army was larger to-day than it was at Kambula, far larger. I was at the Kambula battle. All the army was present to-day. We had very sick hearts in the fight when we saw how strong the white army was, and we were startled by the number of horsemen. We were afraid to attack in the thorns, as we knew you would laager the waggons. We were afraid to cross the river yesterday after the mounted men because of the laager. We were all, by order, at the Umlambongwenya kraal the day before yesterday.

When the King addressed us, he said, "As the Inkandampemyu Regiment would not let the cattle go in as a peace offering, and wished to fight, and as the white army was now at his home, we could fight. That we were to fight the army in the open; to attack it between Nodwengo and Ulundi kraals (where we did fight)." The King also told ns, when we pursued you, not to cross the river, for fear of the guns that would be left in the laager. The King himself, personally, placed the different regiments, and gave us our orders. We were watching and expecting the army would leave the laager and march for the King's kraal. We saw the force when it started to cross the river, and surrounded it, as we had been ordered to do. Yesterday we all thought we should have an easy victory if you came into the open. The two cannon taken at Isandhlwana were at Nodwengo, and are now at the King's other kraal in the thorns. No one knows how to use them. The white man who writes the King's letters is a trader. He came trading in the beginning of the year. The King has his movements always watched. His property is not touched; he is a lame man. A white man was taken at the Zlobani and taken to the King, who ordered him to be taken back, and said he was to be let go near Kambula. The army is now thoroughly beaten, and as we were beaten in the open, it will not reassemble or fight again. No force is watching the lower column (Crealock's), and no force has been sent there. How could there be, when all the army was here to-day. We mustered here by the King's orders at the beginning of this moon (about ten days ago). We had not been called out before. I have never heard that Dabulamanzi wanted peace, or wanted to go over to the white people.

List of Regiments and Corps Present.

Corps	Regiments
Undi	Tulwana
"	Ndlondhlo
"	Indlungenqwe
"	N'kobamakosi ("Uve" with them)
Usixepi	Nokenke
Umlambongwenga	Udududu
Umkandampemvu	Umcityu
Likaxi	Umxopo
"	Ndloko
"	Amakwenkwe
Bulawayo	Noumgeni
Ndukwza	Ndukwya
Nodwengu	Isangu

2. Our front was attacked by the Ndloko and Amakwenkwe; right flanks by Tulwana, Indlungenqwe, and Nodwengu; left flank by Ndlondhlo, Nokenke, Udukusa, Udududu, Usumgeni, Umxopo; rear by Umcityu, and Nkobamakosi.

3. On the 2nd July, at a meeting attended by the six following chiefs, and others of importance, it was resolved to send to Lord Chelmsford the " Royal Coronation White Cattle." When about five miles from our camp, the Umcityu Regiment prevented their being driven to us, resolving to fight. There were present at the meeting:—Mnyamane; Usirayo; Umavingwana; Cetuga (son of Mangwendo); Palane (second in command of

the Nkobamakosi); Untuzwa (brother of Seketwayo).

4. Cetywayo and Mnyamane were at the Umlambongwenya kraal on the evening of 3rd July, and probably saw the fight. Dabulamanzi and Umavingwana were seen near the Nodwengu kraal on the 4th.

* * *

Lord Chelmsford's Official Account of the Battle of Ulundi.

The General, writing from Head-quarters, Entonganeni, on the 6th of July, says:—

"My last despatch, dated June 28, will have placed you in full possession of the situation on that date of that portion of Her Majesty's forces under my immediate and personal command, and of our relations with Cetywayo. These forces were about to leave this place for the Valley of Umvolosi, with ten days' provisions, and about two hundred waggons, the remainder of the stores, together with all the tents and waggons, &c., being left behind in an entrenched position here. I was at that time aware that a very considerable force was collected on the left bank of the river, and I reported that until I received from Cetywayo compliance with the demands I had already communicated to you, I should continue my advance to Ulundi. The advance was commenced on the 30th of June, and the camps of the Flying Column and 2nd Division were formed that day at a distance of nine or ten miles from the Umvolosi River. Two messengers from Cetywayo were seen by me about mid-day. I have the honour of enclosing a copy of the message sent to him, which at their request was reduced to writing; likewise a copy of the written communication received by me through Mr. Vign, the white man with the Zulu chief. 'Die messengers brought with them the sword of the late Imperial Prince Louis Napoleon, which, for safe custody, was sent back to the fort here, the messengers were desired to take charge of the cattle which had been sent in to me at Entonganeni, as I wanted to return them now I was advancing; but they refused to take them, on the plea of the delay it would cause in their return to the King. On the following day (July 1) our advance was continued over a difficult country, where the waggon track passed through bush of cactus and mimosa trees. After considerable labour on the part of the troops in clearing the road and levelling the drifts, the Column reached the vicinity of the River Umvolosi at about one p.m. The enemy's pickets fell back on our approach, and no opposition occurred this day to our taking up our positions on the right bank of the river; at one time, indeed, large bodies of Zulus were seen to move from Ulundi to certain positions in our front, which made me anxious to get our camps formed as speedily as possible. By dusk our position was perfectly defensible, and our cattle and horses had been watered at the river. On the ensuing day (July 2) the camp of the 2nd Division closed up to that of the Column under Brigadier-General Wood, and our entrenched camp, with a small stone fort, was formed on a plan that would enable a small garrison to defend it, leaving the remainder of the force free to operate, unencumbered by any waggons, in such a manner as might be deemed desirable. The Zulu force did not show itself this day; no messengers arrived from the King. A large herd of white cattle was observed being driven from the King's kraal towards us, but was driven back shortly afterwards. As no message had been received from. Cetywayo the following morning (July 3), and as considerable annoyance was offered to our watering parties by Zulus firing on them, I arranged for a reconnoissance to be made by Lieutenant-Colonel Buller, C.B., with his mounted men, as soon as the time allowed for meeting my demands had expired. The cattle sent in by Cetywayo on June 29 were driven across the river to him during the morning. Lieutenant-Colonel Buller crossed the river by the lower drift to the right of our camp, and was soon in possession of the high ground on our front and the Undabakaombie kraal. The object of Lieutenant-Colonel Buller's reconnoissance was to advance towards Ulundi, and report on the road, and whether there was a good position where our force could make its stand if attacked. I was also anxious, if possible, to cause the enemy to show its force, its points of gathering, and plan of attack. Lieutenant-Colonel Buller completely succeeded m the duty entrusted to him. Having collected his mounted men near Undabakaombie from the thorny country near the river, he advanced rapidly towards Ulundi, passing Unodwengo on his right. He Had reached the vicinity of the stream Untukulwini, about three-quarters of a mile from Ulundi, when he was met by a heavy fire from a considerable body of the enemy lying concealed in the long grass around the stream. Wheeling about, he retired to the high ground near Unodwengo, where he commenced to retire by alternate portions of his force in a deliberate manner. The Zulus were checked; but in the meantime large bodies of the enemy were to be seen advancing from every direction; and I was enabled, with my own eyes, to gain the information I wished for, as to the manner of advance and points from which it would be made in the event of our forces advancing to Ulundi. Though the Zulus advanced rapidly, and endeavoured to get round his flank. Lieutenant-Colonel Buller was able, to retire his force across the river with but a few casualties. He informed me of a position which, on the following day, my force occupied, and which subsequent events showed was admirably adapted for the purpose I had in view. I consider that this officer deserves very great credit for the manner in which he conducted this duty. That night the Zulus were moving about in large bodies, as testified by the sound of their war songs, but they in no manner interfered with us. At 4 a.m., the 4th of July, the troops were silently roused, the bugles, however, sounding the reveille at the usual hour— 5.15 a.m. I left the camp, with all the waggons, oxen, &c., garrisoned by the 1st Battalion, 24th Regiment and casualties. Colonel Bellairs, C.B., D.A.G., at my special request, remained in command of them. At 6.45 a.m., the force, as per return enclosed, crossed the river. Lieutenant-Colonel Buller's mounted men, going by the lower ford, seized the high ground on our front without opposition. Passing over a mile of very bushy ground, the force marching in a hollow square, ammunition and intrenching tool carts, etc., in the centre, the guns moving also in the square in such positions as to enable them to come interaction on each face without delay, we reached the high ground between the kraals Undabakaombie and Unodwengo at 7.30 a.m. The mounted men were now out, covering our front and flanks, while the 17th Lancers covered the rear. By this time our advance from camp was evidently observed, and dark clusters of men could be seen in the morning light on the hill tops on our left and left front. To our right, where the largest number of the enemy were believed to be, we could see but little, as the mist from the river and the smoke of their camp fires hung heavily over the bush below. Leaving Undabakaombie to our left (this kraal was burnt by our rear guard), I advanced to the position referred to by Lieutenant-Colonel Buller; this was about 700 yards beyond Unodwengo, and about the same distance from the stream that crossed the road halfway to Ulundi; this was high ground uncommanded from any point, and with but little cover beyond long grass near it. At this point I wheeled the square half right, so as to occupy the most favourable part of the ground. The portions of the Zulu army on our left and left front were now formed in good order, and steadily advancing to the attack; masses also appeared from the thorn country on our right and passed round to Unodwengo and to our rear, thus completing the circle round us. The battle commenced at 8.45 a.m., by our mounted men on the right and left becoming engaged. Slowly retiring until the enemy came within our range, they passed into our square, which now opened with artillery and rifles. Shortly before 9 a.m. the Zulu army attacked us on every side. The Unodwengo kraal, a vast assemblage of huts, probably numbering 400 in number, afforded good cover for concealing the movements of a force, which appears to have been the Ulundi, Ugobamakosi, Uve, and Umbakauli regiments. No order was to be seen in their movements, which was caused (so state prisoners) by these regiments having been taken by surprise by our early and silent advance. Hurrying up from their bivouacs, they had no time to form up separately; but, in a cloud, advanced to the attack beyond the cover of the kraal. The fire by which they were met, however, from our right face proved too heavy, and the bulk of these regiments failing to advance, rapidly passed to their left and joined the Umcityu Regiment, which was pressing up to the attack in a determined manner. As the ground here fell suddenly, and cover was afforded them in this advance, men were killed within thirty yards of the companies of the 21st Regiment, forming the rear face at this point. The fire of the enemy from a few minutes to 9 to 9.20 was very heavy, and many casualties, I regret to say, occurred; but when it is remembered that within our comparatively small square, all the cavalry, mounted men, natives, hospital attendants, &c., were packed, it is a matter of congratulation that they were not heavier. The fire from the Artillery and Infantry was so effective that within half an hour signs of hesitation were perceivable in the movements of the enemy. I then directed Colonel Drury-Lowe to take out the 17th Lancers. Passing out by the rear face, he led his regiment towards the Unodwengo kraal, dispersing and killing those who had not time to reach the shelter of the kraal or the bush below, then wheeling to the right), charged through the Zulus, who, in full flight, were endeavouring to reach the lower slopes of the mountains beyond. Numbers of the enemy in this direction, who had not taken part in the actual attack, were now firing, and, momentarily strengthened by those flying, were enabled to pour in a considerable &e on the advancing Lancers below them. Our cavalry did not halt, however, until the whole of the lower ground was swept, and some 150 of the enemy killed. Many of those they had passed in their speed had collected in a ravine to their rear; these were attacked and destroyed by our mounted natives. The flight of the Zulu army was now general; the slopes of the hills were, however, beyond the reach of our already fatigued cavalry, and, having no fresh troops to support him, Colonel Drury-Lowe exercised a wise discretion in rallying his men. Lieutenant-Colonel Buller, meanwhile, had posted the Mounted Infantry so as to fire into the flank of the retiring enemy, and the remainder of his mounted men, making for the country beyond, killed some 450 in the pursuit. Our 9-pounder guns were shortly afterwards moved from the rear and front faces of the square, and made excellent practice on the enemy retreating over the hills to the east on our left rear, and between Ulundi and the River Umvolosi. As soon as our wounded had been attended to, and were fit to be moved, the force advanced to the banks of the stream near Ulundi, while the mounted men and cavalry swept the country beyond. Ulundi was fired at 11.40 a.m., and the kraals of Qikazi and Umpambongwena shortly afterwards. At 2 P.M., the force commenced to return to its camp on the right bank of the Umvolosi, which it reached about 3.30 p.m. By sunset every military kraal undestroyed up to this time in the valley of the Umvolosi was in flames. Not a sign of the vast army that had attacked us in the morning was to be seen in any direction. By the statements of the prisoners attached, it would appear that nearly the whole available Zulu army was under Cetywayo's command this day. By Mr. Vign's statement, it would appear he considered it to be 20,000; by others it is put down at 25,000, or even more, and was larger than that assembled at Kambula; it must have formed on a circumference of some ten miles. It appears that Cetywayo himself arranged the disposition of the forces, and that they considered they would have no difficulty in defeating British troops if they advanced in the open, away from their waggons. I feel I have a right to say that the results of the battle of Ulundi, gained by the steadiness of the infantry, the good practice of the artillery, and the dash of the cavalry and mounted troops will be sufficient to dispel this idea from the minds of the Zulu nation, and of every other tribe in South Africa for ever. It is difficult to compute accurately the loss of the Zulus on this occasion, as the extent of ground over which the attack was made, and the pursuit carried on, was so great; but judging by the reports of those engaged it cannot be placed at a loss number than 1,500 killed. The loss of the Zulus killed in action since the commencement of hostilities in January, has been placed at not less than 10,000 men, and I am inclined to believe this estimate is not too great. I regret to state that, in addition to the casualties in killed and wounded, the Hon. W. Drummond (in charge of my Intelligence Department) is reported missing; it appears he was last seen riding alone near Ulundi, at a time when a considerable number of Zulus were still hovering about. On the 3rd of July, Major Upcher, commanding the forts here, reported that Lieutenant Scott-Douglas, of the 2nd Battalion 21st Regiment, in charge of the signalling stations, had not returned here. I fear it must be considered certain that Mr. Drummond, Lieutenant Scott-Douglas, and the corporal 17th Lancers, have fallen into the hands of the enemy. I have taken upon myself to disregard the instructions I have received, and am sending this despatch direct, furnishing a copy to Sir Garnet Wolseley, who is with General Crealock's Division. I trust that this action will meet with your approval."

***

The following is the official text of the final messages which passed between Lord Chelmsford and Cetywayo just before the battle of Ulundi:—

Message from Lord Chelmsford to Cetywayo.

"June 30th, 1879.

"1. If the induna 'Mundula' brings with him (1,000) one thousand rifles taken at Isandwhlana, I will not insist on 1,000 men coming to lay them down if the Zulus are afraid to come. He must bring the two cannon and the remainder of the cattle; I will then be willing to negotiate.

"2. As he has caused me to advance by the great delay he has made, I must now go as far as Umvolosi River to enable my men to drink. I will consent, pending negotiations, to halt on the farther (Ulundi) bank of the river, and will not burn any kraals until the 3rd of July, provided no opposition is made to my advance to the position on the Umvolosi, by which day, the 3rd of July, by noon, the conditions must be complied with.

"3. If my force is fired upon, I shall consider negotiations are at an end; and to avoid any chance of this, it is best that 'Mundula' should come to my camp to-morrow at day-break, or to-night, and that the Zulu troops should withdraw from the river and its neighbourhood to Ulundi.

"4. I cannot stop the General with the coast army until all conditions are complied with; when they are so, I will send, as speedily as possible, a message to him."

***

The message from the Zulu King to Lord Chelmsford runs as follows:—

"June 30th, 1879.

"The King called me this morning to write this letter to your Worship, General Lord Chelmsford:—

"He brings with bearers a sword that belonged to the Prince of England (so they say, I do not know, of course), to-morrow morning the two 7-pounder guns and a lot of oxen will leave tomorrow morning to bring at your Worship's feet.

"For Cetywayo,

"C. Vign, Trader.

"Sir,—P.S.—If the English army is in want for the country, please do me a favour to call for me by bearer, that I might get out of the country. I went into the country to buy cattle for blankets.

"And be your obedient servant, C.V.

"P.S.—My really believing is, that the King wants to fight, but the princes or his brothers they want peace; also the people wants to fight.

"The bearers are Umvousie Englishmen."

The following note was written in pencil on the envelope:—

"P.S.—Be strong, if the King send in his army, they are about 20,000.

"In haste, your obedient servant, C.V."

APPENDIX K.

SIR GARNET WOLSELEY'S COMMISSIONS.

VICTORIA, by the Grace of God, &c., &c., to our trusty and well beloved SIR GARNET JOSEPH WOLSELEY, Lieutenant-General, &c., &c.,

Greeting, —

Whereas we did by certain Letters Patent, under the Great Seal of our United Kingdom of Great Britain and Ireland, bearing date at Westminster the 15th day of July, 1856, in the 20th year of our reign, erect the district of Natal, in South Africa, into a separate colony to be called the Colony of Natal:

And whereas, by the said Letters Patent, and by certain other Letters Patent, under the Great Seal, bearing date at Westminster, the 22nd day of December, 1869, in the 33rd year of our reign, and by certain other Letters Patent under the said

Great Seal, bearing date at Westminster, the 22nd day of May, 1872, in the 35th year of our reign, we did make provision for the Government of the said colony:

And whereas by the said Letters Patent of the 15th day of July, 1856, we did ordain that the said Government should be administered by a Governor duly commissioned by us, or in the event of his death, incapacity, or absence from our said Colony, or if no Governor should have been commissioned by us, by a Lieutenant-Governor appointed by our Warrant under our Sign Manual and Signet; and whereas we did, by our Warrant under our Sign Manual and Signet, bearing date at Windsor, the 3rd day of July, 1875, appoint our trusty and well-beloved Sir Henry Ernest Bulwer to be our Lieutenant-Governor of our said colony, with powers and authorities therein mentioned; and whereas we are now minded to appoint a Governor to administer the government of our said colony during our pleasure:

Now know you that we, reposing especial trust and confidence in your prudence, courage, and loyalty, do by this our Commission appoint you, the said Sir Garnet Joseph Wolseley, to be, during our pleasure, our Governor and Commander-in-Chief in and over our Colony of Natal and its dependencies:

And we do hereby authorise, empower, and command you to do and execute all things that belong to the said office of Governor and Commander-in-Chief, according to the provisions of our said several Letters Patent above recited, and according to such instructions heretofore given by us to our Lieutenant-Governor for the time being as are now in force, and according to such other instructions as may from time to time be given to you under our Sign Manual and Signet, or by our order in our Privy Council, or through one of our Principal Secretaries of State, and according to such laws as are now or shall hereafter be in force in our said colony.

2nd. And we do require that before entering upon any of the

duties of the said office you do cause this our commission to be read and published in our said colony, in the presence of the Chief Justice, or of some other judge of the Supreme Court of the colony, and of the members of the Executive Council thereof; and that you do then and there take before them the oath of allegiance in the form provided by an Act passed in the 31st and 32nd years of our reign, intituled "an Act to amend the law relating to promissory oaths," and likewise the usual oath for the due execution of the office of Governor, and for the due and impartial administration of justice, which oath the said Chief Justice or Judge is hereby required to administer.

3rd. And whereas it may be to the advantage of our service, that our Lieutenant-Governor should continue to take part in the administration of the government of our said colony, notwithstanding that you, our said Governor, are present therein; now, therefore, we do hereby authorise and empower our Lieutenant-Governor for the time being, with your sanction and approval, to exercise all or any of the powers and authorities conferred upon the Governor by any of our said recited Letters Patent, or by any of our instructions above referred to (except the power of granting a pardon or remission of sentence to an offender convicted of crime, and the power of assenting in our name to Bills passed by the Legislature, or of reserving such Bills for the signification of our pleasure thereon).

4th. And further know you, that we do hereby appoint that this our present commission shall not supersede our commission under our Sign Manual and Signet, bearing date at Windsor, the 3rd day of July, 1875, in the 39th year of our reign, appointing our trusty and well-beloved Sir Henry Ernest Bulwer, Knight Commander of our Most Distinguished Order of St. Michael and St. George, to be our Lieutenant-Governor of our Colony of Natal; but that as long as you are able to act as such Governor aforesaid, under these presents, our aforesaid commission, dated the 3rd day of July, 1875, shall be taken and deemed to be subject to the superior powers conferred by this commission.

5th. And we do hereby command all and singular our officers, ministers, and loving subjects in our said colony, and all others whom it may concern, to take due notice hereof, and to give their ready obedience accordingly.

Given at our Court at Balmoral, this 28th day of May, 1879, in the 42nd year of our reign.

By Her Majesty's command,

(Signed) M. E. HICKS-BEACH.

(Signed) G. J. WOLSELEY,

Governor.

Proclamation by His Excellency Sir Garnet Wolseley, Lieutenant-General, &c., &c.,

Whereas Her Majesty the Queen of the United Kingdom of Great Britain and Ireland, and Empress of India, has been graciously pleased by a commission, dated at Balmoral, the 28th of May, 1879, in the 42nd year of her reign, and passed under the Royal Sign Manual and Signet, to appoint me to be Governor and Commander-in-Chief in and over the Colony of Natal and its dependencies:

And whereas, under and by virtue of the above-recited Commission, the Lieutenant-Governor of the Colony of Natal, Sir Henry Ernest Bulwer, appointed such by warrant under the Royal Sign Manual and Signet, bearing date at Windsor, the 3rd of July, 1875, is authorised and empowered, with my sanction and approval, and subject to the exceptions hereinafter stated, to exercise, notwithstanding my presence in the colony, all or any of the powers and authorities conferred upon the said Governor of the Colony of Natal by certain Letters Patent, issued under the Great Seal of the United Kingdom of Great Britain and Ireland, and bearing date respectively, at Westminster, the 15th of July, 1856, in the 20th year of the present reign, the 22nd of December, 1869, in the 33rd year of the present reign, and the 22nd of May, 1872, in the 35th year of the present reign, or by any such instructions heretofore given to the Lieutenant-Governor of the Colony of Natal as are now in force, or by such other instructions as may from time to time be given to me under the Royal Sign Manual and Signet, or by order of Her Majesty the Queen in her Privy Council, or through one of Her Majesty's principal Secretaries of State, and according to such laws as are now or shall hereafter be in force in the said Colony of Natal, the power of granting a pardon or remission of sentence to an offender convicted of crime, and the power of assenting in Her Majesty's name to Bills passed by the Legislature of the Colony of Natal, or of reserving such Bills for the signification of Her Majesty's pleasure thereon, being excepted:

Now, therefore, I do, in pursuance of, and by virtue of, the powers vested in me as Governor of the Colony of Natal and its dependencies, and conferred upon me by the Royal Commission above recited, bearing date at Balmoral, the 28th day of May, 1879, in the 42nd year of the present reign, hereby proclaim my sanction and approval of the exercise, notwithstanding that I may be present in the said colony, by Sir Henry Ernest Bulwer, Knight Commander of the Most Distinguished Order of St. Michael and St. George, Lieutenant-Governor in and over the Colony of Natal, by virtue of a commission under the Royal Sign Manual and Signet, bearing date at Windsor, the 3rd day of July, 1875, of all or any of the powers and authorities conferred upon the Governor of the Colony of Natal by any of the above-recited Letters Patent, or by any of the Royal instructions above referred to, and according to such laws as are now, or shall hereafter, be in force in the said Colony of Natal; subject, however, to the following exceptions, viz., the power of granting a pardon or remission of sentence to an offender convicted of crime, and the power of assenting in the name of

Her Majesty to Bills passed by the Legislature of the Colony of Natal, or of reserving such Bills for the signification of Her Majesty's pleasure thereon:

Now, therefore, I do hereby command all and singular Her Majesty's officers, ministers, and loving subjects in the Colony of Natal, and all others whom it may concern, to take due notice hereof, and to govern themselves and give their ready obedience accordingly.

God Save the Queen,

Given under my hand, and the Public Seal of the Colony of Natal, at Government House, Pietermaritzburg, in the Colony of Natal, this 28th day of June, 1879.

By His Excellency's command,

C. B. H. MITCHELL,
Colonial Secretary.

***

Subjoined is the Commission by the Queen appointing Sir Garnet Wolseley special High Commissioner for South-East Africa:—

Victoria, by the Grace of God, &c., &c, to our trusty and well-beloved Sir Garnet Joseph Wolseley, &c., &c., greeting: —

Whereas we did by our commission under our Sign Manual and Signet, bearing date at Osborne House, Isle of Wight, the 27th day of February, 1877, in the 40th year of our reign, appoint the right trusty and well-beloved councillor, Sir Henry Bartle Edward Frere, Bart., Knight Cross of our most honourable order of the Bath, Knight Grand Commander of our most exalted order of the Star of India, our Governor and Commander-in-Chief in and over our Colony of the Cape of Good Hope, to be our High Commissioner for the territories of South Africa adjacent to our said colony, or with which it might be expedient that we should have relations, and which were not included within the territory of either of the two Republics then established in South Africa or of any:

And whereas the territory of one of the said Republics (theretofore known as the South African Republic) has become, and is now part of our dominions, and is known as the Transvaal territory:

And whereas we are minded to constitute and appoint a special High Commissioner for South-Eastern Africa, who may act in our name and our behalf, and in all respects represent our Crown and authority in respect of the native tribes in the territories of South Africa to the northward and eastward of our Colony of Natal and of our said Transvaal territory, and further, may hold communication with the president or representatives of the Republic of the Orange Free State, or with the representatives of any foreign power:

Now know you that we, reposing especial trust and confidence in the prudence, courage, and loyalty of you, the said Sir Garnet Joseph Wolseley, of our special grace, certain knowledge, and mere motion, do by these presents constitute and appoint you to be our High Commissioner for the territories of South-Eastern Africa, which are situated to the northward and eastward of our Colony of Natal, and of our Transvaal territory, and are not included within the territory of the said Republic, or of any foreign power, and for the transacting of any business which may be lawfully transacted by you with the aforesaid President or representatives. And we do further require you, by all proper means, to invite and obtain the co-operation of the Government of the said Republic, or of any foreign power, towards the preservation of peace and safety in South Africa, and the general welfare and advancement of its territories and peoples.

2nd. And we do hereby authorise and empower you, as such our High Commissioner, in our name, and our behalf, to take all such measures, and to do all such things in relation to the native tribes in the territories of South Africa to the northward and eastward of our Colony of Natal and of our Transvaal territory, as are lawful, and appear to you to be advisable for maintaining our said possessions in South Africa in peace and safety, and for promoting the peace, order, and good government of the tribes aforesaid, and for restoring and preserving friendly relations with them.

3rd. And we do hereby authorise and empower you, by instruments under our hand and Seal, to appoint so many fit persons as you shall think necessary (in the interest of our service) to be your deputy commissioners, and by the same, or other instruments, to define the districts within which such deputy commissioners shall respectively discharge their functions. And we do hereby authorise and empower every such deputy commissioner to have and exercise within his district such of the powers and authorities hereby conferred upon you, our High Commissioner, as you shall think fit to assign to him by the instrument appointing him. Provided, nevertheless, that the appointment of such deputy commissioner shall not abridge, alter, or affect the right of you, our High Commissioner, to execute and discharge all the powers, authorities, and functions of your said office.

4th. And further know you, that we do hereby appoint that these presents shall not supersede our said commission, bearing date the 27th day of February, 1877, appointing the said Sir Henry Bartle Edward Frere, to be our High Commissioner for the territories of South Africa above described; but that so long as you are acting as such High Commissioner as aforesaid under these presents, our aforesaid Commission, dated the 27th day of February, 1877, shall be deemed to be suspended in respect of any measures to be taken or things to be done in relation to the native tribes aforesaid, situated to the northward and eastward of our Colony of Natal, and of our Transvaal territory, and not included within the territory of the Orange Free State or of any foreign power.

5th. And we do hereby command and require all our officers and ministers, civil and military, and all the inhabitants of our said possessions, with their territories and dependencies, and all other our loyal subjects in South-Eastern Africa, to be aiding and assisting unto you, the said Sir Garnet Joseph Wolseley, as High Commissioner.

Given at our Court at Balmoral, this Twenty-eight day of May, One Thousand Eight Hundred and Seventy-nine, in the forty-second year of our reign.

By Her Majesty's command,
(Signed) M. E. HICKS-BEACH.

APPENDIX L.

Immediately after Sir Garnet's second arrival in Pieter Maritzburg, the Chief of the Staff published the annexed general orders; the first showing the actual redistribution of the troops. Staff, and special service officers, and the second their general distribution, for the completion of the campaign, the capture of Cetywayo, and the resettlement of Zululand under the new scheme of rearrangement and partition.

Head Quarters, Pietermaritzburg, Natal, July 26, 1879.

1. The following re-distribution of the Troops and Staff in South Africa is published for general information:—

COMMANDING THE FORCES IN SOUTH AFRICA.
- His Excellency General Sir Garnet J. Wolseley, G.C.M.G., K.C.B.

Personal Staff.
- Military Secretary—Brevet Lieutenant-Colonel Henry

Brackenbury, R.A.

Aides-de-Camp.
- Brevet-Major H. McCalmont, 7th Hussars.
- Captain E. L. Braithwaite, 71st H.L.I.
- Captain E. F. Lord Gifford, V.C, 67th Foot.
- Lieutenant A. G. Creagh, RA.

General Staff.
- Chief of the Staff—Brigadier-General G. Pomeroy Colley, C.B., C.M.G.
- Orderly Officer—Lieutenant Hardy, Rifle Brigade.
- Deputy Adjutant General—Brevet-Colonel Bellairs, H.P., C.B.
- Deputy Quartermaster-General—Lieutenant-Colonel East, H.P.
- D.A.A. and Quartermaster-General for Intelligence Duties—Captain Maurice, R.A.
- Commanding R.A.—Colonel Reilly, C.B., R.A.
- Commanding R.E.—Lieutenant-Colonel Steward, R.E.
- Commissary-General—Commissary-General Sir E. Strickland, K.C.B.
- Commissary-General Ordnance—Deputy Commissary-General Wright.
- Paymaster—Staff-Paymaster Morris (Hon. Major).
- Principal Medical Officer—Surgeon-General Woolfryes, C.B., M.D.
- Principal Chaplain—Reverend C. J. Coar, M.A
- Inspecting Veterinary Surgeon—Inspecting Veterinary Surgeon T. P. Cudgin.

Lines of Communication and Base.
- Inspector-General—Hon. H. H. Clifford, V.C, C.B., Major-General.
- Aide-de-Camp—Lieutenant Westmacott, 77th Foot.
  A.A. & Q.-M.-Genl

- Major Butler, H.P., C.B., Durban.
- Major Webber, R.E., Landmann's Drift.
- Lieut.-Colonel Hale, R.E., Port Durnford.

D. A. A. & Q.-M.-Genl
- Capt. W. R. Fox, R.A., with Ins.-General.
- Brevet-Major Hon. H. J. L. Wood, 12th Lancers, Baker Russell's Column.
- Captain Yeatman Biggs, R.A, St. Paul's.
- Capt. Patterson, 16th Foot, Point, Durban.

Specially employed:
- Bvt.-Colonel Walker, C.B., Scots Guards, Fort Pearson.
- Captain Stewart, 3rd Dragoon Guards, Clarke's Column.

Commandant Remount Establishment
- Major J. C. Russell, 12th Lancers,

Clarke's Column.
- Commanding—Lieutenant-Colonel Clarke, 57th Foot.
- Orderly Officer—Lieutenant Towers-Clark, 57th Foot.
- Principal Staff Officer—Captain Hart, 31st Foot.
- Staff Officer—Lieutenant Harford, 99th Foot.
- Commanding Mounted Troops—Major (Local) Barrow, 19th Hussars.
- Orderly Officer Captain Hon. W. Elliott, 93rd Foot.
- Senior Commissariat Officer—Commissary Reeves.
- Senior Medical Officer—Surgeon-Major Giraud, M.D.
- Royal Artillery—Gatling Battery, and one division N-6, Major J. F. Owen, R.A.
- Royal Engineers—One Officer and twenty men, Capt. Blood, R.E.
- Imperial Infantry—57th Regiment, Major Tredinnick.
- Imperial Infantry—3-60 Regiment, Major Tufnell.
- Imperial Infantry—80th Regiment, 5 Companies, Major Tucker.
- 2nd Squadron Mounted Infantry—Major Barrow.

Colonial Troops.
- European—1st Troop Natal Horse, Captain de Burgh.
- European —Lonsdale's Horse, 2 Troops, Captain Lumley-Hickson.
- Native—Jantji's Horse, Captain C. D. Hay.
- Native —Mafunzi's Horse, Captain Nourse.
- Native —Natal Native Contingent, 4th Battalion, Captain Barton, 7th Foot.
- Native —Native Pioneers.

Baker Russell's Column.
- Commanding—Lieut.-Col. Baker Russell, C.B., 13th Hussars.
- Orderly Officer—Captain Bushman, 9th Lancers.
- Staff Officer—Captain Woodgate, 4th Foot.
- Attached for duty—Capt. Hon. R. A. J. Talbot, 1st Life Guards.
- Commanding Mounted Troops—Captain Brown, 1-24th.
- Senior Commissariat Officer—Deputy Commissary Coates.
- Senior Medical Officer—Surgeon-Major Cuffe.

Imperial Troops.
- Cavalry, one squadron K. D. Gds.
- Royal Artillery, N-5 Battery: Lieutenant-Colonel Harness, R.A. Royal Engineers,
- 94th Regiment: Lieutenant-Colonel Mai thus. 1st Squadron Mounted Infantry: Captain Browne, 1-24th.

Colonel Corps.
- *European*: Lonsdale's Horse, 1 Troop: Frontier Light Horse: Commandant D'Arcy. Transvaal Rangers: Commandant Raaf. Natal Mounted Police: Captain Munsell.
- *Native:* 2nd Battalion Natal Native Contingent: Major Bengough, 77th. Mounted Natives.

The following officers now on the Staff of Divisions or Brigades will rejoin their regiments:

Major Walker, 99th Regiment, A.A.G.; Lieutenant Hutton,

60th Regiment, A.D.G-.; Lieutenant Brewster, K.D.G., Provost Marshal; Lieutenant Phipps, 1-24th Regiment, Orderly Officer; Captain Montagne, 94th Regiment, Brigade Major; Captain Chater, 91st Regiment, Deputy Provost Marshal.

The following officers now on the Staff of Divisions or Brigades, or employed on special service, will be provided with passages to England:—

Brevet-Major Grenfell, 60th Rifles, D.A.A.G., Head Quarters; Brevet-Major Robinson, Rifle Brigade, A.AG.; Brevet-Major Gossett, 54th Regiment, A.Q.M.G.; Captain Harvey, 71st Regiment, D.A.Q.M.G.; Major Clery, Staff Officer, Flying Column; Captain McGregor, 29th Regiment, Brigade Major (on breaking up of Brigadier Rowland's Brigade); Brevet-Lieutenant-Colonel Wavell, 41st Regiment; Captain Brunker, 26th Regiment; Captain Doyle, 2nd Dragoon Guards; Major Bayley, 31st Regiment; Captain Justice, 108th Regiment; Captain Wavell, 1-9th Regiment; Lieutenant James, R.E.

The following Regiments will be placed under orders of readiness for embarkation—17th Lancers, 2-3rd Regiment, 1-13th Regiment, 1-24th Regiment. All details and employed men of these Battalions will rejoin their Head Quarters. The 17th Lancers will hand over their horses to the King's Dragoon Guards, under arrangements to be made by the Inspector-General Lines of Communication and Base.

Army Head Quarters remains at Pietermaritzburg until the morning of the 30th inst.; will leave Rorke's Drift on the morning of 3rd August, and on the 6th will reach Entonganeni.

By Order, G. POMEROY COLLET, *Brigadier-General, Chief of Staff.*

General Distribution of Troops:
- Harness's Battery, Baker Russell's Column.
- Sandham's Battery, Port Durnford, pending farther orders.

- Le Grice's Battery, Pretoria, one division, Clarke's Flying Column.
- Ammunition Column will be detailed hereafter.
- Ellaby's Battery, St. Helena.
- Tremlett's Battery, Cape Town.
- Owen's Gatling Battery, Clarke's Column.
- Royal Engineers will be detailed hereafter.
- 1st K.D.G's H.-Qrs. and 1 Squadron, Utrecht.
- 1st K.D.G's H.-Qrs. and 1 Squadron, Pretoria.
- 1st K.D.G's H.-Qrs. and 1 Squadron, Baker Russell's Column.
- 1st K.D.G's H.-Qrs. and 1 Squadron Rorke's Drift, 1 troop selected as General's escort.
- 17th Lancers, Pinetown Camp, for embarkation; hand over horses to K. D. Guards; India.
- 1st Squadron Mounted Infantry, Baker Russell's Column.
- 2nd Squadron Mounted Infantry, Clarke's Column.
- 2-3rd "The Buffs," Pinetown Gamp, for embarkation; Straits Settlements.
- 2-4th Regiment, Luneberg and Pretoria,
- 1-13th Regiment, Durban, for England.
- 2-21st Regiment, To mass at Koppie Allein, when they can be withdrawn from Zulu forts, for service in Zululand or Transvaal, as required.
- 1-24th Regiment, Pinetown Camp, for embarkation to England.
- 2.24th Regiment, Utrecht, Conference Hill, and Fort Cambridge.
- 57th Regiment, Clarke's Column.
- 58th Regiment, Landman's Drift, Head Quarters, Posts from
- Dundee to Fort Evelyn, when no longer required with Ulundi convoy.
- 3-60th Regiment, Clarke's Column.
- 80th Regiment, Pretoria, Head Quarters, 5 Companies,

Clarke's
- Flying Column, and Detachments at Lydenburg and Middleburg.
- 88th Regiment, Pinetown Camp, when no longer required at Fort Chelmsford and Etshowi.
- 90th Regiment, St. Paul's, Head Quarters, and Detachment at Kwamagwasa.
- 91st Regiment, Umlalosi, Head Quarters, and Detachments at Forts Durnford and Chelmsford.
- 94th Regiment, Baker Russell's Column.
- 99th Regiment, Pietermaritzburg, Head Quarters, Detachments at Durban, Fort Pearson, Greytown, Rorke's Drift, and St. John's River.

By Order,
G. POMEROY COLLET, *Brigadier-General,*
Chief of the Staff. Pietermaritzburg, July 26, 1879.

APPENDIX M.

THE GENERAL'S DESPATCH.

Sir Garnet Wolseley's despatch to the Secretary of State for War, announcing the capture of Cetywayo, is as follows:—

Army Head-quarters, Camp, Ulundi, Zululand,
September 3, 1879.

Sir,—I have the honour to report that after a well-sustained pursuit through a most difficult country, extending over sixteen days, Cetywayo, the ex-King of Zululand, was captured on the 28th ult., by a patrol under the command of Major Marter, King's Dragoon Guards, to -whom every praise is due for the skilful manner in which the capture was effected.

Cetywayo is now on his way to Capetown, accompanied by some of his wives and servants. He will be detained as a State prisoner at large in the Cape Colony, under the authority of an Act to be passed for that purpose by the Cape Parliament.

On the 1st inst. I held a meeting attended by nearly all the great chiefs of Zululand, most of those who from bodily infirmities or other sufficient causes were unable to attend, being represented by their principal councillors. I explained to the assembled chiefs how the country is in future to be divided among them, and the terms upon which they are to be appointed to rule over their respective territories as independent chiefs. I have addressed a despatch to the Secretary of State for the Colonies, giving full details of the arrangements I have made for the future government of the country, through which I have every reason to believe that peace will be permanently secured, and the Zulu military power, which has so long threatened the peace of South Africa, be for ever broken up.

I now feel, therefore, in a position to report that the Zulu war has been satisfactorily concluded. Her Majesty's troops can now return to Natal, where, with the exception of those to be retained for the garrisons of South Africa, they will be encamped at Pinetown to await the arrival of transports to take them to their respective destinations. The 1st Battalion 13th Light Infantry, and the 1st Battalion 24th Regiment, have already embarked for England.

Lieutenant-Colonel Clarke's Column is now on the march to Natal, via St. Pauls and Entumeni. It will cross the Tugela at the Middle Drift. Upon reaching Natal, all the levies and irregular troops belonging to it will be disbanded. Lieutenant-Colonel Baker-Russell's Column will be broken up as soon as Oham, Cetywayo's brother, has been re-established in his own district, and when, with the assistance of Lieutenant-Colonel Hon. G. Villiers, whom I appointed Special Commissioner to Oham's armed forces, Lieutenant-Colonel Russell has obtained the submission of the turbulent and semi-independent tribes inhabiting the north-west corner of Zululand and the disputed territory there bordering upon the Transvaal. I expect that a show of force in the district will be sufficient to effect this object in a very short time.

I have already had the honour of reporting to you the strength of the garrisons I propose retaining, at least for the present, in the several provinces of South Africa, and from which detachments will be provided for Mauritius and St. Helena.

Almost all the hired land transport is now being discharged, and I hope I may soon be in a position largely to reduce the amount of Government transport still retained.

To-morrow I intend marching from this with the Headquarters Staff and a small personal escort direct to Utrecht, en route for Pretoria, which place I hope to reach about the 1st proximo.

Our patrols have visited the most distant localities of Zululand, testing thereby the completeness of the submission of the chiefs and the peaceable condition of the country. I have in this way been able to extend our topographical knowledge of Zululand, and by actual survey, as well as by reconnoissances, to lay down on paper with very tolerable accuracy its rivers, mountains, &c.

I believe that at least 5,000 stand of arms have been now collected and destroyed. Those upon whom I rely most for information estimate at about 8,000 the total number of guns in Zulu-land before the war. Assuming that this somewhat underestimates the number, I think we may calculate that at least one-half of the firearms in the country have been taken or voluntarily surrendered by the chiefs coming in to submit. A considerable amount of gunpowder and ammunition has also been destroyed.

The successful action fought near this spot on the 4th of July last has been the only engagement with the enemy since I assumed command of the troops in South Africa. In this action I took no part. Lieutenant-General Lord Chelmsford having commanded there in person, and made all preliminary arrangements, all the merit of that victory is due to him. The subsequent operations have happily been of a bloodless character, but their successful accomplishment depended upon a nicety of calculation and a precision of arrangement only to be expected from a very able and experienced Staff, such as that which I am fortunate enough to have with me, presided over by that ablest of Staff officers, Brigadier-General Sir George Pomeroy Colley.

These operations, immediately leading to the capture of the King, have been carried out by the troops of the column under Lieutenant-Colonel Clarke, 57th Regiment, who has performed the duties of his responsible command in the most highly efficient manner. The officers and men under him have worked most cheerfully, though the stimulus to exertion given by the presence of an armed enemy was wanting; indeed, the conduct of all the troops in the field, British and Colonial, since I assumed command, has been admirable.

Of those who have toiled unremittingly throughout this war no one is more deserving of special mention than Major-General the Hon. H. H. Clifford. Since his arrival in South Africa he has been in charge of the base and of the lines of communication, a charge which I thought it necessary to extend when I assumed command. On him has devolved the heaviest part of the work connected with the concluding operations and reduction of the force. No one could have worked with more earnest zeal than he has done, not only to keep the troops in the field supplied with everything they required, but to do so without unnecessary or extravagant expenditure of public money. By him great economy was introduced into the administration and a most salutary check established over the outlay of all public money.

As this despatch is to announce to Her Majesty's Government the successful termination of the military operations in Zululand,

and the peaceable settlement of the country, I venture to send it to you in charge of my Aide-de-Camp, Captain Lord Gifford, V.C, whom I recommend to your favourable consideration. Lord Gifford was actively engaged in pursuit of Cetywayo from the day when the first patrol was sent out, and at the time when the capture was made was watching with a small body of men the kraal into which he had traced the King, with the intention of effecting the capture at nightfall.

I have, &c.,

G. J. WOLSELEY, General.

THE RESIDENT IN ZULULAND.

The subjoined memorandum by His Excellency Sir Bartle Frere, with reference to the powers which are to be conferred upon the Resident to be appointed under the new order of things in Zulu-land, is a most important document, as indicating the line of policy which will be pursued; but it must be regarded only as a draft of what the instructions will be, giving their general drift, but at the same time not being final:—

Memorandum on the Appointment of a Resident in Zululand.

The Resident will exercise a double function, not only as the representative of British interests, but as responsible for explaining the views and wishes of the British Government to the Great Zulu Council. He will exercise in that Council a potential influence in all national questions, and especially with regard to the management of any territory which, having once been effectually claimed by the Transvaal Government and under its flag, will henceforward, by the adjudication of the boundary commissioners, be' held to be Zulu territory.

2. It is intended that in that district individual rights of property which were obtained under the Transvaal Government shall be respected and maintained, so that any Transvaal farmers, who obtained rights from the Government of the Republic, and who

may now elect to remain on the territory, may possess, under British guarantee, the same rights they would have possessed had they been grantees holding from the Zulu King, under the guarantee of the Great Zulu Council.

3. The Resident will probably require an assistant, and one of these two officers will have his station in the north of Zululand, probably at some point in the immediate neighbourhood of the old hunting road.

4. For the other station, a position will be selected in Zululand near the coast, and probably not far from the Tugela Drift and the south main road into Zululand.

5. In either case the position will be chosen for convenience of living as regards salubrity, and supplies of wood, water, grass, &c., communications with the interior, and, above all, security against ambuscades and sudden attack, and facility for withdrawing, if necessary, to a more defensible position within the British border.

6. The station, with a suitable arrondissement carefully marked out and beaconed to prevent intrusion of unauthorised native habitations for a couple of miles round the Residency, will be declared,
and should by legislation receive the position of British territory, trifling offences within which can be disposed of by a cantonment magistrate, serious offences being sent for trial to the High Court in Natal.

7. Provision should be made for a suitable escort, the strength of which will be fixed by the General commanding. It should not exceed what is needed to secure the personal safety of the Resident, or his establishment, against a sudden surprise.

8. Shops, and other private dwellings of persons connected with the Residency or escort, will be placed within the limits of the station, according to instructions which may from time to time be issued by the Cantonment Magistrate.

9. The Resident will be the medium of all communications between the Zulus and the British Government, and will communicate, as the case may require, with the High Commissioner, the Lieutenant-Governor of Natal, the Administrator of the Transvaal, and other British authorities.

10. His presence, or written authority, will be necessary to all criminal jurisdiction over Europeans for offences committed in Zululand.

11. He will have a power of veto on any order for the expulsion or fining of any person of European descent who has once been allowed to reside in Zululand by the Kling's license, or by unrevoked and tacit permission of residence for one year.

12. In any criminal trial of a person of European descent, the Resident will either preside himself or sit as assessor to the King, and have a veto on all stages of the proceedings.

13. It will be the Resident's duty to see that the promises made by the King at his coronation are properly observed, and to bring immediately to the notice of the High Commissioner any case in which the King may infringe any of such promises, and decline or evade giving immediate redress.

H. B. E. FRERE, Governor and High Commissioner.
Pietermaritzburg, November 27, 1878.

ABOUT CODA BOOKS

Most Coda books are edited and endorsed by Emmy Award winning film maker and military historian Bob Carruthers, producer of Discovery Channel's Line of Fire and Weapons of War and BBC's Both Sides of the Line. Long experience and strong editorial control gives the military history enthusiast the ability to buy with confidence.

The series advisor is David McWhinnie, producer of the acclaimed Battlefield series for Discovery Channel. David and Bob have co-produced books and films with a wide variety of the UK's leading historians including Professor John Erickson and Dr David Chandler.

Where possible the books draw on rare primary sources to give the military enthusiast new insights into a fascinating subject.

www.codabooks.com

The English Civil Wars

The Zulu Wars

Into Battle with Napoleon 1812

Waterloo 1815

The Anglo-Saxon Chronicle

The Battle of the Bulge

The Normandy Campaign 1944

Hitler's Justification for WWII

Hitler's Mein Kampf - The Roots of Evil

I Knew Hitler

Mein Kampf - The 1939 Illustrated Edition

The Nuremberg Trials Volume 1

Tiger I in Combat

Tiger I Crew Manual

Panzers at War 1939-1942

Panzers at War 1943-1945

Wolf Pack - the U boats

Poland 1939

Luftwaffe Combat Reports

Eastern Front Night Combat

Eastern Front Encirclement

Panzer Combat Reports

The Panther V in Combat

The Red Army in Combat

Barbarossa - Hitler Turns East

The Russian Front

The Wehrmacht in Russia

Servants of Evil

www.ingramcontent.com/pod-product-compliance
Lightning Source LLC
Chambersburg PA
CBHW021139160426
43194CB00007B/633